HUNTER KILLERS

THE DRAMATIC UNTOLD STORY OF THE ROYAL NAVY'S MOST SECRET SERVICE

IAIN BALLANTYNE

An Orion paperback

First published in Great Britain in 2013
by Orion
This paperback edition published in 2014
by Orion Books Ltd,
Orion House, 5 Upper St Martin's Lane,
London WC2H 9EA
An Hachette UK Company

1 3 5 7 9 10 8 6 4 2

A CIP catalogue record for this book is available
from the British Library.

ISBN: 978-1-4091-3901-0

Typeset by Input Data Services Ltd, Bridgwater, Somerset

Printed and bound by CPI Group (UK) Ltd, Croydon, CR0 4YY

The Orion Publishing Group's policy is to use papers that
are natural, renewable and recyclable products and
made from wood grown in sustainable forests. The logging
and manufacturing processes are expected to conform to
the environmental regulations of the country of origin.

Every effort has been made to fulfil requirements with regard to
reproducing copyright material. The author and publisher will be
glad to rectify any omissions at the earliest opportunity.

www.orionbooks.co.uk

To the Royal Navy submariners who fought and won the Cold War and their families, not forgetting the shipbuilders, the support staff and good friends in the United States Navy submarine force.

CONTENTS

The Primary Theatre of
Cold War Confrontation

Scale: |___| 500 miles

BATTLE MAP

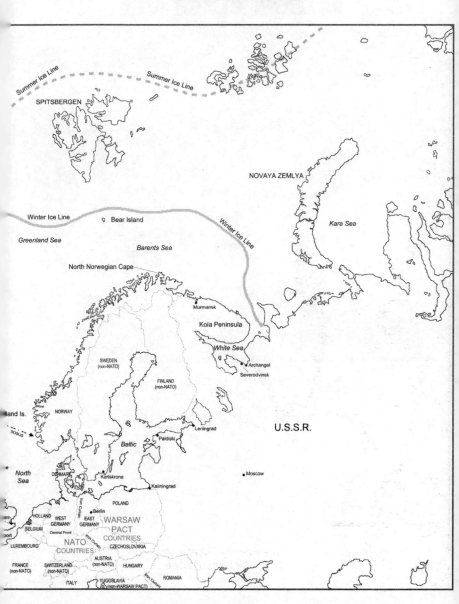

INSIDE AN IMPROVED VALIANT CLASS SSN

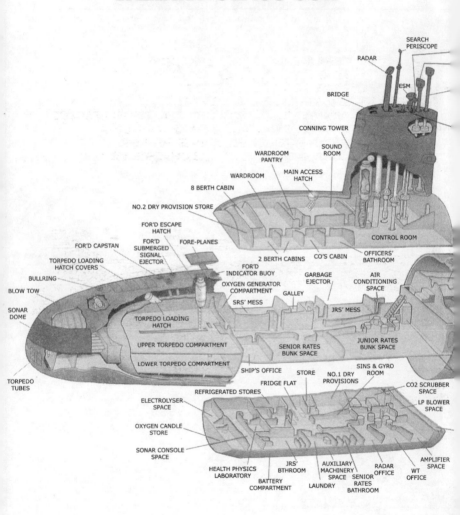

DISPLACEMENT.............4500 TONS
LENGTH.......................285 FT
BEAM...........................33 FT
DRAUGHT.....................27 FT
ARMAMENT...................SIX 21in. TORPEDOES TUBES
PROPULSION.................NUCLEAR REACTOR
UNDERWATER SPEED......OVER 20 KNOTS
COMPLEMENT................13 OFFICERS 100 MEN

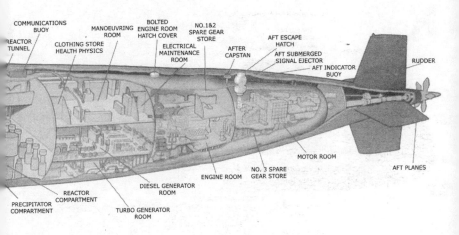

WIRELESS TELEGRAPHY

SNORT INDUCTION

SNORT EXHAUST

ATTACK PERISCOPE

COMMUNICATIONS
BUOY

REACTOR
TUNNEL

CLOTHING STORE
HEALTH PHYSICS

MANOEUVRING
ROOM

BOLTED
ENGINE ROOM
HATCH COVER

NO.1&2
SPARE GEAR
STORE

ELECTRICAL
MAINTENANCE
ROOM

AFTER
CAPSTAN

AFT ESCAPE
HATCH

AFT SUBMERGED
SIGNAL EJECTOR

AFT INDICATOR
BUOY

RUDDER

MOTOR ROOM

AFT PLANES

ENGINE ROOM

NO. 3 SPARE
GEAR STORE

DIESEL GENERATOR
ROOM

REACTOR
COMPARTMENT

PRECIPITATOR
COMPARTMENT

TURBO GENERATOR
ROOM

DIESEL FUEL
OIL TANK

1 | PIRATES OF VALOUR

'They'll never be any use in war and I'll tell you why:
I'm going to get the First Lord to announce that we
intend to treat all submarines as pirate vessels in
wartime and that we'll hang all the crews.'

Admiral Sir Arthur Wilson, Controller of the Royal Navy, 1901

Since the early days of the twentieth century the Silent Service, as the submarine arm of the Royal Navy is known, has won 14 Victoria Crosses. This is more than any other branch of the British fleet. Even old Arthur Wilson, who won the VC himself, for engaging the enemy in hand-to-hand combat during the Sudan campaign of 1884, would surely have admitted the undersea warriors he loathed so much were pretty brave fellows.

In the case of submariners there has always been an added level of valour. This was especially so in the early days, when they also had to contend with utterly appalling, life-threatening conditions posed by the very vessels in which they went to war.

Wilson was not alone in taking a dim view of submariners. There were many others in the Royal Navy who regarded the new breed of pirates in their midst as offering dubious military worth.

How on earth could one of those tiny, impertinent boats be allowed to affect a battle at sea? For a start, the people who operated them were dangerous eccentrics, lacking discipline and simply not gentlemen. Arthur Wilson also allegedly blustered that submarines were 'underhand and damned un- English!'

Anyone associated with submarines was, so the doubters believed, to be regarded as a criminal, indeed a lunatic. Right from the earliest days of British submarine operations, the sanity of men who ventured beneath the waves in their 'boats' – they were not even proper ships – was a matter of debate. Who else but a madman would go to war under the sea, inside a tiny metal tube that, in most cases, did not even boast a toilet? During the First World War submariners were sometimes forced to stay submerged for many hours at a time. With no recourse to fresh air or means of dumping human waste overboard they had to do their business, so to speak, in a bucket.

Sometimes the air became so foul a submarine's own engines stopped working, as if out of protest at the sheer horror of it all.

Inside a submerged boat the stench of urine and faeces was combined with sweat and grease, the aroma of unwashed bodies and filthy clothes. Fresh water was invariably in short supply, so submariners would not bathe for days, if not weeks. Not for them a shave each day nor crisp clean clothes. The food could be equally foul.

Aside from the enemy's homicidal intent, the boat herself could spring a leak or suffer some form of catastrophic mechanical failure that might kill everybody. Or at least make the chances of survival close to zero.

The Engineer-in-Chief of the Royal Navy, Sir John Durston, disowned the early British submarines. He pointed to the danger posed by running petrol engines in an enclosed space with no means of ventilation while submerged. He did not want the deaths of sailors from carbon monoxide poisoning on *his* conscience. The embarkation of white mice as an early-warning device was another eccentric facet of the weird world of submarining. If their little lungs couldn't cope with the foul and fetid atmosphere then it wouldn't be long until the humans couldn't either. Durston suggested submersibles were unviable until a different means of propulsion could be found. Elsewhere, the Director of Naval Construction totally rejected submarines. He regarded them as lunacy, what with their blundering around beneath the waves with no means of seeing where they were going. Navigation was by guesswork. Their primitive periscope used a knuckle pivot on the outside of the hull, so it could be swung up, rather than extended vertically from inside the boat as later became the practice.

The image also rotated as the scope rotated. It was better than no sight at all, but not much. As if that wasn't bad enough, while submerged the switch controls for the electric motor sparked frenetically. At any moment they might ignite petrol or diesel fumes, creating an inferno that burned both mice and men to a crisp.

Running on the surface with the hatch open, during recharging primitive batteries emitted poisonous gas. Death was a close companion for the early British submariners.

Their clothes, whether ashore or out on the ocean, *always* stank of petrol or diesel fumes, with a hint of vomit. The first generation of British boats rolled wildly while on the surface in anything but a flat calm sea, so throwing up was a normal activity. Then there was the customary tinge of excrement (more of that shortly) and the aroma of cooking grease to finish off the distinctive scent of the submariner.

Those boats lucky enough to possess some form of toilet had to follow a careful procedure to evacuate the offending faecal matter. The toilet pan had to be pumped out by hand or with the assistance of high-pressure air. While submerged it was essential not to use up all the air in the boat, so the toilet pan was not cleared until absolutely necessary. This meant quite a pile of human waste. Sometimes there would be a blowback during the pan evacuation process. The unfortunate sailor – most often the new boy in a crew – would get blasted in the face. Consequently, the wise submariner would adopt the tactic of sidling in crablike, head well below the top of the pan. He would operate the various levers and valves with utmost caution. If there was blowback it would cover only his clothes, hands and hair. The submarine stank most on its return from a patrol. The crew would have no idea how bad it was – or how much they reeked – for their olfactory senses had long ago been desensitised.

In those submarines lacking a toilet efforts were made to deploy the bucket when the boat was surfaced. The submariner did his business by hovering over it while the receptacle sat on the casing. The contents were then tipped over the side. In those boats blessed with a toilet, the trick was to make sure the expulsion of its contents while submerged did not betray the submarine's position to the enemy. Air bubbles and brown stuff on the surface were a dead giveaway.

Despite all this, there were those who saw the game-changing nature of the submarine. For Britain's navy also produced modernisers who seized the day with vigour. Admiral Sir John Fisher – regarded with hostility by traditionalists because of his fervent belief in technological change – welcomed the revolution offered by the torpedo and 'Submarine Boat' combination. Fisher was outraged both by admirals afloat and politicians ashore who saw submarines as 'playthings'. Admiral Lord Charles Beresford was a particular foe of Fisher's, the two men diametrically opposed ideologically, cultivating a bitter feud that at times burst into the public arena and scandalised the nation. Beresford, a confirmed battleship man, contemptuously labelled submarines 'Fisher's toys'.

· Despite such opposition, between 1902 and 1905 the Admiralty built thirteen A Class submarines. The growth matched the rise to prominence of Fisher. In October 1903, while serving as Commander-in-Chief at Portsmouth, he wrote: 'It is an historical fact that the British Navy stubbornly resists change. A First Sea Lord told me on one occasion that there were not torpedoes when he came to sea and he didn't see why the devil there should be any of the beastly things now!' Fisher declared that no invasion force would dare assault England 'with these invisible demons known to be near'. Six months later he wrote to somebody he described as *a High Official*: 'It's astounding to me, *perfectly astounding*, how the very best amongst us absolutely fail to realise the vast impending revolution in naval warfare and naval strategy that the submarine will accomplish.' Fisher was sworn in as First Sea Lord – the head of the Royal Navy – on 21 October 1904 (Trafalgar Day). And so the man who wrote at the beginning of 1904 that 'Satan disguised as the Angel of Light' couldn't persuade the Admiralty submarines would be a decisive weapon was now in charge of British naval policy. In addition to getting rid of dozens of old and weak surface warships, Fisher accelerated development of the submarine in British service. By January 1910, when he retired for the first time as First Sea Lord, the Royal Navy would have 61 operational boats.

The piratical aspect of submarine warfare during the First World War shocked many people. There were numerous instances of appalling casualties among non-combatants, not least the sinking of the liner *Lusitania* on 7 May 1915 by *U-20* with the loss of nearly 1,200 lives. The majority of them were civilians, including women and children. For centuries warfare against commerce had been conducted with a certain amount of decorum. The objective was to capture ships and take their goods, not to send them to the bottom with mass bloodshed. Such chivalrous practices were not possible in an era of steel ships, long-range guns and submarines armed with torpedoes. Merchant vessels were to be sunk along with their cargoes. Early submarines had to surface to conduct an attack. To linger too long invited destruction by the enemy. Besides, the practice of making one's fortune via prize money had been outlawed. There was no incentive any more. New industrialised warfare required destruction of enemy capacity to wage war and denial of essential resources. It was difficult to put a prize crew aboard a ship anyway, and submarines were too small to take aboard survivors without endangering themselves. There were still meant to be rules of conduct with reference to civilian lives being preserved where possible. Submarine warfare, particularly unrestricted, as practised by the Germans had, though, outraged civilisation. Even as the Allies agreed armistice terms with the Kaiser in October 1918, a U-boat torpedoed a mail ship in the Irish Sea, not once but twice, just to ensure she went down. Nearly 200 people drowned, again including women and children. Allied leaders called for an end to the German U-boat campaign. The USA's President Woodrow Wilson branded its pursuit replete with 'illegal and inhuman practices'. The British politician Arthur Balfour declared the U-boat crews 'brutes'.

A few German submarine officers were tried for war crimes, including some from *U-86*. After sinking the hospital ship *Llandovery Castle*, in June 1918, they had ordered survivors attacked, ramming lifeboats and shooting at them. Allegations of war crimes were laid against the Royal Navy, too. The notorious Q-ships, covert armed merchant vessels, had lured many a U-boat to destruction. Often they worked in conjunction with British submarines.

To early-twentieth-century sensibilities it was all rather beastly and shocking. Submariners were agents of horror, of underhand, dirty warfare in which innocents were slaughtered.

During post-war conferences there were demands for the submarines to be outlawed. The British, who had nearly been brought to their knees by Germany's U-boat campaign against trade, were determined to get rid of submarines altogether.

Their delegation went to the 1921–22 Washington naval arms limitation conference with that objective firmly in mind. The USA was not positive towards the idea, or it might have succeeded. Both France and Japan were against getting rid of submarines. As ever, the junior navies – particularly the rising economic powers of America and Japan – were rather keen on vessels that nullified the superiority of the top fleet.

For, even after discarding many of its First World War-era warships, the Royal Navy remained the most powerful maritime force on the planet. Having failed to ban the boats, attempts were made to civilise submarine warfare. Admiral of the Fleet Lord Chatfield, who had been one of Britain's chief negotiators at Washington, was a confirmed surface warship proponent. He was sceptical of submarine warfare being regulated: 'No such rules will affect the murderer in his use of any weapon which he may possess,' he observed, 'and to which he had devoted money and training.' An irresistible weapon, the submarine had only just begun to show its potential.

It was here to stay.

The purpose of submarines remained stalking their prey with utmost stealth, to strike with total ruthlessness and then disappear. They would continue to be as feared and loathed as any pirate.

The British were not being idealistic when they argued for the abolition of submarines, but rather were seeking to preserve their advantage. For the time being the battleship was still king of the sea while cruisers were policemen of the empire. Submariners, along with naval aviators,

were the new boys and even after the First World War their unconventional ways still provoked distaste among the ranks of the naval
traditionalists in the 'black shoe' surface navy. Nobody wanted to believe a tiny submarine with its handful of torpedoes, or fragile biplanes
carrying the same type of puny weapons, could negate the mighty walls
of steel safeguarding Britain and its empire.

The submarine – a primitive platform of uncertain use and unknown
capability at the beginning of the century – in the Second World War
influenced the course of war in three theatres. It took the offensive on
occasions when surface ships could not and into places they dared not
stray. It became an effective anti-surface ship weapon and even a submarine killer.

The best British submarine type of the Second World War was the
Triton Class (or T-Class), with 53 of them completed between 1936 and
1945. Royal Navy submarines, while playing their part in the Far East,
were inferior to American vessels. They lacked range and suffered from
sweatshop living conditions, thanks to an absence of proper air conditioning. The Americans, who had overcome a critical handicap in faulty
torpedoes, deployed big air-conditioned submarine cruisers, fitted with
search radar sets, night periscopes with built-in radar, and highly effective VHF radios. Predatory US Navy boats brought Japan's economy
to its knees. Some argue that it was not necessary in practical military
terms to drop the nuclear bombs on Hiroshima and Nagasaki because
the submarines had already achieved victory.

This was the submarine as a strategic weapon in addition to its proven
ability as a tactical menace.

In European waters the casualty rate among undersea warriors was
horrendous. Of 25,000 men who saw service as submariners in the Royal
Navy during the Second World War, 3,142 perished and 359 were taken
prisoner but this was a much lower attrition rate than among their
German counterparts.

A total of 759 U-boats were destroyed, with 28,000 young men losing
their lives, a casualty rate in the Kriegsmarine's 41,000-strong submarine arm of almost 75 per cent.

Valour in the face of the enemy was, though, not found wanting
among the ranks of the British submariners. Between 1939 and 1945, eight
Victoria Crosses were awarded to Royal Navy submariners for outstanding bravery. The citation for the VC awarded to Lieutenant Commander
David Wanklyn, captain of the legendary Malta-based submarine HMS

Upholder, said that he exhibited 'courage, coolness and skill'. They were qualities possessed by many of Britain's pirates of valour. During the Second World War, British submarines sank 1.35 million tons of enemy shipping, including seven cruisers, 16 destroyers, 36 submarines, and 46 minor warships. They damaged three battleships, 11 cruisers, three destroyers and two submarines.

In the decades that followed the end of that conflict, the risks British submariners faced would be considerable. Not just for the new breed of undersea warriors, but also the whole human race, navigating the treacherous waters of the Cold War. And to begin with the Royal Navy would field a submarine force containing many vessels that had seen their share of war service.

2 | OFFICERS AND REBELS

Launched early in 1944, at the legendary Cammell Laird shipyard on the Mersey, HMS *Subtle* saw combat in the Far East, where she was once severely depth-charged by Japanese destroyers after firing torpedoes at a cruiser.

By the time 19-year-old Tim Hale joined her in the summer of 1955, she had been modernised and remained a reasonably capable boat – not a bad vessel in which to begin his career.

Taken away from the bosom of his family in 1949 and plunged into the environs of Britannia Royal Naval College (BRNC), Dartmouth, Tim Hale was born on 27 August 1935. A scion of Devon landed gentry – he numbered judges, generals, a bishop, bankers and businessmen as well as landowners in his family – he joined the Royal Navy in 1949, among the final intake of boys aged 13. From then on cadets would have to be at least 16 years old.

Hale's family had wanted him to go to Winchester School but young Tim decided he'd rather be in the Navy. He was following a tradition of military and naval service in his family dating back hundreds of years.

One of his forebears, Captain Bernard Hale, had commanded the frigate *Castor* on the West Indies station in 1801, where unfortunately he died of disease. Bernard's father was General John Hale, who as a young officer had been with Wolfe at Quebec in 1759. He later founded the 17th Lancers, one of the British Army's most famous cavalry regiments.

Tim's father, Paymaster Commander Windham Hale, was a Royal Naval Volunteer Reserve (RNVR) supply officer, serving in the Navy throughout the Second World War. He saw action in the cruiser *Kenya* on the Malta convoys and battleship *Valiant* out in the Far East.

August 1945 was a month Tim Hale never forgot: on the 6th a nuclear bomb was dropped on Hiroshima, followed three days later by another wiping out Nagasaki; on the 15th war with Japan officially ended for Britain; on the 18th his father lost his life. Commander Hale was knocked off his bicycle, returning from a fishing expedition up the river Tamar. The happy Hale family home – a 250-year-old country house near Honiton – was filled with sorrow and anger at the cruel injustice of it all. Tim's tenth birthday nine days later passed without great joy, one to forget rather than remember. With three children to bring up alone, three years later his mother gave her permission for Tim to enter BRNC. It was a career that at the time many young boys wanted to pursue but Tim had no particular naval heroes other than his late father.

After successfully completing the first phase of the academic side of his education at Dartmouth – qualifying as a Midshipman at the end of 1953 – Hale served at sea as a cadet. His first surface warship was the Second World War-era cruiser *Devonshire*, in British waters, followed by the aircraft carrier *Triumph* in the Mediterranean. He also spent time in HMS *Sheffield*, another cruiser. Hale's final surface warship, as the Senior Midshipman, was the carrier *Bulwark*, only commissioned into service in late 1954, and on sea trials in home waters.

Hale was soon tasked with choosing which branch of the Navy he would like to serve in. Being a fiercely independent non-conformist – in his own words 'a bit of a bloody rebel' – Hale didn't fancy the conventional spit-and-polish ways of the surface fleet. He'd had enough of that at Dartmouth.

Becoming an aviator or submariner was preferable to anything else and so he joined HMS *Subtle* in May 1955, at wind-blown Portland on the Dorset coast. The boat was commanded by Lt Cdr Bobby Camplin, who would write in a confidential character assessment that Sub Lieutenant Hale 'was quick to learn and showed interest in technical matters, but needs to develop a sense of responsibility and his powers of leadership'.

Hale took his first dive in his stride, showing no anxiety at all about being confined in what war-time German submariners dubbed 'an iron coffin'. His maiden voyage under the waves took place off Portland when *Subtle* was acting as a target for frigates on exercise with Flag Officer Sea Training (FOST).

Hale's eager eyes took in all the many varied activities connected to diving, including the First Lieutenant making sure all the hatches had been shut properly and then giving orders to dive.

'That didn't seem too much of a problem,' thought Hale, who was more impressed with the excitement offered by the boat's subsequent trip up the canals to Brussels. After some alcohol-lubricated diplomacy with the locals, *Subtle* headed back to sea and for waters off Scotland to take part in Flag Officer Submarine's (FOSM's) so-called 'summer war'.

She would be stalked by friendly frigates while, in turn she would try to 'kill' them in practice torpedo runs. *Subtle* sailed on the surface to make better time. As she ploughed through rough seas, headed out into a stormy stretch of ocean called the Iceland–Faroes Gap, conditions aboard ship were appalling. *Subtle* was a tiny submarine in huge seas and Hale made an astonishing discovery. While most of those around him were chucking their guts up, he felt fine. And hungry.

'I consumed all the cheese and biscuits when the other officers were off their food and the galley couldn't cook. When weather eased and people fancied some biscuits and cheese, they found they couldn't. The "fucking Subbie", as they called me, had eaten it all.'

The dangers inherent to Hale's new profession were shockingly brought home on his boat's return to port. As she entered harbour *Subtle*'s men saw efforts being made to raise her sister submarine *Sidon* from the bottom of Portland Harbour. The last time they had seen her, she was floating alongside the depot ship, HMS *Maidstone*.

Ultimately *Sidon* would be beached on Chesil Beach and never go to sea as an operational submarine again. *Subtle* inherited bottles of spirits from *Sidon*'s wardroom bar stock, for the wine merchant Saccone and Speed had written off the booze. Hale and his shipmates drank a toast to the memory of comrades who had lost their lives in the other submarine.

At 08.25 on 16 June 1955, while *Subtle* was *en route* to Brussels, one of two High Test Peroxide (HTP)-propelled torpedoes carried by *Sidon* was being slid into a tube. It accidentally went past the top stop and triggered the engine start lever. HTP fuel igniting within the confines of the tube caused the subsequent explosion. Because *Sidon* was closed up for a move, her torpedo-loading hatch was shut. The only way the force of the explosion could vent was into the boat. Even though there was no warhead fitted the blast tore through the two forward watertight bulkheads, killing a dozen of *Sidon*'s crew and severely injuring seven others. Everyone forward of the Control Room was killed. It also blew open the torpedo tube bowcap, allowing a massive ingress of water.

Fire consumed the forward section of the boat as toxic smoke filled the interior, flames shooting out of the conning tower hatch, which was the only one open. An onlooker saw 'pieces of equipment and furniture, hats and coats, flung into the air'.

The aft escape hatches clanged open and men emerged, jumping overboard to escape the inferno and fumes. A rescue team put aboard from *Maidstone* assisted *Sidon*'s surviving 37 able-bodied men. Twenty-five minutes after the initial explosion – and despite strenuous fire-fighting efforts – the boat sank. A naval doctor who went down into the boat from *Maidstone* died and was posthumously awarded the Albert Medal.

With *Sidon* on the bottom of Portland Harbour in 36ft of water, *Maidstone* transmitted the signal every submariner dreaded: 'SUBSUNK.'

When *Sidon* blew up, Hale's fellow Dartmouth term mate, Sub Lt David Eliot, was working on the boat's casing – it was by chance that he wasn't in the torpedo compartment in the fore ends. That he might have lost a friend in that fashion, rather than to enemy, was thought-provoking for Hale.

'In those days being in the submarine service was a bit risky, as such incidents, involving somebody being killed, were not unusual, but we put up with it and carried on.' Hard-drinking runs ashore helped to take the edge off the stress, and Hale soon proved he could hold his own.

Sidon's accident was a precursor to the *Kursk* incident 45 years later, in which the Russians lost an Oscar II Class cruise missile boat thanks to the same cause: unstable HTP again being used as a propellant in torpedoes. While the British recognised in the 1950s that it wasn't worth the risk, the Russians had a different philosophy.

To continue Hale's naval education there were eight months on the Junior Officers War Course at the Royal Naval College in Greenwich. He luxuriated in exploring the many local pubs and pursuing the young ladies of the capital city. With his fellow officers, he lived in grandly ornate buildings that dated back to the end of the seventeenth century, for the college was originally a hospital and retirement home for invalid naval veterans. In 1873 it became the staff college for the Navy, training generations of seafaring warriors in strategy and tactics. Hale ate his meals in the splendour of the Painted Hall, beneath epic ceiling decorations by James Thornhill celebrating British sea power. Despite a growing reputation as a roisterer, Hale still managed a first-class pass in all the courses. Switching venues to Portsmouth, he was required to spend nine months split between various training establishments learning the arts of navigation, gunnery and anti-submarine warfare among other things. Hale also passed the submarine Officer Training Course at HMS *Dolphin* – the Gosport home base and headquarters of the Submarine Service – with flying colours.

In the 1950s, with the Navy still on station in far-flung bases around the world, there were some exotic places in which to serve, even for submariners, and Hale wanted a posting to Australia. He knew a rather attractive young lady who lived there but it was not available, so he asked for a billet in the Mediterranean.

In July 1957, Hale joined the 1st Submarine Squadron (SM1), at Msida Creek, Malta, where HMS *Forth* was mother ship. His boat was to be HMS *Totem*, the squadron's most modern submarine. Hale would spend six months in *Totem*, and had already qualified as a Lieutenant that June.

He asked if he could put his second stripe up. The captain, Lt Cdr Brian Mills, required that Hale gained his watch-keeping certificate first, to prove he could take charge of a submarine responsibly. Eventually putting up his second stripe in December 1957, he would have the increase in pay back-dated to the date he made seniority.

Back at Britannia Royal Naval College, in September 1957, the independent-minded Rob Forsyth was disenchanted at being treated like a schoolboy rather than a young adult.

'As a bit of a rebel, I resented the discipline of "old navy" since Victoria's time being imposed on 18-year-olds [for by then that was the minimum age of cadets]. The seeds of my move to submarines were sown, because the surface navy ruled the roost at Dartmouth with all its mind-boggling tradition and formality. The staff was accustomed to managing – actually more like bullying – children into a naval way of doing things. They had no idea how to manage older teenagers like myself, other than to continue in the same vein.'

Born in July 1939, two months before the outbreak of the Second World War, in which his father saw action with the RNVR, Forsyth grew up far from the ocean in leafy Warwickshire and Hertfordshire. He devoured stories of the Navy in action, his father inculcating a love of the sea. One of Forsyth's earliest memories was aged five hiding in the front garden of the family home by the drive gates, across which he and his brother had arrayed a banner saying: 'Welcome Home Daddy'. He had no idea, though, what his dad might look like as he had been away at war for so long. 'When the gates were opened there was a naval officer in uniform with his cap at an angle. I think that is when I decided to join the navy because I liked the cap.'

Forsyth's sailor dad infused his son with a work ethic, telling him: 'If you want to get anywhere in life you should give it everything you have. Half-measures are never enough.' This had an enormous impact on the youngster and it would govern his attitude to life.

In 1955, at the age of 16, just a decade after the end of the Second World War, Forsyth was applying for a scholarship to Dartmouth. After spending four years at a grammar school, he would switch to two years at a private school, where it was thought the regime would better prepare him for the naval college. During his first two years at Dartmouth, by day Forsyth learned naval lore, basic parade ground drill and seamanship. In the classroom, aside from in-depth study of Admiralty seamanship manuals, the cadets were also taught applied maths, physics, a language (Spanish for Forsyth), naval history, astro navigation, terrestrial navigation and communications. Gunnery, Anti-Submarine Warfare (ASW), mine-sweeping and an introduction to naval aviation were also served up. The last was most exciting, with flights in a Tiger Moth biplane trainer and Dove air navigation aircraft, though airsickness was not so enjoyable.

Meanwhile, what kind of Cold War at sea would Hale and Forsyth – one still learning his seagoing trade in the second-line boats and the other a cadet – soon join? It is impossible to understand the arena they and others would one day enter without first voyaging across the landscape of the early Cold War under the sea and through some of the major events that shaped it. Out there in the vast, cold ocean was a secret conflict being waged by submarines – on both sides – that owed much to Nazi technology.

3 | THE FORMIDABLE ELECTROBOOT

F orays by British submarines into dangerous waters off northern Russia could only happen thanks to Hitler's scientists and engineers.

In the closing weeks of the Second Word War a special commando unit, which boasted James Bond's creator, Ian Fleming, as one of its operational planners, had raced for Nazi technological secrets. It wanted to secure them before they were destroyed or the Soviets got them. One of the key achievements of 30 Amphibious Assault Unit (30 AU) was capturing snorkel technology and also advanced submarines at Kiel on Germany's Baltic coast. The British amassed nearly 100 surrendered German submarines at the Northern Irish port of Lishally, near Londonderry.

The Type XXI U-boat was a revolutionary kind of submarine, with high-speed batteries providing up to 17 knots submerged. This was extraordinary when the most Allied boats could manage submerged was 9 knots. Snorkel masts enabled Germany's advanced diesel submarines to stay submerged – and safe from enemy attack – while venting generator fumes, recharging their batteries and sucking in fresh air.

Capable of impressive submerged endurance, via use of the snort mast (as the snorkel became known), the Type XXI had a sleek, supremely hydrodynamic hull form, with no external guns other than cannons mounted within the fin.

Combined with boosted battery power delivering high underwater speed a Type XXI did not have to surface to attack a convoy. It could fire 18 torpedoes (three salvoes) in around 20 minutes, which was as long as it took any other submarine to load a single torpedo.

The Type XXI could manage 50 hours submerged on batteries at full capacity (charged), an endurance that could be doubled by reducing energy consumption by 50 per cent. Other submarines could only achieve half an hour submerged on battery power, or 24 hours if they shut almost all equipment down. Using the snort to recharge the batteries, the prime objective for a Type XXI was an entire patrol submerged (and it took only three hours' snorting to recharge batteries). It was also very stealthy at low speeds, using what were called creeping speed motors (on rubber mountings) to absorb noise. The Type XXI could safely dive up to 440ft (90ft deeper than the most modern Second World War-era British submarine), with a crush depth of more than 1,000ft.

Fortunately for the Allies only two 'electroboots' ever deployed on combat patrol during the Second World War. Crew training, technological defects common to any cutting-edge technology, and intensive bombing kept the majority of the 120 'electroboots' non-operational. They were captured or destroyed. Even more remarkable were Type XVIIB boats, which used air-independent hydrogen peroxide propulsion, removing the necessity to even poke a snort mast above the surface.

Following a series of top-level meetings, it was decided the British, Americans and Russians should each have ten U-boats of all varieties, the remainder to be scuttled in Operation Deadlight.

The Soviets had limited contemporary experience on the open ocean in any kind of warship – during the Second World War the Red Navy fought mainly in littoral waters or operated along rivers and other inland waterways.

As a result the Russians requested that Royal Navy crews sail their allocated U-boats to Leningrad. The Soviets hid their lack of confidence on the high seas behind claims that they were being given defective submarines. The British had, though, delivered detailed seaworthiness assessments of the boats to their new owners.

The Americans, who took two XXIs, would base the design of their new Tang Class upon the Nazi boat type. They also reconstructed some of their newer Second World War-era submarines, under a programme entitled Greater Underwater Propulsive Power, or GUPPY, to incorporate German innovations.

Some Type XXIs were even pressed into service, the British operating two. While one was scrapped in 1949 after running on trials, the other was given to the French. They commissioned seven ex-German U-boats into their fleet, one of the Type XXIs seeing service into the late 1960s.

Even the Swedes, neutral during the conflict, recognised the necessity of acquiring revolutionary U-boats if their own navy was not to lose its status as a leading submarine operator. They raised *U-3503* – scuttled inside their territorial waters – from the bottom of the Baltic and towed her to a naval base. Experts carried out a dry-dock inspection of her innovations before the submarine was scrapped. In the mid-1950s, when they needed to revive their submarine arm as part of NATO, the West

Germans adopted a similar practice, locating U-boats sunk during the war and raising them.

Faced with a sudden need to match the West's operational capability the Russians made the most of their inherited U-boats. Four of the ten they received from the British were Type XXIs, seeing service in the Soviet's Navy's Baltic Fleet for nine years. They also wasted no time in replicating the Type XXI in the Zulu and Whiskey classes of diesel boat. The British decided to implement what they had gleaned from the XXIs in a radical reconstruction programme for some of their T-Class submarines. Eight boats, including HMS *Taciturn*, were taken in hand between 1950 and 1956. Cut in two, they had a whole new section inserted containing two more electric motors and a fourth battery. It gave them a submerged top speed of between 15 and 18 knots but this could only be maintained for a short period. There were no external guns – these were removed as part of the rebuild – for they were given sleek streamlined outer casings. A large fin enclosed the bridge, periscopes and masts. Space was also made for specialist intelligence-gathering equipment.

Taciturn and her reconstructed sisters were known as the 'Super-Ts'. Externally she bore little, if any, resemblance to the submarine that had emerged from the Vickers yard at Barrow-in-Furness in the north-west of England in 1944. *Taciturn* was blooded in action against the Japanese. She sank a number of small vessels and also joined forces with her sister submarine *Thorough*, both using their 4-inch deck guns to bombard shore targets. The first to receive the Super-T conversion, *Taciturn* was a perfect solution for cash-strapped Britain, almost bankrupted by the Second World War, yet needing to match the rising threat of Russian naval power. Construction of brand-new boats was not possible for some years. Submarines built to combat Hitler's Germany and militaristic Japan were refashioned using the fruit of Nazi science to become the best Britain could send against the Soviets.

It was Vice Admiral Sir Geoffrey Oliver who proposed the Royal Navy's much reduced submarine force should take the war to the enemy.

Staking out Soviet submarine bases in the Kola Peninsula and on the shores of the White Sea, they would eliminate the threat before it could break out into the vastness of the Atlantic. Oliver, who first went to sea as a midshipman in the battleship *Dreadnought* in 1916, also saw action in the Second World War as a cruiser captain. He had even commanded carrier strike forces, so was a well-rounded tactician, though never a submariner. His April 1949 paper – written when Oliver was Assistant Chief of the Naval Staff (ACNS) – gave impetus to the conversion of *Taciturn* and her seven sister boats into Super-Ts. If things turned hot they would sink Soviet boats in the Barents Sea, hunting down and killing them with torpedoes, or laying mines.

The precedent for using submarines to destroy other submarines had been set in the recent world war. British boats sank 36 enemy submarines, while the Americans claimed 23 Japanese. All but one of the targets was sunk while on the surface. The distinction of hunting and killing an enemy submarine while both were submerged fell to Lieutenant James Launders in HMS *Venturer*. His successful attack on *U-864* off Norway, on 9 February 1945, remains the only one of its kind and was achieved after *Venturer* trailed the zig-zagging enemy boat for some hours. Having fixed the German's position – and likely future track – via ASDIC, Launders fired a spread of four torpedoes, at 17-second intervals. *U-864* managed to evade three, but steered into the path of the fourth and was blown apart.

By the mid-1950s Britain's navy simply had to be more aggressive and push its submarines forward, to repeat Launders's remarkable feat in order to make up for withered global sea control capability. It had not only ceded supremacy on the high seas to America, but was facing relegation into third place by the burgeoning maritime might of the Soviets. Even before the Second World War Stalin had been urging Red Navy chiefs to build a battle fleet that would break free of the traditional coast-hugging role. Within three months of the fighting in Europe ending, Stalin decreed the USSR should create a powerful ocean-going navy. Unfortunately, the vessels that started to come off the slipways, such as Sverdlov Class cruisers, were outmoded before they were launched. They replicated Nazi technology without taking it much further.

May 1955 saw the creation of the Warsaw Pact, which militarily melded the USSR with its satellite states in Eastern Europe to counter NATO.

Emboldened by Kremlin concessions to protests for more freedom in Poland, on 23 October 1956 200,000 Hungarians took to the streets, objecting to the presence of Russian troops in their country. Their revolution was brutally suppressed by the Red Army. Around 20,000 Hungarians paid with their lives for daring to try and cast off the Soviet yoke.

Even as Russian tanks crushed dreams of democracy on the streets of Budapest, the Soviets were threatening nuclear war against Britain and France in response to an invasion of Egypt.

The Americans did not back their Second World War allies' bid to take back control of the Suez Canal by force, while the new Soviet overlord, Nikita Khrushchev – supporting the fervent Arab nationalist leader Colonel Gamal Abdel Nasser – warned he would unleash 'rocket weapons' against London and Paris.

Despite a measure of military success, it was President Dwight D. Eisenhower's fury at his allies going it alone that forced them, ultimately, to withdraw from Suez. The Cold War had turned nasty, but open warfare between the two armed camps had been avoided. Beyond confrontations on land, lethal shadow boxing between the naval forces of East and West was already a facet of the Cold War confrontation.

In April 1956 the mysterious disappearance, and probable murder, of a frogman trying to spy on Soviet warships within sight of *Taciturn*'s home base in Gosport heightened tension.

The Russians were returning the courtesy of a British naval diplomatic mission to Leningrad the previous year. As the aircraft carrier HMS *Triumph* and her escorts sailed up the river Neva, they passed building yards containing dozens of surface warships and submarines in various states of completion. Many in the British naval community had refused until then to believe the Soviets really were undertaking such an ambitious programme. Their hosts had not actually meant to leave so much on display. When the British naval squadron sailed back down the Neva, smokescreens were generated in front of the building yards. With *Triumph's* height as an aircraft carrier, it was still possible for naval intelligence specialists to take photographs.

When the Russian Navy sent the cruiser *Ordzhonikidze* to Portsmouth she carried no less a person than Nikita Khrushchev. On the British side there was a great desire to learn as much as possible about the Russian warship – a temptation too hard to resist, especially as she was parked in the centre of the Hampshire harbour.

Lionel 'Buster' Crabb, a well-known veteran of daring underwater exploits in the Second World War, was ordered by MI6 to see what he could find out about the *Ordzhonikidze*. Crabb had already covertly inspected the propulsion of a Sverdlov Class cruiser in 1953 – *Sverdlov* herself, when the vessel was anchored at Spithead for the Coronation Review of Queen Elizabeth II – discovering an innovative bow thruster. Three years later it was worth seeing what else might be below the waterline. Crabb stayed at the Sally Port Hotel in Portsmouth with his MI6 handler, who signed the register as 'Mr Smith'. After the former naval officer departed to carry out his dive, 'Mr Smith' cleansed the room of

Crabb's civilian clothes and other belongings. Newspapers were soon carrying stories about Crabb disappearing on an espionage mission. The Navy maintained he was testing new diving equipment in Stokes Bay, just down the coast, rather than diving in Portsmouth Harbour. Soviet sources said sailors aboard the cruiser had spotted a frogman. An official complaint was lodged with the Foreign Office. Nobody publicly admitted to anything. The head of MI6 was forced to resign by the Prime Minister, Anthony Eden, for launching an ill-advised mission without specific authorisation by the government. The Navy had allegedly assisted MI6, providing a boat and a naval officer to support Crabb's dive.

It was claimed the local Special Branch squad sent someone to rip out relevant pages in the hotel register.

The furious British government cancelled various military intelligence-gathering operations, including deploying submarines into the Barents Sea. This caused massive loss of face for the Royal Navy but in the absence of British boats taking part, the Americans received a confidential briefing on surveillance skills from Cdr John Coote. He had captained the Super-T boat HMS *Totem* on at least one recent spying mission in the Arctic. At one stage *Totem* had to surface so one of her officers, Peter Lucy, could carry out temporary repairs to a defective S-band search-receiver. Mounted in the periscope it picked up potential threats by detecting radars of searching aircraft and surface vessels. Normally such a procedure required a workshop, but *Totem* was hundreds of miles from home. Lucy would be working solo in the housing at the top of the fin and if the Russians loomed over the horizon Coote would dive the boat under him. Lucy would have to swim for his life and, if captured, probably suffer a grisly fate at the hands of Soviet interrogators. Several months later, Cdr Coote told senior British naval officers and the US Navy that intelligence gathered on the Soviet Navy in the Barents had revealed a weakness in its ASW capabilities. To gain such an edge risks were justified.

Not long after Coote showed the Americans how valuable Royal Navy missions in the Barents were, the British PM was warned that without them the US–UK defence relationship was at risk. It was felt the Americans would press ahead with the submarine surveillance programme anyway, denying the British access to data collected. Eden was still worried about the possibility of such forays sparking a hot war, so he remained true to one of his favourite sayings: 'Peace comes first, always.'

Eden's subsequent Suez misadventure led only to national humiliation and his resignation, in January 1957. Harold Macmillan, a firm supporter of the Anglo-American 'Special Relationship', succeeded him. The new PM authorised resumption of British participation in submarine deployments to the Barents. He was only too well aware that Soviet military doctrine was following a new direction that would require intelligence gathering in Northern seas. For while Khrushchev agreed with the need for a powerful global navy he saw there was no point in trying to match Western strength, but rather to outflank it. A battle-cruiser programme was cut, the number of Sverdlovs under construction revised downwards. Khrushchev announced a 'Revolution in Military Affairs', which sought to steer the Russian armed forces away from huge, lumbering conventional formations, to smaller high-tech units. They would deploy missiles with nuclear warheads.

Many of these new weapons would, from the 1950s onwards, be tested at firing ranges and detonation test sites located on the island of Novaya Zemlya. The Barents, Arctic and Kara seas washed its shores, but it was from the western side that it was most approachable by submarines.

To Khrushchev nuclear weapons were a means to achieving superpower punch while enabling a reduction in military spending, diverting resources instead to the civilian economy. Submarines armed with missiles would be a key component of the USSR's defence revolution. To enact this element Khrushchev turned to a man he had served alongside during the 1941–45 war, Sergei Gorshkov, making his old comrade in arms Commander-in-Chief of the Soviet Navy in 1957. The ascent of Gorshkov would reinvigorate the Soviet Union's naval forces and make them more aggressive, both in home waters and overseas.

On 9 June 1957, what remained of a corpse in a diving suit – minus head and hands – was found in the sea off Chichester. It was difficult to identify, although a scar on a knee was supposedly a match for Crabb. While an inquest recorded an open verdict the coroner decided that, on balance of probability, it was him. One popular theory was that Crabb had been spotted by the Russian cruiser's own frogmen on security duty. He had either been captured alive and taken aboard ship or killed in the water. More recently it has been suggested Crabb was sucked into the *Ordzhonikidze*'s screws. When at anchor in a foreign port, the cruiser turned them vigorously from time to time as a standard counter-measure against snooping frogmen.

With Crabb apparently suffering a grisly fate at the hands of the Soviet Navy – during a spying mission just a few hundred yards from *Taciturn*'s home berth at HMS *Dolphin* – did any submariner need to be reminded the Cold War could be fatal?

4 | YOU MUST NOT SAY A WORD

When she set sail from Portsmouth on 4 September 1957, HMS *Taciturn* headed west and then up through the Irish Sea.

As would be typical of many submarines of the nations actively engaged in the Cold War under the sea, the front line was joined the moment *Taciturn* left her home base.

There was no fixed line of trenches to signify the point where combat conditions prevailed – distinct from rear areas where there was little if any risk of conflict. On land a carefully delineated Iron Curtain existed, across which tanks and troops of each side dared not trespass for fear of sparking a massive conflict. For submarines and the men who operated them, the front line was fluid and intermingled, stretching all the way from the deep ocean to coastal waters.

As *Taciturn* cast off from the jetty, newspapers were carrying reports on a big Russian naval exercise, which was to be held in Arctic waters between 10 September and 15 October.

The Kremlin issued warnings for all foreign ships to stay out, as live ammunition would be used. Legally of course, *Taciturn* was perfectly at ease to operate within the Barents Sea. If she made her presence felt by cruising on the surface, within international waters, there was nothing the Russians could do about it, technically speaking. However, they regarded the Barents as exclusively theirs. Strangers should keep out.

Around a fortnight before HMS *Taciturn* left Portsmouth the Soviets conducted a successful test flight of an 8K71 Intercontinental Ballistic Missile (ICBM). It was launched from the Baikonur Cosmodrome in Kazakhstan, describing an arc of some 6,000km to splash down in the Pacific. If the Russians could put a warhead on such a missile – as they undoubtedly would– it would tear up the rules of the game in the East–West stand-off.

At that stage of the Cold War, to deliver their nuclear weapons the Americans relied on B-52 bombers, while the UK's Royal Air Force (RAF) was also in the vanguard of countering the Russian threat, operating the Vulcan and Valiant. NATO estimated 16 million Russians could be killed or injured via raids on key Soviet cities by the British V-Force before the American B-52s got anywhere near their targets.

The Valiant had been used on strike missions against Egyptian troops during the Suez Crisis. Proving its conventional lethality, it performed well in a role that harked back to the days of the Second World War, but in any conflict with the Soviets the West's bombers would spend their time dodging flak and surface-to-air missiles.

Rockets travelled at thousands of miles an hour, invulnerable to anti-air defences, and the NATO bombers' home airfields would be easily destroyed. America and NATO's promises of protection for Europe seemed rather hollow. The US Air Force's Atlas ICBM would not achieve a successful test flight until late October 1958 and it was not ready as an operational weapon until a year later.

Taciturn was now being sent into Soviet waters to find a chink in the foe's armour, to try and give the West an edge in some fashion while it struggled to catch up in the ICBM race.

Aside from recording individual war vessels in sound and vision, noting data on weapons and radar performance – all useful tools if it came to war – NATO submarines studied naval base infrastructure. They also observed how Soviet vessels manoeuvred at sea and noted any tactical bad habits.

To know an enemy's vulnerabilities – and capabilities – without him realising you had gained that insight awarded the possessor a killer edge. And that was the point of *Taciturn*'s mission to the Barents. It was not to sink enemy vessels, but to get close enough to record the distinctive sound signatures of Soviet warships.

Early on 6 September, shortly after the boat had dived, her captain, Lt Cdr Roche O'Connor, made a broadcast promising his men he would soon explain as much as he could about their important mission.

For the next five days the boat would remain submerged and carry out an exercise, trying to sneak into a formation of NATO surface vessels. It was an important dress rehearsal for the mission ahead, to see if the boat could spy on warships without being rumbled. Thereafter *Taciturn* would head for the submarine depot ship HMS *Adamant*, anchored in Rothesay Bay, off the Isle of Bute, to take on stores.

Sailors would be able to write to their families, leaving their letters with the post room aboard *Adamant* to be forwarded after the boat departed. To preserve operational secrecy, none of *Taciturn*'s men were allowed to telephone home. O'Connor advised his men the boat would be dived for most, if not all, of the subsequent seven weeks. He warned: 'We must remain completely and utterly undetected by friend and foe.'

Furthermore, if the Russians caught them, it would be 'unpleasant and most dangerous'.

The chart table was to be screened. Only a select few officers with the correct level of clearance would know the boat's exact position.

Radio silence would only be broken in an extreme emergency. On returning to the UK they must not speak about what they had been doing. Most chilling of all, they and their families would for some time be monitored by the security services. O'Connor cautioned: 'You must not say a word to even your wives or mothers.' Concluding the briefing he explained lights must be switched off where and when possible, to conserve battery power. The boat would run in Defence State 2, which meant ready to go deep at any moment. Throughout whatever lay ahead, the captain's ability to take the right decision in moments of crisis – retaining his cool while others around might be losing theirs – would be essential to the survival of *Taciturn*. In the eyes of a 22-year-old rating, Leading Engineer Mechanic M. Hurley, who worked in the machinery spaces, O'Connor was 'first and foremost a gentleman'.

In the 1950s, when notions of Kipling-style gentlemanly bravery in the face of the enemy still resonated, this was a true tribute and sign of respect. An officer could have many personality faults, but so long as he was a gentleman he could be forgiven a lot. Writing about O'Connor in a secret diary, Hurley observed of his captain: 'He knows his job, is patient, polite and understanding. Unlike many submarine skippers he never cracks or shows signs of irritation under strain (and if he did it would be understandable). Very popular with the crew and is considerate to them. In all one could not ask for a better man as Captain.'

As the Cold War increased its intensity, those qualities of cool command in the face of pressure and also a genuine care for the welfare of sailors would remain vital. Steely courage and technical competence, not forgetting an ability to think fast – and to come up with solutions to problems that only a non-conformist mind could find – were also important. There was no accessible chain of command beyond the confines of a solo submarine in hostile waters. The buck stopped with the captain.

And Lt Cdr O'Connor was determined to make absolutely certain his crew were in the right mindset. They must understand the mission they were embarking on could require the ultimate sacrifice.

Who knew what the Russians would do to his men if they were caught snooping around in the Barents Sea? Grabbing the hand-mike for the public broadcast system, O'Connor gave his men a resolute, steely call to action:

'This will be a wartime patrol – we must get good results.'

Aboard *Taciturn* as she headed for Soviet waters was an officer unlikely to have been a product of Dartmouth.

To handle her forthcoming penetration of the Red Navy's domain, *Taciturn* had a specially embarked team of experts, ready to apply their dark arts. One was a Lieutenant Commander called Lucas, which seemed extremely likely to be an alias. Of portly build, he had the appearance and manner of a foreigner, with a hint of an accent. Pleasant in nature, he was inevitably the object of much curiosity. *Taciturn's* men speculated 'Lucas' was actually Russian and someone suggested he could speak up to 14 languages. Hurley confided to his diary that 'one thing is certain – he has made this trip for a useful purpose and will make use of some unusual talents'. Lucas would probably have been gainfully employed listening in to Soviet wireless transmissions. As such 'Lucas' was a key advisor to O'Connor. Whether he was Russian or came from some other East European nation, he was playing for high stakes. Should *Taciturn* be cornered and her crew captured, he could expect only brutal interrogation and execution.

Despite rough seas, on Sunday, 8 September 1957, as she edged up through the Irish Sea, *Taciturn* used her snort mast. Having taken in air and vented fumes, the snort was lowered. To conserve battery power, carbon dioxide absorbers were kept off and oxygen generators not used for much of the day. It was important to push the envelope of dived endurance.

Hurley wrote in his secret diary that conditions became 'quite stuffy'. If anyone wanted to smoke it was almost impossible to light a match thanks to a lack of oxygen. Smoking was an essential morale boost for sailors under pressure, a refuge from the strange pressures of their trade, even though it poisoned the atmosphere.

As time wore on people got out of breath very quickly and there was bad news on the fresh-water front – the patrol was estimated to last 47 days, but already there was only enough left for 20.

The consumption rate had to be reduced radically.

Shaving would be out of the question.

As *Taciturn* ventured into the middle of the unsuspecting group of NATO warships for her tactical exercise, the boat suddenly rocked violently from side to side. Had practice depth charges been dropped?

Word soon spread that *Taciturn* had actually struck an uncharted rock pinnacle.

The Control Room requested damage assessment reports from throughout the boat, which fortunately discovered no leaks. O'Connor ordered the submarine to periscope depth. Once he had checked there were no lurking surface ships to collide with, *Taciturn* surfaced and headed for the depot ship HMS *Adamant*. As soon as the boat was secured alongside, divers were put over the side to inspect *Taciturn*, finding only slight damage. It was nothing that would impede the mission.

Adamant was sent to Rothesay in late 1954, to support the Scottish-based 3rd Submarine Flotilla, but she didn't mind accepting visitors like *Taciturn*. The depot ship was a floating one-stop shop, built during the Second World War as mother ship for submarines operating with the Eastern Fleet against the Japanese. While alongside her, submariners would sling their hammocks in *Adamant*'s mess decks, while the officers moved into cabins. Aside from providing somewhere for sailors to live and eat, *Adamant* – whose Ship's Company included shipwrights, metal-workers, ship fitters and even coppersmiths – was host to workshops in which both heavy and light machinery could be mended. Torpedoes could be repaired and fresh ones supplied. During the 1950s she would be mother to half a dozen boats at a time, supplying power and fresh-water supplies, to relieve strain on their own systems. On this occasion an outbreak of Asian flu meant nobody was allowed off the submarine. The depot ship lowered stores over the side, restoring the boat's food lockers and replenishing fresh-water tanks. A false deck was created over storage boxes in passageways; fruit and vegetables were kept either hanging up or packed into fridge compartments alongside fresh meat.

At 06.20 on 10 September 1957 *Taciturn* slipped from *Adamant* and headed north. The warning klaxon for diving sounded twice and she began to submerge, the bridge team clambering down ladders within the fin. The last man down from the bridge shut and secured the hatches. Lieutenant Commander O'Connor went to the periscope and took a quick look, a senior rating stepping forward behind him to secure the lower hatch.

The priority was to immediately assess *Taciturn*'s own noise levels, to see if anything might give her away to Soviet sonar and hydrophone operators. A frequent source of such giveaway sounds would be cables or other fixtures, such as anchors, not secured properly within the outer casing.

After checking her own noise levels, and satisfied *Taciturn* was not generating 'rattles', the boat was 'trimmed'. This was necessary to ensure she was neutrally buoyant and neither heavy by the bows or by the stern.

In a Super-T boat like *Taciturn*, the main ballast tanks were on the outside of the pressure hull, although there were also two supplementary internal ballast tanks as well. As *Taciturn* dived she vented air out of the top of the tanks, with water entering the bottom via free flood holes. To surface the vents were shut. Compressed air – stored in bottles and used sparingly – was released into the top of *Taciturn*'s main ballast tanks, forcing water out of the bottom, creating positive buoyancy.

As she dived at the beginning of her journey to Arctic waters, the boat's fore hydroplanes (on the bows) and aft hydroplanes (on the rudder) angled down and up respectively.

Rather like an aircraft's flaps, hydroplanes function by water flowing over them creating pressure, in the case of a diving submarine forcing the bows down and the stern up. Propellers push the boat forward and under at the required speed. Once the submarine is below the surface, small internal tanks are filled to adjust the weight and longitudinal stability of the boat

This is a process known as 'catching the trim'. Ensuring all this went smoothly would be the First Lieutenant, assisted by the Chief Stoker who probably knew more than the officer (by virtue of long experience).

They were responsible for calculating changes in internal weight, such as the amount of stores aboard, as well as torpedoes, fuel and the number of people – their collective weight, together with personal kit and any equipment they might have brought aboard – not forgetting engineering stores. These were computed and appropriate adjustments made to the internal tanks – known as the auxiliary and compensating tanks – which had been dipped, to gauge the levels while *Taciturn* was at *Dolphin*. The First Lieutenant did this again when the boat was alongside *Adamant*, arriving at a figure of so many thousand gallons of water, representing the adjustable weight. *Taciturn* therefore modified her displacement by pumping more water into, or pumping it out of, the internal tanks. This aimed to give the boat perfect balance in water. It meant that once dived, and having achieved neutral buoyancy, *Taciturn* could hover under the surface, both props stopped. Or she could be manoeuvred with ease and precision at very low speeds. Until trim was achieved the boat would only be taken to periscope depth – 60ft – but if sea conditions were still too rough the submarine would go deeper. Calm was essential to achieving proper trim.

Once cruising under the water – the boat switching from diesel generators to batteries – *Taciturn*'s direction, while achieving trim, was controlled by a combination of the rudder, aft hydroplanes and forward hydroplanes all working together. Satisfied trim had been achieved and no noise was being made, Lt Cdr O'Connor ordered the boat to surface. The men controlling the hydroplanes turned wheels that angled both sets of hydroplanes up. As soon as *Taciturn*'s fin was clear of the water, and fresh air coming into the boat via the open hatch, a low-pressure air blower was used to blow the remaining water out of the main ballast tanks. In rough weather the LP blower would be run every hour to keep the tanks full of air.

After making good progress on the surface, at 10.00 on 12 September radar picked up a possible ship contact, so the boat dived and began snorting.

It seemed likely *Taciturn* would not surface for many days. O'Connor explained over the broadcast system that not only would this reduce the chances of being seen but also make for a more comfortable ride. The sea got rougher and rougher and it appeared something had broken free under the casing, but by 15 September the weather had eased. *Taciturn* surfaced and two sailors were sent out to fix the anchor back in place. They had not been at work long when an aircraft was detected by radar. The two men were called back inside and *Taciturn* executed a crash dive.

The Officer of the Watch reported sighting a surfaced submarine through the periscope. Silent Routine was imposed, with all movement to be cautious and no loud noises. Unfortunately it appeared the anchor had broken loose again. After a period snorting, *Taciturn* surfaced shortly before 05.00 on 17 September. An hour later the submarine dived, hoping to have finally fixed the problem, but apparently not. The anchor really had been secured, so what could it be? One of *Taciturn*'s senior ratings remarked to Hurley, rather sourly: 'We might as well tow a bell for the amount of noise we are making.' As there was no sign of any potentially hostile activity, except a fleeting aircraft contact, the submarine surfaced, making yet another determined effort to stop the noise.

If they couldn't, the mission might have to be abandoned.

5 | AN EMBARRASSMENT ...
OR DEAD

It was now two weeks since *Taciturn* had left Portsmouth, with the boat's men restricted to just one wash a day for hands and face. There was only enough water for one full body wash a week per man. Everybody was beginning to stink and the rancid body odour was far from pleasant in such a confined space, although submariners cultivated a tolerance for it.

The boat's interior was damp and chilly, with an increasing amount of condensation, caused by warm bodies and hot-running equipment in a cold hull. Some sailors guessed *Taciturn* was within the Arctic Circle and speculated the submarine sighted had been a Russian. The mysterious noise persisted, forcing the boat to surface and dive three times during the night of 18 September. Lieutenant Commander O'Connor considered abandoning the mission. There was no way they would remain safe in Soviet waters with such a giveaway. Hurley reflected in his diary: 'it was pointless to go on as, if located, we would either be a grave embarrassment to HM Government or dead!'

That morning an aircraft contact, moving very fast, was picked up 200 miles away. It seemed from the electronic signature that it was a Soviet Badger bomber. The big jet eventually passed right overhead, travelling at 550 mph. Hurley noted: 'It's our first real contact with our "Comrades".'

At 17.30 on 19 September the boat surfaced; a potential source for the noise was found in the casing and thrown overboard.

Hurley by now had a boil and felt dreadful, with a heavy cold.

The Coxswain – a senior rating, third-most important man in the boat after the captain and First Lieutenant – told Hurley he would find a means of curing it. Had *Taciturn* possessed a naval doctor he might well have lanced the boil and drained the pus away. That was an extremely painful process and might have risked reinfection or the infection spreading, particularly with so little water available to wash. The Coxswain used a warm compress to bring pus to the surface and, once this had been done several times, the boil burst of its own accord.

*

As *Taciturn* got closer to Soviet waters O'Connor stepped up silent running and decided to make a broadcast, stressing the need for absolute stealth.

'In many ways we have managed to cut down on noise but from now on we will have to be really quiet all the time. There must be no crashing around with stores, no shouting or hammering or dropping hatch covers.'

He gave them as much detail on the mission as he was allowed: 'I am unable to say where we are. But we are in the operational area and for 48 hours, starting from yesterday afternoon, we are in a heavily patrolled U-boat area [Soviet submarine patrol zone]. During the subsequent 48 hours we will cross a line into an area heavily patrolled by both submarines and surface vessels. On the other side of that line is an area that will be most interesting and keep us very busy.'

They would be evading Russian attention while getting close enough to record intelligence. The boat stopped snorting at 02.30 with the intention of not doing so again for at least 24 hours to minimise potential exposure. *Taciturn* would reduce use of machinery to only the essentials, conserving battery power and keeping noise down.

There would be no hot meals during the day – just sandwiches for lunch (no banging around the galley with pots and pans). It also reduced the drain on battery power and ensured people could stay at their stations and not move about to go and get hot food.

Taciturn crept forward at minimum speed, reducing prop noise. Any sailors off watch were ordered into their bunks. Most lights were turned off, as were nearly all heaters. They must conserve the battery at all costs.

Hurley was soon afflicted with a rumbling stomach, scribbling down his thoughts as he lay in his bunk: 'We bake our own bread, which soon goes. Tea, milk, sugar and water must be watched carefully and often dinner is very small as it's cold, though normally supper is a good large meal. It's not that we are starved so much as the long gaps between good meals (which are really good) and the fact that, if one is hungry, there is no bread to fill up on as is normal. But before we are through things will be a lot worse.'

Water consumption was still too high – some 300 gallons a day – but offset by a distiller creating fresh supplies.

The First Lieutenant warned if water usage continued to exceed 250 gallons daily he would shut off the supply completely. No mugs of tea, no washing at all or indeed *any* activity that required water, for at least 12 hours. The rations state was not good either – there was food for 19 days left, but the boat was expected to be out a further 29.

As if all that wasn't trying enough, because *Taciturn* was not going to surface for some time, rubbish could not be ditched overboard. The stench of trash added to that of filthy bodies, made an almost unbearable combination. Hurley noted in his diary: 'things are becoming tighter and the living harder'.

A sub-surface contact was reported during the Morning Watch, with a strong likelihood of a Russian submarine.

This was no surprise as they were well into the home waters of the Red Banner Northern Fleet.

Taciturn faced the dilemma of staying deep to remain undetected, or coming up to periscope depth and raising her Electronic Counter Measure (ECM) mast to spy on Russian activity. There were several air contacts and more signs of a Soviet submarine nearby.

Taciturn became a tomb – silent, cold, dark, with only the on-duty watch out of their bunks. The captain banned anything but 'necessary movement'.

During the evening of 22 September, as *Taciturn* cautiously poked her snort above the waves, telegraphists listened in on the wireless frequencies. They picked up a transmission from a Russian submarine, only 7,000 yards away (not even four miles).

Even when that potential threat melted away, *Taciturn* ceased snorting every hour so sonar operators could listen for any Russians nearby. It meant the batteries were not fully charged by dawn and it was dangerous to poke the snort mast above the surface during daylight. Tempers frayed, people flashing up at the slightest provocation. Hurley put it down to 'boredom, lack of regular food, cold and headaches (which most people seem to have) and Rum, which is I think the main cause'. Yet, without the daily ration of rum to take the edge off things, life really would be beyond a joke.

There were indications of a determined effort to flush out *Taciturn*. Mysterious vibrations and bumps reverberated through the hull, which were possibly the Soviets chasing phantoms with depth charges. A message was passed along from the Control Room asking if anybody had heard an actual explosion in the water. In the early evening of 23 September, *Taciturn* detected a Soviet submarine very close. People moved as silently as possible to Listening Stations, using slow deliberate motions to avoid bashing into anything and creating noise. They taped the sound signature of the Russian boat. Over the next 63 minutes, the target did plenty to give itself away, using a snort mast and also active sonar pings.

Was it a Whiskey or a Zulu? There were plenty of them around, with Soviet yards constructing 262 between 1950 and 1957 (236 Whiskeys and 26 Zulus). The British boat's conversion to Super-T had taken more than two years to complete (from the end of 1948 to the spring of 1951) and her displacement was now 1,740 tons submerged. The Whiskey was 1,350 tons and a Zulu weighed in at 2,350 tons dived. *Taciturn* was more than 293ft long, the Whiskey 249ft and Zulu 295ft. As foes they were well matched.

Taciturn picked up various unidentified noises before again detecting the definitive sound of a submarine. The British boat closed down the distance to make further recordings but the contact faded.

A snowstorm offered an opportunity to snort under cover, reducing surface visibility by obscuring the tip of the mast. It didn't last long. Likely-looking blizzards were spotted elsewhere through the periscope but nothing came *Taciturn*'s way, so she was unable to snort again. The air grew fouler and increasing efforts were made to reduce battery consumption.

Lieutenant Commander O'Connor's orders stated that if *Taciturn* knew the Russians had spotted her she was to head home immediately.

A really determined search was now being made by the Soviets in the area where *Taciturn* had first detected a Russian submarine. There was a lot of air activity over that patch of sea. Up to three destroyers were carrying out search patterns. O'Connor concluded he had no choice but to withdraw.

Once inside a NATO exercise area *Taciturn* would be permitted to break radio silence, letting FOSM and the Admiralty know the patrol had been concluded. It was estimated they would reach the UK in around seven days. O'Connor took *Taciturn* as deep as he could and piled on knots to leave the Soviet patrol line far behind. Later, when *Taciturn* returned to periscope depth, the ECM operators picked up aircraft, two of which appeared to be running search patterns. At 20.00 on 27 September, *Taciturn* surfaced, remaining there for 24 hours, a strong swell making it difficult for her men to sleep as the boat rolled badly. Overnight Lt Cdr O'Connor was able to send his signal.

The boat would make the final part of her passage home on the surface, *Taciturn* proceeding down through the Minches, lids shut, snort mast bringing in the fresh air while getting rid of fumes and foul odours.

Hot meals were back on the agenda.

In his diary Hurley reflected on the peculiar and arduous existence of submariners: 'no one really can know what life in a boat is like, not even the General Service [surface navy] ratings until they do a trip. Some of it is unbelievable: the condensation which is like rain at times, the fog, literally, [inside the boat] when we surface quickly, the varying pressure when snorting on one's ear drums, the damp and cold and absolutely cramped style (35 bodies in a [bunk] space smaller than our kitchen at home), lack of water, fresh air, daylight, sleeping in one's clothes for weeks. No one is a hero because of this and no one really grumbles, but anyone who says submariners have an easy life and don't deserve the extra pay ought to see for themselves.'

On 3 October *Taciturn* came alongside at Faslane, the small, very basic submarine base at the Gareloch, in the mouth of the Clyde. Hurley was unimpressed, declaring it 'just a small enclosed gravel area with little or no facilities and when we arrived no depot ship either'.

The day *Taciturn* reached Faslane, Russia launched Sputnik 1, the first man-made vehicle to be successfully sent into outer space. A fortnight later a US Navy submarine came into Faslane, dropping off a package, which was taken to the US Air Force airhead at Prestwick Airport. The American submariners whom *Taciturn*'s men socialised with claimed their package contained film of Sputnik being sent into the heavens. This was unlikely, as it was launched from Kazakhstan, a long way from any sea a Western submarine might penetrate.

The Russians were, however, conducting nuclear weapons tests on Novaya Zemlya. As with the British submarines, aside from the captain and a select few, nobody in the American boat knew exactly what they had been doing or precisely where. They did know that it was cold, damp and dangerous, and that the Soviets didn't want them there.

6 | WE MUST LIVE IN SILENCE

Having orbited the earth 1,400 times, gathering data on the upper layers of the Earth's atmosphere and analysing radio signals in the ionosphere, on 4 January 1958 Sputnik 1 fell from the heavens.

A shooting star burning its path across the sky, Sputnik's rise and fall deeply alarmed the Americans, who feared they were emasculated by Soviet predominance in space.

As Sputnik's orbit decayed, Senate Majority Leader Lyndon Johnson warned: 'Control of space means control of the world.'

Supremacy in outer space, Johnson feared, would make the Russians 'masters of infinity'.

And if that wasn't alarming enough – suggesting the Kremlin wasn't just hell-bent on world domination but something *much bigger* – Johnson felt Sputnik was the precursor of a bid to seize 'the power to control the earth's weather, to cause drought and flood, to change the tides and raise the levels of the sea, to divert the gulf stream and change temperate climates to frigid'.

At the end of January 1958 the Americans finally caught up in the space race with their Explorer 1 satellite successfully achieving orbit. Funded by the US Army, it was packed with equipment to study cosmic rays and micrometeorites. Parity had been achieved, even if American national pride was dented at coming second. Lyndon Johnson's lofty words were headline-grabbing stuff, but a surer sign of Soviet intent to menace the West lay in the shipyards of Arctic Russia, where the Kremlin continued its bid for hegemony under the ocean, *across inner space*. In February 1958, work was under way on designing the first Red Navy nuclear missile submarine, the Hotel Class boat *K-19*. Construction would begin by the end of the year, at the SEVMASH yard in Molotovsk, on the White Sea. Fortunately for the West, when it came to ballistic missile submarines it was the Russians playing catch-up.

If anything possessed world-shattering power, it was a submarine laid down at Groton in Connecticut on 1 November 1957 and named after the first President of the United States. USS *George Washington* was the first of the American fleet's ballistic missile submarines (SSBNs).

Commissioned in December 1959, she was capable of carrying 16 Polaris A-1 missiles with a range of 1,000 miles.

The five George Washingtons would be followed by five boats of the Ethan Allen Class, completed between August 1961 and January 1963. The US Navy was also soon building Lafayette Class SSBNs.

Of crucial importance to the new ballistic missile submarines would be the information provided by the Transit 1B satellite launched into outer space during April 1960. By 1964 it was enabling ships to gain an instant and stunningly accurate fix on their positions. It handed the West more Cold War supremacy than any Sputnik or 'Spam in a can' mission – as an air force officer in Tom Wolfe's *The Right Stuff* put it. Did you *really* need men and monkeys in space capsules to gain an edge on the other side?

Transit 1B provided data crucial for military operations, feeding it to the US Navy's first-generation SSBNs so they could get accurate fixes on their positions, which was a key tool for targeting their missiles.

The Russians had nothing to compare.

Their Hotel Class SSBNs, introduced into service between 1958 and 1962, were nuclear-powered but carried only three missiles, with a range of 370 miles. The Golf Class carried the same, while converted Zulu Class boats boasted just two, and in both cases with a similarly short range. Both the latter were conventionally powered, with all the short-comings that entailed. Early Soviet ballistic missile boats also suffered the handicap of having to at least partially surface in order to launch – their fin had to be poked above the waves, as the tubes were enclosed by it.

The British at the time had no nuclear-powered or nuclear-armed sub-marines at all.

The warhead of just one Polaris missile possessed destructive power in the order of 600 kilotons of explosive. To gauge its potential for destruc-tion, it's worth noting that the 'Fat Man' bomb dropped on the Japanese city of Nagasaki in August 1945 generated an explosive yield of just 21 kilotons. Producing heat approaching 4,000°C and creating winds of more than 600 mph, 'Fat Man' killed at least 40,000 people immedi-ately. By the end of the year a further 35,000 had died. Just one Polaris missile warhead would be capable of killing and maiming hundreds of thousands if not millions via its explosion, fall-out and long-term effects.

Each one of the three R-13 missiles carried by the Hotels had a war-head with an explosive yield of approximately a megaton – equivalent to one million tons of TNT or around 48 times bigger than the explosive power of the 'Fat Man' bomb. The range limitation meant the Soviet SSBNs had to operate within certain areas to hit American cities, giving them much less haystack to hide in than the US Navy's Polaris boats.

Aside from the ability to conceal a boat in the vastness of the ocean, where even a Soviet SSBN would stand more chance of surviving elimination than land-based silos and jet bombers, the submarine-launched nuclear missile would also, hopefully, be less accident-prone.

For example, on 11 March 1958, just three days after *Taciturn* sailed on her second deep-penetration mission into the Barents, a US Air Force B-47 Stratojet bomber accidentally dropped an atom bomb on the small settlement of Mars Bluff, South Carolina. The Mars Bluff incident made headlines worldwide, but when it came to submarine intelligence gathering, there had actually been one serious mishap, though it did not involve the British.

The American fleet's early forays into the north were stained with failure of a spectacular kind. The diesel-electric spy submarine USS *Cochino* had been lost off the coast of Norway in August 1949. It garnered global headlines as the Soviets protested about 'suspicious training' in Russian waters. Having forward deployed to operate from Londonderry, *Cochino* had sneaked into the Barents to try and pick up traces of Soviet nuclear weapons tests. *Cochino* failed to find anything of significance, and while she was weathering heavy seas her batteries suffered several explosions after water poured down the snort mast.

Fortunately the submarine USS *Tusk* was in close company – so the two boats could practise hunter-killer tactics – and was able to save all but one of the surfaced *Cochino*'s men. Unfortunately *Tusk* lost seven of her own men during the rescue operation. The US Navy learned that in stormy Northern seas on covert missions, air-independent boats might be best. Nearly a decade on the Royal Navy was still gambling on the consummate skill and ability of its sailors to operate diesel boats fitted with snort masts.

In March 1958 as *Taciturn* headed North, Lt Cdr O'Connor made a broadcast to his crew, telling them: 'Here we go again.'

He couldn't explain exactly where they were going, but warned: 'We must live in silence and water will be rationed, so watch your consumption of it.' *Taciturn*'s captain issued the usual cautions against talking about the mission once they returned.

The mysterious Lt Cdr Lucas joined *Taciturn* again, but new to the boat were a Lieutenant Block of the US Navy, Dr Newman (a civilian sonar expert) and a specialist radar and communications officer named Lieutenant Payne.

The mysterious Lt Cdr Lucas, who it appeared was actually a Pole, kept a low profile but the American was standing watches. His accent provoked amusement when he made broadcasts. Like the drawling Yank sailor in the 1955 Hollywood movie *Mr Roberts* he prefaced them with: 'Now hear this! Now hear this!'

Dr Newman established a permanent presence in the Sound Room to analyse sonar contacts. Lieutenant Payne was ensconced in the Wireless Transmission and Radar offices, scrutinising Russian transmissions and surface contacts.

On 27 March, O'Connor told *Taciturn*'s crew they were going into waters crowded with Soviet activity. There would be a particular threat from submarines, so everybody had to be extra quiet. After the batteries were charged, explained O'Connor, 'we will be slithering our way in'.

Within minutes of this pep talk there was a contact alarm, but it proved to be nothing. The boat moved in towards the coast. At 11.30 the sound of five explosions reverberated through the water, with a sixth soon after.

It sounded like exercise charges being dropped.

The Sound Room picked up what might be a submarine, but closer listening revealed two trawlers.

Taciturn detected a motor torpedo boat, so positioned herself on the vessel's likely path to record prop noise. The target passed overhead at 30 knots. Once the Sound Room gave the all clear, Lt Cdr O'Connor gave his crew a warning about water consumption: 'We will stay here until the job is done, even if it means we have no water every other day, to conserve what we have left.'

By 31 March the daily consumption rate was down, from around 300 to just 55 gallons. The situation was slightly alleviated by running the distiller to make more, but only when the Sound Room could guarantee there were no Soviet forces nearby to hear it.

Taciturn's sonar operators did catch a trace of a Russian cruiser, but the most exciting moment so far came on the afternoon of 1 April. O'Connor caught sight of a sleek, bullet-shaped jet going very fast, using the submarine's Special Fit periscope to capture stills and moving footage.

The mystery jet appeared to be involved in an interception exercise with two other aircraft. Both the captain and Lucas studied it via the periscope but could not immediately identify what it was. The MiG 21 had first flown in 1955, and would enter service with the Soviet Air Force in 1959. Perhaps they caught sight of some trials for the new type?

Taciturn was now within the Kola inlet itself, for land was visible on three sides. Proceeding with utmost caution at periscope depth O'Connor inspected the landscape. On top of some buildings a radar antenna could be seen revolving. Everything was covered in a light dusting of snow.

The risk of discovery rose commensurately, but there was a problem with the snort mast, which meant it took longer to charge the battery. That couldn't be good in waters infested with ships that might attack at any moment. The submarine withdrew and sought deeper water.

Three days later, on 4 April – Good Friday – *Taciturn* was still in dangerous waters, resuming her espionage mission, but ended up under attack. The submarine's assailant was a Skory Class destroyer, her silhouette sharply visible against the morning sun in the East.

Lieutenant Commander O'Connor was scanning the surface through his periscope and suddenly caught sight of the hard-charging Skory – capable of an impressive top speed of 33 knots – spray creaming away from the Soviet warship's bows. Snapping the handles of the periscope up, O'Connor sent it back down into the well – removing a telltale aiming point on the surface. He ordered the planesman to take HMS *Taciturn* to 120ft.

The Skory's geared turbines screamed louder and louder.

Leading Engineer Mechanic Hurley listened tensely as the destroyer passed right overhead, the noise reverberating through *Taciturn*'s hull like an express train steaming through a tunnel.

The Skory made a sharp turn, coming straight back, dropping three depth charges as *Taciturn* went even deeper, to 220ft. The explosions were extremely loud and very close. In his head O'Connor visualised the Skory on the surface, trying to read the mind of the Soviet captain.

Would he remain convinced his lookouts had spotted a periscope?

Provided nobody in *Taciturn*'s crew made a wrong movement, dropping something with a clatter, shutting a hatch carelessly, or even talking or coughing – they would be okay. The Russian warship's hydrophone operators would not be able to back up the visual sighting. The Skory's primitive sonar would find it difficult to get a good echo now *Taciturn* was in a colder water layer.

Exhaling cautiously – as if even that might alert the foe above – breath hanging in the cold damp air, O'Connor looked across at the hydrophone operator and raised his eyebrows.

Was the Soviet destroyer coming back?

In response, he received a gentle shake of the head.

It appeared they had got away with it. O'Connor ordered the submarine back to 60ft and put the periscope up.

Its narrow head cutting through the surface, throwing off feathers of spray, as it revolved the scope's lens twinkled in the sunlight. O'Connor took a quick all-round look then pulled the scope down.

The Soviets were always ready with depth charges if there was even the slightest confirmation of a foreign submarine in their backyard

Taciturn edged up to the 12-mile limit of Russian territorial waters, detecting Riga Class frigates, a type of simple, tough, unsophisticated surface combatant cheap to build in large numbers. The most formidable threat posed to *Taciturn* was the Riga's brand-new RBU 2500 system, which some of the modernised Skorys also possessed. It was capable of hurling up to 16 depth bombs into the sea in rapid succession.

O'Connor had to decide whether it was worth the risk of entering Russian waters. Should she be caught cold and forced to surface *Taciturn* could not claim to have strayed inside by 'accident'. The Russians might be justified in sinking *Taciturn*, killing the crew, or at the very least interning survivors. They were, after all, not averse to launching missiles and fighter jets to intercept America's U-2 spy planes, the aerial equivalent of *Taciturn*, which had been penetrating the USSR's airspace since 1957.

In waters off the Kola Peninsula, as he considered his next course of action, O'Connor had to weigh up the objective of his mission – intelligence that could possibly save lives in some future war, contrasted with immediate risk to his own men. He decided to back off a little, taking the submarine deeper. *Taciturn*'s men stood down but were called back to duty on detection of a vessel nearby.

From the prop noise and roughly tuned diesels, it was a trawler or a Red Navy support vessel rather than a warship. Bringing the boat to 60ft, O'Connor popped the periscope up, turning it 360-degrees.

Through the choppy spray, in the distance he spotted the towering masts of what might be a Sverdlov or Chapaev Class cruiser, passing by in international waters. The Chapaevs, built in the late 1940s, were armed with a dozen 6-inch guns, as were the younger Sverdlovs. At 18,000 tons the latter were some 3,000 tons bigger. Capturing a Soviet cruiser on tape or film was well worth it, but even with an impressive submerged speed of up to 17 knots, it was impossible for *Taciturn* to catch her. Around four hours later a cruiser and escorts were spotted a mere two miles away, passing down the British submarine's starboard flank; close enough for successful recordings of the vessels' distinctive sound signatures. After charging batteries via the snort mast during the early hours of the following morning, O'Connor again took *Taciturn* deep, to give his sailors a respite. The boat had been dived for 15 days, retaining the submarine's most valuable asset and its primary defence.

Stealth.

Invisibility.

By 20 April *Taciturn* was heading south, and homeward bound. It improved conditions aboard enormously, the boat getting warmer and with less condensation. Hot meals were back on and those who were off-duty were no longer confined to their bunks. Life was on the up.

That evening Hurley was allowed a look through the periscope and thought he spotted what might be Norway on the port side; turning the scope he saw the last rays of the sun dancing on the gentle ripples of *Taciturn*'s wake. On 21 April the boat surfaced for the first time in 34 days, but no hatches were opened as the weather was too bad. When *Taciturn* came in to *Dolphin*, the Captain in command of the squadron was extremely relieved. Hurley reported: 'he had heard nothing from us for seven weeks and because of our engine problems we were late!'

In October 1957, while *Taciturn* was making her first foray into the Barents Sea, Admiral Lord Louis Mountbatten and the defence minister, Duncan Sandys, went aboard USS *Nautilus*.

The world's first nuclear-powered attack submarine (SSN) was visiting Portland and took them to sea off the coast of Dorset for five hours.

It was a powerful display of cutting-edge technology Britain would need to invest in to stay in the Cold War game.

As First Sea Lord, Mountbatten recognised it would be fatal for the UK's own efforts to acquire an SSN capability to lose momentum. Therefore, in March 1958, he invited Admiral Hyman Rickover – boss of the US Navy's nuclear submarine programme – to Britain for discussions on how to get around a serious roadblock.

Simultaneous with a rather depressing meeting in the Ministry of Defence, where the latest inertia in British SSN reactor development was discussed, Mountbatten held another nearby. It concluded with him and Rickover shaking hands on a deal to acquire an American propulsion system.

With a typical display of showmanship, Mountbatten then took Rickover along to the other meeting, revealing the agreement to the astonishment of all present. It would give the British time to perfect their own reactor, while ensuring the Royal Navy could benefit from the experience of getting an SSN to sea up to three years earlier than might otherwise be the case.

The forthcoming HMS *Dreadnought* shared a lot with the US Navy's Skipjack Class internally, not least the reactor and power plant, though externally she was more of a hump-backed whale than a shark in shape. Her foreplanes were not on the fin like a Skipjack SSN but either side of the bows. In return for the reactor, Rickover did impose a request that the British should accept American training and safety practice. Royal Navy submariners were schooled in a simulated SSN reactor compartment at a shore base in the USA, also going to sea in American boats to qualify in running a nuclear powerplant. Rickover at that time personally selected every officer appointed to serve in the American nuclear-powered submarines – via a gruelling and often eccentric interview process. He insisted that he should have the same powers in selecting the captain and other officers of *Dreadnought*.

Mountbatten deftly side-stepped this, insisting Rickover needn't worry. The Royal Navy would select its best and brightest for the job.

'You have selected me,' Mountbatten told him, 'and you can safely take the rest on trust.'

The British had actually discussed proposals for a submarine utilising nuclear power during the Second World War, but other naval construction projects took precedence. After the war the creation of land-based nuclear power stations was considered more important.

At Dounreay, northern Scotland, in the spring of 1958 construction began of a replica submarine reactor compartment. Inside this facility – the Admiralty Test Reactor Establishment – the future hunter-killer submarine's engineers would learn how to run a sea-going reactor.

All American nuclear submarines would also use the Submarine 5th Generation Westinghouse reactor fitted to *Dreadnought* until the introduction into service of new Los Angeles Class SSNs in the mid-1970s.

For years it was claimed Rickover was fiercely against giving away such cutting-edge American technology to the British.

It has emerged in recent times that the dedicated anglophile was actually very much for it. Admiral Mountbatten had such a good rapport with the fearsome Rickover that he referred to him as 'My dear Rick'.

In return, the UK gave the Americans details of research into other areas of submarine design. Mountbatten also cultivated a good relationship with the head of the US Navy, Chief of Naval Operations Admiral Arleigh Burke. They had secret discussions as far back as 1955 on the possibility of the UK joining the American Polaris strategic missile programme.

Thanks to the technology transfer from Westinghouse, Rolls-Royce swiftly and safely put *Dreadnought*'s reactor together, except with steam turbines from English Electric. Everything else was of both British design and origin. This solution meant the submarine had a British fore end and an aft end that was American. A British-origin Type 2001 sonar array was installed in the bows of the new SSN. As active sonar, it possessed a huge power output while there was also to be a British-origin sonar set for passive detection at long range. Laid down in the Vickers yard at Barrow-in-Furness on 12 June 1959, *Dreadnought* would cost £18.5m to build. A measure of the care and attention to detail during the 18-month construction process was more than 7,300 x-rays taken of the welds – from the pipework in the reactor system to the hull itself – to ensure they would not give under the extreme pressures the deep-diving boat would experience.

Meanwhile, Tim Hale was informed, while serving in the old Second World War-era submarine *Sanguine* in the Mediterranean, the Admiralty was gathering in officers who had been top of their respective training classes at HMS *Dolphin*. They would be *Dreadnought's* seaman officers. Appointment to this plum job required Lt Hale to make a return to Greenwich, for more training between April and July 1959. Before that he was sent to serve as Navigating Officer in the old *Taciturn*. Still worn out by her forays into the north, she had been declared unfit to dive after the usual two years' service between refits. This would remain the situation until room could be found in a dockyard to put her ills right again.

To occupy *Taciturn's* crew, and give them a rest after their Arctic adventures, she was sent on a recruiting cruise around Britain, visiting 14 different ports in the hot, sweaty summer of 1959.

Cardiff was port number nine, and *Taciturn* arrived there on 6 June. Aside from being the fifteenth anniversary of the D-Day invasion, Hale had other reasons to remember that particular visit. It was where he met his first wife, Penelope Boothby.

During a 12-month nuclear science and technology course at Greenwich, Hale learned to appreciate the innovative tactical benefits of nuclear-powered submarines. They had unlimited power to run life support systems, more powerful sensors and weapons systems, without needing to shut anything down to preserve battery power.

Nuclear submarines were non-air breathing, so they did not have to potentially expose themselves to the enemy, in order to vent fumes or take in air. Those were the kinds of life-or-death advantages Britain's undersea boat warriors could do with on their missions against the Russians.

Even so, the dawn of that new era was still some way off. While Hale was at Greenwich a creaky old Super-T would go once more into dangerous waters, her crew risking their lives to bring home some intelligence treasure.

In June 1958 Lt Cdr Alfie Roake was appointed captain of HMS *Turpin*, which had seen service in the Pacific during the closing stages of the Second World War.

In December of 1950 she had entered Chatham for her Super-T conversion – second to receive the major rebuild – returning to the fleet in September 1951. For Lt Cdr Roake the process of preparing *Turpin* for dangerous missions into the Barents was not initiated until summer 1959, with a visit to the Old Admiralty Building in London. He received a formal briefing on what was required. Roake later visited GCHQ at Cheltenham, the top-secret hub of Britain's global espionage network, for further briefings.

Of the utmost value to the *Turpin*'s captain were secret patrol reports written by *Taciturn*'s Lt Cdr O'Connor. *Turpin* had also been deployed to the North before, in the summer of 1955.

Sailing in her – and without the benefit of any formal submarine training at all – was 21-year-old 'Sparker' Tony Beasley, a rating specialising in the dark arts of electronic surveillance who was also a budding Russian linguist. When a transfer boat took Beasley and three other specialists out into the Solent to board a vessel, they had no idea their destination was a submarine. Seeing *Turpin* emerge from the evening mist, their hearts dropped into their boots. They suspected that weeks of discomfort and danger lay ahead.

And so it proved.

For Beasley the worst moment came when *Turpin* was at periscope depth, sucking up intelligence while snorting. He was listening to Soviet warships carrying out radar sweeps when he realised he had picked up their short-range Q-Band. That meant the foe was *very close.*

And getting closer by the second.

Beasley suspected it meant the Russians had spotted *Turpin*'s snort mast and periscope. They were about to be rammed.

Well schooled in submarine movies, if not the reality of submarining practice, Beasley yelled out: 'Dive! Dive! Dive!'

All hell broke loose in *Turpin*'s Control Room. The boat went under with the mast and scope still up. Water flooded into the submarine until the snort flap closed. Caught up in the scrum, Beasley was hit by the one-ton periscope as it descended, sustaining a serious shoulder injury.

The Sound Room picked up at least two Soviet destroyers, their screws thrashing through the water overhead.

Things hit the water.

Depth charges.

Fortunately, *Turpin* found a cold water layer at 120ft that was difficult for the crude Russian sonar to penetrate but still endured a three-hour assault.

Having survived that encounter, Beasley and *Turpin* spent more than a fortnight off the Russian coast. The embarked specialists ticked off items on a radar, sound signature and photographic target list.

At one stage *Turpin* was temporarily forced to withdraw, surfacing for a running repair on one of her intelligence-gathering aerials. Dived again, and moving closer than ever to the coast at periscope depth, Beasley and other operators picked up multiple converging Soviet radars. The boat withdrew her periscope and went deep as warships criss-crossed overhead.

This time the depth charges were set to explode below 120ft, one of them even bouncing off *Turpin*'s outer casing before it detonated.

The explosion grabbed the submarine and shook it vigorously.

As charges exploded above, below, to either side, the submarine was rocked violently. *Turpin*'s then captain, Lt Cdr B. Rowe, took her down to 280ft, close to the limit. A cold water layer finally hid the boat from the searching Soviets. Their enthusiastic depth charging continued but now at a distance.

Shutting down as much machinery as possible, including propulsion, *Turpin* drifted, a current pulling the boat into mortal danger – a minefield.

A rasping scrape along the hull was followed by a *twang*. The mines were secured to the seabed by wires. One of them had snagged on part of the superstructure. Fortunately, rather than being pulled down until a sensitive prong hit the casing and exploded, the mine broke free. Ordering revs on the engines, Lt Cdr Rowe eased *Turpin* out of peril.

After reaching safety off the coast of Norway, the boat surfaced for an inspection of potential external damage.

She was not a pretty sight – large parts of *Turpin*'s superstructure had been blown off by depth-charge explosions; both scope and snort were all bent out of shape; part of the rudder appeared to have been ripped away; the fin was all bashed in and torn. The sonar dome was no more;

radio aerials were gone; there was a 30ft gash down the starboard outer casing. Serious though all that was, *Turpin* still had propulsion and essential life-support systems. She could dive in an emergency. Staying on the surface, *Turpin* made a light signal to a passing British trawler, explaining she had no means of radio communication. *Could they please pass a message on to the Navy requesting submarine depot ship HMS* Maidstone *at Portland prepare to receive them?* Temporary repairs would be made before the boat headed back to Portsmouth.

In autumn 1959 *Turpin* faced her sternest test. Alfie Roake had seen action in the same waters as a young officer in a cruiser on the Allied convoy runs to Murmansk and Archangel. Recalling frozen seas, he made sure he dug out his old woollen long johns. Like all submarines heading to the far North *Turpin* took aboard torpedoes with fully armed warheads so she could strike with maximum lethality if attacked.

For politicians – wary of bad headlines and being accused of pushing the world to the edge of war – sending a submarine on a covert mission to spy seemed a much better bet than a recce aircraft. Several of them had been shot down and airmen killed. In reality, the potential for much worse disaster was considerable. A serious error by a submarine captain could mean a lot more lives lost, or people captured for propaganda purposes. Submariners' families and loved ones might never know what had happened to their lost sons, husbands and lovers. At least the Soviets returned the corpses of fallen airmen. Even the wreckage of the downed aircraft could be recovered but not so any submarine sunk. The sea could swallow all sorts of embarrassments.

Alfie Roake mused on the fate of submariner spies: 'We flew no "Jolly Roger" listing our achievements and had no special welcoming party – we left and entered harbour like "a thief in the night" ... We had no feed-back as to how we had done, and a verbal enquiry elicited a non-committal reply ... Meanwhile, we were all ordered not to breathe a word about our adventures ...'

The hatch was shut on 21 October 1959 and *Turpin* did not surface for 39 days. *Turpin* was a ghost boat, whose whole modus operandi was to not exist. Roake was glad of *Turpin*'s special super-quiet screws and worked hard with his sailors to eliminate potential sources of noise. The boat was packed with specialist equipment, for sonar and radar intercept, with wires trailing everywhere inside the vessel. Her pennant number was painted out and escape hatches were welded shut. This was standard practice, to prevent them from being blown open during depth-charging.

On the way around the south-west of England the boat's new film and stills periscope cameras were tried out, shooting some stunning vistas of the Isles of Scilly.

Contemplating the weeks ahead, Roake knew that, after the Soviet threat, tedium would be his next-worst enemy, so he devised a weekly routine to combat boredom. There would be inspections of the boat on a Saturday, a religious service on a Sunday, with a film show later on the same day.

A broad choice of music was also taken aboard. Reflecting everybody's taste, a selection of records had been tape recorded, ranging from pop to classical, which would be broadcast over the speaker system when the noise did not risk detection by the foe. As O'Connor had done before him, Roake reminded his sailors that everything they did must remain secret, even from their nearest and dearest.

Snorting as she passed the tip of Scotland and all the way up around the Norwegian North Cape, *Turpin* passed into what her captain called 'Indian country'. Roake fretted over the conflicting demands of good practice with the periscope – a quick all-round look and then down to minimise chances of visual or radar detection – against the surveillance requirement. The latter required the stubby little aerial mounted on the scope to be exposed as long as possible, for it was the main portal for ingesting intelligence data. Roake made sure everybody adhered to 'Silent Routine', requiring, among other things, careful use of wheel spanners and suchlike. If one was dropped, the resulting clang would be a gift to any listening foe.

With aircraft and helicopters frequently buzzing overhead, Roake felt like 'David against Goliath, in my small diminutive "T" boat of some 1,320 tons [sic] carrying out a tiny pin prick of an operation against a colossus. We were on our own with the nearest support and succour thousands of miles away.'

As with *Taciturn*, water usage was a problem but the distillers were only used when the boat was snorting, due to the drain on the battery and the noise generated. Their output was a pathetic 10 gallons an hour.

The stoker minding the distiller had to be togged out in warm clothes and clad in oilskins as he was sitting amid a 'gale of wet icy air' sucked in by the snort, a layer of ice forming around the nearby Engine Room door.

A graph was kept on view for everybody to see the amount of fresh water consumed each day and what was left. *Turpin*'s men didn't shave and only had a full body wash – 'a sluice down' – once a week. A single mug of water daily was allowed for cleaning teeth.

Because of the constant Arctic night at that time of year, red lighting was used almost around the clock, which made for tired eyes and dulled senses. One of the engineer officers wore red braces to keep his trousers up and these became invisible in red lighting. His brother officers joked about his trousers falling down because he had forgotten his braces. The red lighting even played tricks with the food. The boat's staple diet was Italian plum tomatoes and under red lighting these too would become invisible.

The submarine did not have a doctor embarked, but rather a book of medical advice, plus a few surgical instruments. It was up to the captain to judge the best course of action. One of *Turpin*'s Electrical Artificers became sick and after much head scratching and consulting the 'book of words' Roake decided the man had polio.

'We were in a very vulnerable situation, and unable to break radio silence. With no one to ask, you have to make your own decisions and decide your own priorities – rather as in Nelson's day. Supposing he had some contagious disease or died? Do you head for home? Bury him at sea – in "peace time"? These are the sort of questions that go through your mind ... Fortunately the man recovered.'

On 29 November 1959, after covering 4,320 miles, HMS *Turpin* returned to port, while on 1 December, far away from the tiny submarine, there was an extraordinary outbreak of mutual co-operation between the two sides in the Cold War. An agreement was signed making Antarctica a demilitarised continent, used only for scientific research. The northern polar regions continued to be a venue for the most dangerous game.

It was a beautifully bright spring day in 1960, during *Turpin*'s second espionage mission under Roake's command. At minimum revs, *Turpin* closed slowly on the target unseen by anyone on the bridge of the Soviet boat, the sea flat calm, and he captured excellent beam-on portraits.

Roake adjusted the focus of the periscope, placing the cross hairs on a November Class attack submarine. His finger pressed the trigger of a camera attached to the scope clicking off some frames. The narrow aperture of the attack scope – and the need to minimise detection risk by only raising it for a few seconds – required Roake to shoot the Soviet submarine in a series of looks. The films would be developed and then prints stitched together to form a patchwork showing the November in full detail from end to end.

Of radical appearance – with a space age streamlined fin and rudder – the Soviet SSN was very fast and deep diving, but noisy. It made more of a racket than even Soviet diesels, which might explain why *Turpin*'s stealthy approach was undetected. The November's hull was covered in anechoic coating that made her hard to find on sonar, but here she was sitting on the surface and Roake had caught her cold.

The first November Class boat was *K-3*, also known as *Leninskiy Komsomol*, which got under way on nuclear power in July 1958, so it was quite a coup to catch her. The Soviets were still trying to figure out how to use SSNs and she was undergoing exhaustive trials. Having captured the November on film, Roake ordered *Turpin* to dive under the Russian boat.

To his horror, the November decided to dive at exactly the same moment – *right on top of him*. The hydrophone operators said they had clearly heard the clunk as the Soviet vessel's main ballast tanks vents opened, followed by the sound of rushing air exiting them and water flooding in. Roake took *Turpin* deeper and faster to get out of the way. Roake thought it 'an exciting moment'.

The patrol resumed and there were 'bangs and bumps' at a distance, which may have been depth charges. There was a heart-pumping moment when the British boat's hydrophone operators heard what sounded like torpedoes heading their way. Just in case, Roake ordered *Turpin* deep and turned the boat towards the oncoming threat, hoping to comb the possible tracks. The Sound Room picked up a Soviet submarine snorting and, using his scope, Roake spotted both the snort mast and the periscope of the foe. Possibly the most dangerous moment came when half a dozen Soviet destroyers homed in on *Turpin*. She was already at maximum silent running and going even deeper. Roake felt he 'took every evasive action in the book' but still could not shake them off. Caught on the horns of a dilemma, he considered he 'couldn't speed up too much, nor run pumps, as this would have given them a confirmed contact [noise]: so we got heavier and heavier, deeper and deeper, with the stern sagging, and the shafts grinding ...'

Turpin managed to level out at 425ft. When Roake later related this to a naval architect on the staff of Flag Officer Submarines, he was informed a further 50ft and his submarine's hull might have collapsed.

By going deep Roake had successfully shaken off the Soviets. He considered it 'altogether a lucky escape: and I know how it feels to be hunted for real. Good training – but not very nice!'

A further problem presented itself when the wire that raised the periscope started to fray; if it snapped the patrol would be over. The wire had to be unravelled and then re-reeved, which was far from easy at sea. Roake felt it was a case of 'needs must when the Devil drives'.

The boat rose to shallower depth, in order to lessen water pressure, and the periscope was raised up to the deckhead. Metal cotter pins were inserted through brackets on the deckhead and on the periscope. Without the pins, when they took the hydraulic pressure off, the periscope would have dropped to the bottom of the well. They might not have been able to get the scope up again.

The submarine went deep for the work to be carried out, hydraulic pressure taken off and the wire removed. The new wire was fitted without mishap.

On the way home, *Turpin* snorted her way through shallow waters off Norway facing two hazards – wrecks of warships from previous wars that littered the seabed and trawlers. From past experience Roake knew how keen the latter were to snare a submarine, so they could claim compensation for damaged nets. 'On this occasion they were unlucky,' he recorded with satisfaction.

Surfacing on 16 March, at 07.42, *Turpin* had again broken the Super-T record, having been submerged for 42 days in total, sailing 5,533 miles. During the voyage back Roake offered one of his Engine Room stokers a look through the periscope, which for some unknown reason the man refused.

'He had seen no daylight until we were alongside [at Portsmouth] – on both patrols.'

Turpin returned without fanfare. Senior officers Roake reported to did not even acknowledge where he had been or what his boat had been doing. Offloading his laundry at home – all of which reeked of diesel fuel – Roake was later amused to see his saggy, unsightly long johns hanging on the line in the garden. They had done the convoy run to northern Russia during the Second World War when he served in a cruiser. Now he'd worn them during a submerged espionage mission in the same waters. Roake imagined the raised eyebrows of his neighbours – never in a million years would they guess where his old thermals had been.

The US Navy was keen to show off its latest Skipjack Class hunter-killer, to foreign civilians as well as friendly naval officers. She was a showcase for the shape of things to come in the Royal Navy. Commissioned at the end of July 1960, USS *Scorpion* departed her home at New London Submarine Base on 24 August, the two-month deployment enabling the SSN to be worked up to full front-line efficiency.

A former naval officer turned national newspaper defence correspondent, Desmond Wettern got his ticket for a tour of *Scorpion* when she visited the UK. Wettern was amazed by what he found. Familiar with the grim conditions British submariners experienced on long-distance deployments, Wettern was particularly impressed with the air conditioning and condensers

The latter meant, he wrote, 'there is ample water always available'. Wettern noted that bunks did not have to be folded away every day. They even provided privacy, via curtains, and each one had a reading light. Knowing how important good food was to preserving crew morale, Wettern was awestruck by the lunch menu available. It included 'grilled steak, sautéed mushrooms … green beans, bread, butter, coffee'. The boat was, though, 'dry', with no alcohol except for that used in the submarine's duplicating machine ink. Meanwhile, within a few weeks of completing the Greenwich nuclear course Tim Hale was on his travels again. Only this time he was off to sea not in an old British diesel, but aboard *Scorpion*. Spending part of October 1960 in her was a revelation not only for Hale but also *Dreadnought*'s future captain, Cdr Peter Samborne. He had already spent time in American SSNs as part of his training for *Dreadnought*, a privilege generously provided to a number of hand-picked British officers and senior ratings by the USN. 'To be aboard an SSN at sea was incredible,' reflected Hale, 'the speed and the endurance, the general capabilities of such a boat cannot be matched by a diesel. Though it was fairly noisy compared to later nuclear-powered boats, noise was not such a priority in 1960.'

Hale and Samborne were in *Scorpion* – commanded by Cdr Buzz Bessac – for a big NATO-run exercise called 'Rum Tub', in which the American SSN attacked carriers, an exhilarating experience for young Hale. For *Scorpion* a favourite means of outwitting the opposition was to hide at the core of their battle group. The SSN would sneak in under the carrier herself, made invisible by the noise of the big ship's screws.

Diesels might not have been able to even catch fast carriers, but as Hale discovered, *Scorpion* – the world's most advanced attack boat at the time – could even outpace them. 'The cry went up aboard *Scorpion*: "Get the URG!" – the Underway Replenishment Group [supply ships] – or "get the Flat-top", the carriers. And they did. It was a revelation – to be able to track them via powerful sonar from 20–25 miles, and close on the target at 25 knots.'

Launched by Her Majesty the Queen on 21 October 1960, the new British SSN was as much a naval revolution as the battleship *Dreadnought* of 1906. Like that predecessor, the Cold War SSN was a huge leap in capability. The Edwardian ship was a technological marvel – the first all-big-gun battleship, with steam turbine propulsion, a type only used in destroyers until then.

The reactor of submarine *Dreadnought* produced steam, which via the geared turbines drove a single shaft connected to the large screw. Battleship *Dreadnought* used coal for its heat source, while the SSN had enriched uranium. Should the reactor fail there was a diesel generator and battery to provide auxiliary diesel-electric propulsion.

In fact there was duplication of essential systems throughout, so if anything went wrong – as it could in the dangerous trade of submarining – there would be a good chance of achieving salvation. At that stage, though, there was no duplication of SSNs – *Dreadnought* was one of a kind in the Royal Navy. If the Silent Service was to be truly effective against the Soviet menace there would have to be more of them. In the meantime the Russians sought to nullify any advantage a new breed of British submarines might offer by stealing their secrets from right under the noses of the Admiralty.

10 | THE PORTLAND SPIES

Acquiring and adapting Nazi technology at the end of the Second World War had worked for both sides in the early years of the Cold War. Yet, while the West used it as seed corn to grow new ideas, the Soviets ploughed an increasingly barren furrow.

In the State-controlled, centrally disorganised economy of the USSR, innovation was not encouraged, and so the Soviets sought to steal what they could not create themselves from the capitalist, free enterprise West.

One means of obtaining advanced technology was to insert agents into Western business concerns. Via industrial espionage the Kremlin sought knowledge that could be adapted for defence purposes. Or Russia's business emissaries simply formed above-the-board partnerships with Western industry. Best of all was acquiring the latest technology by subterfuge. That required not submarines sent into dangerous waters but a few dedicated espionage operatives, able to exploit the open nature of democratic society.

Retired Royal Navy war veteran Harry Houghton was ideal for Russia's purposes but he was of a starkly different background to the Cambridge spies who betrayed their country on ideological grounds.

Rising to the rank of Master-at-Arms – the senior rating responsible for enforcing discipline aboard a warship – Houghton was an alcoholic who somehow persuaded people he was trustworthy.

After leaving the Navy he became a civilian clerk in the Admiralty and in 1951 was posted to the British Embassy in communist Poland. At that time positive vetting – checking the background of those in a position to access secrets – was a patchy affair. People who presented obvious security risks sometimes slipped through the net.

Never one to turn down an evening of merry-making involving copious amounts of booze and a chance to chase women, Houghton was soon spotted by Polish intelligence. He made it easy for them, dabbling in the black market, trading in coffee and medical drugs, mixing with well-known shady characters. Heavy drinking gave Houghton a loose tongue.

Always on the lookout for weak characters they could exploit, the Poles constructed a blackmail honey-trap, photographing the married

– but soon to be divorced – ex-sailor in a compromising position with a woman. Fortunately, it had already become obvious to his British bosses that Houghton was a deeply unsuitable character to have roaming the streets of Warsaw. A naval attaché reported he was 'unsuitable … self-confident, affable, and easy going, rather objectionably familiar with the girls of the Embassy staff, obviously fond of a drink to judge by the smell of his breath in the early mornings'.

In 1952, with his black market activities found out, he was called home. The Admiralty unwittingly made the error of then sending him to work in the top-secret Underwater Detection Establishment at Portland, Dorset. Houghton was transferred from Polish intelligence handlers to the Russians, who were delighted to have a spy placed inside one of their top targets.

To gain better access to secrets – for his own job was not in a terribly sensitive area – Houghton, by then aged 55, began an affair with Ethel Gee, a 46-year-old spinster who secured a job as a clerk in the Drawing Office Records Section at Portland. Contained within it were plans for the new Type 2001 sonar of HMS *Dreadnought*. Work was simultaneously under way at Portland on perfecting submarine stealth and a new kind of variable-depth sonar. Also in their embryonic stage were designs for a new type of submarine to carry nuclear-tipped ballistic missiles.

Portland had gained importance from the late 1950s onwards because various centres of Admiralty underwater research and testing were closed and their work concentrated at the Dorset base.

Analysis of first-in-class tests for all British warships, including submarines, was conducted there. The Americans, who had entrusted nuclear reactor technology and other secrets to Britain, were later furious the Royal Navy had been so easily penetrated.

Desmond Wettern, the British national newspaper naval correspondent who had visited USS *Scorpion*, thought truly significant information made it to Moscow. It was amazing how similar the Soviet Navy's new Yankee Class SSBN (first commissioned November 1967) was to the UK's Polaris vessels (lead boat HMS *Resolution* commissioned October 1967). Scrutinising the case, Wettern wondered if secrets the Soviets gleaned via Houghton and Gee enabled them to suddenly make this gigantic leap forward in submarine design. Portland was a good source of such intelligence, for its experts had completed an Admiralty review into the practicality of the Polaris system in July 1960. It judged that the complexities were enormous and not easily mastered. Yet in record time the Russians were able to send an SSBN to sea that would match the

UK's forthcoming Resolution Class boats. The Yankee was identical in length and uncannily similar in appearance, and carried 16 missiles, just like Polaris.

It was, Wettern observed, comparatively easy 'to obtain information in a free society'. All you needed was the weak link in the chain.

That was Harry Houghton.

Signs that he was up to no good were not absent. His former wife suspected he was spying for the Russians and in 1956 passed on her suspicions to a naval welfare officer. He reported them higher up the command chain, but nothing was done about it. Nobody in the Naval Service could believe one of their own would be a traitor. Houghton might be a rogue with a fondness for drink and chasing women, but surely such allegations were just his ex-wife being bitter over the divorce?

It was a mole codenamed 'Sniper' working for the USA's Central Intelligence Agency (CIA) inside the Polish security apparatus that triggered events leading to the uncovering of the Houghtons' treachery.

'Sniper' said there was a Soviet agent inside Portland and his name began with an H. At first it was suspected the spy was an officer. Who else would have access to highly secret information?

Scrutiny of likely candidates on the Navy List – a record of Britain's commissioned naval officers past and present – did not offer up a likely-looking chap. 'Sniper' said the man had been recruited while working at the British Embassy in Warsaw. His name was possibly Huiton.

'Sniper' was able to produce evidence of Portland material passed to the Soviets. The field of suspects was narrowed down to Houghton, who was now on the staff of Portland's Port Auxiliary Repair Unit. A surveillance team was assembled to see if he did anything, or met anyone, suspicious. They soon found out that his girlfriend worked in a very sensitive area and the two of them were consorting with a character identified as Gordon Lonsdale. This man claimed to be a Commonwealth citizen, having been issued with a Canadian passport in January 1955. In October the following year he had enrolled on a course at the School of African and Oriental Studies in London.

In reality he was the linkman for an effort to protect Soviet submarines from detection and facilitate better tracking of NATO's. One contemporary account of what would ultimately become known as the Portland Spy Ring case declared: 'Soviet leaders realise that the value of their 700 submarines is diminished as long as the West possesses the means of tracking them accurately.' Three deep-cover espionage operatives were ordered into Britain specifically to bring home information on Western sonars, how they worked and were put together, so the Russians could copy them. Houghton and Gee were the point of access and Lonsdale was the most overt of the three deep-cover agents. MI5 watchers observed a series of meetings between Lonsdale and Houghton, including at least one where they enjoyed a convivial pint at the Maypole Pub in Surbiton.

Trailed on to the Metropolitan line of the London Underground, Lonsdale got off at Ruislip and went to a bungalow occupied by Peter and Helen Kroger, whom he had visited before. Their house was already under observation. Whereas Lonsdale was a flashy character, the Krogers seemed unlikely spies. Posing as an antiquarian book dealer, Mr Kroger, aged 51, went to work in London most days. Aside from the 48-year-old Mrs Kroger's occasional bouts of heavy drinking – the results it was said of unhappiness at being childless – the couple appeared the embodiment of suburban respectability. During the summer Peter Kroger played cricket, arousing laughter with his habit of using the bat as if he was playing baseball. He and Helen also enjoyed holidays around Britain, especially in Devon and Cornwall.

The Krogers' comfortable bungalow was actually a radio transmitting station and they were really Morris and Lona Cohen, both Americans by birth. They had helped the Rosenbergs – spies executed in America for stealing nuclear weapons secrets – but had successfully evaded capture. The antiquarian book business was used as a cover to send secrets out of the country. Such was his success that Kroger soon had a small office on the Strand. Microdots were secreted inside some of the many books he mailed all over the world.

As for the linkman, there really had been a Gordon Arnold Lonsdale, born in Canada. At the age of seven, in 1931, his mother took him to live in her native Finland and during the Second World War the Soviets somehow acquired his papers. The original Lonsdale died in 1943 but it wasn't long until he was reborn, but if anyone had ever cared to check the new Lonsdale physically, his penis gave him away. The real Lonsdale had been circumcised and also had a distinctive scar on one of his legs. The fake Lonsdale was actually Konon Molody, who had worked as a Red Army agent behind enemy lines during the war. He only returned to his native land just before hostilities, having been sent to live with a relative in California during the 1930s. In 1951 Molody – by then an import–export specialist, fluent in English, German and Chinese – was recruited by Soviet intelligence.

Assuming the Lonsdale identity, he took passage to Canada in 1953 on a merchant vessel, gaining entry using the Finnish papers.

Lonsdale became a resident of Vancouver and applied for a full Canadian passport, then headed for Britain. An out-going, larger-than-life character, with a taste for the ladies, Lonsdale soon set himself up in business selling and renting jukeboxes and one-armed-bandit machines to pubs, nightclubs and cafes.

Not terribly successful with money matters, he was always short of funds and maintained a large overdraft. Surveillance continued until January 1961, when a trip to London by Houghton and Gee provoked an intricate operation to round up the entire Portland Spy Ring. The British authorities had to act, as 'Sniper' had been forced to defect. There was a risk the Russians would issue recall orders to Lonsdale and the Krogers.

The operation involved at least 40 operatives from the intelligence services, some of whom were deployed in cars and vans to trail a Renault Dauphine driven by Houghton from Dorset to Salisbury railway station.

A light aircraft flew parallel to the car's route, tuned into a radio transmitter secretly attached to the Renault.

Cunningly positioned in the railway carriage, some observed Houghton and Gee from behind newspapers. Watchers were also hidden among the throng on the Waterloo station concourse. Others followed the couple to and from Walworth market, and used the cover of a crowd milling about a used car lot opposite the Old Vic theatre.

The man who arrested the trio was Detective Superintendent George 'Moonraker' Smith, who had won his spurs hunting down IRA cells trying to bomb London and later gathered up Nazi agents.

Nestled inside Gee's shopping basket was a tin containing films with more than 300 exposed frames on them. For Houghton had photographed 230 pages in a book named *Particulars of War Vessels*, conveying detailed – and highly secret – information. He had even photographed naval architects' drawings of HMS *Dreadnought*. Also packaged up for the Soviets were Admiralty Fleet Orders, revealing key alterations and modifications to British warships and their combat systems. As if all that wasn't enough, the basket contained secret documents on sonar systems and other sensitive matters. Houghton and Gee were handing over these secrets to Lonsdale for £125 in cash – three months' salary for Gee and two months' pay for Houghton. Gee thought her lover's friend – whom she had met on previous trips to London – was Cdr Alex Johnson of the

US Navy. She believed they were only helping a friendly nation.

Shocked to have been arrested, Houghton declared during a subsequent interrogation at Scotland Yard: 'I have been a bloody fool!'

'Moonraker' Smith also arrested the Krogers. Searchers were stunned by the power of the radio sets they found concealed in the bungalow, capable of sending encrypted messages to Moscow Centre. The Krogers and Bunty Gee pleaded not guilty. Houghton offered to give evidence against his co-accused, a further act of betrayal, which was declined by the Crown. His transgressions were just too severe.

A search of Houghton's cottage in Dorset discovered Admiralty papers concealed inside a large radio cabinet and also a plan of the naval base at Portland. Inside a box of matches were instructions for a meeting with Lonsdale in London.

At the home Bunty Gee shared with elderly relatives a further search discovered a list of questions on secret anti-submarine sonar. In some of her handbags were notes on naval documents that might be worth copying for the Soviets.

During the trial Lonsdale refused to speak and inquiries in Canada provided few clues. He remained cool throughout his interrogation and subsequent trial in March 1961, reading a spy novel to pass the time.

He refused to admit his true identity, though 'Moonraker' Smith was sure Lonsdale was a Soviet agent. Gee and Houghton were each sentenced to 15 years in prison, and after being released in May 1970 were married.

In 1969 the Krogers, who had received the same length of sentence (20 years each), were sent to Russia, in an exchange for a Briton arrested in the USSR for distributing anti-Soviet leaflets. Lonsdale preceded them by five years, also under a swap. According to the official biography of Molody on the Russian intelligence service web site, in late 1970 he died of a stroke 'like his father', aged 47. He collapsed while mushroom picking near Moscow.

HMS *Dreadnought* was a new concept – a hunter-killer, or Fleet, submarine – and she had obviously aroused great curiosity in the Kremlin, hence the efforts of the Portland spies. A chance to serve in her was something ambitious British naval officers could aspire to.

Clearly bright new horizons beckoned for Tim Hale and the Royal Navy's other trailblazing nuclear warriors selected for the first crew, but for Rob Forsyth the future was not yet settled.

After the stultifying boarding school routine of Dartmouth, Sub Lt

Forsyth had been sent in July 1960 to start his career aboard minesweepers based at Port Edgar in Scotland.

On joining the 100th Mine Counter Measures Squadron, serving in the Ton Class vessels *Appleton* and *Lewiston,* Forsyth found there were serious tasks at hand. Many thousands of Second World War-era mines still lurked in British waters and they needed to be found and destroyed.

Things went downhill when he was sent to the air defence frigate HMS *Chichester* in April 1961. In the relaxed and informal care of the minesweeping squadron, a freshly minted officer was given time for robust work in the enthusiastic fashion to be expected of lively and intelligent young men. Slack was given for the occasional transgression. This would not be the case in the steely man-o'-war the 21-year-old Forsyth now joined. The enforcer of discipline and general standards of behaviour aboard ship was the First Lieutenant. He and Forsyth did not rub along well, especially as the youngster bucked against the formality of the surface navy.

War clouds were gathering in the Arabian Gulf and rather than heading for Singapore as expected *Chichester* was diverted to loiter off Kuwait. The oil-rich emirate had been made independent of the UK in June 1961, but signed a treaty allowing it to call in British military assistance if threatened. The Iraqis were gathering tanks and troops on Kuwait's borders. By July the helicopter carrier *Bulwark* had arrived to put ashore several hundred Royal Marines. The strike carrier *Victorious* wasn't far behind, nor was *Chichester*. After a period using her powerful air search radar to detect potential Iraqi threats, the frigate settled down to a mundane routine, much to Forsyth's disgust.

Friction with the First Lieutenant continued, reaching such a pitch that one day the captain called Forsyth to his cabin and told him: 'We'll have to do something about you.'

Over gin and tonic the two discussed how he could enjoy a fulfilling naval career more suited to his character. The captain suggested submarines. Forsyth was not so sure, but the captain told him straight: 'Firstly, you have taken the Queen's shilling so do as you are ordered and secondly, if you don't you will probably be court-martialled.'

In fact, a transfer had already been arranged. Landed at Mombasa, Forsyth made his own way to Nairobi, where he was booked on an RAF flight home a week or so later.

Arriving at the spiritual and educational home of the Submarine Service, HMS *Dolphin* in Gosport, Forsyth felt he had stepped back in time to 'a WW2 atmosphere – there were wooden huts heated by pot-bellied coke stoves, 1940s diagrams on the walls, school desks on plank floors'.

Located in Fort Blockhouse – the much-rebuilt ancient fortress at the core of the HMS *Dolphin* base – the trainees spent most of their time in the classroom. A major objective was to impress upon them how easily they could cause disaster through lack of attention to detail. Above all they must listen to what their instructors told them. The chief instructor, a grizzled old war veteran, told the future submarine officers: 'When we finally do allow you lot to sea, you will not qualify unless you can walk through the submarine blindfold and identify every single valve.'

He paused for effect, casting a flinty gaze around the classroom.

'If you can't do that in darkness,' growled the chief instructor, 'with water flooding in, you will kill everyone.'

Forsyth was impressed, thinking: 'That *is* serious.'

A litany of potentially fatal incidents was unveiled. For every dreadful incident the grizzled old instructor had an appropriate story to put the fear of God into the students.

They heard of people being sucked out of a submarine when they opened a hatch without making sure the pressure inside was equal to that outside (and of course some novice was to blame). Then there was the potential for explosions of excrement caused by improper use of the heads (toilet) system – covering the inexperienced miscreant from head to foot (which served him right, really). Submarines had apparently hit the bottom when depth gauges were shut off from the system (and some young idiot forgot to re-open them). And let's not forget the time water poured down through the open conning tower hatch after some green-gilled fool forgot to clip it shut. The trainee submarine officers also listened in awestruck silence to tales of being depth-charged by the Germans during the Second World War – *yes, some of the instructors really were that ancient.*

They weren't averse to telling yarns about good and bad Commanding Officers (COs) either. The bad ones usually drank too much, or rather had too much booze at the wrong time. They should also be aware of practical jokes, especially from ratings who wished to show their dislike of officers, including the Steward in one boat who allegedly caused a stink by pinning a kipper to the underside of a Wardroom table.

Forsyth's first extended period at sea in a submarine seemed to be one big practical joke. 'Completion of the course was followed by a very short appointment to HMS *Aurochs* – for six weeks – to gain my sea qualification before joining a boat properly. She was a Second World War submarine still equipped with a gun. Nobody warned me how wet submarines would be and I had a bunk on the deck next to the ward-room. The first night at sea I was washed out of it.

'I thought we were sinking. Nobody had ever told me about the everyday occurrence of the Atlantic Ocean pouring down the conning tower. *Aurochs* had a low bridge, which encouraged ingress of water. To handle it you had a canvas tube called an elephant trunk, which connected the bottom of the conning tower to another canvas arrangement called the birdbath, all hung from the deckhead pipes. The water would be pumped out into the boat's bilges, though occasionally it overflowed. One time when we were on the surface in bad weather, I was working at the chart table, with the birdbath pressed up against my back and the sound of torrents of water flowing into it was most unsettling for a novice.'

There were signs, though, that submarines were a much better fit for Forsyth. For a start, the rigid divide of 'them' (ratings) and 'us' (officers) was not there, with the interplay between the two based on mutual respect (or not, depending on the personalities involved and their competence).

As for getting to know a submarine and all its many valves, pipes and systems blindfold, that was not a joke, but a reality. Forsyth would have just a few weeks to learn it or he was out of the Submarine Service. His early days as a submarine officer would plunge him into a confrontation between navies that took the world to the brink of destruction.

In deep water off the Western Highlands of Scotland, the diesel boat *Auriga* concluded her latest pre-deployment exercise. Rising to periscope depth, the submarine extended her aerial, picking up an electrifying signal from Faslane. The FLASH – highest-priority message – instructed her to return with speed 'and store for war'.

Auriga surfaced and headed south, coming around the Mull of Kintyre. As the boat approached the Isle of Cumbrae, in the mouth of the Firth of Clyde, lookouts spotted other British submarines also making speed on the surface. There was a real danger of collision, but fortunately crunches were avoided, despite near-misses. The inevitable intrusion of a Soviet spy trawler 'with more aerials than the *Queen Mary*', as one submarine officer put it, did not help. As the bridge crew negotiated the traffic, inside the boat Rob Forsyth and the rest of *Auriga*'s sailors listened to local radio news broadcasts piped over the speakers. The airwaves pulsated with reports about the rapidly escalating Cuban Missile Crisis. This was obviously why they had been ordered to prepare for war.

Lieutenant Forsyth thought this was very exciting, especially as it meant he would soon have real live torpedoes in his care rather than dummy fish. Newly promoted, and having passed the blindfold test, he found his new responsibilities included being the boat's Assistant Torpedo Officer. Leading Seaman John Cumberpatch, the experienced Leading Seaman who really ran things, assured the young officer that everything would be fine.

Those 13 days in October 1962 were among the most terrifying of the Cold War; it was one of the few occasions when the civilian population was acutely aware of how thin was the dividing line between humanity's survival or extinction. It all came just a year after 12,000 people had crowded into Trafalgar Square in London to protest against the US Navy's Holy Loch-based ballistic missile submarines.

In March 1961 the USS *Patrick Henry*, carrying a full load of nuclear-tipped Polaris missiles, had entered British waters, surfacing after a deterrent patrol that had set a record of 66 days and 22 hours.

That autumn hundreds of protesters crowded around the gates of the

Scottish naval base chanting 'Ban the Bomb' and 'Go home, Yanks'. In London protests peaked on Battle of Britain Sunday. Four thousand police officers penned in the demonstrators, who included church leaders, the actress Vanessa Redgrave and the playwright John Osborne. The police aim was to stop them marching on Parliament. Now, 13 months later, it appeared the protesters' worst fears about the threat to humanity were about to be realised.

In reality, the closest the USA and Soviet Union, indeed the world, came to nuclear annihilation was not due to the missiles on Cuba, but because of an unseen deployment of Russian submarines. It was these boats Britain's Cold War underwater warriors would be tasked with finding and, if required, destroying.

Precursors to the Cuban Missile Crisis were American involvement in the Bay of Pigs invasion – a total disaster for the newly elected President John F. Kennedy – and bruising encounters at a Vienna summit with the Soviet leader, Nikita Khrushchev.

On 17 April 1961, anti-communist Cuban renegades staged an invasion of their home island in the Bay of Pigs, their aim to depose Fidel Castro. Organised by the USA's Central Intelligence Agency, it failed spectacularly. Ordered to pull out after three days of fighting, two CIA operatives and 175 Cuban renegades escaped, leaving behind 75 dead and 1,500 rebels who surrendered to a Castro force numbering 30,000 troops.

The US Navy had provided an escort for the invasion ships. Forbidden from engaging in hostilities, these warships now picked up those who got away. Less than a week earlier President John F. Kennedy had vowed the USA would not use force to get rid of Castro.

In the immediate aftermath of the Bay of Pigs he continued to deny America was involved. His new administration, taking over the project from the previous Eisenhower regime, had failed to get a grip on the CIA's plans. Choosing to proceed, but in a half-hearted fashion, the new President was seen as duplicitous and weak. America's humiliation was absolute, with Kennedy forced to confess on 21 April 1961 that the USA had been responsible for organising and launching the misadventure.

The principal bone of contention at Vienna in early June 1961 was, though, not Cuba but Berlin, the former German capital. It was still administered (and occupied) by the Russians, Americans, British and French but marooned in communist East Germany. In typically crude rhetoric, Khrushchev called it the 'testicles of the West'.

The mighty Red Army could easily surround the West's troops in Berlin, hold them hostage and then squeeze.

Hard.

President Kennedy let Khrushchev know he would meet Soviet aggression with a commensurate response. The Soviet leader, a veteran of Stalingrad, where he allegedly forced Russian troops into battle at the point of a gun, gave a typically aggressive response.

'Force will be met by force,' he warned.

Kennedy, a battle-scarred US Navy veteran, gave a steely rejoinder: 'Then, Mr Chairman, there will be a war. It will be a cold, long winter.'

Berlin remained an open city, espionage capital of the world, a thorn in the side of the Soviets. It was a tricky commitment for the West, but a beacon of democracy in the totalitarian East.

Neither side could back down.

Khrushchev wanted Kennedy to sign a treaty that handed the whole city to the East Germans. The President refused to do so. Kennedy indicated the USA was only interested in retaining its foothold in the western half rather than insisting on access to the eastern portion. Taking this as his cue, Khrushchev ordered the erection of the 100-mile-long Berlin Wall, permanently cutting off east from west. Construction started on 13 August 1961. Khrushchev also announced the imminent testing of an unprecedented 100-megaton nuclear weapon. It was nicknamed the 'Tsar Bomba' – *the emperor of all atomic bombs.* Western paranoia was increased by the Russian lead in the space race – in April 1961 Yuri Gagarin had become the first human being to orbit the planet Earth.

An alleged Russian advantage in nuclear missile numbers over the USA reinforced a perception that West was falling behind East.

Anxious to boost Western morale and his own position, Kennedy revealed spy satellites had discovered the reality – Soviet missile capability was far behind the USA's.

The Americans certainly possessed a marked lead in strategic destructive power at sea.

The Russians sent their submarines out from the Kola Peninsula, in the Arctic, and from Kamchatka, in the Pacific, needing to cover vast distances before they got anywhere near launch range. A forward base for submarines in Uncle Sam's backyard, such as Cuba, might help close the gap.

With his nation ten years behind American long-range missile capability, Khrushchev thought it worth 'throwing a hedgehog at Uncle Sam's pants'.

Nothing could achieve this better than a massive influx of weapons into Cuba, to safeguard it against further invasion and secure a base from which to export Marxist–Leninist ideology.

Khrushchev felt psychologically stronger than Kennedy. He believed in any face-off he would be able to bully the President into backing down.

The Soviets sent not only Ilyushin-28 bombers to Cuba, capable of carrying nuclear weapons, but also medium-range nuclear-tipped missiles that could hit targets over 1,000 miles away. They deployed thousands of military personnel, constructing launch pads for long-range missiles with a 2,500-mile range. Khrushchev ordered the secret deployment of these weapons to the Caribbean island in late May 1962.

The entire US intelligence apparatus failed to detect their delivery. President Kennedy did not see reports on them until the missile bases were almost finished. In August the Russians were asked exactly what was going on. They prevaricated suspiciously before issuing a denial on 7 September. On 14 October the first photographic evidence of Soviet long-range nuclear missiles on Cuba was obtained.

The island is only around 90 miles away from Florida, so there was nowhere in the USA beyond their reach.

America had not been threatened directly with bombardment during the Second World War, though German submarines had preyed on shipping off its east coast. The idea of enemy bomber raids being mounted from Cuba, Soviet missiles launching from the island, a substantial Russian naval base and the presence of major ground forces was deeply disturbing. The Russian bear wasn't just seeking a toehold in Uncle Sam's backyard but squatting on his doorstep. For Kennedy, who felt he had not been tough enough with Khrushchev at Vienna, it was a decisive test of resolve. Analysis of photographs taken by a U-2 spy plane revealed launch pads and bunkers.

The leaders of the US Air Force and US Army told the President to mount an all-out attack to eliminate the missile sites before they became operational.

He realised this could also destroy mankind; an uncontrollable escalation leading to SSBNs launching Polaris missiles while Russian boats within range nuked the USA. Strategic bombers of the UK and America would fly on suicidal missions to deliver atomic slaughter to the heart of the Soviet Union. The naval-minded Kennedy believed nuclear weapons should be the last resort rather than the first choice. Eight carriers and 175 other naval vessels were rapidly deployed by the US Navy's Atlantic

Fleet into the Caribbean. Soviet ships would be stopped and searched under a 'quarantine', which was to all intents and purposes a blockade, though the latter was actually prohibited by international law, except in time of war. On 22 October, Kennedy told the world Russian missiles were present on Cuba.

The day President Kennedy made his revelation, the British submarine *Alderney* was at sea in the Atlantic with units of the Canadian fleet. While she provided a training target for an ASW exercise, another British boat, *Astute*, was alongside in Halifax, Nova Scotia, her crew on an extended run ashore.

Canada had no submarine arm in the early 1960s, but was able to utilise three British vessels – the 6th Submarine Division (SM6) – towards which it paid a substantial amount in operating and maintenance costs.

Mixed RN and Royal Canadian Navy (RCN) crews enabled the latter service to cultivate a core of trained submariners for the day when Canada would field its own flotilla. Both governments had agreed control of the Halifax-based submarines would be returned to the Royal Navy in time of war.

On 22 October 1962 *Alderney* stopped pretending to be a Soviet submarine trying to sneak into Canadian territorial waters. While the RCN surface vessels withdrew unexpectedly and disappeared elsewhere, she remained at sea somewhere off Halifax, not clear about what the sudden emergency might be. That evening she was called in to take on fuel.

While alongside at the refuelling jetty, Cdr Ken Vause, boss of SM6, came aboard and gave a briefing, in which he explained what was happening in the outside world. War stores were to be taken aboard immediately and the submarine would deploy before the sun came up. *Alderney* would patrol just north-east of the Grand Banks to detect and then trail Soviet submarines.

Astute had already departed. The previous evening *Astute*'s officers had been dining on French cuisine ashore in Halifax, when someone in the restaurant switched on the radio. They listened in shocked silence to President Kennedy announcing the naval 'quarantine' of Cuba.

It seemed just one small step from war.

Racing back to base, *Astute*'s officers had watched, with more than a pang of envy, as Canadian warships put to sea. The situation was already tense out in the North Atlantic. NATO units had for some days been tracking a Soviet submarine 300 miles off the coast. As they helped ships cast off, the British submariners – most of whom were unmarried and would be at a loose end – promised departing Canadians they would make sure their girls had some good company. Sadly, there would be no amorous pursuits, for Cdr Vause gave orders for *Astute* to get ready for war. She would take aboard a full outfit of torpedoes and as much food as possible.

There had been no direction either way from the UK on what SM6 should do, but with the world in a crisis that could easily tip over into conflict, Vause decided his submarines would be better off at sea than languishing in harbour. Senior officers in the RCN approved his decision.

The involvement of British submarines was, though, potentially a grey area. It was agreed control of the boats would stay with the Canadians provided they were not given orders to actually wage war.

They could carry out surveillance on the picket line waiting for Soviet submarines heading south, arrayed along the Sound Surveillance System (SOSUS) line, which acted as a sonar fence. Connected to listening posts ashore, it was a network of hydrophones embedded in the bottom of the Atlantic. It could detect submarine activity all the way from US shores to Scotland (and beyond). Anything trying to stray through it would be detected and a NATO boat then sent in to carry out close shadowing.

To cover himself Vause wrote a letter to FOSM in the UK, informing his national service boss of what was happening, but he sent it via sea mail. It seemed Vause did not want to be second-guessed by people not on the scene.

The American 'quarantine' started at 09.00, Washington DC time on 24 October. An estimated 25 vessels thought to be carrying weapons, or weapons-related cargos, were heading for Cuba. President Kennedy applied extra pressure on the Soviets by explaining Polaris missile boats were deployed and in position to fire. B-52 bombers carrying nuclear weapons were also ready. The USA's land-based silos were on enhanced levels of stand-by.

Kennedy's preferred option was for the naval 'quarantine' to work.

It would be up to the Soviets to make the first aggressive move.

The Kremlin was informed that if the USA was attacked then it would surely finish things.

TO SEA WITH SEALED ORDERS

Somewhere to the east of Newfoundland *Astute*'s Navigator, Lieutenant Toby Frere, was finding it difficult to determine exactly where his boat was, for she lacked an operational navigation aid such as Decca or LORAN to obtain a fix. The Decca Navigator System (no longer used) was, much like the still extant Long Range Navigation (LORAN), a radio navigation aid using low frequency signals from beacons on land to gain a fix.

With no other means, Frere used a sextant, determining the position of the planets and the stars in relation to his boat. It was a device, and skill, dating back a couple of centuries. Aside from surfacing to enable Frere to take navigation fixes, *Astute* also emerged from the deep at certain times to tune into the BBC World Service.

This was not for reports on the missile crisis, but so one of her officers could pick up the latest stock market news and assess how his investments were faring amid all the turmoil.

The American stock market had dropped 2 per cent the day of Kennedy's speech revealing the presence of missiles on Cuba. The UK stock market was similarly volatile. When dived *Astute* used her Type 186 sonar to try and detect Russian boats, with some assistance from US Navy Maritime Patrol Aircraft (MPA); so far, without success.

Should the crisis develop into war the Canadians in *Astute*'s complement, including a native Indian cook looking after the Wardroom and a French Canadian officer, would be in a difficult position. Canada was obliged by a mutual defence pact to deploy its maritime forces in support of the US Navy, as well as being a founder member of NATO. However, in 1962 its government was far from supportive of the Kennedy administration's actions.

Rear Admiral Kenneth Dyer, Flag Officer Atlantic Command (FOAC), had other ideas. A Canadian who was trained at Dartmouth and saw service in the old British battle-cruiser HMS *Hood*, commanding various warships during the Second World War, Dyer decided it was essential his nation honour its defence commitment to the USA. His orders said his vessels should join a surveillance line from 'the northern tip of the Grand Banks' down to the 'southern end of Georges Bank' but no further south.

Should the UK join the USA in combat operations, both *Astute* and *Alderney* would switch to national control along with the Canadian sailors in them. There was no way they could be replaced at sea without endangering the boat by forcing her to surface and get them off. They would not, anyway, want to let their shipmates down.

Canadian sailors in *Astute* and *Alderney*, including Lt Peter Haydon who was Navigating Officer of the latter, found one signal from Rear Admiral Dyer had a distinctly chilling effect on bravado.

In the event of war, so the admiral decreed, they must ensure they were not captured with 'CANADA' shoulder flashes still on their uniforms. Nor could they even be caught dead with them. They must cut them off.

Maintaining a watch off the Grand Banks, surfacing every now and then to get a navigation fix and check the stock market, *Astute*'s men tried to maintain their normal equilibrium, coping with the usual eccentricities of submarine life and the strange habits of shipmates.

A priority each day was to try and evict the First Lieutenant, Tod Slaughter, from his bunk, as early as possible. It was located in the wardroom, right above where the table was erected and set each day for breakfast. If they tried to start eating while he was still in his pit, Slaughter would invariably wake up and tumble straight into the middle of the breakfast spread.

His brother officers, crammed in tight around the small table, looked on appalled as Slaughter put his feet in the butter and knees in the marmalade and knocked over the coffee pot.

Yelling their outrage as he carved his path of carnage, they suffered the further insult of being shoved here and there while Slaughter squeezed himself into his anointed position at the head of the table.

He never failed to yell:

'*Where's my breakfast!?*'

This provoked a volley of curses from the Steward, a Canadian Indian, working in the small pantry just outside the wardroom.

He tolerated abuse from nobody, at any time of the day. If the officers really pissed him off, the Steward would shape the breakfast rolls by squeezing the dough in his armpits.

Slaughter made a grab for the nearest packet of cigarettes, ignoring protests that he had no rights to any of them, and lit up. The only one to take any of this with equanimity was the Engineer Officer. A mature

Lieutenant, he had endured numerous skirmishes with Slaughter over cigarette rights.

Wearing a resigned smile on his face, the Engineer regarded the First Lieutenant with toleration born from years of trying to find innovative means to cope with the most demanding technical difficulties. To see off Slaughter's nicotine-hungry forays he had taken the extraordinary measure of writing his name on each cigarette.

Surfacing for the stock market check on October 25, *Astute* managed instead to pick up radio coverage of a speech to the House of Commons by the Prime Minister, Harold Macmillan. MPs had been called back from their annual recess for an emergency debate on the Cuban crisis and the Prime Minister – a family friend of President Kennedy – was voicing strong support for the USA. In private he was trying to persuade the US leader to call off the quarantine.

As a former naval officer Kennedy perhaps understood the ability of maritime forces to exert deterrence better than Macmillan, whose military service had been in the Army.

In Parliament Macmillan did not reveal any participation by UK naval vessels. The letter from SM6 to FOSM in the UK had yet to arrive, so the Prime Minister was blissfully unaware of *Astute* being at sea to actively support the quarantine. The Americans were by no means viewed as victims in the crisis. In response to a question from one socialist MP, anxious that British merchant vessels should not be stopped and searched while on lawful business, Macmillan explained the Americans were mounting a limited embargo. Its aim was to stop nuclear weapons being transported to Cuba. Macmillan suggested UK-registered vessels were unlikely to be involved in *that* kind of trade.

At Faslane Rob Forsyth's boat, *Auriga*, was also being prepared for potential combat. The young Lieutenant was, truth be told, bottom of the pile and only allowed to work in the torpedo compartment under the strict supervision of the redoubtable Leading Seaman Cumberpatch. Determined to show he was up to the job, Forsyth set about earning the respect of the ratings rather than expecting it by divine right. His fellow officers also pushed him hard – by their example and also constantly emphasising the high standards needed – to get a firm grip on the job. He learned a lot from the Engineer Officer about how the complex mechanism of a submarine worked. Forsyth wanted to do well, because he found the job absorbing and also out of self-preservation.

'My wish to be usefully employed was more than satisfied by the twin tasks of keeping my submarine safely afloat – or rather not sinking her – and preparing for war.'

Already he had his sights set high and decided he would like to be a submarine captain one day. He soon discovered that, in the closed confines of a boat, in close company with all sorts of strong-willed, colourful characters, it wasn't possible to be friends with everybody all the time.

'We did not all get on, but in general you didn't tell people you didn't always like what they said or did, because it would make life unlivable. It has been said to me that submariners are difficult people to get along with, period. To outsiders they may sometimes appear to be spiky and aggressive but naturally they think themselves the best thing since sliced bread at doing what they are trained to do, i.e. close with the target with all possible speed and sink it. This requires aggressive thinking. But on board, in the confines of their submarine, somehow they still managed to get on together.'

Auriga's dummy torpedoes were taken off and live war shots brought aboard, amid much swearing from those tasked with carrying it out. It involved rigging various pulleys to unload and load the weapons by extracting or inserting them via hatches. The Assistant Torpedo Officer was allowed to take part only under the strictest supervision of Petty Officer Art Bodden and Leading Seaman Cumberpatch, who thought Forsyth 'a very keen young lad'. This was a considerable tribute from a seasoned submariner who had seen his share of officers, both good and bad.

The 25-year-old Cumberpatch, from Corby in Northamptonshire, had joined the Navy in 1953. His father was a soldier in the First World War, while his brother was in the Royal Marines during the Second World War.

He received basic training in the HMS *Ganges* shore establishment, at Shotley, Suffolk. A Boy Seaman, aged 16, one day Cumberpatch was asked by an instructor what he wanted to do with his naval career.

He replied, without hesitation: 'Submariner.'

Cumberpatch didn't mind being 'a sardine in a tin' and later, on going to HMS *Dolphin*, thoroughly enjoyed submarine training. When he passed out as an 18-year-old baby submariner in 1955, his first boat was HMS *Tapir* and by the age of 20 he was also married.

Joining *Auriga* in 1961, Cumberpatch was well adjusted to serving in an arm of the Navy where he found 'damn good camaraderie', regarding it all as 'good fun'.

'But you had to know your job. You were close knit and you had get on with people.'

Living conditions were a bit rough and ready in the fore ends with all the torpedoes and their associated equipment. 'Eighteen of us used to sleep in there – nine either side in canvas bunks – stacked three high.'

Luckily he had a middle bunk. Anybody in the top one ran the risk of getting soaked by condensation dripping off the inside of the hull, so they slept under a plastic sheet. The men shared the fore ends with food, not least fresh vegetables, including nets of onions and sacks of potatoes, which Cumberpatch didn't mind peeling when watch-keeping. It was quite a therapeutic activity. Bread was stowed on torpedo loading racks out of the way. The loaves soon acquired a hard shell of mould on the outside – formally known as penicillium. That had to be peeled off as well before people could eat any of it.

There were officers who were 'a pain in the arse' but most of them knew what they were doing and with the green ones, well, you helped them along a bit. While Forsyth – just a lad compared to Cumberpatch – might be in charge on certain aspects it was just as well he watched and learned during the delicate – and potentially lethal – business of handling torpedoes. So long as Cumberpatch put 'Sir' on the end of his necessarily forthright advice and instructions it was within acceptable bounds.

Contemplating the real thing being loaded aboard instilled a real sense of responsibility in Forsyth, who appreciated the deadly statistics.

'A Mk8 torpedo weighed 3,000 lbs, was 21 feet long and we carried about 18 of them. Loading them through a hatch, stacking them in racks and later loading them into torpedo tubes using very antiquated gear was not for the faint-hearted. If you got it badly wrong, then it could kill someone. No one was going to let me give the orders until they were sure I had the drill right and understood the dangers. That is when I realised the real meaning of being a submariner. Teamwork and safety were critical. The torpedo compartment crew helped me learn my job because team safety was more important than officer–crew relationship. Stripes on the arm did not mean you knew your job until you had proved it.'

A mountain of food also had also to be stowed away, including boxes of tinned peas and tomatoes, which were stacked in a passageway, creating a false deck. This was covered in plywood. Unsuspecting submariners who misjudged the height between the false floor and various pipes, valves and bits of equipment, banged their heads. More curses were uttered.

With sealed orders taken aboard, *Auriga* cast off, exited the Gareloch and pushed out into the Clyde. Her captain, Lt Cdr Mike Wilson, opened the envelope. He was instructed to form a picket line with American and British submarines, way out in the Atlantic – on likely Soviet submarine routes south – working also with surface warships and MPAs. Once again there were numerous submarines all trying to squeeze through the same narrow waters. The Soviet spy vessel trailed them as closely as it dared. *Auriga*'s bridge team waved goodbye to the Russian before disappearing into their boat, as she dived. Once in position, *Auriga* soon picked up several Soviet submarines. They must have been going at speed, for, as one of the British boat's officers observed, 'their turbine whine could be heard more than 20 miles away'.

Auriga tracked the Russian boats for a while, using her HF radio to pass on details of the contacts to NATO's Commander-in-Chief Atlantic and also to the Admiralty in London. The Soviets passed out of range to the south.

The Canadian government remained unconvinced the crisis posed a direct threat to its own sovereign territory but Rear Admiral Dyer continued tasking his units on 'training activities'. These just happened to involve searching for possible submarine activity.

Astute and *Alderney* were positioned with American boats at the northern gateway to the Grand Banks, sweeping to and fro, their sonar operators straining to pick up signs of Soviets racing past.

By the time *Alderney* had reached her picket station Russian submarines committed to the crisis were themselves more than likely off New York and Halifax or even in Cuban waters.

Rather than searching randomly in the vast Atlantic, it made sound tactical sense to loiter near Soviet spy trawlers – frequently used by Russian boats as communication relay stations. It was also worth shadowing vessels that resupplied Moscow's boats at sea. With this special quarry in mind, *Alderney* placed herself north-east of the Strait of Belle Isle, hoping to catch a submarine on the surface.

More than 180 American naval vessels, including the new nuclear-powered strike carrier USS *Enterprise*, along with 30,000 US Marines embarked in various amphibious ships, had by now entered the Caribbean. The navies of the Dominican Republic, Argentina and Venezuela reinforced US Navy efforts.

All this would be held in check provided there was no aggressive action by the Russians, including breaching the quarantine.

Soviet vessels must stop and be searched. Any submarines detected would be forced to surface by non-lethal explosive charges. They were expected to obey the international code message 'IDKCA' – conveyed to them via underwater telephone – which signified:

Surface or be destroyed.

It was the biggest of bluffs and Kennedy must have prayed fervently his old Vienna antagonist would not call it.

The period of maximum peril came on 26 and 27 October, with eight Russian cargo ships approaching the quarantine line. The USS *Essex* – configured as an ASW carrier – and an escort group of destroyers went to meet them.

A submarine was detected submerged between two of the merchant vessels. *Essex* flashed her instructions for the Soviet ships to stop and be searched. The submarine was instructed: 'IDKCA.'

Rather than press on, provoking gunfire and depth-charge attacks, the Soviet group capitulated. Over the next few days all Russian submarines surfaced. Unknown to the Americans until after the Cold War, four of the Foxtrot Class diesel-electric patrol submarines deployed to Cuba were armed with nuclear-tipped torpedoes. Their captains were authorised to fire these weapons if they came under attack. Russian land forces on Cuba also had Frog tactical nuclear missiles and permission to use them against American naval landing forces and their supporting ships. Submarines were the only Soviet naval vessels involved in the Cuban Missile Crisis. The only way the Kremlin's boats could have seen off the US Navy's quarantine enforcers would have been to use their nuclear-tipped torpedoes, which would have started a Third World War. There was no interim measure, such as long-range surface warships to counter American carriers and destroyers by jostling with them for possession of the sea. It was a lesson the Russians took to heart immediately. Khrushchev, the man who once declared there was no need for a large, modern surface fleet, staged a *volte-face*. To conclude that Russia believed submarines were a useless weapon in the Cold War would be an error. As the coming years would confirm, fielding a balanced fleet with powerful surface units, *and above all submarines*, was still the Kremlin's ultimate aim.

It fell to a militant left-winger, and Labour MP for Salford East, Frank Allaun, to bring a chill to a House of Commons debate on 30 October. A life-long pacifist and anti-nuclear weapons campaigner, the former *Manchester Evening News* industrial correspondent called for American atomic weapons to be removed from British soil. He wanted SSBNs based at Holy Loch sent home. He told his fellow MPs that, as the crisis peaked just a few days earlier, he had been shaken to his core.

'I went upstairs and looked at my children, who were asleep, and wondered what kind of future, if any, they were going to have. I guess that parents throughout the world had the same sort of reaction. I have maintained for some years that mankind's chances of survival are only fifty-fifty. In the light of the events of the last few days, however, I would say that the odds have considerably worsened.'

Allaun feared a future crisis might actually push the world over the edge. He likened the East–West confrontation to a game of chicken on a vast scale. The primary protagonists – the USA and USSR – took with them 'unwilling passengers', namely 'every man, woman and child in the world'. He was 'extremely grateful that Mr Khrushchev swerved aside at the last moment. If he had not done so, my children might not have been able to sleep in peace in their beds tonight.'

Allaun said it didn't help that Russia perceived itself as a nation surrounded by nuclear missiles every bit as close and threatening as those unwisely positioned on Cuba.

He pointed out newspapers were reporting that an American Polaris missile submarine had put to sea from Holy Loch. 'As we sit here tonight that submarine is probably prowling somewhere on the bottom of the ocean near the frontiers of Russia,' speculated Allaun. 'If Khrushchev had reacted, that submarine would have escaped any retaliatory blow. It would have been safe. But we in Britain would not have been safe. We would have been the victims if an atomic attack had taken place.'

The crisis spluttered out but submarines were still on patrol.

Astute had a brief supply break at St John's before returning to sea. The key moments of tension in the Cuban Missile Crisis in the North Atlantic actually came after the maximum moment of peril had passed in the Caribbean.

Spearheaded by the Canadian ASW carrier *Bonaventure*, the two British submarines and 24 of Canada's frigates and destroyers were sweeping an area 1,000 miles in length and 250 miles broad. On 5 November a Foxtrot boat was detected by the destroyer HMCS *Kootenay* close to the Georges Bank; in total 11 Russian submarines were being trailed simultaneously. Unhappy at this turn of events, a couple of Soviet spy trawlers made aggressive lunges towards *Kootenay*, but she hung on to the contact. The US Navy subsequently took up the baton when her target sailed further south.

While its government dithered over supporting the Americans, Canada's Atlantic-based warships and the submarines of SM6 acquitted themselves well, for between 23 October and 15 November it is estimated 136 submarine contacts were made.

Alderney was stood down on 8 November, sailing back into Halifax on 10 November, while *Astute* came in four days later. The submarine crews needed to blow off steam. The young officers, somewhat unkempt and stinking after weeks in their floating prisons, headed for the bar in the naval base wardroom.

While his Royal Navy shipmates from *Alderney* were ordering their drinks Lt Haydon, as a Canadian, was dismayed to be singled out by the RCN Base Commander. Haydon was told that before entering he would need to bathe and visit the barber. The stinking, lank-haired, unshaven British were one thing, but no Canadian officer might soil the atmosphere of the wardroom bar. Not on his watch. Hearing of this, Cdr Vause was furious, storming into action. He forcefully told the Base Commander his young submarine officers had been more or less at sea for two months, including almost four weeks on war patrol. Furthermore, Vause bellowed:

'They are going to get drunk, get laid and have a bath.'

If the Base Commander wanted to continue with his ban then, warned Vause, he would go and see what Rear Admiral Dyer had to say about it.

Quailing in the face of this onslaught, the Base Commander lifted the ban. *Alderney's* officers, including Haydon, set about the task of getting drunk with gusto. Joining them in raising a glass, Vause suggested they should get their hair cut as soon as possible, in order to at least look more presentable. On the other side of the Atlantic, once she too was stood down from her own missile crisis patrol, *Auriga* returned to Faslane and finished off her work-up for deployment to Canada. Then it was time for a transatlantic passage.

While not on duty Lt Forsyth relieved the boredom by playing uckers (a traditional naval board game like a superior version of Ludo) and scat (a complex card game in which the objective is to get rid of all the cards in your hand, even if that means cheating).

There was a more serious pursuit at hand, though, with a proposed attempt to carry out the longest-distance snort ever by a Royal Navy submarine. It was even announced beforehand that *Auriga* would make the entire voyage without surfacing. In the event, halfway across, a severe sewage tank defect forced a change of plan. It meant excrement could not be evacuated from the submarine. There was a mightily unpleasant build-up in the sewage system. A revolting odour permeated the boat, requiring *Auriga* to surface and stay there, in order expel the fumes and get rid of the offending faecal matter. While Forsyth was not to clock up a record-breaking snort passage, he was impressed by the ingenuity shown in providing a temporary solution to the problem. 'A heads seat was rigged inside the fin, with the waste falling down to where seawater washed over the hull. There was a large following sea, which occasionally flushed the toilet and its occupant from below as he sat there. A toilet vacant/engaged notice was hung in the control room!'

Leading Seaman Cumberpatch took the toilet arrangements in his stride, literally. 'This is cracking,' he remarked with deep sarcasm as he climbed up into the fin to do his business, wearing an oilskin, a towel around his neck and some toilet paper stuffed in a pocket. Buffeted by the incoming sea spray – wiping his face with the towel – it was far from ideal, but there were worst things in life. *Weren't there?*

Grateful to reach St John's, Newfoundland, *Auriga* was met by a group of press on the quayside, eager for news of the record-breaking achievement. The reporters were welcomed aboard and into the wardroom, where the officers of *Auriga* – now showered and in their best uniforms – were quizzed about their supposed ground-breaking feat. It was confessed that it had not actually been possible, *due to unforeseen technical problems.*

It was at this precise moment that the senior rating charged with maintaining the submarine's sewage system knocked on the door, to make his progress report on repairs. Holding aloft a fork smeared with brown slime and himself ponging rather noxiously, he announced: 'I think we have found the cause of the problem!' Noses wrinkling, the assembled reporters had a good idea what the 'technical difficulty' was.

The only way to blow off steam after such a horrendous transatlantic crossing was for the men of *Auriga* to get roaring drunk. The rest of Canada regarded St John's – in their eyes a charming imperial outpost still living in the Edwardian era – as eccentrically old-fashioned, condescendingly wondering if the locals could even read or write. British submariners cared little for any of that, just so long as the girls were pretty and the bars welcoming. They also enjoyed the conveniences of St John's (*Auriga*'s ratings were permitted to visit an icebreaker alongside in port to use that vessel's showers and heads). Living ashore, but required to report for duty aboard the boat in the morning, some *Auriga* submariners, including Forsyth, suffered hangovers so bad they could barely manage to crawl into the shower. Forcing limbs to work, controlling raging headaches and queasy stomachs, somehow they also made it to the submarine. Once they reached Halifax, the ratings of *Auriga* did not live aboard the submarine but in HMCS *Stadacona* a stone frigate shorebase.

A January 1963 send-off for a submarine going home to Britain featured a rousing alcohol-fuelled sing-along by *Auriga*'s men and the departing crew. This ended with a rousing rendition of 'This Old Hat of Mine' and one lad was thrown out into the snow for fun. Aboard *Auriga*, under the tutelage of the redoubtable Cumberpatch, Forsyth was shaping up well, the Leading Seaman going as far as to suggest he was 'a very, very good officer ... and not a bad lad'.

The fact that Forsyth never appeared to get flustered was an excellent quality. Forsyth also knew when not to upset Cumberpatch unnecessarily, such as after the deck had been cleaned – it was important nobody got it dirty again straight away. So, when exiting the submarine via the fore end hatch, the trick was to jump from the accommodation space door across to the lower rung of the ladder. Or else walk on the deck and receive a telling-off. In such small ways did officers and men build up respect for one another.

Firmly established at Halifax, and integrated into SM6, the *Auriga* was worked hard, often sailing at weekends to be on station in the diving area when the faster Canadian surface ships arrived. She would stay out for up to three weeks. The warships used to arrive on a Monday afternoon and *Auriga* would spend all week exercising with them. No sooner had the surface warships departed for home at the weekend than Canadian sub-hunting aircraft would turn up to play war games. When the surface ships returned on the following Monday, it used to irritate the submariners that the Canadians could not even be bothered to bring out the mail.

During one of these deployments *Auriga* took part in sea trials that sought to make it easier to trail Soviet submarines. A Canadian boffin had come up with the idea of dropping dozens of 'floppy magnets', which it was hoped would create a noise nuisance, clinging to the target boat's hull and flopping around. *Auriga* was tasked with being a guinea pig for this bright idea. A Neptune sub-hunting aircraft flew over *Auriga*'s position, unleashing a blizzard of the things. While some might have fallen away into the deep, others duly hit, and attached themselves to the British submarine.

As *Auriga* tried to make herself as stealthy as possible, despite these tiny magnetic parasites, another SM6 submarine attempted to detect her. Sailors inside the target vessel, including Rob Forsyth, flinched at the God-awful, ear-splitting football-rattle din. Not surprisingly, the sonar operators in the other boat beamed in delight at how easy it was to detect and track *Auriga*. The floppy magnets created a big problem. When *Auriga* surfaced they slid down the hull and remained firmly fixed inside the casing, on top of the ballast tanks. Any stealth the boat possessed was nullified by the continuing noise nuisance. They couldn't find, and remove, all of the 'floppy magnets' until the submarine went into dry-dock at Halifax.

The infernal things were dropped on the Russians, too; the crews of several Foxtrot Class boats were reportedly driven to distraction. Realising there was no point in continuing with their deployments they headed straight home. In general, though, the Soviet submarines were already so noisy there was not much difficulty in finding them regardless of floppy magnets.

Such pursuit of innovation – outlandish as it might seem – was a symptom of NATO's desperation to find ways to offset the Soviet Union's greater submarine numbers. Admittedly many of the USSR's boats were of pre-Second World War vintage, but a lot were modern and capable of global operations, with more and more nuclear-powered vessels entering service. The Russians had 30 armed with missiles and a dozen nuclear-powered boats deployed at any one time. The Americans fielded around 150 submarines of all types, but with better SSNs and more powerful ballistic missile boats. The Royal Navy had 54 submarines of mixed vintage. Just one of them was nuclear-powered, the *Dreadnought*.

In late 1962 Britain's Vice Admiral R. M. Smeeton, who was deputy to the alliance's Supreme Allied Commander Atlantic (SACLANT), glumly summed up the situation. He told a group of politicians from the various NATO nations: 'the Soviets have today the largest submarine force the world has ever known. We must assume that this force has a simple mission ... it is to divide and destroy the physical structure of NATO ...'

This, he felt, would be achieved 'not by frontal attacks on our defended territory but by the infiltration of submarines into our geographical core and from there striking out at the soft and exposed area behind our fighting front. The mission of the Soviet submarine force is obvious, the danger to our alliance is ever present ...'

He revealed that it wasn't possible for NATO navies to create conditions for victory in the Atlantic without resorting to nuclear weapons. The upper hand could only be maintained by obliterating Northern Fleet bases to remove the Russian boats' means of support.

'We simply do not have enough forces,' the Vice Admiral conceded.

It was currently only possible, with the limited conventional maritime forces at NATO's disposal, to harass the Soviets – to conduct surveillance of their operations – and demonstrate the alliance's resolve to contest the oceans.

'We can take steps to make sure the enemy is fully aware of where his course of action is leading him without using nuclear weapons,' explained the admiral. 'But we cannot go to war that way.'

SACLANT had too few ASW ships and Maritime Patrol Aircraft;

nor did it have enough submarines. As far as the admiral and other senior officers were concerned, Moscow not only had a bigger navy, but also a more modern one. For their part the Soviets feared the ability of the West's aircraft carriers. Operating in the North Atlantic and Mediterranean they could place nuclear-armed strike jets even closer to the heart of Mother Russia than ever before.

They also worried about the advent of American ballistic missile submarines packing far more destructive power – and with greater reach – than their own could muster. With their less capable boats and missiles, the Soviets sought to use ice cover to gain advantage by getting closer to their targets in the USA. Nuclear devastation could be inflicted on American cities in just a few minutes – something that gave Washington real pause for thought and made NATO determined to get in there.

There is surely no more dangerous an environment in which to operate diesel-electric submarines than under ice. They need to surface at regular intervals, to take in oxygen and expel fumes from their diesel engines.

Otherwise both battery life and air will soon run out, with the suffocation of the Ship's Company. The boats themselves will plummet to a frozen doom. For British submariners of the early 1960s it was just one more instance of pushing the parameters of that envelope of risk. Going under the ice was considered to be a necessity, for it was potentially a sanctuary for Soviet submarines waiting to unleash nuclear missiles.

The US Navy had some years earlier realised there was an urgent need for nuclear-powered boats to ensure their submariners could survive and fight in the ice-bound far North.

The Royal Navy, too, must soon field nuclear-powered attack boats, for diesels were profoundly unsuited to the task. Until then, Britain's Arctic undersea warriors, including Rob Forsyth, did not know if their next venture beneath the ice would be their last. They took risks their American allies would never contemplate.

For example, having been built at the end of the Second World War to carry the war to Japan, SM6's A-Class boats did not possess the sort of heavy-duty heating necessary to cope.

It got so cold inside that icicles formed. Temperatures were never much above freezing. Even using the inadequate heaters they did possess provided its own dilemma. The more heat they pumped out, the faster the boat's batteries were drained. Levels of CO_2 were, as ever, a problem. They were monitored very carefully, and scrubbers used to clean the air, supplemented by oxygen generators. They did not produce a lot of oxygen; nor was the air scrubbed that effectively – it took a long time to restore the atmosphere.

Fortunately the foul air could be changed via snorting, but under the ice the snort mast obviously could not be raised. The only salvation would be smashing through it to gain access to the air.

The polar ice cap, noted one US Navy submarine captain, is 'composed of huge chunks and floes, varying greatly in size and thickness, grinding one upon the other, creating the effect of a solid mass'. Another American submarine officer, Cdr D. McWethy, taking a flight over the Arctic Ocean during the late 1940s, was astounded to see hundreds of cracks in the ice (called leads) and gaps between floes (known as polynya). He realised it would, theoretically, be possible, even with a diesel-electric boat, to operate under the ice. During the Second World War, the Germans had ventured into the Arctic with U-boats – in the early autumn and summer when conditions permitted – penetrating deep into Siberian waters from bases in Norway.

Even though their commanders felt sure they could navigate under ice, always finding some place to surface, they still had a number of close calls, including losing periscopes. During attacks on Soviet shipping, torpedoes were sometimes set off when they hit ice on their way to target.

A boat had to be tough to survive the Arctic, with a fin robust enough to batter through the sheet ice without sustaining unacceptable damage. The British, who also experimented with submarine operations in the polar regions during the Second World War, showed an early interest in seeking out Soviets under the ice. Aside from the challenges of operating a boat and keeping sailors alive in such extreme conditions, there was also a need to explore limitations of new British torpedoes and find means of communicating orders to, and receiving reports from, submarines deployed in such zones.

There were also attempts to gain an edge over the opposition by putting polar research stations on large floes in the ever-shifting drift ice. Sometimes, in reality, they were listening posts packed with equipment for detecting submarines. That kind of caper possibly provided inspiration for a best-selling novel by a former Royal Navy sailor, and Second World War surface navy Arctic convoy veteran, Alistair MacLean. In *Ice Station Zebra*, first published in 1963, a US Navy nuclear-powered submarine ventures under the ice towards the North Pole. Allegedly sent on a mission to rescue scientists who have survived devastating fires at a British research station, the American boat carries an MI6 agent. His mission is to recover a film dropped by a Soviet reconnaissance satellite – on which are images of every land-based nuclear missile silo in the USA. The film had been deposited near Ice Station Zebra, where – desperate to recover it – Russian agents started the fires and murdered a few people.

The USS *Dolphin* is the main location for most of the drama, suffering several accidents under the ice, including fire and flood, even having her reactor shut down and going to auxiliary battery power. At one point she fires a torpedo to blow a hole in the ice when there is no polynya to be found.

Her highly skilled crew ultimately brings *Dolphin*, and the satellite film, to safety. MacLean was influenced by a number of real-life events – ventures by American nuclear-powered submarines under ice, the space race and East–West tension, and the 1959 loss of a film container from a US intelligence-gathering satellite over the Arctic. The Soviets were said to have recovered it.

In recent years it has emerged that the CIA in May 1962 was involved in exploits to counter Soviet listening stations that could have come straight from the pages of a novel. Even if he did not know details of the CIA mission, MacLean certainly did plenty of research into under-ice operations by submarines, providing a chilling insight into the risks. In *Ice Station Zebra* the captain of the *Dolphin* remarks: 'if anything happens to the reactor or the steam turbines or the electrical generators – then we're already in our coffin and the lid screwed down. The ice-pack above is the coffin lid.'

In real life, the USA's Office of Naval Research, Defense Intelligence Agency and CIA put together 'Operation Coldfeet'. Two 'intelligence collectors' were parachuted onto the ice close to a drifting, and recently abandoned, Soviet research station. The Russians had conducted an evacuation because they believed the ice would soon crush it. After seven days collecting intelligence the two men were picked up in breath-taking fashion by a specially converted former B-17 bomber. Using a so-called 'Skyhook' it plucked them and their intelligence goodies from the ice and reeled them in. The CIA has revealed they brought home 'valuable information' on how the Soviet Union was utilising its scientific research stations. 'The team found evidence of advanced acoustical systems research to detect under-ice US submarines,' a CIA document reveals, 'and efforts to develop Arctic anti-submarine warfare techniques.'

Two months before Operation Coldfeet the two Halifax-based British boats *Alderney* and *Astute* assisted the US Navy nuclear-powered attack submarines *Seadragon* and *Nautilus* in under-ice training. The Brits played Russian boats operating in the Gulf of St Lawrence, one of the likely firing positions for their ballistic missiles. With a range of between 300 and 325 nautical miles, Soviet submarines lurked in waters stretching from the eastern seaboard of North America all the way up to off Nova Scotia.

The ice in the Gulf of St Lawrence formed and thawed each year. It was not as dirty as that which stayed all year around, but it was up to 5ft thick, with the ice keels a further 25ft deep.

With infinite caution *Alderney* edged under the ice, her captain using the periscope to assess the keels. During the day he was able to make them out due to sunlight through the translucent ice but in the pitch-black night *Alderney* was forced to rely on sonar. The primitive upward-looking echo sounder was not without its flaws (such as not being able to tell the difference between thin sheet ice and open water). It was pretty useless when trying to surface at any time, never mind at night.

Trying to bash your way through ice, even if only three feet thick, tested the nerve of even the most mentally robust. The psychological strain increased dramatically when a diesel-electric boat didn't have a lot of battery life left and air was getting fouler by the second. Adding to such troubles, not all vents were covered with fairings. Even if a boat could find somewhere to burst through, the vents might freeze up. It wouldn't stop the submarine from surfacing but might prevent the boat from diving. In the event of war, under the ice all efforts would be focused on surviving the experience rather than fighting. Even when not actually under the ice, in the Arctic periscopes and masts could still be easily damaged by even small amounts of floating ice. Ruptured seals could let in water, too. Using the thin, fragile attack scope was definitely not advised – it might get bent. It was very difficult to hunt another submarine under the ice, anyway – too much clutter on the sonar.

Alderney's Lt Peter Haydon remarked drily: 'It was indeed an adventure and I think most of us would agree that we were often a little apprehensive, especially when the battery was very low and there was no sign of open water.' The most an SSK (a diesel patrol submarine) could hope to manage was what Haydon described as 'quick ventures under fringe ice'. To take a submarine right under the ice sheet – where it grew thick – was 'a questionable exercise'.

The mere thought of a fire under the ice sent a shudder through any submariner, especially if combined with battery life seeping away as a boat tried repeatedy, and failed, to smash through. Not only would you have a fire consuming all the oxygen, but your crew would be fighting for breath as the submarine filled with noxious fumes. There was no means of escape and each time you tried to break through your battery got weaker, death that bit closer.

Flood was also a desperate prospect. Should a boat spring a leak she'd swiftly fill up with water, drowning her occupants or freezing them to death. The pressure would squeeze more and more water into the boat until it sank like a stone.

Rob Forsyth found *Auriga*'s under-the-ice adventures introduced him to a new dimension in discomfort. 'Inside the boat was wet – hot breath and bodies – cold hull – water running everywhere; condensation dripping on you, including on the charts, which – like some of the bunks – had to be covered in plastic. The inside of the hull was nominally clad in cork to keep the condensation down. That would only work with the air conditioning on and we couldn't use it because of the drain on the battery.'

To the forefront of everybody's minds as *Auriga* slid under the ice was, of course, a desire for the boat to have a polynya nearby at all times. *Auriga* endeavoured to be no more than half an hour from one.

'I suppose it could be described as a mixture of excitement and fear,' conceded Forsyth. 'The word was passed around if people heard that we had found one. There was no room for error at all.'

Auriga's under-ice operations focused primarily on the perennial challenges of navigation and survival, the upward-looking echo sounder remaining a lifesaver despite its imperfections.

Providing added assurance the boat could be extracted from a tricky situation was a sharp edge around the top of the fin – handy for cutting through ice. An optical illusion did not help the process of identifying the way ahead or where to smash through. Forsyth witnessed this phenomenon when he took a look through the periscope. 'You could see the boat's bow through the periscope and due to the refraction everything above you seemed to be in front – most disconcerting.'

It had been recognised that Maritime Patrol Aircraft could be extremely effective working with diesels, so *Auriga* refined her co-operation techniques. The American diesel boat USS *Grenadier* had proved the efficiency of such a team in May 1959. She chased a Soviet missile-armed Zulu Class submarine until the latter was forced to surface, finding a Neptune MPA low overhead, bathing her in a searchlight and taking numerous intelligence photos.

It was the first concrete proof that Soviet submarines were ranging across the Atlantic and operating not far from the US coast. Such a triumph was still an exception rather than the rule.

A chilling illustration of how thin the line was between life and death – how submarining was an inherently hazardous profession – was provided one time, just after *Auriga* emerged into open water.

The boat was trying to evade NATO ships practising their ASW techniques. The captain decided the most effective means of avoiding their attentions would be to sit on the bottom. Some 300ft of cold, impenetrable water overhead would hide *Auriga* from their sonars.

The submarine settled gently on what everybody assumed was the seabed. They waited, keeping as silent as possible until the warships moved away. Deciding it was time to bring *Auriga* up again, the captain ordered a small amount of compressed air blown into the ballast tanks, giving the boat a touch of positive buoyancy.

She refused to shift. With the battery low, the other best option – piling revs on the screws to drive her up – was fraught with risk. Use all the battery power up and they would die a long, slow death stuck to the bottom.

To young Forsyth the captain didn't seem overly perturbed, and so he did not feel too worried, at least not at that stage. It was decided to put a full blast into the tanks while simultaneously turning the screws. Apparently the boat only had enough compressed air to do this once. Sub Lieutenant Forsyth realised *Auriga* was in a tight spot. His exciting life as a young submariner might soon be snuffed out in the darkness and freezing cold.

Tanks blown.

Revs on the screws.

No movement.

Everybody in the boat swallowed their rising fear. Many a prayer was muttered. There was a slight trembling underfoot, the depth gauge needle began to decrease: 300ft ... 280ft ... 260ft ... 200ft ...

Prayers answered.

Auriga's ascent gathered pace rapidly, the boat shooting to the surface. The sea erupted, *Auriga* leaping above the surface, smashing down to settle amid hissing, collapsing spray.

Lieutenant Forsyth – he had been promoted in March 1962 – was ordered up to the bridge. Pulling on his foul-weather jacket, hauling himself up the first few rungs into the tower, he released the clips, unlocking the lower lid. He climbed up, repeating the process for the upper lid. As it swung upwards, freezing cold water deluged him. Shaking it off, Forsyth climbed onto the bridge itself. His nostrils were assaulted by an incredibly foul smell. Wondering what on earth it could be, he looked over the side of the fin and found stinking black mud covering it.

'It was quite apparent the CO had chosen the wrong place to bottom and we had been in primeval ooze. The depth gauge, which might have shown us settling slowly deeper, had obviously been blocked by mud, as had the propellers and the vent holes at the bottom of the ballast tanks. In retrospect that was the probably the nearest that I came to really perishing in a submarine.'

Even amid melting bergs it appeared there could be potentially fatal hazards. During one episode in the early 1960s, the A-Class boat *Alcide* strayed into what one of her sailors described as 'the top of a huge pocket of fresh water, the remains of an iceberg'. Frederick Rodgers went on: 'With the difference in water density between salt and fresh we immediately became very heavy and dropped like a stone. Only when we exited at the bottom of the [melted] berg did we regain our buoyancy.' How deep *Alcide* went exactly was not known, possibly as much as 800ft. Had the melting iceberg created just a few more feet of fresh water, the boat's momentum might have gone beyond the point of no return.

The adventures of their boats deep into, and under, the ice zone surely persuaded the British that such operations were not viable in war conditions unless deploying a nuclear-powered boat.

As a mere submersible, a diesel boat's natural environment was still the surface, despite an ability to hide from a foe under the sea. In the Second World War, technology allowed submarines to stay dived for longer. Developments such as the snort enabled greater exploitation of sub-surface stealth. Through modification and reconstruction, utilising Nazi advances, old Second World War-era boats like the A Class and the Super-Ts were able to push the limits of underwater endurance and speed. In seeking an elusive potential foe in the formidably hostile North Atlantic – trying to achieve superiority over the Soviets through training and operational skill, if not numbers – the British submarine force would simply need to field boats that could stay down for a long time, were deep-diving and not desperately in need of snorting to draw in oxygen and charge batteries.

As the most junior officer on the boat Rob Forsyth was detailed off to be Duty Officer aboard *Auriga* at Halifax on Christmas Day 1963. He watched the movie *On the Beach* projected on a screen erected in the wardroom. The only other member of the audience was his wife, Maureen, who had by then joined him in Halifax. Released in 1959, *On the Beach* starred Gregory Peck as the captain of the American nuclear-powered submarine USS *Sawfish* (named *Scorpion* in the Nevil Shute novel it was based on). It depicted the aftermath of a nuclear holocaust in which the captain's family and those of his sailors have been exterminated.

It is not long before the *Sawfish* sets sail for the last time, departing her temporary refuge in Australia, which is among the last places on Earth yet to be consumed by radiation. Peck's captain leaves behind a new lover (played by Ava Gardner). The submariners are doomed to die at sea. The submarine used to play *Sawfish* was the Royal Navy boat HMS *Andrew*, sister vessel to *Auriga*, which seemed to make the movie all the more poignant.

Just over a year on from the Cuban Missile Crisis it hardly made for cheerful viewing. Sitting very close together in sombre silence, each lost in thought, Rob and Maureen watched the stars of the film part, to each die alone in the fallout from a nuclear war. It truly was President Kennedy's 'cold, long winter ...'

Smile wrapped around his face, Lieutenant Tim Hale was perched high above the sea on the *Dreadnought*'s bridge as she surged through the ocean. The only noise was the clack and snap of a small Red Ensign rippling violently in the wind, its cable dinking against the radar mast. It was underscored by the gentle whisper of the sea parting. Ahead, the boat's big fat nose pushed out a huge bow wave. In her wake the water frothed and boiled. The forward planes – extended either side of the nose just above the surface of the water – were wreathed in ribbons of fine mist.

On the aft outer casing spray leapt up as the sea was sucked over her black hull. Smashing and crashing, it dissipated with a hiss.

There was no sound of straining diesels, or smells of cooking food coming from the galley vents – just the brine in Hale's nostrils, the spray wetting his cheeks. Speed picking up, the huge screw revolved faster, *Dreadnought* digging her tail into the sea, lifting her front end out of the water.

Hale marvelled at the ever-bigger bow wave.

The sheer, brute power being displayed was awesome.

This is fantastic, he thought.

Altering course south, the rudder pulled the stern down; the second bow wave moved aft of the stern.

He stared over the side of the fin, enthralled by a manoeuvre that would for some years remain exclusive to *Dreadnought*.

The submarine leapt forward. Planing across the surface of the ocean, she clocked up 19.5 knots. Three more than any other nuclear-powered boat could manage. With the second bow wave at the stern, *Dreadnought* cocked herself up and remained perched on the first one. The foreplanes gave lift on the bow, with the after plane angled at 10 degrees up to put the stern down. This was *Dreadnought* 'on the step'. *She's flying*, thought Hale, *how long before she takes off?*

Unfortunately, although she could dazzle and thrill as she skimmed across the surface of the Irish Sea, *Dreadnought* could not yet dive, for that milestone lay a little way down the road.

In December 1962, Britain's new wonder submarine – the Royal

Navy's first Submersible Ship Nuclear, or SSN – was at sea for cosmetic reasons. The submariners expressed the cynical view that what were usually called Preliminary Sea Trials were, in reality, *Political* Sea Trials.

They were happening because the Civil Lord of the Admiralty, Ian Orr-Ewing (whose portfolio included overseeing the nuclear submarine programme) found himself fending off furious MPs in Parliament.

Why was it was taking so long to get the new submarine into service?

The minister said Vickers was working as fast as it could and trying hard to stop shipwrights and boilermakers falling out over job demarcation. He hoped it would be solved with help from the trades unions.

Orr-Ewing decided to ask the Navy to take *Dreadnought* to sea even if she could not yet function in every respect – just so there was some visible sign of progress. *Dreadnought* had begun the process of testing equipment and machinery at the beginning of 1962, with her reactor going critical on 1 December. Critical meant the reactor had reached the point where it was self-sustaining due to the chain reaction of colliding neutrons, but with no power available yet. Once there was sufficient heat to produce steam, there would be power to drive the machinery. The turbines would start turning, capable of delivering the electrical load to operate the entire submarine and also create propulsion. Before going to sea, the engineers would need to report: 'We are self-sustaining, with power available for operating the whole ship.' This they duly did.

The *Dreadnought*'s men had been working hard with Vickers (despite industrial disputes) to get the boat ready for sea – and in that sense they were at the very heart of their nation's Cold War effort.

Dreadnought was a marvel – able to stay submerged for weeks, if not months, at a time, so long as her food lasted. She could go very fast, cover huge distances in record time to catch and destroy anything the opposition had. Commissioned on 17 April 1963, the Navy naturally made a big thing out of *Dreadnought*'s official entry into the fleet, aiming to garner as much publicity as possible. Flag Officer Submarines, Vice Admiral Sir Horace Law, gave a presentation, aiming to amaze the press with as much science as possible, while keeping reporters blind to one seemingly embarrassing fact. Even so, a reporter from the *Daily Express* rose from his seat and asked: 'What are the weapons that *Dreadnought* will have?' FOSM adroitly dodged the issue, indicating his Public Relations Officer should parry that one. 'We have been extremely open,' said the PRO, 'and I can assure you that this excellent vehicle will have suitable weapons.'

*

As the lead boat of her breed in the RN, *Dreadnought* was pushed to the limit in a series of deep dives, something that would reduce her life due to structural flexing. As she flew through the water – banking, climbing and plunging at speed – *Dreadnought* had a helmsman (controlling the rudder and foreplanes) and a planesman (controlling the afterplanes). It was possible for both planes and rudder to be controlled from one position. The planesman sat at a control column, which had a wheel, very much like that used in airliners. *Dreadnought* even had an automatic pilot.

The Control Room was lined with equipment possessing lots of dials but actually the capacious interior was rather austere.

There was no end of technological marvels enclosed within *Dreadnought*'s large hull. To ensure pinpoint accuracy in determining her position without the benefit of astral navigation, or needing to consult any external source that might give her away, there was the Ship's Inertial Navigation System (SINS). This utilised three gyroscopes – one pointing at the centre of the Earth and two orientated on the north–south and east–west axes – that tracked minute changes in course during a submarine's voyage, using the boat's point of departure as the primary reference point.

Added input was needed every now and then to check for variations, such as a fix by observing landmarks or the stars via the periscope, or a radio navigation aid such as LORAN.

To celebrate her Anglo-US qualities – American powerplant in a British submarine – the reactor compartment bulkhead, with its massively thick door to shield everyone from radiation, was christened Checkpoint Charlie (in honour of the American-controlled crossing between East and West Berlin).

A scrawled note on a board beside it declared the reactor 'critical'.

To keep everyone at peak performance there were air conditioning and also air- and water-purification systems, which were fundamental to the boat's ability to dive and remain dived (without needing to suck in any air) for months.

There were showers, even a laundry – unprecedented comforts, absent in earlier British submarines. Senior and junior rates had their own messes either side of the galley, with chairs and dining tables, and were served meals on a cafeteria system. A small lift transported the same food from the galley to the wardroom for the officers.

One 1960s naval pundit declared: 'Accommodation for her crew is of a standard which it was impossible to attain in any previous submarine.'

Films could be shown in one of the messes, on a proper screen, rather than in the cramped torpedo room on a bed sheet. Hale's excitement at being in the realm of a nuclear-powered submarine left him in a state of incredulity. It was such a different world from the diesel boats: '*Dreadnought* was so much bigger, with three decks rather than one. The hull shape was radically different of course and the equipment packed into the boat was so much more sophisticated. You had lots of fresh water, so you could wash. You grew up as submariners saying: "We will wash on Saturday whether dirty or not."'

All steam plants must distil fresh-water supplies, to make up for leaks and losses. In *Dreadnought* this meant there was a fresh-water supply for the crew, too. Hale could wash any day he liked.

Dreadnought did not have to snort – she could make oxygen and get rid of CO_2. The new SSN had unlimited power and her galley team could cook and do all sorts of things without worrying about draining the battery.

As *Dreadnought*'s commissioning Torpedo Officer, Lt Hale was well acquainted with the so-called advanced weaponry possessed by the sleek new killer of the deep. Britain's inaugural SSN relied on Mk8 torpedoes of 1929 vintage for her teeth. Though the Navy might have been reluctant to reveal that snippet – worrying it didn't fit in with the cutting-edge technology stance – in fact the Mk8 (capable of more than 40 knots) was a proven, extremely reliable and hard-hitting torpedo. It would turn out to be more reliable in some cases than the successors the Navy would ultimately develop, even though it was free-running without wire guidance. Hale got to grips with a torpedo compartment radically removed from any he had seen before.

'We had six tubes and it was all so well designed that you could move and load torpedoes so much easier than diesel boats, with their lack of space, small number of reloads and no power-loading machinery. The tubes were also water ram discharge. If you put air into the back of a torpedo to push the weapon out of the tube – as was the case in previous types of submarines – then it could create a huge bubble. This was a giveaway to any enemy looking for you. With a water ram discharge – like a giant water pistol – you use sea pressure rather than air pressure to shoot the torpedo out the tube. You don't produce the giveaway bubble.'

The *Dreadnought* had the ability to fight the enemy at high speed without the inconvenience of slowing down to a crawl every time she needed to fire a torpedo. In diesel boats a torpedo could not be launched at the enemy above 7 knots. This was perhaps acceptable in an era in which submarines principally sought to evade other war vessels, with incidences of submarine versus submarine combat rare. In the Cold War, with the advent of the hunter-killer, slowing down dramatically to use your main weapon system was not wise. Setting sail for test ranges off Gibraltar, one of *Dreadnought*'s key aims was to see how fast she could go while firing torpedoes. Hale and his team were really put through their paces.

'We went faster and faster – from six to nine, to 12 to 18 knots. At 18 knots the torpedoes got damaged on exit. If firing an unguided torpedo, the maximum recommended speed at the time of discharge depends on whether the weapon will get clear of the tube without damage from collision with the bow fairing. We still got up to 21 knots and managed to fire a torpedo but in the end it was recognised you probably should do no more than 15 knots maximum for the Mk8. Wire-guided torpedoes would require a maximum ship speed of 6 knots whilst the outboard dispenser was reeling out the control wire. This was to avoid damaging the guidance wire.'

Another massive leap forward in terms of offensive war-fighting was the immensely powerful Type 2001 sonar the Soviets had been so keen to gain insight into via the Portland spies. With a limitless energy supply from the reactor *Dreadnought* could detect threats using active sonar at unprecedented ranges for both ships and submarines. Subsequent years, though, would see active pinging kept to an absolute minimum by both sides in the undersea Cold War. 'We did a lot of sonar trials and there were no power limitations,' Hale revealed, 'and we transmitted huge chunks of sound energy into the water. *Dreadnought* could do active ranges of 20 miles.'

The Type 2001 could be 'ripple all', putting lots of power into the array, broadcasting on all its transducers or a more selective 'searchlight' pulse into a specific vector. As an early variant of the new breed of sonar, active pinging on the Type 2001 was not a subtle affair. 'It was a massive noise, even inside the boat, and we had special earplugs, but never used them. Active sonar is not always a good idea because you tell everyone where you are – therefore you apply it for a very specific purpose.'

The need for the SSN to be ready as soon as possible was starkly illustrated by a 1963 incident in which a British diesel boat was damaged.

It led to the Norwegians demanding to know more about circumstances surrounding the appearance of a severely damaged Porpoise Class boat in their waters. Bordering the Soviet Union, Norway was anxious no incidents should spark something serious. The British said their submarine had been caught in the middle of a Soviet Navy exercise.

Detected by a Kamov Ka-25 Anti-Submarine Warfare (ASW) helicopter equipped with dipping sonar – basically a giant hydrophone on the end of a wire – she was cornered. Russian frigates and destroyers then pursued the British boat, and it appeared likely she had even been rammed; whether on purpose or by accident was not clear. With battery power close to running out and with watertight integrity compromised, the boat made a break for the safety of Norway.

Soon there would be more than just one SSN to take on such missions in Russia's backyard. Even as *Dreadnought* was finished, construction of the first Royal Navy SSN with a British reactor, *Valiant*, began and a third attack boat, *Warspite*, was ordered.

With the advent of *Dreadnought* British submariners would operate at depths never before envisaged. After studies by the Royal Navy's own medical professionals it was judged pointless for them to attempt a free-ascending escape from a sunken submarine any deeper than 600ft. This led to the advent of Deep Submergence Rescue Vehicles to (hopefully) retrieve them. The fresh generation of submariners would be entering arenas of risk-taking in which there would be no room for error, or rather where mistakes would be more costly. The old-style cavalier ways of winging it would not retrieve the situation at such depths and among those who would take on the new challenges were Dan Conley and Doug Littlejohns.

They were among the first wave of Baby Boomers, those born in the immediate aftermath of the Second World War – between 1946 and 1955 – who reached adulthood in the 1960s and 1970s.

Dan Conley entered the world on 9 September 1946, the same year Austria was carved up into four zones of occupation by Britain, America, Russia and France. There were also war crimes trials under way in Japan and Germany. Born in Edinburgh, Conley spent the first two years of his life in the Scottish capital before his father reacquired the family trawler, *Golden Dawn*, which had been taken into naval service during the war.

Conley senior took the family to Campbeltown and set about re-establishing his fishing business. Dan's father had been a Warrant Officer in fast torpedo boats during the Second World War. Submarines would sometimes come into the old fish quay in Campbeltown itself, young Conley's gleaming eyes devouring their sleek black shapes. Watching from the upper deck of his dad's fishing boat, he was intrigued by not only the submarines but also the men who emerged from them.

They scampered around their boats' outer casings, wearing big chunky white jumpers. They sported jauntily tilted sailor's hats, swapping jokes and banter as they secured their boats alongside.

Conley's father contracted tuberculosis and as he could no longer go to sea, *Golden Dawn* was sold and the family moved to Glasgow, where Dan finished his schooling. Submarines still exerted their spell whenever he saw them, either at a distance on the Clyde or during Navy Days at Rosyth Dockyard. Conley won a Royal Navy Scholarship at the age of 15 and two years later, in September 1963, he and other new-entry cadets were marched up the hill from the centre of Dartmouth to the college, beginning the process of becoming naval officers.

His first taste of life at sea in a submarine came as a Midshipman, in November 1964. Conley was told to turn up early one Tuesday morning at *Dolphin* and make his way aboard the Super-T boat HMS *Totem*.

'I soon discovered there were no officers around and the only person in the Wardroom was a rating trying to acquire some gin to polish the lenses at the top of the periscopes. About 30 minutes before getting under way the officers arrived en masse. Soon we were proceeding down the Solent towards the open sea, where a force eight gale was whipping up.'

Totem dived amid turbulent seas to the south of the Isle of Wight. Thrown around even when submerged at periscope depth, a number of mock attacks were subsequently carried out. Following a brief introductory tour of the boat, Conley was allowed to have a go on the forward hydroplanes, while he was also invited to try out his navigation skills. With *Totem* back alongside, Conley's day at sea was over. He had enjoyed it and felt that submarine life was ideal for him.

The Naval Service was in Doug Littlejohns's blood, in a line stretching back to before Trafalgar. He numbered among his forebears ship's surgeons. In the late 1930s, with war clouds looming over Europe, his father volunteered to train as a Swordfish torpedo-bomber telegraphist/gunner.

At 6ft 4in tall he was, though, too big to fit into the cockpit. Switching to destroyers – a move Littlejohns believes probably saved his dad's life – he served as a Chief Petty Officer (CPO) Telegraphist. During the war Littlejohns senior was appointed to the staff of Britain's most successful fighting sailor of the 1940s, Admiral Sir Andrew Cunningham, and later worked for the legendary Admiral Lord Louis Mountbatten. Doug's dad also worked for Mountbatten during the admiral's time as Commander-in-Chief of the Mediterranean Fleet in the early 1950s and later when he was First Sea Lord.

As a CPO Telegraphist, Littlejohns senior ran the Whitehall-based communications centre via which Mountbatten transmitted and received signals to and from naval bases and warships worldwide.

With a Scottish mother and English father, and born at Galston, Ayrshire, near Kilmarnock, on 10 May, 1946 young Littlejohns moved with his family to Plymouth in Devon, where his father ran the Mount Wise naval HQ Communications Centre.

One of Doug's treasured memories from childhood was being allowed to watch from the First Sea Lord's office in the Admiralty as the Guards brigade staged Trooping the Colour.

It was a very hot day in the summer of 1956 and the ten-year-old Littlejohns sat on the ledge of the sash cord window, dangling his legs outside. He counted the young Guardsmen as they fainted on parade with a loud crash. Coming over to see who had collapsed, Mountbatten peered out and ruffled the youngster's hair. At the time the First Sea Lord was heavily involved in creating a flotilla of nuclear-powered submarines for the Royal Navy. Littlejohns feels it would have delighted Mountbatten to know the lad sitting in his window would one day command one.

While in Tim Hale's day Dartmouth provided secondary school education for its future officers, by the 1950s it had contracted the job out. There were plenty of grammar and public schools that could do the job of general education as well, if not better.

Conley and Littlejohns won their scholarships under the Murray Scheme, which had been introduced three years after Forsyth's intake. Forsyth was trained under the Cost Scheme – two years at college, with some sea time in vessels of the Dartmouth Training Squadron. The Murray Scheme involved an initial Dartmouth year, with cadets spending the second year at sea as a Midshipman. For their third year they returned to the college as Sub Lieutenants doing the Academic Year.

There were 240 young men admitted to Dartmouth – including Littlejohns – in the September 1964 intake, but even though it was an age of the sky's the limit in post-war meritocratic Britain, the majority of the naval college's young men still came from the upper echelons.

At the beginning of 1965, following the conclusion of Dartmouth term one, came sea time in the anti-submarine frigate HMS *Eastbourne*, cruising off West Africa down as far as Lagos. On his return to Dartmouth for the summer term, Littlejohns was summoned to the

Captain's Office with seven other cadets. 'I went in there and stood before the Captain. He looked over his half-moon glasses and revealed: "You have been selected to go to university – aren't you pleased?" I said "yes" to get out of there.'

In the Cold War there were four breeds of submarine officer – the Marine Engineers, who ran the propulsion system; Weapons and Electrical Engineers, who ensured the weapons systems worked; Supply Officers, who handled the logistics; and Executive Officers, who navigated the boat and took the tactical decisions. Only the last category could ever command a submarine, or even be selected to take the ultra-demanding, five-month Commanding Officer's Qualifying Course (COQC).

This formal course for training potential future submarine captains was introduced during the First World War. When lives were at stake, even in normal submarine operations away from the enemy, it was of utmost importance both that the man in command was technically skilled and that he wouldn't crack up under pressure.

The COQC was otherwise known as 'The Perisher', for if you failed it your career in submarines perished.

The common precursor in the pre-nuclear era was time as a First Lieutenant, performing duties as second-in-command of a submarine. With the dawn of nuclear-powered submarines even the Executive Officer (XO) would be a Perisher graduate. For Tim Hale, the route to Perisher was via six months as XO in the new Oberon Class diesel boat HMS *Osiris*, which had only been completed in January 1964.

He didn't get much of a break before finishing one job and starting the next. 'I left *Dreadnought* and flew to San Francisco on Friday, 6 October 1964, for my brother Charlie's wedding. I came back on the Sunday night, joining *Osiris* at Faslane on the Monday. My allocated "leave between appointments" had been all of 72 hours.'

Osiris was a step change from the old Second World War-era diesel submarines. Outwardly the Oberons looked the same as the P-boats. German submarine technology had been used as the basis for the Royal Navy's Porpoise Class diesel-electric boats, the first all-new type constructed for the Royal Navy post-WW2. The subsequent Oberons were a radical advance in several technical areas, including sonar. They were probably the best diesel boats built by either side at the height of the Cold War.

Like their Porpoise Class predecessors, machinery and other equipment was soundproofed for stealthy running. Oberons had advanced diesel-electric propulsion to achieve a high underwater speed of 17 knots and a cruising speed on the surface of 12 knots. They were fitted with a new and much improved Electronic Surveillance system for detecting hostile ship and airborne radar, and also intelligence gathering. There was an attempt to provide rudimentary air conditioning and also effective climate control whether operating in the Arctic or tropics. It was such a heavy draw on the battery it was rarely used. Mechanical oxygen generators and CO_2-absorbent canisters were also intended to keep air fresh, but again, if they were run for too long, they would drain the battery.

The Oberon Class boats' hulls were made of high-grade steel. This allowed deep diving, to around 600 ft, which was several hundred feet more than Second World War-era diesels. The use of fibreglass and plastics in the fin and casing reduced radar signature when on the surface. The O-boats were so good Australia, Canada, Brazil and Chile bought them. However, they were still diesels, so living conditions aboard *Osiris* compared with *Dreadnought* remained a little basic. Hale's time in an O-boat served to remind him how diesels worked after five years in the nuclear world. Beginning the submarine command course in March 1965, he soon found out there could be such a thing as over-confidence.

'I thought I knew it all. I was trying to do too much. I just wasn't *getting it* with four weeks to go before the end.'

A lot of the Perisher revolved around the safe use of the periscope to ensure the submarine was not about to be rammed by an enemy surface warship. Hale was taking too many chances, using the scope too much.

'I thought I was going to fail,' was his blunt recollection of that tricky phase. The officer in charge of the course, known as Teacher, twice took over during an attack run and sent the submarine deep.

Conceding control to Teacher was a real black mark. Hale found Perisher was as much about character calibration as anything else. In the hard-drinking 1960s it was not unknown for Teacher to see how would-be submarine captains performed under pressure, deliberately keeping them up in the bar of the hotel where they stayed. Feeling the strain and needing to release tension, Hale got really drunk one night, only managing three or four hours' sleep. With an early call in the morning, it was his turn to act as captain and take the boat out to sea, to get her in position for that day's tests. Far from increasing Hale's chances of failing, the hangover actually improved them.

'I was tired and slowed up. Suddenly, I wasn't trying to do too much, just did the basics, which worked. I got my confidence back, realised I had been going at it too hard. I have found that if you get all cocky and think you have it sorted then life can come and cut you down to size. That's what nearly happened on my Perisher.'

There were two groups of students, one each in the pair of submarines allocated to Perisher. Hale's group proved to be an outstanding bunch, achieving the first 100 per cent pass in six years. In the other boat one of the candidates failed. Qualifying for submarine command that July at the age of 29 – most peacetime submarine captains were well into their thirties – Hale felt he was ahead of the curve.

'I had been in submarines for eight years. I was a two-and-a-half-ringer [a Lieutenant Commander] and I got my first command before I was 30. I was thinking: "Wow, isn't this terrific?" I had been working extremely hard under pressure for such a long time. Now I went away on holiday to Spain with my lovely lady, my beloved Di, who then became my wife for over 40 years. It was the best holiday of my life – I was deeply in love with Di and had passed Perisher. Life couldn't get any better.'

Hale's first submarine command would threaten to rain on his parade, for she was not a relatively modern Porpoise or Oberon, but the old reconstructed T-Class boat HMS *Tiptoe*.

Tiptoe's exploits in the early Cold War were marred by misfortune – a series of incidents that made Hale wonder if he was being awarded command of a boat that habitually wrecked people's careers. In the summer of 1955, while moored alongside a wooden jetty in Tromsø, Norway, she was hit by a merchant vessel of more than 2,000 tons' displacement. Pushed under the structure, *Tiptoe* suffered considerable damage. At least it provided an excuse to give her a Super-T rebuild.

In January 1964 *Tiptoe* suffered the embarrassment of running aground on a sandbank in the Clyde during a spell of thick fog. Then, in July 1965, while submerged at periscope depth off Portland, she was in collision with the frigate HMS *Yarmouth*. In each case the submarine's captains were court-martialled and severely reprimanded. Now it was Tim Hale's turn to joust with fate and overcome *Tiptoe*'s clumsy reputation.

Hale took command in the immediate aftermath of the Portland incident and his first task was taking *Tiptoe* up through the Irish Sea to Birkenhead for repairs at the Cammell Laird shipyard.

'Of course we hit terrible weather – dreadful gales.'

Tiptoe could not submerge to evade the worst of it, as might otherwise be the case, for the periscope damage prevented her from diving. Hale, in the first week of his maiden command, faced a nightmare passage, in a submarine whose crew had been traumatised by their recent collision.

A desperate situation required drastic solutions.

'I remember being very tired and very scared in the bloody awful weather. With a low bridge, a Super-T like *Tiptoe* was always taking waves – very wet in any sea state. We would put the guys in the bridge and tie them in, so they couldn't get washed away, and then the conning tower hatch was shut, leaving them to it. One time, in very bad weather and visibility, I tied myself into a corner of the bridge, telling the Officer of the Watch (OOW), who was also tied down for safety, that I was there if needed.'

Tiptoe's bows dug into an angry, frothing ocean. Hale's innate resistance to seasickness came in handy as he stuffed himself into his corner, waves and spray crashing over the rim of the tower. Cap secured on his head by its strap, a foul weather jacket hood pulled over it for extra protection, he was so dog-tired he fell into a deep sleep. Undisturbed by the waves and spray or any emergency, *thank goodness*, Hale slept for a couple of hours. It was an awesome display of *sang froid* in the face of a howling gale. If the CO could have a kip in the corner, then the Officer of the Watch felt he could stick it out, too.

Somehow they got the boat to the Mersey, and Hale's career survived this early test of his mettle.

As the submarine was temporarily handed over to the care of Cammell Laird, he couldn't help but contemplate how narrowly he had avoided the fate of his immediate predecessors. *There but for the grace of God go I.*

It would not be Hale's last tricky moment in *Tiptoe*. After a series of successfully completed training exercises, in March 1966 the men of the accident-prone boat were rewarded with a visit to Hamburg, epitome of the Swinging Sixties.

Top attraction for lusty young sailors was of course the notorious Reeperbahn, a string of bars, brothels and nightclubs that was like a magnet for mariners visiting the north German port. Hale regarded Hamburg as 'a terrific run ashore' and felt it would be good for his lads to blow off steam. The only thing that lay between *Tiptoe*'s men and fleshpots of delight was safe passage up the Elbe.

The boat reached Cuxhaven at the mouth of the river late, so it was decided to spend a night at anchor, awaiting a pilot in the morning.

At around 03.00 a sentry posted on the submarine's bridge observed what looked like the lights of various ships sliding past.

He used the intercom to ask the rating on watch in the Control Room if he had any idea why they might be heading out to sea. The watch-keeper immediately twigged it was *Tiptoe* moving, not the other vessels. The boat had swung with the tide and her anchor was dragging. Prick-ling with anxiety, realising that at any moment the submarine could run aground – or collide with another vessel – the watch-keeper immediately called the First Lieutenant, Mike Cooper.

Cooper leapt out of his bunk, checked the situation via an all-round look on the periscope, and pressed the klaxon button, sending a blood-curdling alarm throughout the boat. Shocked out of their slumber, men struggled into their clothes, heads spinning and hearts thumping. Fuelled by adrenaline they clambered through hatches and up ladders, making their way to positions in the Control Room or on the bridge. Others stood by in the machinery spaces or ready to operate valves and other systems.

Dreading that he was about to fall victim to the same curse as had befallen his predecessors, Lt Cdr Hale went up to the bridge, calling out:

'Harbour stations! Slow ahead both!'

In his head he cursed the bloody Elbe and the bloody *Tiptoe* and his bloody luck. *This boat was going to get him after all.*

Hale turned the submarine into the tide, taking her into deeper water. The casing party got the anchor hauled in while the Navigator took a fix through the periscope. Had *Tiptoe* remained where she was, when the tide went out she would have been stranded.

They had been very lucky.

Hale decided to stay on the bridge all the way up the Elbe to harbour. The weather made his foul mood even worse for 'it was bloody cold, with an east wind from Russia'.

Having picked up the River Pilot, as *Tiptoe* approached the port of Hamburg she swapped him for the Harbour Pilot. Hale greeted this man with a tight smile, barely suppressing residual fury at the turn of events. 'He told me the berth, and I headed for it. The first three heaving lines all missed and we drifted off in the current. I shouted at the casing party, and swung the submarine around to try again, noticing that the Pilot was grinning. I snarled at him, too. The second try was successful, heaving lines made it and we secured about 09.00. I asked the Harbour Pilot down below, saying I would sign his pilotage chit. In my cabin I offered him a large slug of Scotch, which he accepted, and we drank. I then asked him: "Why were you smiling as we missed the first time?" He said that he had not heard bad language like that since he too had been a submarine captain, at the end of the Second World War.' Hale considered the middle-aged Harbour Pilot afresh. The German wore a worn old waterproof jacket and a grubby, extremely battered cap.

Its peak shaded wise eyes set in a weathered face. It was still possible to imagine him as a young submarine captain, one of Germany's legendary Grey Wolves. Leaning forward to pour the former U-boat commander another shot of Scotch, Hale told him: 'We have the greatest respect for yourself and your comrades.'

The two submarine captains clinked glasses to the veterans of both sides in the war and, of course, lost shipmates.

Having narrowly evaded disaster on the Elbe, after a raucous few nights of well-deserved relaxation along the Reeperbahn, *Tiptoe* sailed for England. Leaving the Swinging Sixties ashore, Lt Cdr Hale took *Tiptoe* back out to sea, ordering course for Chatham Dockyard, where she would go into refit. His time in command over, he had avoided the court-martial hat trick and now headed for the Maritime Tactical School based at the Military College, Woolwich. His course in tactics proved both amusing and interesting as, among other things, he met a number of old friends.

Next stop was Whitehall's dusty offices and a job in the Department of Naval Intelligence. Hale's task was to assess the success, or otherwise, of Royal Navy patrols in the Barents. He applied his brain to producing an Exercise Area Plan in order to identify specific zones used by the Soviets in a similar fashion to the Portland Areas utilised by the British for their warfare training. It also identified Russian firing ranges where new weapons were tried out. They were a useful place to loiter and gather intelligence. Having spent five months ashore Lt Cdr Hale was awarded his second submarine command, this time the 20-year-old HMS *Artemis*. A rebuilt Second World War-era diesel design, with a high bridge on top of the fin, telescopic snort induction and decent sonar, she was, though, another boat with a chequered past.

In 1954 *Artemis* allegedly suffered sabotage when someone detonated a smoke grenade in her engine room. Two years later she was in collision with a trawler in home waters, but undamaged. In 1963 – during a period when she was operating from Halifax as part of SM6 – she failed to report in as scheduled, triggering an air and sea search, but happily soon surfaced.

Fortunately, Hale's six months in command during 1966/67 passed without any similar adverse incidents. He regarded it as the happiest period of his life, for he had married for the second time, to Di two days before taking command of *Artemis*. Meanwhile, recently out in the Atlantic the SSN he had helped bring into service got a taste of going up against the Soviets.

At the end of January 1967, the UK, USA and USSR became joint signatories of the Outer Space Treaty. Among other things, this committed them to refrain 'from placing in orbit around the earth any objects carrying nuclear weapons or any other kinds of weapons of mass destruction or from installing such weapons on celestial bodies'.

While peace may have reigned in outer space, on Earth it was a different matter, for aside from proliferation of nukes based in submarines and elsewhere, so-called small wars raged across the face of the planet. The Cold War face-off in the North Atlantic also remained tense and an early February 1967 pursuit of a Russian submarine caused major alarm at the highest level of government in Britain.

The potentially 'awkward incident', as one civil servant described it, possessed an added edge, as it coincided with a visit to the UK by the Soviet premier, Alexei Kosygin. He was holding talks with the Prime Minister, Harold Wilson, who was working with the Russians to try and broker a peace agreement between Hanoi and Washington to end fighting in Vietnam.

The Americans were not happy at the British and Russians working together, especially when Wilson had refused to commit the UK militarily on the US side in South-East Asia. The Russians were supplying North Vietnam with missiles that were shooting down American planes. Washington was also concerned that its primary military ally in the Cold War was getting rather too cosy with the putative foe.

It was the most high-profile visit to the UK by a Soviet leader since Khrushchev's unfortunate call at Portsmouth in a warship 11 years earlier. This time the Soviet delegation came by airliner. Instead of the British security services sending a frogman on a spying mission that ended badly, they worked with their Russian counterparts to ensure it all went smoothly.

For Harold Wilson, news that British naval forces were in hot pursuit of a Soviet submarine would be most unwelcome and, initially, the information was kept on a need-to-know basis within the MoD.

There was no point in worrying the PM unnecessarily – but the problem would really explode if the press got a sniff of it. The potential for such incidents to escalate had been firmly planted in the broader consciousness by a recent UK-made movie called *The Bedford Incident*. Released in October 1965, it depicted the pursuit of a Russian diesel submarine in waters off Greenland. The Soviet boat is kept down until her air has almost run out, launching a nuclear-tipped torpedo when the destroyer USS *Bedford* accidentally fires anti-submarine rockets.

Fourteen months later, an episode involving *Dreadnought* seemed tailor-made for turning fiction into fact at precisely the wrong moment. Outer space might be safe, but the seas off the British Isles remained a danger zone.

At 10.30 a.m. on 6 February – the same day premier Kosygin's airliner touched down on British soil – a Shackleton MPA of the RAF picked up a contact about 100 nautical miles to the north-west of Malin Head. Having already dropped a string of sonar buoys as part of a major ASW exercise with the Royal Navy, the aircraft was able to maintain contact for the next 90 minutes, classifying it as 'probably a submarine'.

At 12.35 p.m. the contact was picked up again. Following standard procedure, Flag Officer Scotland and Northern Ireland (FOSNI) – senior officer co-ordinating the exercise and also responsible for safeguarding local waters – was asked what he wanted to do about it.

FOSNI ordered three frigates, two diesel submarines and *Dreadnought* to break off their exercise. His orders were clear: the British naval force was to 'close the submarine's position for the purpose of hunting her'.

It was not the first time, nor would it be the last, that a Russian boat poked its nose into a Royal Navy exercise. It was the misfortune of this one to blunder into a string of sonar buoys and then to encounter *Dreadnought*. The British SSN detected her at great range and for the next five hours, like beaters flushing out grouse, the formidable array of combined British air and sea power played with the hapless Soviet. It was one thing for a single submarine to trail a target, and for a contact to fade away after a few hours, but this interloper was caught cold and could not get away. The tricky prospect of having to do something decisive to conclude the hunt now presented itself.

Should the Royal Navy frigates drop reduced-strength depth charges? What about allowing *Dreadnought* to close in and possibly fire a torpedo set to run wide as a warning shot? With two other submarines and the frigates all sharing the same space of water it was getting very congested. *Rather dangerous.*

There might be an underwater collision, or some other unfortunate mishap. In time of war the answer would be simple: the nearest member of the hunting group with the best chance of destroying the enemy would deliver a killer blow. But this was nominally a time of peace between the UK and Soviet Union.

Intelligence sources believed the Soviet submarine was a Whisky Class diesel that departed the Baltic on 22 January. This information was fed to *Dreadnought* via a radio message while a request for clarification on what to do next was sent back up the line to FOSNI. He decided to phone the Secretary of State for Defence, Denis Healey, who responded that 'during the period of Mr Kosygin's visit, it would be best to avoid any action which might carry the risk of an awkward incident'.

The hounds were called off.

The British huntsmen returned to the pretence of hunting down and killing a Soviet fox rather than doing it for real. Shackletons continued monitoring the situation to ensure the intruder withdrew properly.

A year earlier there had been an incident that had gone even further. On that occasion the Royal Navy had been allowed to bring about a satisfying exposure of a cheeky invader.

A Romeo Class submarine – a relatively new type of diesel-electric boat – was caught hanging around waters in the approaches to the American SSBN base at Holy Loch (also conveniently near routes used by submarines to enter and exit Faslane).

The Soviets, like their UK counterparts on missions to the Barents, were keen to listen in on NATO radio transmissions, particularly the use of a new system it was rumoured enabled British and American submarines to communicate with each other while submerged. The Northern Fleet had also tasked the Romeo with noting deployment patterns of American SSBNs and gathering intelligence on acoustic signatures of individual vessels.

Like *Taciturn* a decade earlier, the Soviet boat was forced to snort while her diesels recharged batteries, also poking her periscope above the waves to make visual observations. She extended an aerial to try and intercept signals traffic. This all risked exposure, the Russian boat sneaking as close as possible to British territorial waters, if not edging into them. A key target for the Soviets was *Dreadnought*, which their spies in the UK informed them was possibly visiting Holy Loch. The Russians were unclear at the time about whether or not she was armed with some new variety of nuclear-tipped missile. Over the course of several days some interesting signals traffic was analysed by the Romeo's embarked intelligence specialists. Growing in confidence, the Soviet boat made a foray well into the UK's territorial waters, little realising that SOSUS – which had detected its first Soviet diesel boat as early as 1962, during the Cuban Missile Crisis – identified exactly where and what kind of boat she was.

SOSUS regularly tracked US Navy SSBNs making their journeys right across the Atlantic to Holy Loch. Prowling British surface warships and submarines, with help from SOSUS, now fixed the Romeo's position.

It was time to send this particular snooper packing back to Russia and British warships and Shackletons closed in.

Forced to surface twice, the captain of the Romeo obtained permission via radio from Northern Fleet headquarters to abandon his mission, taking his boat home on the surface. The Romeo was shadowed all the way back to waters off the Kola by NATO air and sea units. It was a definite humiliation for the Soviet Navy.

The following year, with everyone walking on eggshells during the Wilson–Kosygin summit, the Royal Navy's punches were pulled.

After the talks in London, the Soviet leader travelled by train to Glasgow. Cheering crowds gave him an ecstatic welcome, though there were peace protesters among them. The same Campaign for Nuclear Disarmament (CND) activists who staged sit-ins outside the Holy Loch Base waved placards, including one declaring: 'Welcome to your target area Kosygin.'

Soviet boats undoubtedly had some of their nuclear missiles targeted on the Clyde. It was also, clearly, a major object of surveillance by Russian submarines, too.

In March 1967, Tim Hale arrived at Portland to join the staff of Flag Officer Sea Training (FOST) as the resident submariner – a shore job overseeing the participation of diesel submarines in combat-training exercises. It meant he could live at Larkbeare, the Hale family home near Honiton, as Portland was only about an hour and a quarter's drive away. The Captain in command of HMS *Osprey*, the FOST shore base, was cynical about how long Hale would stay. He believed the Submarine Service regarded the post as somewhere to park an officer until he could be found a submarine command. Hale assured him that he wanted to stay and told him how how happy it would make Di and himself to settle into a domestic routine. After three days at Portland, and enjoying it, Hale got a call from the Secretary at FOSM. It seemed the XO of *Warspite* – being completed at Barrow – had died in a car crash. FOSM urgently needed a nuclear-qualified CO as the new boat's XO – the captain of *Warspite* at the time was known to Hale: Cdr 'Tubby' Squires, who had been XO of *Dreadnought*.

Hale was one of only three suitable people – and the SSN's commissioning was due in four weeks' time. In terms of a career move it was great – as a family man it was a disappointment. Di was not happy and nor was FOST but the head of the Submarine Service personally wanted him to join *Warspite*. Hale was allowed the Easter weekend off and then went to Barrow.

Fully worked up as a front-line submarine, HMS *Warspite* was to embark on an ambitious shakedown cruise. Originally it was intended she would join a task force of Royal Navy surface vessels covering the withdrawal of British troops from Aden, but that operation was completed in early November 1967 rather than in the spring of 1968.

Leaving the UK as planned, after a call at Gibraltar *Warspite* shaped course for Singapore and was at sea for Christmas. Surfacing south of Ghana to cross the Equator – conducting the usual pagan ceremonies for those who were virgins at 'Crossing the Line' – *Warspite* then dived and did not surface again for 6,000 miles, somewhere well north of Mauritius.

The last sight of land until she rounded the Cape of Good Hope had been the Cape Verde Islands. For the voyage to Mauritius the submarine relied on an artificial horizon sextant, which provided excellent fixes for navigation.

'Allied with a good log and gyro, SINS and frequent echo soundings, the ship's dived position can be known accurately, even on one fix per day,' Hale observed in an account he wrote not long after the voyage. 'Star sights are taken at the same time as the W/T [Wireless Transmission] routine, and so an artificial horizon sextant is essential.'

With a conventional sextant, the height of a particular celestial body – whether it be a star, the Sun or Moon – above the horizon is measured, which, after consulting relevant tables, provides a position line. Sights of two or three different bodies provide several position lines – the intersection of which fixes exactly where you are. Without sight of the horizon – at night for example – a normal sextant can't be used and taking a fix at all is difficult through a periscope. The cunning provision of an artificial horizon sextant actually in the periscope enabled *Warspite* to take a fix any time, day or night.

Hale was an old hand at such feats of underwater voyaging. He had completed a Gibraltar to Norfolk, Virginia, transit in *Dreadnought* during June 1964, the SSN covering 3,140 miles (out of 3,421) dived, with an impressive Speed of Advance (SOA) of 24 knots. After sailing south to use the Exuma sound range in the Bahamas (to test *Dreadnought's* sensors against the best submarines the Americans could offer) the British SSN headed back across the Atlantic, again calling at Gib before going on to the UK. *Dreadnought* had clocked up another 2,950 miles, with 2,805 of them dived.

Dreadnought's course probably cut across the one used by Columbus during his 1492 transatlantic passage, which helped provide conclusive evidence the world was not flat. In July 1964, Hale noted: 'Since commissioning in April 1963 *Dreadnought* has travelled 30,000 miles dived, only 13,000 surfaced.' He added mischievously: 'It was nice and quiet at 400 feet, 25 knots, so much so that we are convinced the world is flat.'

As *Dreadnought*'s Sonar Officer, Hale had a keen interest in accurate navigation. The Navigator, Lt Mick Milne-Home, used an echo sounder fitted in the bottom of the SSN's hull to send pulses of sound to the ocean floor.

The reflections provided depth readings. Compared with a chart showing the topography of the Atlantic, they revealed the boat's position. In such a process the submerged boat sails across several contour lines, careful not to run parallel to them. The Navigator must choose an area of ocean that is not featureless. On *Dreadnought*'s run across the Atlantic, she was given what Hale described as a moving haven, which was basically a mobile exclusion zone. For *Dreadnought*'s transatlantic transit, 100 miles of water ahead and 100 miles astern, plus 50 miles on either side, was kept clear of friendly submerged traffic. It was only valid for a certain amount of time.

Dreadnought – moving at an allowed average speed of 20 knots – could only rely on water space exclusivity for a fixed period, enough to enable her moving haven to pass through, before submarine traffic was again allowed to enter a particular area. Failure to stick to the timetable would compel an SSN to surface, in order to remove the risk of collision. Time allowed to slow down and take navigation fixes was limited. As *Dreadnought* shot through the Vacapes Areas – the Virginia Capes operating area, a zone thick with US Navy submarine traffic – the moving haven was reduced to 20 miles ahead and astern, with five miles on each side.

Hale learned not to put his faith entirely in bottom contour charts. The American ones used by *Dreadnought* – the British were still in the process of compiling their own – were not completely reliable.

'Some of the contour lines have obviously been drawn with a certain amount of artistic licence,' he noted at the time, 'there are various discrepancies with soundings on British charts, but combined with [readings provided by] the 773 Deep Echo sounder the answer produced is good. The 773 gives a sounding at over 25 knots and over 3,000 fathoms.'

Dreadnought took a sounding at least every 15 minutes and, explained Hale, 'plotted it on a tracing paper overlay'. He added: 'This is particularly useful when tying in a line of soundings with an outstanding feature like an escarpment or sharp peak.'

For *Warspite*'s record-breaking voyage more than three years later, the boat possessed an array of exceedingly detailed Admiralty charts produced by the UK Hydrographic Office with all the known soundings.

On the roof off Mauritius, a helicopter flew out with the mail and, after a mere four hours, in which the submariners took full advantage of fresh air in their lungs (and sunshine on their pallid skins) the SSN dived.

Christmas was celebrated at a depth of 300ft as the submarine made speed for Singapore. On Boxing Day – the boat maintaining the same depth – there was a 'Smoker's Concert' in the fore ends during which everyone was allowed to light up. The two-hour variety show of *Warspite* talent was of mixed quality.

'There was a guitar-playing group (good),' Hale observed in a contemporary review, 'the Wardroom Wallahs brass band (dreadful), a locally produced locally written skit (hilarious), various personal appearances (various), and a sing-song at the end (noisy).'

The carbon dioxide content in the fore ends rose from 0.8 to 2.1 per cent, which was on the cusp of lethal. Hale remarked with some wonder in its aftermath: 'We all seem to be very much alive!' Whereas smoking in diesel boats was banned, or heavily regulated, there was no limit in SSNs, at least not in the late 1960s. If smoking was allowed in tube trains, cinemas and restaurants, why not submarines with a far better regulated atmosphere? A diesel while submerged did not have the power to operate air purification equipment continuously, but that was not the case in nuclear-powered *Warspite*. She had all the energy needed.

There are three means of keeping the air clean in an SSN.

Electrolysis: When a current of electricity is passed through an electrolyte – in this instance seawater – it produces oxygen and hydrogen. The hydrogen is pumped over the side and the oxygen circulated around the boat. *Carbon dioxide scrubbers*: The air is circulated over a heated amine solution that absorbs the CO_2 and this is also removed from the boat. COH_2 *burners:* They burn off the CO to CO_2 and also burn the hydrogen – this is all to get rid of the impurities in the air.

The air inside Hale's nuclear-powered submarine was far purer than that of the world outside, which had its own distinct aroma, none more so than the pungent Malay Peninsula. *Warspite* surfaced for a run through the shallow Malacca Straits to Singapore on 29 December. Hale reflected: 'It was a change to see ships, sit in the sun on the bridge, smell the warm wet air of the tropics. After our canned air one could see the advantage of fresh air, but it did make the boat far more warm and sticky when dived.'

With 14,000 miles trailing astern, *Warspite* reached Singapore on New Year's Eve. After some shore leave not dampened by heavy rainstorms, on 17 January 1968 the SSN set sail to take part in a big fleet exercise.

Led by the carrier HMS *Eagle*, it was staged off Gan, part of the Maldives Islands that had been a naval base until 1957, when it was transferred to the RAF. It was surrounded by very deep waters, which were excellent for nuclear submarine operations.

Heading once again for Mauritius, the first leg of her long journey home, *Warspite* weathered Cyclone Ida by diving to 200ft, before surfacing and entering harbour. The SSN sat at a buoy on the diesels, so she could shut down the reactor and give the back afties (nuclear engineers) some shore leave, as otherwise they would have to keep watch.

On 18 February, *Warspite* departed Mauritius and dived, not surfacing properly again until the Canary Islands, 7,000 miles later.

Off the Cape the submarine exercised with a South African Air Force Shackleton maritime patrol that requested some photos.

'We broached, but did not fully surface,' reported Hale. 'Even so, the aircraft was so low that our captain reckoned he was looking down on him.'

The tip of the periscope was 45ft above the waves, so the aircraft must have been *very* low. Submerging fully again, *Warspite* headed north, obtaining a radar fix on the Cape Verde Islands, which, Hale noted drily, 'hadn't moved, luckily'. Reaching Gib on 7 March, Hale summed up the submarine's achievement: 'We thus completed 433 hours continuously shutdown [sic], during which the air purification machinery proved its capabilities. The proof? We were all very much alive!'

After shore leave, *Warspite* sailed with only 1,500 miles between her and home, pausing in waters off Cornwall to let Shackletons of the RAF see if they could find her. There was some evasive manoeuvring while dived which, Hale remarked, involved 'fast stuff that shook up the corners, and the bodies, which was no bad thing after a long passage'. Faslane was reached at 5.00 p.m. on 14 March and, keen on statistics, Hale broke down the voyage: '*Warspite* covered 30,350 miles since leaving the UK in November. During this time 94 days were spent at sea, 28 in harbour giving leave.' This averaged out 'at 323 miles per day at sea and 250 per day overall.'

Peacetime long-distance voyages were one thing, but could a nuclear-powered submarine operate below the waves at full war pitch for such extended periods? And could it be done without damage to both machinery and fragile human minds and bodies? Time, and missions into the Russian Bear's backyard, would tell.

In December 1967 Sub Lt Dan Conley joined the diesel boat HMS *Odin*, operating from Faslane. He was both Torpedo Officer and also Casing Officer, which he discovered involved being responsible for the maintenance and workings of the upper, external part of the boat.

It was not an easy start, recalled Conley, as the submarine was entering her annual inspection period. Nerves were frayed trying to get the boat in shape. 'Everyone was focused upon bringing *Odin* up to the highest levels of cleanliness and presentation. This would be followed by two days at sea, with the boat put through her operational paces. I didn't initially feel part of it, at least not until after the inspection. I had a fairly ragged time, being detailed to help paint and clean out the fore-ends, much to the embarrassment of my senior rate in charge. He clearly did not want his new boss to be around during the final compartment preparations. Also, I had to remain ashore for the operational sea inspection, receiving the displeasure of the CO when I was not there on the jetty to meet the boat when *Odin* returned to harbour unexpectedly early.'

Conley suddenly wondered if submarines were for him, but as the inspection became just a bad memory things improved. His mentor and training officer was the XO, Lieutenant Geoffrey Biggs, who boosted his confidence by letting Conley take charge of the boat as OOW. The thrill of his new calling didn't last long, for Conley was next drafted to *Sealion*, finding her in a very poor state. If there was a submarine that embodied a Navy running its diesel boats too hard and for too long, it was this one, the last of the Porpoise Class to be constructed. With her build completed just seven years earlier, by 1968 she was worn out, particularly by two missions to the Barents in 1966/67.

Rob Forsyth had served in her between 1964 and 1966, just before she deployed on the Northern patrols. Now Conley was joining *Sealion* in April 1968 as Navigating Officer. Not only did the boat need a deep refit, but her crew was exhausted. *Sealion* was a Faslane-based submarine but when Conley first clapped eyes on her she was in dock at Portsmouth. She had been there for nearly two months while having two new propeller shafts fitted.

'At that stage *Sealion* was not in good shape – filthy, with crew morale rock bottom,' recalled Conley. She stank abominably, possessing her own particularly unpleasant aroma, for over the years all sorts of noxious stuff had spilled into the bilges, including milk and curry powder. It all needed to be hosed out and disinfected. A few weeks later *Sealion* emerged from dry dock and was put alongside the jetty in HMS *Dolphin* to get ready for sea.

Heading north for Scotland, *Sealion* needed to be worked up again for operations and in May 1968 entered a series of training exercises in which she would be observed by sea riders from her parent unit, the Faslane-based Third Submarine Squadron (SM3). One of those officers was Rob Forsyth, whose special responsibility was sea training of sonar operators.

As a senior Lieutenant, who just a few years earlier had been *Sealion*'s Sonar Officer, it was a return to familiar surroundings.

During dived navigational exercises in the Clyde the CO was, to Conley's alarm, 'like a raging bull. Rob provided advice at the chart table, was very kindly disposed to me and clearly sympathised with my predicament as a fiery captain yelled at everyone.'

Conley was tasked with navigating *Sealion* around the Isle of Arran dived at night. The boat's command team and crew were also asked to execute a series of potential combat scenarios while hunted by both helicopters and surface warships. *Sealion* was required not only to show the squadron sea riders how well she could lay mines, but how carefully she could penetrate an enemy minefield. A photo-reconnaissance scenario required images of shoreline targets taken via the periscope camera, without being detected. All of these demanding work-outs put pressure on Conley.

As Roake's exploits off Russia had showed nearly a decade earlier, they were all essential survival skills, including how to handle extreme fatigue. And at times, even though he was a junior officer, Conley felt as if the entire fate of the work-up – success or failure – rested on his shoulders.

It was a stiff baptism of fire. Emerging exhausted but without committing a major cock-up, Conley felt it proved he could handle extreme pressure. *Sealion* passed the work-up period successfully but the CO was relieved earlier than anticipated. The new captain was lacking in experience and confidence, as this was his first command. He would evolve to become an effective CO and man-manager. Before departing the previous captain surprised Conley by revealing he had confidence in the young officer's abilities.

After Dartmouth and training at sea as a midshipman Doug Littlejohns had been sent to university in September 1966. His original intention was to more deeply acquaint himself with the world of Virgil and Plato by reading Classics before becoming a naval aviator. 'My A Levels were Pure and Applied Mathematics and Latin, so the Navy improbably concluded that a degree in Economics might be more useful than familiarity with the Ancient World.' Typically single-minded, Littlejohns rejected that idea and instead opted for reading a brand-new subject – Mathematics and Computer Science, from which he would graduate with a First Class Honours at Reading

His original career choice was suddenly altered. 'Halfway through I was told I couldn't be a fast jet pilot, because the Navy had spent too much on my education for me to be killed by a flight deck accident. There were six Executive branches to choose from and I was invited to list them in order of preference. In a fit of pique I decided to put "submarines" in all six. I thought aircraft and submarines had a war-like aspect and would be exciting and I liked that. With becoming a naval pilot denied to me, I didn't fancy any other branch except submarines.'

The Navy decided it was important not to let its students become too immersed in university life, so it was arranged for Littlejohns to spend time in the old diesel boat HMS *Ambush*.

He first joined her at *Dolphin* on a Sunday afternoon in the summer of 1968, after a rousing wardroom party. The next day he was officially welcomed aboard by her Commanding Officer, Lt Cdr Chris Wood. *Ambush* was a late-Second World War build, which had carried out snorkel trials in the late 1940s and in 1951 was the last vessel to hear anything of the submarine *Affray*. She picked up the latter's desperate distress call. *Affray* was lost with all hands in the Hurd's Deep, close to the island of Alderney in the English Channel

By 1968 *Ambush* was decidedly long in the tooth and Littlejohns's maiden dive was a good illustration of how sometimes it is better to take a leaky boat deeper. 'We went out in Portland exercise areas and I saw water pissing in through the conning tower hatch. I thought: "We are going to die." Chris Wood took such things in his stride and ordered the boat to dive deeper, the lid sealing itself due to water pressure.'

Although not a Second World War veteran, the captain of *Ambush* was a prime example of the buccaneering post-war breed. Littlejohns felt he was 'a tremendous CO and a charismatic man. If the Submarine Service was peopled by men like him then I had made the correct decision.'

This was still a navy in which clinical professionalism did not rule out making life as enjoyable as possible. Wood, who enjoyed a joke, tried to keep things upbeat and also to lead by example. That extended to lessons in the art of hard drinking (and how to recover from it and still exert effective command). The night before Littlejohns's first experience of one of Portland's famous 'Thursday Wars' – a weekly multi-threat training exercise – the CO decided to take the university student for a beer and skittles evening at a local pub. Returning to the boat, Wood woke up the duty officer. Several of the other officers also turned to, and they all 'slurped some whisky into the small hours', recalled Littlejohns. 'I felt somewhat groggy at 06.00 when we sailed but Chris was all smiles and raring to go. It was a lesson learned.'

To be a submarine officer Littlejohns must know how to work hard after playing hard – and conduct himself with grace and humour. Wood also gave the youngster responsibility early, for despite nominally being a passenger, Littlejohns pulled bridge watch-keeping duties like everyone else. This thrilled and delighted him, for while some of his fellow university students were smoking dope and going to anti-war demos, he was in charge of his very own submarine. The less than savoury realities of life as a submariner were not long in coming, pungently illustrated by one officer possessing feet so smelly it was enough to make Littlejohns gag.

As a novice, he was given the top outboard bunk on the port side in the wardroom. With condensation running down the inside of the hull on one side, it had a valve right in the middle, which meant he had to adopt a foetal position curled around it each night. It was also right over the end of the wardroom table where the First Lieutenant sat for breakfast. This posed the problem of turning to in the morning without standing in the poor man's breakfast. He did not always succeed: 'More than once I had to clean egg and bacon off my socks.'

Aboard HMS *Ambush* in the Bay of Biscay, en route to Lisbon, there was concern the CO's golf swing was under threat after an injury to his hand. Littlejohns learned that Lt Cdr Wood had devised a means of getting around it. When the boat next surfaced he climbed up onto the casing – with the Leading Cook acting as his caddy – and, using his favourite driver, hit several potatoes off into the sea.

Littlejohns was amazed by the First Lieutenant of *Ambush*, who 'knew every rivet of the boat and did it all by feel', which meant he could command the submarine with pure instinct for the old lady's limitations. This remarkable officer had served in A-boats for eight years before moving on to an O-boat for a six-month stint prior to the Perisher, which he passed.

A new First Lieutenant arrived, straight from *Dreadnought*. The diesel boat's men, Littlejohns included, were amazed to see he 'brought a slide rule and liked to do it all by numbers. He even wore uniform.'

The old and bold veteran submariners of *Ambush* didn't like it, for they still sported pirate rig, which Littlejohns had also enthusiastically adopted.

'My favourite outfit was an almost Dayglo orange shirt – a gift from my mother – which I could never have worn at home for fear of ridicule.'

The notorious slide rule failed to persuade the Chief Stoker as to its effectiveness, especially as the results of the First Lieutenant's trim calculations were far from reliable.

The Chief Stoker shook his head and grumbled, spending all night pumping and transferring thousands of gallons of water. The scientific way of doing the trim was clearly at odds with instinctive reality. *Ambush* was so light she took half an hour to dive. Nevertheless, there were elements of diesel boat veterans' intuition that would transfer successfully across to the nuclear boats. Inside such men there was what one submarine officer has dubbed 'a hard kernel of experience'. The strength of character – the ability to act by instinct allied with a cool head – came from the hard school of the diesels.

The first-ever visit by a nuclear-powered submarine to Plymouth's naval base was a big deal – an example of 1960s Britain on the cutting edge of science and technology. SSNs had previously only visited the spectacular closed amphitheatre of the Sound, dropping anchor just inside the Breakwater.

They had never actually made their way through the Devil's Narrows and up the Hamoaze to Devonport. In advance of *Warspite*'s milestone port call, from 21 to 23 August 1968, spokesmen for the Navy were emphasising there would be 'no possibility of a nuclear explosion even if an accident did occur'.

Apparently, someone walking down Royal Parade in the city centre would receive 'more radiation from cosmic sources' than from living aboard the SSN.

Plenty of people turned out to watch *Warspite* sail in, with all the car parking spaces on the Hoe seafront taken. Hundreds of people pressed onto the promenade, packing every available inch along its railings.

There were also keen observers aboard a Russian tug named the *Geraitchesky*, ostensibly towing a floating crane from Odessa to Tallinn in Estonia. She had turned up the day before *Warspite* sailed in, dropping anchor right in the deep channel that snakes through the Sound, and which all submarines and warships must navigate if heading for Devonport. Claims that a Russian trawler also shadowed the SSN as she approached Plymouth were firmly denied by the Navy.

Traversing the Sound, *Warspite* slid past the entrance to Sutton Harbour. This was where Elizabethan seadogs once sallied forth to tackle the Spanish Armada and to push back the frontiers of English exploration in the New World. Nearly 400 years later, with her screw churning up the same waters, *Warspite* turned wide past the Soviet tug. No doubt somebody aboard the Russian vessel took plenty of photographs.

A reporter who visited *Warspite* as a guest of her new Commanding Officer, Cdr John Hervey, noted with relish: 'Submariners usually step ashore with a faint smell of diesel fumes clinging to their clothing; atomic submariners have a "nuclear" body odour that marks them as members of the new elite!' Among the VIPs welcomed aboard *Warspite* for a tour was Tim Hale's mother. She stunned him with a revelation about a family connection between the SSN and an earlier British warship bearing the same name.

As a young girl during the First World War she had visited the previous *Warspite* – a super-dreadnought battleship completed by Devonport Dockyard in 1915. She told her son: 'Uncle Monty was the captain.'

Anyone with knowledge of British naval history knew the legend of *Warspite*'s amazing fight against the whole German fleet at the Battle of Jutland. That his great uncle was the ship's captain was astonishing to Hale.

Now, at the height of the Cold War, the great nephew of Capt. Montague Philpotts was the command-qualified XO of Britain's latest capital ship. Both old and new ships were cutting-edge for their day. The super-dreadnought was the second capital ship in the British navy to have oil-fuelled boilers, enabling her to carry eight 15-inch guns at high speed. *Warspite* and her four battleship sisters were the most feared vessels of their type in the world. At more than 31,000 tons' displacement when fully loaded with ammunition and oil, 645ft long and with a beam of 90ft, battleship *Warspite*'s top speed was 25 knots. She needed a crew of approximately 1,000 men. Her nuclear-powered namesake, now nestled along the same sea wall at Devonport, had a dived displacement of 4,500 tons, was 285ft long and had a beam of 33ft, with a top speed submerged of 30 knots and crew of around 100 men. Despite the disparity in size and smaller Ship's Company, the new *Warspite* was being depicted as the latter-day equivalent of the old battlewagon. Eagerly scribbling reporters visiting the SSN heard how she was a Fleet submarine. Goggle-eyed, one newsman wrote: '*Warspite*'s control room looks like a space vehicle – and she behaves and handles just like an aircraft. She can even perform aquabatics.'

In their off-duty hours, so the hacks reported, when not preparing to hunt down enemy ships and submarines, the crew of this formidable space age vessel occupied themselves listening to 'taped music and films'. They also liked 'playing bridge, chess, tombola and the naval form of ludo'. Soon the men of the SSN would be engaged in an altogether more deadly game.

Across the globe the rising tempo of operations and increasing heat of the East–West face-off were pushing both sides to the limit amid a turbulent international scene.

The year 1968 had begun with the Soviet-sponsored North Vietnamese Army (NVA) delivering a shock to American forces by besieging US Marines at Khe Sanh combat base. A few weeks later the NVA and Viet Cong launched a countrywide offensive across Vietnam, taking temporary control of Hue City; a suicide squad infiltrated the grounds of the US Embassy in Saigon. The situation was only retrieved after heavy fighting and many casualties. The news didn't get any better for the Americans. In late January a North Korean boarding party seized control of the spy ship USS *Pueblo* close to Pyongyang's territorial waters. Her crew was imprisoned and tortured, some of them subjected to mock executions. They would be released in December that year after being forced to sign confessions to spying.

The USA itself was convulsed with Civil Rights protests, while in London an anti-Vietnam War demonstration outside the US Embassy in Grosvenor Square turned into a mass riot.

Further signs of a world spinning out of control were provided by a terrorist bombing campaign in Germany and the assassinations of both the American Civil Rights leader Martin Luther King and Presidential candidate Bobby Kennedy.

In the United Kingdom, there were marches through the streets of Ulster calling for fairer treatment of the Roman Catholic minority. These sparked a violent reaction from the Protestant majority that in turn provoked dark warnings of retaliation from the Irish Republican Army (IRA). In France a general strike saw students, workers and Leftists clashing with police, bringing insurrection to the streets of Paris and nearly causing the downfall of the government of President Charles de Gaulle.

On the other side of the Iron Curtain, the so-called Prague Spring in which Czechoslovakia tried to throw off the shackles of Soviet domination was crushed when Moscow sent in thousands of tanks and 200,000 troops to suppress it. Looming over all this was the spectre of nuclear annihilation, with both sides continuing to test new atomic weapons. There was a series of incidents, which reinforced the impression that the world was dicing with disaster. In late January 1968 an American B-52 strategic bomber caught fire while on a nuclear deterrent patrol, the crew abandoning it in mid-air. The aircraft crashed onto sea ice just off a US Air Force base at Thule in Greenland. Carrying at least four thermonuclear weapons, the B-52 exploded on impact, its payload destroyed. Radioactive fragments were scattered across the ice, some of which melted, hot debris plummeting into the cold ocean. The Golf Class missile boat *K-129*, with her 98 sailors, was lost on 8 March 1968 in deep water to the north-west of the Hawaiian Islands. The Russians believe to this day that an American hunter-killer collided with their boat. In reality, a catastrophic mechanical or structural failure, crew error or even accidental weapons detonation was to blame. Not enemy action. On 24 May 1968 nine Russian sailors were killed by radiation when the November Class attack boat *K-27*, based at Gremikha, suffered a severe reactor accident. Nothing could be permitted to endanger the breakneck speed of Russian naval construction even though such incidents proved standards were slipping to a lethal degree.

The West was not immune to submarine disaster.

At the end of May 1968, the Americans lost the nuclear-powered attack boat USS *Scorpion*, which Tim Hale had voyaged in less than a decade earlier. Armed with at least two nuclear-tipped torpedoes, the *Scorpion* disappeared along with her 99-strong crew in 10,000ft of water, approximately 400 miles south-west of the Azores. Unfounded allegations that she was destroyed during a duel with a Russian boat soon emerged. To this day there are those who believe *Scorpion* was sunk by a Soviet submarine in revenge for the supposed deliberate sinking of *K-129*. Such claims reflected the increasingly close-quarters East–West rivalry at sea, where the traditional dominance of the West was being stretched to breaking by burgeoning Russian naval power.

British submariners were working very hard to counter Moscow's rising maritime strength. The Yanks might have more submarines, but no fleet was more adept at penetrating the Soviets' backyard than Britain's.

This was because it had to send its two Special Fit SSNs – *Valiant* and *Warspite* – back time after time. The USN – with a larger number of submarines and captains to choose from – generally sent each of its boats on a single high-risk Barents Sea penetration.

One American submariner would pay his own awestruck tribute to *Warspite*'s daring: 'She's the easy rider, she does the Sneaky Petes no other boat can do.'

The British SSN had received her Special Fit capabilities at Chatham Dockyard in Kent, where nuclear submarine refits were carried out. It made her supremely suitable for operations 'up North'. She could now pursue four types of intelligence – ACINT (Acoustic Intelligence), COMINT (Communications Intelligence), SIGINT (Signals Intelligence) and ELINT (Electronic Intelligence). Such equipment – much of it operated by the specially trained riders – was not fitted to every submarine. It indicated a level of technical capability that placed *Warspite* on the cutting edge of Cold War espionage.

In John Le Carré's *Tinker Tailor Soldier Spy*, first published in 1974 but set a few years earlier, the Soviets place a mole – nicknamed Gerald – at the heart of MI6. He ensures false naval intelligence is lodged successfully with the British. The Admiralty and MI6 are fed a bogus report on a Soviet naval exercise in the Black Sea and Mediterranean within hours of it allegedly being drafted by a Russian admiral.

This is all very clever, but, in the real Cold War, sending a Special Fit boat to spy on the Soviets was a better bet, sucking in raw data. Granted, no Western nuclear-powered submarines operated in the Black Sea, but anywhere else could be spied on by an SSN. No need to risk trusting potentially misleading sources in Moscow when you could get information direct. The nuclear-powered submarine was the ultimate undercover operative, a deep-penetrating mole of unsurpassed power and stealth.

A nuclear boat doesn't need to risk exposing itself to snort air and expel diesel fumes. It is not limited by depending on battery power while submerged, so is fast and covert.

Tim Hale, *Warspite*'s XO in 1968, summed up the life-or-death differences between diesels and SSNs. 'In a nuclear-powered submarine you can come up where and when you want to. It is a platform upon which you can hang a lot of Special Fit equipment, because the power is available. An SSN is larger and noisier than a diesel boat using its battery – due to the machinery associated with nuclear power – but it has more speed. It also has unsurpassed underwater endurance and sheer power. More people can be carried, including intelligence specialists.' And the espionage 'product' brought back by the Special Fit SSNs was, according to Hale, 'irreplaceable'. *Warspite* would, he revealed, 'watch the Soviet Navy through the periscope doing their manoeuvres. We listened to them talking to one another, quite often in uncoded, clear language. We recorded their signals, their messages, and tried to figure out what they meant. We recorded their missile firings and their torpedo firings and what they said during them.'

For the British, losing just one nuclear-powered Fleet submarine would, aside from the fatalities and resulting public scandal, create a serious gap in the order of battle.

By the end of 1969, the Royal Navy would have 45 submarines, with only eight of them nuclear-powered (four SSNs and four SSBNs). It compared poorly with the Americans and Russians. In 1953 the US Navy was an all-diesel force of 110 boats. By 1968 it fielded a force of 156 submarines, both diesel and nuclear. Nine years later, the USN Submarine Force would operate only three diesels, but had 115 nukes in commission. In 1969, the Soviet Union possessed 375 submarines, with 60 of them nuclear-powered.

The late 1960s and early 1970s were dangerous at sea, with Russian surface vessels deliberately going as close as they could to British and American warships. Soviet submarines – aware of their high noise levels – were determined to make up for what they lacked in stealth by aggressively shaking off shadowers.

Neither the NATO powers nor Russia could hide surface ship incidents in quite the same fashion as collisions between submarines, out of sight beneath the ocean.

In May 1967 upper-deck guardrails were ripped away and hulls dented when Soviet and American destroyers clashed in the Pacific.

That was nothing compared with an episode in which a Russian warship cut across the bows of a British warship in the Mediterranean. On the night of 9 November 1970, *Ark Royal* hit the Kotlin Class destroyer *Bravyi* amidships and would have cut her in two had the carrier's captain not ordered his ship to go full astern just seconds before impact.

While NATO navies tempered aggression with the knowledge that the lives of their sailors were precious and each individual naval unit was a scarce commodity, the Soviet attitude was typically totalitarian, regarding both as expendable.

Being run down by a surface warship was one thing, but facing an Echo II charging like a mad bull in a Crazy Ivan – a sudden 180-degree turn to take an aggressive look at anyone lurking astern – was the most dangerous game in town. A big cruise missile-armed nuclear-powered boat, the Echo II was relatively easy to track due to noisy machinery and, in fact, so lacking in mechanical stealth it was rarely taken above 10 knots. You still wouldn't want to tangle with such a big, tough beast.

There is no such thing as a non-serious collision between dived submarines, especially nuclear-powered.

Figures for the exact number of undersea collisions are hard to come by, but in the mid-1970s a report to Congress by the US Navy admitted to nine such incidents in waters close to the Soviet Union between 1965 and 1975. For their part the Russians confessed to seven crashes involving their submarines and those of the US Navy in the period 1968–87. They regarded using boats as battering rams to be a legitimate tactic. Admiral Sergei Gorshkov, hardline boss of the Soviet Navy, issued a severe reprimand to the captain of the Hotel Class nuclear missile submarine *K-19* for *not* ramming an American attack boat. *K-19* had turned to check her baffles, surprising the USS *Nautilus*, a serious collision only narrowly avoided. In late 1969 *K-19* didn't let him down, barging into an American submarine in the Barents Sea.

When *K-129* blew up off Hawaii she was being shadowed by USS *Swordfish*. Horrified sonar operators in the American attack submarine listened to the groaning wreck of the Soviet boat sinking to the seabed nearly 17,000 feet below.

The Russians mounted a forlorn recue effort, but it was an American submarine, the USS *Halibut*, which found and – deploying a remotely operated submersible – photographed the remains of the *K-129*, in August 1968. Some years later a CIA-funded expedition using the *Glomar Explorer* – a ship constructed for the task by the reclusive Hollywood movie mogul and industrialist Howard Hughes – retrieved the for'ard part of *K-129*.

It included her weapons section, also containing the remains of half a dozen sailors. As *Glomar Explorer* raised the wreckage the Russian boat's missile compartment – including a trio of SS-N-5 missiles – fell away into the deep. The mediocre quality of construction discovered during detailed inspection of what was retrieved proved shocking. It included poor welding, imprecise joins between hull plates and wooden beams used to buttress the hull. The Americans and British would never send such a submarine to sea.

Admiral Gorshkov summed up the Russian attitude to the dilemma of quantity over quality when he remarked: 'Better is the enemy of good enough.' It was also the primary foe of his young sailors. A naval high command that would risk the lives of its men in such boats could hardly be expected to give the West's sailors much quarter.

October 1968
The Greenland Sea

Bubbles gurgled as they trickled over the bows of HMS *Warspite*, hydroplanes wheezing as minor adjustments altered the boat's depth. The man-made killer whale's rudder turned gently, her slick cigar-shaped hull sliding easily through the ocean. Her multi-bladed bronze screw was a blur as it propelled the submarine at high speed, little streams of bubbles eddying off the edges. She flew gracefully under water, *Warspite*'s outer casing a uniform matt black but with a scum line of green algae running from bow to stern. It divided the third of her visible when surfaced from that part always concealed below water. Her killer whale's teeth came in the form of the torpedo tubes concealed behind small doors in her nose, well below the algae line.

Warspite hit a cloud of shrimps that chattered nervously, filling the ears of the submarine's sonar operators with a sound like a sizzling frying pan. The darkness swallowed up *Warspite* again, but the shrimps would chatter on for hours, providing a slight but telltale indication of the submarine's passing. She was heading deep into the Arctic, up around the corner beyond the North Norwegian Cape, infiltrating the Russian Bear's backyard. *Warspite* was penetrating a zone heavily populated not only by crustaceans but also by the deadly Cold War foe.

Entering the Barents Sea, the submarine left a trail of frustrated lust. Minke whales feeding on herring were distracted from their grazing by the intruder, which they took to be an attractive female. At only 23ft in length, the amorous Minke were dwarfed by *Warspite*. That didn't stop the whales from flicking their white-banded tails to turn and give chase. After filling their lungs with air the Minkes arched their spines and plunged in hot pursuit. Even their efforts, giving chase at 16 knots, were no match for *Warspite*'s speed. After 20 minutes, the whales were forced to surface for more air while *Warspite* sped east, swallowed up once again by the polar abyss.

*

Ten years on from *Taciturn*'s exploits, the Barents remained the most dangerous place on Earth for a British or American submarine to operate. Those caught intruding could still expect maximum lethal force from the Soviets. HMS *Warspite*'s men had long ago accepted the hardships of submarine life: the weeks of separation from family and loved ones, never seeing the outside world, enclosed within the giant metal tube that was both their home and workplace. They toiled in the depths, compensated by marginally better pay than sailors in the 'skimmers' (surface warships).

The extra money helped mollify their wives and girlfriends to accept the demanding mistress that was the highly secretive Submarine Service. *Warspite*'s men sublimated their fears of a terrible death in some underwater accident, or violent confrontation, into the professional pride of belonging to an elite. They were members of an elite-within-an-elite, for the crews of the nuclear-powered boats were the handpicked best of their branch in the Navy. Rigorously assessed – to ensure they had the strength of personality to cope with being confined in an underwater war vessel for long periods – they were also security-cleared.

They were worked hard but thanks to the specialist nature of their missions there were no spare hands in a pool ashore to be put on board to give some of *Warspite*'s sailors a break.

It meant a demanding schedule but ensured they were a tightly knit team with an extremely high level of professionalism and esprit de corps.

One of their number put it this way: 'I have never served with a better set of people in my life – we only had us and everybody had to pull their weight.' As far as the world beyond inner space was concerned, the *Warspite*'s men might as well have been on the Moon. The scale of endeavour they were undertaking, hermetically sealed within their submarine, was every bit as daunting as that confronting America's astronauts.

The outer space East–West face-off was the overt flipside of the covert rivalry within inner space. Apollo 7 was scheduled to launch around the same time *Warspite* was in Russian waters. The spacecraft's three-strong crew included two US Navy officers. Their mission was to test a new command module for a forthcoming Moon shot, orbiting the earth for eleven days. After years of lagging behind the Soviets in outer space, the Americans hoped to gain supremacy over Earth by putting a man on the Moon first.

Meanwhile, out there in the murky ocean *Warspite* operated at war pitch at all times, her men taut as a wire. The rest of the Navy might be loafing on beaches during runs ashore in tropical climes, or confined to port because of sparse fleet fuel allowances, but *Warspite* had a supremely critical task to perform and the nuclear power to achieve it.

Her mission into the North was so vital to national security that it was sanctioned on the personal approval of the Prime Minister. The consequences of *Warspite* being caught could at best be a diplomatic protest from the Kremlin. At worst it could mean the death of her entire crew.

By the late 1960s, putting a submarine into the Barents – or *up around the corner* as the submariners termed it – was like gently slipping a fist inside a scorpion nest. You hoped not to touch the sides or make any noise that might disturb the occupants. There was little room for manoeuvre if caught by the Soviets, who would be stirred up into an angry frenzy.

The battle space was laid out on a one-dimensional paper chart. For all *Warspite*'s nuclear age technology such as SINS, she was still partially reliant on the sort of navigational aids used by Queen Victoria's sailors.

The Admiralty first published the standard North Polar Chart in 1875. It was the fruit of earlier ventures into Russian waters by hydrographic survey ships of the Victorian navy.

Back then they were seeking to counter the Russian imperial threat. Just 20 years earlier, during the Crimean War, a British raiding mission was sent into the Arctic. A Royal Navy warship reduced a town in the Kola Peninsula to charred timbers and rubble during a 20-hour bombardment. Simmering enmity between Russia and Britain continued throughout the nineteenth century and into the twentieth century. The complexion of rivalry changed from that of competing empires to a battle between capitalism and communism.

To the uneducated eye the North Polar Chart would have appeared a rather dull, antiquated museum piece, a monochrome effort dotted with a mass of inscrutable figures. Submarine officers could stare at it and gain a very reasonable impression of the dangers they were about to encounter.

They would instantly transpose the figures – the chart's equivalent of contours – into a three-dimensional image in their heads. To stay secure they must remain submerged, and the deeper the better. The chart's figures – soundings – revealed fathoms spooling down rapidly from around 1,000 (6,000ft) on the eastern edge of the Greenland Sea to an average of 500 (3,000ft) past Bear Island, the gateway to the Barents. Close to the Russian coast, it came down to a mere 50 fathoms (300ft).

And less.

Safe periscope depth for a nuclear submarine is 60ft keel depth. In the Barents at 50 fathoms that means 240ft beneath the keel before a boat hits the bottom. In such circumstances, submarines proceed with caution, keeping speed to a minimum, reducing noise levels that may give away their presence. The faster a boat's turbines and other machinery turn the louder the sound signature. A submarine of nearly 5,000 tons' displacement also takes a while to answer the helm. In the shallow Barents, by the time she starts responding it may be too late and the boat will pile into the seabed anyway.

Despite the risks, or rather because of them, the North was still a seductive realm, which British and American nuclear navy submariners considered to be their ultimate test. And the Special Fit SSN crews were secret superstars of their dark art, regarded with awe even by Silent Service comrades. Morale was high because it was a real mission and not an exercise.

Like moths drawn to the flame, the Special Fit boats prowled along the shores of the Kola Peninsula, scrutinising the dull, flat fjords from Polyarny Inlet to Gremikha, at the entrance of the White Sea.

By 1968 there was more firepower concentrated in the naval bases and dockyards that had in recent times mushroomed along the coast of the Barents than any single region anywhere on the face of the planet.

Seeking to hover unseen and undetected on the edge of Soviet combat exercises, or slipping into the approaches of naval bases, the British and American SSNs – like their diesel boat predecessors – tried to discover proof of enemy weapons' performance or tactics. As in *Taciturn*'s day they still sought to record sound signatures of vessels and photograph them along with their sensors and systems.

Skirting, or even penetrating Russian nuclear missile test ranges, they sought to gather evidence of Soviet weapons capabilities. Due to the SSN's almost invisible presence the Russians would, hopefully, be unaware NATO possessed such inside information.

The West's boats might even try and poke a nose into the White Sea itself, where almost 300 years earlier Tsar Peter the Great – the vodka-swilling, sadistic genius who founded the Russian Navy – set sail aboard a yacht that almost sank in a gale.

By late 1968 nuclear-powered submarines were being constructed in unprecedented numbers on the shores of the White Sea, by order of the Kremlin's red tsars. Even for the majority of Soviet citizens much of what was contained by the North did not exist. Nobody was allowed to live within its secret environs, or even leave it, without special permission. Decent human intelligence – or HUMINT as the professional spies called it – was virtually non-existent. There were no major roads or railway lines connecting many of the submarine bases to the outside world – they were accessible only by sea. The North was just bleak, blank space where the detail should be. During the long, deep-frozen winters a shroud of snow and ice made it even more mysterious and foreboding.

Filling in the void of information was top priority for *Warspite* as she took over intelligence-gathering duties from an American attack submarine. There was no communication between the two boats – on the allotted day of departure the Yank stealthily withdrew west and south, her sailors keen to carry their intelligence catch back to their base at Holy Loch in Scotland.

They knew a British boat was taking over and mentally wished the Limeys good luck. What happened next in the Barents on 9 October 1968 has, until today, largely remained shrouded in secrecy. Now, for the first time, the full drama of what *really* occurred can be revealed.

Everything that might produce a giveaway noise had been turned off, from food-mixers in the galley to a tape cassette of the Stones playing in the junior ratings mess. Even officers off watch in the wardroom stirred their tea with great care. While it was highly unlikely the Russian submarine that *Warspite* was shadowing could hear it, the tinkle of spoon against china was still frowned upon. Conversations throughout the boat were hushed, the surface calm masking great tension. *Warspite* knew a Soviet boat was out there, somewhere ahead, but the exact range was unknown.

Lieutenant Commander Tim Hale eavesdropped as the captain, Cdr John Hervey, interrogated sonar operators in the Sound Room.

He was asking them about the depth of the target, but as yet getting no definitive answer, which he desperately needed. Range to target was calculated by a combination of horizontal distance and depth. While *Warspite*'s sonar operators had a handle on the former, they were as yet unable to fix the latter. It was one thing to know you were behind a Soviet submarine, but were you dangerously close?

The British submarine couldn't use active sonar – sending out an exploratory stab of sound energy to fix range to target. To make any overt sound at all would give away *Warspite*'s own location, exposing her to potential attack.

One Cold War-era British naval officer has described submarine versus submarine encounters as single combat *par excellence*. It is a form of hand-to-hand fighting in which, rather than stare the enemy in the eye, you rely only on the sounds you can pick up via powerful passive sonar. That was how you found a chink in the armour of the opponent.

Brushing an unruly lock of hair out of his eyes, Hale scanned the Control Room. Everyone was trying to hide it, but they were *very* tense; like a bunch of expectant fathers waiting for the birth of their first child. In this case, they weren't anticipating a bundle of baby joy, but their first successful trail of a Soviet Navy submarine.

It was what they had trained so hard for and part of the reason why their vessel had recently been fitted with all sorts of special intelligence-gathering kit. *Warspite* had also taken aboard some interesting characters.

The extra bodies raised the total crew from 110 to 125. As with diesel missions in the 1950s, these riders included experts in communications interception – Communications Technicians (CTs). Some of them were Russian-speakers, listening on headphones for giveaway Soviet voice transmissions. Signifying the tight front-line partnership of the American and British fleets in this most dangerous of missions, there was also a US Navy command-qualified Lieutenant Commander aboard. It was a custom often reciprocated, with a British officer in American submarines.

All internal communications crackling along her circuits and intelligence flowing into *Warspite* via her special sensors – indeed just about everything significant influencing operation of the British submarine – was recorded by a 14-track tape recorder and other devices. This was to enable later in-depth analysis, but also to assist tactical manoeuvring in hostile waters. The command team – Cdr Hervey, Lt Cdr Hale and the American officer – had immediate access to it all. They were permitted to ask any one of the riders for their analysis, in order to supplement data obtained by the submarine's own specialists. In such situations, where a threat could emerge at any moment, there was not a second to lose; every piece of input available was to be instantly acted upon. As for the boat they were trailing, the objective was to capture a noise signature.

There was the usual tape library of Soviet submarine prop noises aboard *Warspite*. By comparing the target boat's signature with a past recording they would hopefully be able to identify type and even the individual submarine.

Looking across the Control Room, Lt Cdr Hale caught the eye of a senior rating bent over the tactical plot on which the respective tracks of *Warspite* and the Soviet boat were being noted.

The 'plot' took the form of tracing paper laid over the top of a detailed Admiralty chart. Using a ruler the senior rating carefully drew *Warspite*'s track as it progressed across the paper. He also applied another, representing the Soviet boat. Hale and the tactical plotter exchanged meaningful looks. *Warspite*'s second-in-command smiled and thought: 'The bastard's over there somewhere, isn't he?' Looking into the Sound Room again, listening to the readings called out as the target changed position, Hale frowned. They had still not calculated a definite depth, nor a range.

The problem is, he noted mentally, *finding and identifying the Russian boat is like opening a door and possibly getting a bloody big shock. We don't know whether he is 8ft tall or 6in, a big bruiser or a harmless midget.*

They'd picked up the contact several hours earlier and decided to see where it took them. It was incredibly exciting and also just a little bit nerve-racking. The senior rating in charge of the Sound Room was a 25-year-old Petty Officer, John 'Jumper' Colling, whom Hale knew well, and trusted implicitly, from the time they served together in HMS *Dreadnought*.

A native of Rotherham in the north of England, Colling's two brothers-in-law were in the Service, and he had joined the Royal Navy in 1959, aged 16. Thoughts of becoming a submariner didn't come until he was aboard a wildly bucking surface warship, the Type 14 frigate HMS *Grafton* – which he felt would roll on wet grass – at anchor in Portland.

Feeling queasy and watching submarines departing, he had reflected: *They are sailing out there and going under where there is no bad weather.* The stiff formality of the surface navy was also not something that greatly inspired him. He saw submariners going ashore in their chunky white sweaters and big sea boots and they looked pretty cool.

Having also heard about the extra pay they received, Colling thought: *Now that's my kind of Navy!*

He gained relief from cold and blustery Portland when his ship, by then the Type 15 frigate HMS *Ulster*, visited the Caribbean. Colling also considered a life in the Hydrographic Surveying Squadron, another non-conformist group within the Navy. In the end, he volunteered for the Submarine Service, which he joined in 1963, aged 20. He was already a Sonar Rating and in *Ulster* had specialised in hunting submarines.

The diesel boat *Sealion* was his first submarine but he served just four months in her before she paid off for a refit. He went to *Dreadnought* in May 1964. 'It was the best move that I made,' was Colling's verdict. 'You didn't live in shit any more. The people weren't different – they were still the same sort – but you could bathe and there was a better standard of food.'

Being a sonar specialist was a fascinating trade. 'I thought people in the Engine Room must be bored to tears but on sonar it was a challenge finding the target and identifying it. You could tell the different types of vessels by their propellers, by the numbers of blades etc. Absence of noise indicated a submarine – a boat didn't generate the same level and type of noise a surface ship generates. Later on we got different equipment, new gear to analyse what we were hearing, but back in the early days you analysed it yourself, using your brain. Or you could tape it and slow it down if you wanted to ponder it more analytically. It takes time to get your "sonar ears". Most of it was probably memory – you have heard it before.'

The eager young Sonarmen would test each other by trying to figure out against the clock what kinds of vessel they were listening to.

In *Dreadnought* Hale was Colling's divisional officer, responsible for looking after the well-being and good conduct of 15 sailors in his 'division'. Straight away Hale spotted that Colling – nicknamed 'Jumper' because anyone called Collins or Colling in the Navy carries that sobriquet – had special qualities. He had an instinct for target identification, the intelligence and confidence to call it, providing the key information that would dictate what the captain did next.

Sonar 2001 was also used in *Warspite*, where Colling (as Head Sonarman) found he was in familiar territory. He still lived on his wits to give the submarine her ability to detect and define what was out there.

In October 1968, comparing the sound signature of the Soviet boat with *Warspite*'s tape library revealed the quarry to be an Echo II. Rough hewn though the Soviet vessel might be compared to the British SSN, an Echo II had two years earlier conducted a circumnavigation of the globe, along the way spying on the West's naval forces. The Echo II worked well enough to be taken seriously.

Now, at 18.30 local time, the Echo II shut down a screw, immediately reducing the noise she was generating. The 5,600-ton Soviet nuclear-powered submarine slowed considerably. Now her own noise generation had been reduced, the Echo II's sonar operators sought to pick up tell-tale signs of any shadower trailing in their wake.

JOUSTING WITH 'CRAZY IVAN'

The captain of the Russian submarine would every now and then order a turn so the sonar mounted in the bows of his vessel could have a look behind. If a Western boat was shadowing, the likelihood was it would be astern – in the Echo II's baffles, where sonar could not search, also hiding in the noise created by his own props. For *Warspite*, the trick was to ensure she was not unmasked when the Soviet captain ordered a look. It would require tight manoeuvring to remain astern of the Russian, following around in the turn; or a swift exit to port or starboard, to stay on the target's beam beyond the 'cone' of the sonar's detection capability. Maintaining a trail required everybody to be at the top of their game.

To some in the Sound Room of *Warspite* – trying to maintain a grip on the exact speed and range of their target – the Echo II appeared to be making a turn to port, her stern acting like the hinge around which a door swings.

This was not the case and Tim Hale to this day believes the Soviet submarine captain was profoundly surprised.

'The Russian was shattered to find someone up his arse – literally.'

Perhaps the Echo II's captain was a little too smart for his own good – merely stripping away an element of noise rather than actually turning to take a look astern?

In second-guessing a potential shadower, the Echo II's own specialists could perhaps identify a slight anomaly amid the clutter of chattering shrimp, moaning lovelorn whales and twittering fish.

Or perhaps there was a need for some running repairs on one of the Echo II's propeller shafts, requiring it to be disconnected from the drive? Whatever the reason, the Soviet captain's decision to shut down one of his props was like a motorist speeding in fog suddenly easing up on the accelerator, taking the car behind completely by surprise. At sea, such an incident between two submarines – even if they were only going a few miles an hour – was a lot more serious than a twisted bumper or smashed headlights.

Jumper Colling's sixth sense had kicked in to contradict analysis that the Echo II was turning.

Something was not right

He decided to send a message to the Control Room:

Do not change course whatever you do.

The captain never got it for some reason and *Warspite* turned, believing she was following the Echo II around.

In the Sonar Room, listening with a huge knot of tension tightening in his stomach, Colling felt his worst fears were about to come true.

He tried to yell 'Impact!' but it came out 'Tampax!'

No matter what he shouted, it was too late to make any difference.

As the British submarine turned to port under the stern of the other boat she made physical contact. Her fin scraped along the underside of the Echo II. Aboard the Soviet submarine, sailors were wide-eyed with alarm as the deck tilted dramatically to starboard. Their vessel vibrated violently, shuddering to the force of the collision. Her screws chewed *Warspite*'s fin, blades slicing into its thin skin.

The impact of this first touch had severe consequences, the British SSN heeling dramatically to starboard. In the junior rates mess, where the evening meal was under way, a bottle of ketchup hurtled through the air, just missing Able Seaman Colin Paton. It smashed into a clock, its contents splurging in all directions, dripping down its face. Some of the red sauce hit one of several posters of naked girls taken from soft porn magazines that cheered up the bare white wall panels and locker doors. The ketchup was smeared from one perky pin-up's smile to her soccer socks, and everywhere in between.

Junior rating Ian Wragg was taking a mug of tea with him as he went on watch in the Control Room. His job would be to monitor the boat's propulsion panel. Climbing to the top of a ladder, the collision hurled Wragg one way, the mug going the other, liquid in all directions.

In the junior ratings bunk space Graham Salmon was torn from his slumber and thrown 12ft onto the deck, suffering a cracked ankle.

Inside the Echo II, her captain immediately ordered his boat to surface. Having already rolled once – and retaining considerable forward momentum – the top of *Warspite*'s fin again hit the bottom of the other submarine. This time the British boat heeled over even more dramatically. Tim Hale braced himself, thinking: *Shit, here we go again.*

The consequences were far more severe, pressure on the fin rolling

Warspite 67 degrees to starboard. One sailor only stopped himself from losing balance by bracing his legs against the panelling of the compartment. Walking with the roll, he left big dirty footprints on the deckhead.

In the Sound Room, Jumper Colling – who had been standing centre-stage controlling all the sonar sets, grabbed onto something to stay upright. He frantically checked the sonar equipment was still working. It appeared something had gone terribly wrong with the set mounted in the fin, but the bow-mounted kit still appeared functional.

With the submarine still heeling over and tilting astern, it was a real possibility she might slide to her doom.

One anxious thought intruded into Colling's mind as, acting reflexively, he carried on with the checks:

What is my mother going to think?

In the Control Room, hanging on grimly and desperately willing the boat to come upright, Lt Cdr Hale came face to face with his own mortality.

Among his forebears was the American rebel Nathan Hale, who spied for the Continental Congress during the War of Independence. Nathan Hale's espionage behind British lines earned him the hangman's noose in September 1776. In giving his life Nathan Hale became one of the heroes of American history, famously declaring before he was hanged: 'I only regret that I have but one life to give my country.'

Nearly 200 years later, Tim Hale was also involved in the trade of espionage and now was similarly staring death in the face. During the long, agonising seconds as *Warspite* rolled – showing no signs of returning to upright – behind the mask of a blank face devoid of emotion, Hale's mind was awash with a torrent of chilling thoughts:

This is bloody serious . . .
The water will come in through the damaged conning tower.
I am going to die.

A sailor who lost his grip collided with him, was steadied but in the process delivered a blow to Hale's face.

In the Manoeuvring Room – the compartment in the aft section of the submarine containing controls for the nuclear reactor – the on-watch Engineer Officer, Lt Cdr Frank Turvey, instantly comprehended what had happened.

He made a split-second judgement to counteract automatic safety measures intended to prevent a nuclear accident. It might seem a rather perverse thing to do in such an extreme situation, but the reactor was *not designed* to work at 67 degrees off vertical. It would shut down. Losing power and momentum could result in *Warspite* sliding to the ocean floor. In the shallow Barents, with a maximum depth of just a few hundred feet, there was no room to recover. Turvey operated the Battle Short Switch, over riding automatic safeguards, keeping the reactor on-line.

Warspite rolled back; it seemed to Lt Cdr Hale fairly easily. He judged she must have emerged from under the Echo II, her fin sliding clear.

They had to surface the submarine *immediately*.

When a disaster that could potentially destroy the entire vessel occurred the failsafe was to put the boat on the surface. Making himself heard, speaking loudly but hopefully suppressing any sign of fear in his voice, Hale ordered: *'Full ahead, 30 degrees up, blow main ballast.'* With full speed ahead, the fore and aft planes angled at 30 degrees up, the boat would drive herself to the surface, assisted by compressed-air bottles blowing into the main ballast tanks. This provided maximum positive buoyancy in the shortest possible time. There was just one problem that prevented the order from being executed: *the forward planesman had frozen at the controls.*

His nerve had been shattered – it wasn't his fault the boat had collided with the Echo II and now he was too scared to move.

Without changing course and depth *Warspite* might collide with the Echo II again. This time she might shatter the outer casing, crack open the pressure hull inside, killing everybody with a torrential ingress of freezing water. The torpedoes might explode on impact when *Warspite* hit the seabed. There might also be a serious nuclear incident if the reactor vessel was breached. It had been drilled into Colin Paton that should *Warspite* have a collision while submerged, and he was off watch, he must immediately make for the nearest escape hatch. This was in the Upper Torpedo Compartment. Like everybody else he was responding by instinct and training. *Warspite* was the 23-year-old's first boat and Paton had selected the Submarine Service to do something a bit different from his brother, a Fleet Air Arm veteran. That career choice put him in harm's way, but also gave Paton a chance to play a pivotal role in saving *Warspite*.

A voice blared over the speakers, ordering him to immediately make his way to the Control Room. Struggling out of the Upper Torpedo Compartment and along a passage, he hauled himself up a ladder then – hand over hand – swung from piece of kit to piece of kit across the Control Room. Grabbing on to the back of the seat, he found the terrified planesman had a death grip on the controls.

A desperate situation required instant force, for they might have just seconds to save the boat, and themselves, from destruction.

Paton held on to a piece of equipment with one hand and delivered a rabbit punch to the other man, bringing him back to his senses. Letting go finally, the planesman was pulled out of the seat while Paton hauled himself around and dropped in behind the controls.

There might be tons of water pouring in through the damaged fin, adding so much weight to the boat that they might not be able to get her on the roof. There was not a second to lose.

As Cdr Hervey repeated the order for the boat to surface, Lt Cdr Hale shoved people out the way and lunged at a control panel just behind the planesman's position. On it was mounted a row of four valves known as the emergency blows. They blew compressed air direct from every high-pressure (HP) air bottle into the boat's ballast tanks.

By operating the 'blows', Hale initiated the emergency surface procedure. Eighteen months earlier, during *Warspite*'s construction, he supervised installation of the valves, which were completely new to that class of boat. Now they were *Warspite*'s salvation. Paton complied with orders to steer the boat to the surface, pulling back as she picked up knots.

The SSN leapt out of the water, a terrifying and awesome sight, a huge black killer whale suddenly springing from the deep, then slamming down in a heaving mass of exploding spray.

Once *Warspite* had broken the surface Cdr Hervey decided he needed to find out if there were any Soviet surface warships lurking nearby. With the fin damaged, he couldn't risk opening the lower hatch and climbing up to the bridge for fear of tons of water cascading into the boat.

They couldn't go out of the forward hatch – used only for loading torpedoes – and there was plating screwed down over it anyway.

The quickest and safest means of surveying his surroundings was via one of the periscopes. Realising even this might not be a good idea – with the scopes' true alignment knocked out of place and water seals potentially breached – Lt Cdr Hale tried, but failed, to stop Hervey raising the big search periscope.

It was off kilter but went up without any leaks. With the scope extended the mass of power wires hanging off the bottom would be difficult to get back down into the well – like trying to shove a handful of cooked spaghetti back into a packet. It was decided to keep the scope raised. Not ideal, as *Warspite* would have to maintain extra depth to keep it hidden.

A good grip on the handles, eyes pressed against the lens cups, Cdr Hervey spun the scope. There had been a lunar eclipse three days earlier, creating a Hunter's Moon, bathing the Barents in an eerie blue glow. Now a waning moon shaved the edge off the glowing disc hanging in a starry night sky. Spotting the Echo II nearby, stern on to *Warspite*, Hervey judged it had also carried out an emergency surface.

The Russian submarine captain was, meanwhile, using his own periscope to scrutinise the NATO boat's silhouette in the silvery Arctic moonlight.

Such a situation needed a very cool head on both sides.

Clearly no submarine captain wanted his boat to be in collision with another. Each knew the risks involved in the shadow boxing game played out under the waves. *These sorts of things will tend to happen every now and then in such circumstances.*

What had *never* happened was for two damaged submarines from opposing sides to be on the surface within killing range of each other.

Point blank.

Frayed tempers and an urge for retribution would be understandable after such an incident, turning an accident into an exchange of fire.

To defuse the situation Cdr Hervey put *Warspite*'s stern to the Echo II, then passed word for *Warspite*'s embarked naval doctor and medical assistant to ready themselves for rendering aid to the Soviet boat. Before an offer of help could be transmitted by the periscope's morse signal light, Russian-speaking riders informed Hervey they had picked up a message to Red Banner Northern Fleet HQ. The Soviet captain was reporting the incident to his bosses via wireless. There had been no casualties in the Echo II.

Commander Hervey decided *Warspite* should turn and withdraw to the west and then, as soon as she had been checked over for leaks, dive and get out of there. 'Steer 181 degrees,' he ordered.

'Aye, aye sir, 181 degrees,' Paton acknowledged, trying to hold his course, a degree west of south, by relying on one of the gyrocompasses in the helmsman's panel, but all three failed.

Hale ordered the gyro Electrical Artificer, a senior rating, to make rapid repairs to the Arma-Brown gyrocompass, as it was the fastest to restore on a display alongside the main control panel. The oldest submariner aboard, with a steady nerve, managed to do it within 55 seconds. The captain asked *Warspite*'s various departments for a damage assessment while Hale carried out an inspection of the boat, checking for trouble in likely weak spots. His keenly scanning eyes looked for tell-tale signs of leaks or faltering equipment.

During his walk-through, Hale found stores and bedding had come out of lockers. He told sailors to tidy them away. The torpedo room, containing all its heavy-weapons-handling equipment, the weapons themselves and hydraulic systems, seemed to have survived without damage. The men all appeared physically unharmed, save for Hale himself, who now had a black eye. There was also the badly trampled rating with an injured ankle and bruised back.

After listening to his second-in-command's findings, Cdr Hervey was satisfied the submarine remained safe and ordered *Warspite* dived to 130ft, making 7 knots and exhibiting reasonable stability. Hale suggested going deeper than that, but Cdr Hervey decided it was better to remain relatively close to the surface. More pressure at greater depth might create problems with the boat's battered structure. While the incident was serious, *thank God*, thought Lt Cdr Hale, *it hadn't damaged the boat's ability to float*. Fighting ships require the ability to float, move and fight, in that order. Lose any one of those elements and you've had it.

Sailors in the Echo II were busy trying to free a jammed conning tower hatch, bashing it with a sledgehammer. Once it had been bludgeoned open, the Russian boat's captain climbed up to the Echo II's bridge, to find the other submarine had disappeared. The lights of converging Soviet surface warships twinkling in the night provided him with the comfort of assistance close at hand. That was far from being the case for *Warspite*. She was still hundreds of miles from home.

Following *Warspite*'s hasty withdrawal the USS *Gato* – an American Special Fit SSN already poised to pick up the spying baton – found herself nosing into a hornets' nest. Russian warships were furiously dashing about, searching for the intruder.

They took no care to listen properly, failing to notice a new trespasser intercepting their signals, which were being broadcast in open language. *Warspite*'s misadventure had a positive aspect after all, for the captain of the American submarine, Cdr Al Baciocco (Hale's good friend from his time in *Scorpion*), declared it 'a treasure trove' of intelligence.

That *Warspite* came out of the incident at all was down to the training British submariners receive; Cdr Hervey's cool leadership under pressure; Lt Cdr Hale's instant reactions, blowing ballast tanks to put her on the roof; Lt Cdr Turvey ensuring the reactor did not shut down; the crew's steady reaction in the face of potential disaster.

Retaining reactor power had ensured the boat did not slide to the bottom of the shallow Barents. While she had a 112-cell auxiliary battery, in such extreme circumstances the power it provided might well have been inadequate.

The reactor gave *Warspite* the speed to make a clean getaway. Had she somehow made it to the surface without main reactor power the batteries would not have lasted long. Forced to rely on a set of auxiliary diesel engines – using them for propulsion, powering critical life-support systems and recharging the battery – would have required the British submarine to stay on the surface, to vent fumes and take in fresh air. Neither of the auxiliary power systems could push the boat through the sea at more than a few knots, which compared poorly with her usual surface speed of 15 knots. Dived on nuclear propulsion *Warspite* could normally manage 28 knots or more.

On auxiliary power, the British SSN would have been completely at the mercy of Soviet naval forces, hounded across the Barents by surface warships, helicopters and Maritime Patrol Aircraft.

Enraged by the collision with the Echo II, Admiral Gorshkov's fleet might at worst have actually attacked and sunk *Warspite*, at best cornered her.

Like the sailors of the unfortunate USS *Pueblo* several months earlier, *Warspite*'s men might have been taken prisoner and paraded in front of the world's press. Aside from a propaganda victory, the Soviets would also have snared an intelligence prize of superlative value, packed with the latest Western spy equipment, not to mention the latest submarine technology. Losing reactor power could have handed the Russians all of that.

Worse still, HMS *Warspite* and her men might never have returned.

To escape, after heading south for a short while, *Warspite* went west, then south-west, and then south again. This was all in water approved by NATO Headquarters prior to her deployment and known as the Allotted Escape Route, which operated like *Dreadnought*'s moving haven during her transatlantic crossing in 1964.

The movements of boats were carefully deconflicted by a staff of tactical planners at the NATO headquarters in Northwood, north London. They ran submarine operations much like air traffic controllers manage the complexities of having dozens of airliners aloft at the same time. The added complication with submarines was that once they left port on an operational mission they would no longer be in regular contact.

In *Warspite*'s case, because on 9 October 1968 she was the only Western boat operating deep within Soviet waters off the Kola – therefore at high risk of detection and pursuit – she had been allocated the escape route. No other NATO boats were allowed to enter it during her time in the Barents.

This gave Cdr Hervey and his command team absolute confidence they could bale out at high speed without colliding with another Western submarine. Working hard to control the hydroplanes as the SSN made her exit, Colin Paton remarked to a supervising senior rating that they had experienced a lucky escape. The Petty Officer was not so sure, responding:

'We are not out of danger until we reach a British dockyard.'

Playing on Paton's mind was the time when he saw a British diesel boat in dock at Gibraltar with significant damage after she was 'accidentally' hit by Soviet weaponry. If the Soviets caught up with *Warspite* in their own backyard they would not hesitate to 'accidentally' cause her harm.

Warspite's battered fin was distorting the hydrodynamics of the boat, so much that she listed to starboard at speeds over 7 knots, the degree of tilt increasing as velocity rose. The SSN was now also very noisy, again because of the fin damage, and this made her easier to detect. In fact the top end of *Warspite*'s fin was gone, leaving behind a whole mess of cables and bent metal hanging down inside it. The sonar set fitted into the front was smashed up. Its remains had fallen into the fin. Within two to three days *Warspite* managed to extend her radio mast and tell the Admiralty what had happened. That an incident had occurred would have been passed back by sources inside Russia, but the nature – and severity – of the clash would be a mystery.

'Until then they would not have known exactly what happened to us,' observed Jumper Colling. 'They must have been shitting themselves – they knew something had happened – we could receive messages, but not transmit [until the radio was functioning]. *Warspite* was at least able to pick up the traffic [and hear what others were saying].'

Lieutenant Commander Hale had time to think about what had just happened, asking himself: *How the hell did we get in that position?*

He decided to pay a visit to the Sound Room, sitting down in one of the sonar operator's chairs to analyse the 14-track recording of the collision. Pulling on a pair of headphones, he pushed the start button on the tape deck and relived the most terrifying experience of his life. As the recording unspooled on playback, he could handle only a few moments.

I can't bear to listen any more, he thought, ripping the headphones off. Gathering his courage, a day later Hale listened again. This time he managed to get all the way through, but was caught up in the visceral horror – the scraping and tearing as *Warspite* crunched into the Echo II, stuff tumbling out of lockers, plates and cutlery flying through the air, people making hurriedly for the escape compartments. In some ways worst of all was his voice, and other people's, suppressing terror as orders were given and repeated back. The analytical side of Hale's brain failed to kick in.

He gleaned no clues.

On a third listen through, five days later, he finally comprehended how it had happened. Inexperienced at shadowing a Russian boat so close, the Echo II closing down a screw had been mistaken for a turn. Too close, without knowing the exact depth of the Russian boat, *Warspite* tried to follow her around. The other vessel had not turned at all but was right above them.

For Tim Hale there was a sickening feeling in the pit of his stomach that next time they might not be able to save the submarine. He had stared death in the face and realised instincts and instant reaction made the difference between life and death. 'In such circumstances you don't have time to think. You don't look around and say: "That is water coming in over there, I wonder where it has come from?" By the time you have thought about it you are dead.'

The important thing to do in such an emergency – which *Warspite*'s crew had managed due to their training and professionalism – is to break the cycle of disaster. In a submarine incident the sequence can be as follows: material failure, followed by operator error, causing further material failure. Unless the cycle is broken the end result is destruction and, potentially, the death of every living soul aboard. Hale observed: 'You have to break the sequence. Let's say a valve malfunctions and a guy fails to shut it off or something shuts down the reactor – you may have to put the submarine on the roof, to get the auxiliary diesels on; to provide power; to run the life-support systems; to fight the error.'

When it came to human malfunction, in *Warspite*'s October 1968 collision the only immediately obvious psychological casualty was the planesman. He would put in a request to leave the boat and the Submarine Service the moment he returned home. 'You don't know how people will react under extreme pressure until shit really happens,' said Hale. 'Some of the really good guys you think will be okay suddenly fall apart.' In the aftermath of the collision the Sound Room was a bit jumpy, much more sensitive to noises that might indicate a lurking Soviet.

On the voyage home there was only one other sailor who asked to stop serving in submarines. He approached Jumper Colling, revealing: 'I can't handle this any more, I am frightened.' Colling thought it was brave of the man to admit it.

During a confidential meeting with Lt Cdr Hale on the trip back to the UK the man put in an official request to leave the boat, which was approved.

Once she was well within friendly waters, *Warspite* surfaced and made 16 knots on the roof, white water boiling around her forward hydroplanes as she cleaved the waves. *Warspite* was a powerful and forbidding sight, her nose burrowing a hole in the ocean. This pushed a surging bow wave ahead and threw off creamy paroxysms. The large rudder corrected *Warspite*'s course – the killer whale's tail twitching, with a fury of spume in her wake, which soon fizzled to nothing.

The Senior Engineer Officer, Lt Cdr Bob Isaacs – responsible for safe running and maintenance of all machinery, weapons and life support systems, plus structural integrity of the boat's hull – was asked by Cdr Hervey to take a look at damage to the fin. Lieutenant Commander Hale went up with him, the two men unclipping the lower hatch in the Control Room for the first time since the collision. Fortunately, there was no massive downpour of water but they discovered the fin was severely bent out of shape.

There was no way as she proceeded south towards Scotland's centres of population the SSN could avoid being spotted and even photographed, so *Warspite* was heading for Loch Ewe – just up Scotland's west coast from Faslane and the busy Clyde with all its inquisitive eyes.

A tug and a naval helicopter arrived, the latter off-loading a group of shipwrights who were brought out to the submarine by a small boat. Once aboard, they erected scaffolding around the damaged fin onto which was fixed a tarpaulin painted black. This camouflage, while makeshift, would at least obscure the severity of the damage. At Faslane, the boat would be checked over, and then sail to Barrow for proper repairs.

The Russians mustn't know – and their long-range reconnaissance aircraft and space satellites would be on the lookout. Riding shotgun on *Warspite* during the final stage of the voyage, to fend off any noseyparker civilian vessels, cheeky intelligence-gathering Soviet 'trawlers' or even submarines, was the frigate HMS *Duncan*. Lightly armed, and primarily tasked with fishery protection duties, the *Duncan*'s three 40mm cannons, sonar and Limbo anti-submarine mortars would be sufficient deterrent.

Before she was returned to service in late November 1968, *Warspite*'s fin was replaced entirely with that of sister vessel *Churchill*, then under construction at Barrow. The swiftness with which the yard turned the work around dismayed *Warspite*'s men. They had been looking forward to an enforced break.

Colling expressed their disgust: 'I was thinking we would be there for a few months – having a good time during repairs. We went in there and saw this new fin sitting there waiting for us, and our hopes were cruelly dashed.' At least he suffered no long-lasting effect from the 'iceberg encounter' other than temporarily remaining hypersensitive to noise: 'When in Faslane after the iceberg incident – a seagull flew out of the gash compound – and the noise made us jump.'

News of the incident did not leak at national level in the UK until 19 October, when a story in *The Times* claimed *Warspite* had collided with 'ice on the sea'. According to the Ministry of Defence (MoD), there had been no damage to any systems that might lead to a release of radiation. Furthermore, *The Times* reported, *Warspite* had 'cleared the obstruction with slight damage to her conning tower and other parts of the superstructure'.

An edition of the *North West Evening Mail* – Barrow's local paper – carried a photograph of *Warspite* with the black tarpaulin-covered fin. The workers in the yard were even told by sailors from the SSN that she had struck 'an iceberg'. One yardie responded: 'It's amazing how much paint comes off a lump of ice.' The Ministry of Defence did admit that some sailors aboard *Warspite* were slightly bruised. Tim Hale was under no illusions about what could have happened: 'You are always envisaging situations that might arise where things go wrong. When they do, you will survive if the reaction in the first ninety seconds is a conditioned one, created by endless practice. There is only one way to operate an SSN – with total competence. If it isn't then you are dead.'

What the Royal Navy wanted most of all was to preserve operational secrecy. The Russians might be aware a NATO boat had been damaged, but so long as nobody confirmed it, they could not know *for certain*. Besides, if the British public knew how dangerous the Barents Sea patrols were, there might be protests from the CND and others about the risk of a serious nuclear incident. Such was their importance the Northern missions would continue.

Warspite's logbook entries for October, November and December 1968 to this day remain classified and closed to public scrutiny. That surely wouldn't be necessary if she *really* had hit ice?

The Russians certainly had plenty of evidence *their* boat had not struck ice. For a start ice normally floats and would not be *below* their Echo II. Inside the large gaping hole ripped in the boat they found red glass, matching the sort of navigation lights to be found in the fins of British submarines.

At the end of 1969 *Warspite* received a new Commanding Officer, Cdr John Woodward. He would later find fame as an admiral, commanding the carrier battle group in the British task force that liberated the Falklands from Argentinian occupation in 1982. Back in 1969 nobody would have imagined the Royal Navy going to war in the South Atlantic. Woodward's mind was firmly fixed on countering the Soviet threat.

He has never broken the Silent Service *omertà* that usually precludes talking about the reality behind official statements on collisions with 'ice'.

Woodward has, though, revealed that even a year on the collision was still having an effect among the boat's remaining collision survivors (some sailors had already moved on as part of the usual crew rotation process). Taking *Warspite* to sea to get to know his new boat, Woodward decided to visit the senior ratings, so he could become better acquainted with them.

Handing over command to his First Lieutenant, Lt Cdr James Laybourne – who had relieved Tim Hale as XO in February 1969 – Woodward instructed him that, after sending and receiving wireless signals at periscope depth, he should take *Warspite* deep.

'... go on to fifteen knots, ten degrees bow down to 400 feet ...'

The new captain made his way down through the boat to the senior rates mess, soon finding himself armed with half a pint of beer and enjoying a chat. As expected, *Warspite*'s bows dipped, the deck tilting markedly.

Anxiety manifested itself on the faces of those around Woodward.

'I was watching the most reliable, the most experienced men on board go into total decline over a routine change of depth.'

Woodward felt instant empathy for his senior ratings but was also horrified they had been so mentally hobbled by what he called 'the submariner's unspoken, universal dread'. He suspected their minds were besieged by doom-laden calculations of their own imminent death. Woodward imagined they were thinking: *The hull of this boat will crush at about 1,500 feet. If you start diving at ten degrees down and fifteen*

knots, and do nothing about it, six minutes from now the lights will go out
– permanently.

Without fully functioning senior rates who could handle the pressure, *Warspite* had no backbone. Angles approaching 30 degrees bow down combined with high speed were normal, indeed essential, if the boat was to fight an opponent effectively. This was not a good start to Woodward's first nuclear submarine command. What on earth could have done this to them? *Warspite's* new captain finished his beer, giving no sign he had noticed anything amiss. On returning to the Control Room he took his First Lieutenant to one side, telling Laybourne what he had seen.

'Didn't you know?' the latter asked.

Woodward shot back: 'Didn't I know *what*?'

According to Woodward – sticking to the official line in his autobiography – Laybourne told him *Warspite* had been 'in collision with an iceberg twelve months before'. The XO claimed 24 of the boat's sailors were so badly shaken they refused to ever sail in a submarine again. The boat herself, Woodward discovered, had since the accident not been manoeuvred in a vigorous fashion, to avoid upsetting those survivors who remained.

He decided to reacquaint his sailors with the angles and dangles of a submarine flying underwater, warning his Ship's Company as such.

On the Friday evening of his first week, Woodward had another beer in the senior rates' mess, following a quiet discussion with Laybourne beforehand. The two officers set the stopwatches hung around their necks, Woodward quietly telling his XO: 'In exactly seven and one quarter of a minute's time, go on to twenty knots, put on thirty bow down, and make lots of noise as if you're having problems in the Control Room.'

When the time came, *Warspite's* deck tilted as she went deeper, the internal communications system revealing hectic activity in the Control Room. None of the off-watch senior rates batted an eyelid, carrying on their conversations as normal. As far as Woodward could see, there was not even a drop of beer spilled. He later observed: 'On such psychological tightropes are battles won, or lost.'

No doubt the senior rates had prepared themselves mentally for something happening during the CO's next visit to the mess. Being members of an all-volunteer force, *Warspite's* sailors could ask to leave the boat – and the Navy – whenever they liked. Losing face by deserting your shipmates, giving up submarine pay, or the certainty of a good pension in the case of the senior rates, made it a difficult option. In the aftermath of Woodward's angles and dangles, one sailor did ask to leave.

Years later Woodward would learn of another *Warspite* submariner who had successfully repressed his terror, staying aboard even though the 'iceberg collision' changed him from an extrovert to an introvert. Woodward lacked knowledge of his previous personality, so had no idea. There were others, too, who went on suffering in silence for decades.

The first counselling Colin Paton received for any mental trauma caused by *Warspite*'s 'iceberg' accident would come 30 years later, long after he left the Navy. Paton went into treatment as a result of experiences as a train conductor caught up in the October 1999 train smash at Ladbroke Grove just outside London.

Casting his mind back to the aftermath of the 'iceberg' Paton recalled the only treatment recommended in that case was of the liquid variety: 'When we made it to Barrow, we were gathered into the boat's [junior ratings] mess and ordered to go and have a drink and forget about it. I sent a telegram to my mother in Northern Ireland to say I was fine, thinking she would be worried sick. She had no idea what I was talking about. They didn't even inform our families what we had been through.

'It wasn't until a few days later that the government put out some half-hearted cover story to suggest we had collided with an iceberg. What we really needed was counselling, but the Navy didn't do counselling.'

On 21 July 1969 Neil Armstrong took 'one giant leap for Mankind', the first man to walk on the Moon. That single moment turned Soviet dreams of planting the hammer and sickle flag on territory in outer space to dust.

In the depths of inner space, just under four months later, there was a collision between the American nuclear-powered attack boat *Gato* and the notorious Soviet missile submarine *K-19*.

The latter had in 1961 almost been destroyed when she suffered a catastrophic reactor cooling system failure. This time, cruising at a depth of around 200ft in the Barents Sea on 15 November 1969, the accident-prone *K-19* received severe damage to her bows. She immediately surfaced, but *Gato* made a swift exit from the scene still submerged, which was just as well. Soviet surface warships were sent to search for whoever the intruder was. They would not have pulled their punches had they found the American SSN.

The Russians were particularly angry. President Nixon had authorised *Gato*'s intelligence-gathering mission two days before the USA and USSR were to begin arms limitation talks in Helsinki. The *K-19* was repaired and would return to Soviet front-line missions, despite having her torpedo tubes badly damaged and sonar dome ripped away.

Such incidents, though, remained unknown to the majority of the Earth's population, whose eyes were firmly fixed on outer space as the main arena of superpower competition. Four days after the collision between *Gato* and *K-19*, the Apollo 12 mission saw US Navy aviators Charles Conrad and Alan Bean become the third and fourth human beings, respectively, to walk on the Moon.

While the Americans threw their technological might across the airless vacuum of space to plant the Stars and Stripes, the Soviets struggled and ultimately failed in their own bid, giving up in the early 1970s.

The British, with no manned space flight space programme, were in 1969 pushing back the boundaries of their inner space strategic defence programme. The construction and deployment of the Royal Navy's new Polaris missile-carrying submarines proceeded apace.

Normal routine for the new Polaris missile boats, or 'Bombers', was not meant to involve anything as pulse-racing as dodging hard-charging Soviet surface ships or submarines.

The SSBNs slid through the silent deep for weeks, or even months on end, hoping not to encounter a vessel of any kind.

For their crews, the Cold War was a story of endurance, of painful separation and mind over matter. They might not have to survive the privations of subordinating every aspect of life to preserving battery power in the diesels; nor would they be expected to sneak into the lair of the Russian Bear. Their brethren in the Fleet boat and diesel submarine tribes might scoff at their seemingly sedate existence, but the men of 'the Bombers' had a task that carried psychological pressure every bit as wearing, and responsibilities far higher.

The Royal Navy's stewardship of Continuous At-Sea Deterrent represented a passing of the baton from the RAF's V-Force. The Silent Service assumed the mantle of strategic nuclear defence following a chat between a US President and a Prime Minister on the sun-kissed shores of the Bahamas.

Until that walk on the beach at Nassau in December 1962 the British were officially committed to retaining an air-launched nuclear deterrent. There had been an agreement between Harold Macmillan and President Dwight D. Eisenhower for V-Force bombers to carry the new Skybolt missile, with America funding the entire cost of developing it.

In return the British had allowed the US Navy to utilise Holy Loch as a forward base for SSBNs. By the time Kennedy was elected, Skybolt had technical and cost problems. If it failed, there would potentially be no British nuclear deterrent force. Efforts to develop a UK equivalent had stalled and now the Americans were using Holy Loch – increasing the risk of a nuclear strike on the UK – in return for precisely nothing.

Some in the USA were none too friendly towards Britain securing a nuclear deterrent on Washington's coat tails. A former US Secretary of State, Dean Acheson, summed up the brutal reality for Britain in 1962. He declared: 'Great Britain has lost an empire and not yet found a role.'

The UK was, though, still a world power and had a vital role in NATO. Macmillan concluded that he must get Polaris as an alternative to Skybolt. Fortunately, the Royal Navy had since the late 1950s been studying how to field submarines armed with ballistic missiles. Now it was time to take the feasibility studies forward.

Prior to formal talks, during their meeting at Nassau Kennedy and Macmillan agreed in principle that the USA would supply Polaris.

The RAF was still keen to retain the nuclear deterrent role and proposed a new missile system, named Pandora. This bid failed. Polaris was available, operational and all but invulnerable due to an SSBN's ability to disappear in the vast ocean. Ballistic missile submarines were unseen due to being submerged (with few, if any chances of being sighted by an enemy), unheard (except by those with sophisticated sonars and the training to use them) and of unknown location (a submarine was constantly on the move). An SSBN also had much less reliance on home base support (for fuel and food) than other deterrent sytems, due to the nature of a boat's nuclear power and innate self-sufficiency. The location of an SSBN would only really be known when missiles were launched. Land-based siloes were fixed and their missiles took more time to prepare for launch. V-Force jets relied on exposed airfields and then would have to penetrate Soviet airspace thick with air defence systems. They were also much slower than any ballistic missile.

After formal talks at Nassau a US–UK 'statement on Nuclear Defence Systems' was published. While the Americans supplied the Polaris system, the UK would have to develop its own warheads and construct a new class of submarines. Five SSBNs was thought to be the optimum number. Britain's Polaris boats would be at the disposal of NATO's Supreme Commander Allied Forces Europe. There was, however, a clause that allowed London to deny their use to NATO should it clash with national interests.

Some in the Royal Navy wanted to avoid the deterrent role as they worried it would soak up funds that might otherwise be devoted to new-generation aircraft carriers. With both the USA and Russia opting for submarine-based nuclear deterrent, it was inevitable that sooner or later the UK would have to go down the same route.

Polaris survived the defence cuts of the 1960s, the programme turning out to be a remarkable achievement at a time when others fell by the wayside. To ensure the Royal Navy would have the first of its SSBNs operational as soon as possible, a Polaris Executive was created.

The UK was fortunate in being able to transfer the staff, and expertise, of the Dreadnought Project Team to the Polaris Executive and design of the new SSBNs was soon under way.

On New Year's Day 1963, Rear Admiral Hugh Mackenzie found himself in an empty office in central London. He had a desk and a chair, but the phone was not yet connected. He did possess a rather grand new title: Chief Polaris Executive. Just three days earlier he had received a phone call from the First Sea Lord asking him to stop being Flag Officer Submarines and take on a job of national importance.

*

Lead boat *Resolution* would be followed by *Repulse, Revenge* and *Renown*. Aside from *Repulse* and *Renown*, which had been early-twentieth-century battle-cruisers, the other SSBN names had been carried by full-blooded battleships. A single Polaris missile contained far more destructive power than the entire Grand Fleet of the First World War. Rather than 15-inch guns that could deliver a shell on target up to 30 miles away, the UK's Polaris missile would ultimately, in its final variant, achieve a range of 2,875 miles.

Resolution was commissioned at the beginning of October 1967, then *Repulse* (late September 1968) and *Renown* (mid-November the same year), with *Revenge* the final R-Class into service (early December 1969). Construction of a fifth boat of the class, to be named *Ramillies*, was cancelled in 1964. *Resolution* launched her first Polaris missile on 15 February 1968, a successful test firing off Cape Kennedy, departing for her maiden nuclear deterrent patrol exactly four months later. The *raison d'être* of the British SSBN force was to prevent a first strike by the Soviet Union on the West by guaranteeing a second strike that would inflict massive destruction. There were those who saw such Mutually Assured Destruction (MAD) as lunacy of the highest order. When *Repulse* was launched at the Vickers construction yard, Barrow-in-Furness, on 4 November 1967, it was amid a storm of protest from CND activists. The massive submarine ran aground, remaining stuck on mud flats for 13 hours until the next high tide, at midnight. A whole flotilla of tugs was assembled to ease her off. Looking on anxiously were naval and yard staff, plus more than a thousand spectators munching fish and chips, with transistor radios pressed to their ears to hear the latest news. The CND protesters watched it all glumly. Their loud jeers were drowned out by the cheers of those there to see *Repulse* – which had cost £55m to construct – safely afloat. There was some consolation for CND when the boat bumped the side of a lock as she was brought back into the dock for continued fitting out, but *Repulse* was a tough customer. It caused no more than a scratch.

The Polaris Executive had delivered not only the first SSBN to sea within the required five years but was also overseeing the equally daunting task of creating support bases ashore.

The creek at Gosport was fine as an operating base for diesels but had already been rejected as a home of nuclear-powered Fleet boats. The Polaris force, with submarines twice the size of the new SSNs, and the added complexity of nuclear weapons, had to find somewhere that could also handle the missiles. Deep water, so they could disappear swiftly after sailing for a patrol, was essential and the base needed to be away from any large centre of population for security and safety reasons.

Devonport Naval Base and dockyard in Plymouth was one option considered, and also Falmouth, but in the end Faslane was picked. It was already receiving investment to support the new Valiant Class SSNs. A new ammunition depot was created for the missiles on the shores of Loch Long, at Coulport just over the hill from Faslane itself. The USA was supplying the guidance systems and motors, which were mated with the UK-manufactured warheads in their Re-entry Bodies (ReBs) and then tested to ensure they worked properly. Coulport's job was to assemble the missiles and maintain them. Expansion of Faslane started in 1964 and was completed four years later. First on the agenda was the creation of a Royal Navy Polaris School, so that British SSBN crews could receive their training in the UK rather than the USA. The simulators, classrooms and other components were completed by the summer of 1966.

Deep-water jetties were created, containing the necessary umbilical cords to operate an SSBN's systems while she was alongside – electricity, fresh water for the humans, demineralised water for the submarine herself and sewage pipes to evacuate human waste from the boat. Construction of a floating dock capable of lifting such a large submarine out of the water was ordered so the SSBNs could be maintained at Faslane between patrols. Long refits would take place at Rosyth Dockyard on the east coast of Scotland.

Aside from engineering supply and technical support facilities, and stores, accommodation blocks and married quarters also had to be built.

The requirement for large numbers of submariners in a short space of time led to a training bulge, the Polaris snake swallowing hundreds of people and regurgitating them at Faslane. This requirement competed with the need to train submariners for the diesels and new SSNs, together representing an unprecedented expansion of the Submarine Service.

One young sailor who was to voyage in an SSBN on one of her early deterrent patrols had joined up to see the world. Born in 1948, Michael Pitkeathly grew up in Camberley, an army town in Surrey. For someone hailing from a non-naval background, recruitment advertisements of the mid-1960s suggested the Royal Navy could still offer him a chance to see the world. That idea was certainly foremost in his mind rather than any burning mission to take on the Soviets. He would, though, soon find his horizons restricted to *Repulse*'s shiny new interior.

Pitt.k, as he liked to be known, entered the Royal Navy at the age of 17 in 1966. After initial training at the ratings training school of HMS *Raleigh* in Cornwall, he went to another shore establishment, near Portsmouth, to learn the skills of radar plotting, becoming a Junior Seaman (Radar Plotter).

Pitt.k's first ship was the commando carrier HMS *Albion*, which he joined at the end of 1966, just as she was going into refit at Portsmouth Dockyard. During two years in *Albion*, Pitt.k's experience of the world stretched from waters off Africa to the Far East.

The ship loitered in the Gulf of Guinea for six weeks during the Biafra conflict and covered the withdrawal from Aden, with Pitt.k plotting air and sea contacts on a radar screen using a chinagraph pencil. Such skills would later feed into his career as a submariner.

During *Albion*'s time in the Far East, Pitt.k observed that submariners seemed to have a rather better time than ratings in big surface warships.

Every Royal Navy sailor of that era had, though, to complete a deployment in a surface ship before even asking to join the Submarine Service.

On 18 November 1968 Pitt.k signed up at HMS *Dolphin*, where initial training consisted of ensuring he had a good idea of what was to be expected living and working in a submarine. To introduce the trainees to their future home, they were taken to sea for the day in an old A-boat.

Part 2 training involved schooling in systems belonging to different types of submarine and Pitt.k was selected for SSBNs while others were directed towards diesel boats and Fleet submarines.

The Polaris route was to be the final nail in the coffin for any dreams he might have nurtured about cruising through the tropics enjoying leisurely runs ashore. From what he could gather about life with 'The Bombers', it had more in common with coal mining than anything else.

Having only been to sea as a trainee submariner for a day in the A-boat, Pitt.k was impressed with the sheer size and complexity of *Repulse*.

He asked himself with a mixture of eagerness and anxiety: *How do I fit into all this?* It was a totally different way of life.

'*Repulse* was a new boat – all gleaming decks, shiny stainless steel – brand-new. *Albion* had been covered in layer after layer of paint *everywhere* and showing her age – we were forever chipping it off as she got rusty and painting her again.'

Qualified as he was by this time as an Able Seaman (Radar Plotter 3), or AB (RP3), very little of Pitt.k's job involved radar plotting.

His actual function was to record information from the Sound Room, Electronic Warfare sensors or visual information (from the periscope) onto various plots in the Control Room. Radar was very rarely used on submarines apart from coming into or leaving harbour on the surface.

The standard length of patrol for a British SSBN of the Cold War era was approximately eight weeks with five weeks in maintenance before deploying again. First port of call on returning was to Coulport, where the Polaris missiles were offloaded. The boat would then do what was called a cold move (with the reactor shut down) to Faslane, where there would be a crew changeover. Each SSBN had two crews – named Port and Starboard – to maximise availability for deterrent patrols.

Pitt.k discovered that the pattern was for the recently returned crew 'to generally back up the new crew while the boat was alongside and only once the submarine had gone back out on patrol would you get your leave, which was two to three weeks'.

After that the Bomber submariner would go on a training course, or get some fresh air on an expedition into the Scottish mountains with his crewmates. Some of the Polaris submariners might after a few patrols be given a more substantial break on the staff of a Recruiting Office, or possibly crewing a small Gibraltar-based patrol boat.

Once aboard *Repulse*, Pitt.k was given the less than exalted position of 'messman', cleaning up after senior rates in their mess, their heads (toilets), bathrooms and bunk spaces. He was not very impressed.

'You already knew what the real navy was about, knew how to scrub out, tie knots, what real rough weather was like and generally look after yourself. Being a flunky did not make me particularly happy, nor, should I imagine, would it please anyone who, like myself, was keen to learn submarine branch skills and be a useful member of the Ship's Company.'

Once he had completed both Part 1 and Part 2 training at HMS *Dolphin*, the prize was to pass Part 3 training, the onboard academy that moulded and qualified sailors for life in a steel tube. But Pitt.k and other ratings undergoing training were, as he puts it, 'undoubtedly the lowest form of life on board and rather despised by the fully qualified submariners'.

Even so, they were not without friends.

'The *Repulse* had six Radar Plotters and I was the most junior of them. But they trained you up gradually and I was lucky enough to have a very good, experienced and enthusiastic Petty Officer RP1 who put a lot of time and effort into training me up.'

Those who worked hard at sea also played hard ashore and Pitt.k noticed a change in habits between what he had been used to as a 'skimmer' (in a surface ship) and his new tribe.

'Submariners would tend to go ashore in large groups, whereas in surface warships sailors would go on a run ashore in small groups of three or four. Nobody had cars in those days – we would bus it into Helensburgh and get the bus back. Pubs were not open all day and night back then – the opening times were 10.30 a.m. to 2.00 p.m. and 5.00 p.m. to 10.00 p.m. – so you would cram it down your neck, then all race back to the base for the last hour of drinking at the Trident Club.'

Nobody lived aboard a submarine while in port, except for the duty watch taking care of the boat. Everybody else would move ashore to the barracks or, if the submarine was calling in somewhere overseas, local hotels, with an allowance to pay for meals. The submariner's home at sea, though, was his boat and it was his job to become intimately acquainted with it from end to end, as Pitt.k soon discovered aboard *Repulse*.

'You had to go around the various compartments and when you had mastered the systems inherent to the boat it would be ticked off in your training book. If they wanted me to go in the fore ends and fire a torpedo then they would have been barking mad. But if they wanted me to shut down a bulkhead by isolating an area – shutting a door and shutting a valve – then I could do it. For example, if there was a high-pressure burst – such as a pipe rupturing – I would be expected to isolate it and take emergency action.'

In an emergency the submariner, whoever he was, would seek to break the cycle of a problem, which might affect any one of many systems.

He would also have to be adept at running certain things under emergency local control and know all about what the alarms meant. This was the *whole sailor* – somebody who didn't just know about his department, his compartment, his side of life – but the entire vessel.

Whereas a hunter-killer submarine's job was to find and trail the potential foe, in the Bombers it was quite the opposite. The height of success was to avoid coming anywhere near either friend or foe for the duration of a patrol. Should the command team of the Polaris boat pick up an intelligence report via external communications or the Sound Room detect signs of anything potentially lurking nearby – whether a submarine or surface vessel – they would take *Repulse* in the opposite direction. Keeping things as uneventful as possible was the whole point.

Pitt.k found himself not overly taxed: 'Occasionally, as we crossed shipping lanes, we would get contacts but generally it was all pretty boring and extremely dull.'

The sort of Russian submarines they might pick up were Hotels, Echos and Novembers – all noisy and detected a long way off. It was easy enough for *Repulse* to take a diversion and avoid them.

Deploying on his first patrol, Pitt.k. found a daily routine that delineated the days and enabled him to cope with being inside the submarine for weeks without seeing the outside world. During any one 24-hour period he would pull two periods of watch for four hours each – the 'one in three' system. Efforts were made to ensure he did not pull the same watch at the same time every day. Pitt.k soon became acclimatised to his strange new existence. 'Some people tick off the days until they get back from patrol. I didn't do that. They used to have the familygram – a short 40-word message from family or your next of kin – sent once a week but I didn't bother receiving one as I was not married.'

An outsider might think the topic foremost in men's minds would be their submarine carrying enough destructive power to potentially destroy mankind, or at least make a good start on the process. The rights and wrongs of potentially destroying the planet did not, however, necessarily enter into it. As a junior rating, Pitt.k was representative of the breed: 'I did not think through the bigger issue of the potential mass destruction and I doubt if many of the younger members of the Ship's Company did. You were more interested in getting on with your own particular job or task while looking forward to getting back to Faslane for a bit of leave. Sailors were just doing their job – they didn't think about all the other stuff, but you might at some stage think: "I hope they don't have to fire these things".'

By the time he departed for his second nuclear deterrent patrol aboard *Repulse*, in early summer of 1970, Pitt.k was past the general dogsbody phase. He was assigned to the Control Room to keep the Contact Evaluation Plot, noting the time a sonar contact was made and its bearing on one-inch graph paper. He also helped keep the Local Operations Plot on tracing paper overlaid on a white paper graticule. The latter was a plan view of the tactical situation around the submarine and represented a true picture. A spot of moving light was used to denote *Repulse* while a fan of bearings was worked on in order to provide the fire control solution.

Pitt.k soon discovered his future was not likely to be in SSBNs but rather in some other part of the Submarine Service. 'They sent me on another training course to get rid of me – I really did like my runs ashore too much. The Polaris routine, while excellent for the married men, was a little staid, repetitive and generally very boring for a single lad like me. I was perhaps, a little too lively for Bombers?'

Receiving two months' notice of the training course, in the interim he sailed aboard *Repulse* for patrol number two.

Pitt.k nearly didn't return, coming close to becoming a casualty of the absolute necessity for the Bombers to provide a constant nuclear umbrella for the nation. The risk of one man losing his life was always balanced against the need to preserve that of the many. When Pitt.k was stricken down there would be no evacuation to a hospital ashore.

'About three weeks into the second patrol I went to see the Doc, a Surgeon Lt Cdr, with what I thought was just a sore throat. At the end of our consultation he stuck his finger up my bum and said that I had appendicitis – apparently they can feel up there if it is swollen. They immediately put me into the sickbay and gave me lots of penicillin jabs. I was very ill but they weren't about to compromise the patrol to surface and evacuate me via a helicopter. They sat me up in a bunk so that if the appendix burst, the poison would go downhill. We had a fully qualified Surgeon of course, but the atmosphere aboard a submarine, while good enough to breathe, is not that clean for opening people up. The chances of septicaemia are very high, so I was put in the sickbay to see what happened. For ten days to a fortnight I was sustained by drinking hot mugs of Marmite and Bovril, though I was also on a saline drip. I couldn't wee, so I was getting very bloated and painful. They were getting very concerned, for it was a substantial amount of time, and I was looking fragile. But they managed to subdue the infection. Even so, I was still very unfit and I was kept out of the watch rota. The other RPs were fed up because I wasn't watch-keeping. I was very keen to get back in there and so were they to have me back, although still rather frail.'

The Surgeon might, as a last resort, have opened Pitt.k up to remove the appendix. Had he expired then his corpse would have been stowed in a refrigeration space, but Pitt.k survived.

After returning to Faslane, Pitt.k left *Repulse* on 30 September 1970 but was not sent immediately to hospital as the appendix had calmed down. Travelling to HMS *Dolphin* for his training, he was then drafted to the recently completed nuclear-powered Fleet boat *Courageous*. At the time she was being fitted out at Barrow, where he joined her on 6 November.

As Pitt.k walked over the bridge linking Barrow Island with the mainland, hooters denoted a change in shift at the submarine construction yard. Thousands of workers flooded across the bridge, creating an overwhelming tide it was useless to battle against.

Careful not to lose the kitbag perched on his shoulder, Pitt.k moved aside, leaning against the rail until the crowd had passed. He then resumed his walk towards the Vickers yard.

Courageous had been launched on 7 March 1970. An Improved Valiant Class, her sisters were *Churchill* and *Conqueror*, the former a Barrow boat while the latter was built at Birkenhead on the Mersey. They had the same size and shape of hull as *Valiant* and *Warspite*, but with improved sonar, more efficient propulsion machinery and lower heat signature. Less cooling water was used in the reactor, which reduced the frequency of noisy machinery pumping it around the system. The *Courageous* was purpose-built for the same sort of mission *Warspite* had been carrying out when she had her 'iceberg' bump. Quite a few of the sailors drafted to the new SSN were actually veterans of that patrol. While *Courageous* herself was some time away from putting to sea, her submariners could make 'port visits' and that was how Pitt.k found himself deep beneath the seabed.

Newcastle has always been a popular run ashore for sailors, arising from its many hospitable pubs and friendly females. For Pitt.k, the coach trip over the Pennines to the north-east port was a sign that finally his naval career was looking up. The awarding of extra 'subsistence allowance' (a nice boost to the beer fund) for the group's 35 senior and junior ratings was most welcome. An invitation to visit a coal mine that ran out under the North Sea was a novel break from carousing. Submarining had much in common with mining – men working in an enclosed space with no sight of the world beyond, the challenge of supplying oxygen and light, the risk of sudden death if things went wrong. The submariners also met Newcastle's civic leaders and paid a visit to the brewery where the famous Brown Ale was produced. Following his raucous time in Newcastle, Pitt.k departed *Courageous* temporarily for Royal Naval Hospital Haslar, next door to HMS *Dolphin*, where his appendix was finally removed.

Returning to Barrow, he joined his *Courageous* shipmates in equipment testing and preparing the SSN for her first dive. They often used a life-size mock-up – constructed from wood and located in a large warehouse – to learn how to operate the submarine. It was also the perfect place to hide from those in authority and catch up on sleep. On his way to the mock-up Pitt.k might find himself paying a visit to three pubs. After signing in with the elderly civilian Vickers worker on the entrance to the warehouse, he would disappear into the depths of the mock-up submarine. There followed either a snooze in an obscure corner, to sleep off the beer, or a game of hide and seek with a fellow submariner. Each man would shout out the piece of equipment he was beside. Successfully negotiating the maze in pursuit of his fellow submariner taught Pitt.k the layout of *Courageous*, helping him and the rest of the crew to safely operate the real thing at sea. The new SSN would soon be taking the Cold War to the Russians.

In January 1970 Cdr Rob Forsyth went to Chatham, where he took command of the diesel boat *Alliance*. Constructed towards the end of the Second World War and commissioned in 1947, the 23-year-old boat was in the middle of a major refit. Over the years she had been remodelled extensively and fitted with the latest submarine sonar, and was also capable of firing modern wire-guided torpedoes.

Forsyth had passed Perisher in September 1969 and now he was the man in *Alliance* everyone was looking to for leadership. He realised he must appear 'cool, calm and confident' even though inside he might be 'all churned up' attempting to recall what he had just learned on Perisher. To his men, Forsyth was not an unknown quantity, for the Submarine Service was a small world. His reputation had gone before him, as somebody who was a leading exponent in the dark arts of wielding sonar to find and kill an enemy. Having served at Faslane as one of the team working boats up for front-line deployments he had been a rider in many submarines of the fleet and was a familiar face.

As a 30-year-old Lieutenant he felt 'quite young to have several millions worth of pounds of submarine and 70 or 80 crew to look after', but didn't doubt his ability to command. It was more how well he would perform the task and he wanted to give *Alliance* his best.

At the end of July 1970, she left refit and sailed for Devonport to join the Second Submarine Squadron (SM2). Frequently operating in waters between Scotland and Iceland, HMS *Alliance* had a busy agenda. Occasionally she pursued Russian submarine contacts, but wasn't the best type of boat for that. Forsyth realised his submarine's age made her 'inherently more noisy', enabling the Soviets to easily counter-detect her. It also reduced the effectiveness of *Alliance*'s own sonar because of the background noise she created. The boat's battery capacity was less than P-Class and O-Class boats while *Alliance*'s generators also charged the batteries more slowly. *Alliance* often pretended to be a Russian submarine for British surface warships engaged in ASW exercises, which primarily took place in waters off the north-west of the UK. *Alliance* would try and sneak up on NATO aircraft carriers or frigates. She might also try and hide from helicopters and the new Nimrod MPA but her function was to be detected – to provide a 'predictable target', as Forsyth put it.

'We were once sent to join the Western Fleet as their tame submarine in the Mediterranean and would be invited to dive and be forgotten about for several days.' *Alliance* would then attempt to surprise *Ark Royal* or evade the big carrier's Sea King ASW helicopters.

Alliance was at one stage loaned to the NATO anti-submarine sonar research centre at La Spezia in Italy, where she acted as a target for trials.

All the while, Forsyth was bedding in as the boat's captain, finding his expectations were being met, that he was really enjoying the responsibility of command. 'I thought it was brilliant and could not believe I was being paid to do something I enjoyed so much.'

Once he was over the initial thrill of command, it was clear *Alliance* would not contain him. She was, he realised, simply 'not at the forefront of technology. My ambition was to get into nuclear submarines, where the real Cold War was taking place.'

As an old boat, *Alliance* presented some engineering challenges that required a steady nerve and an absolute faith in physics.

'The stern gland was leaking and needed repacking – it was underwater with a propeller on the end, so it was tricky. We had to put the team in the back end of the submarine, along with everything they needed to do the job, and shut the compartment door. We then put pressure on it – just enough to keep the water out – but not so much it threatened the health of the sailors doing the work. They still suffered some discomfort.'

Had it all gone wrong the compartment could have flooded and everyone in it would have drowned. The willingness to take that risk on behalf of the whole crew won the engineers new respect from their shipmates.

As his first command, *Alliance* holds many good memories for Forsyth. She also presented what he feels was the only time in his career as a submarine captain when he was truly frightened.

This most trying of moments came in January 1971 during a voyage to Gibraltar for exercises in the Mediterranean. The battery was low as *Alliance* had been playing hide and seek with Maritime Patrol Aircraft in the South West Approaches of the English Channel.

Entering the Bay of Biscay, she encountered a storm in the order of gale force 8–9. Even submerged – normally a good way to escape bad weather – the boat suffered an extremely rough ride.

Alliance was heading south and beam on to gigantic swells surging in across the Atlantic from the west. The boat rolled badly, with water pouring down the snort mast.

The sea was constantly washing over the top of the snort mast, forcing the head valve to shut and open constantly. As soon as it shut, a vacuum was created in the boat. Forsyth kept an eye on the vacuum gauge in the Control Room. 'Green was okay. Yellow could only be sustained for a relatively short time. Red meant *stop snorting NOW* because oxygen levels were unacceptably low with the reduced barometric pressure. We were in the Red mainly!'

Below normal barometric pressure a vacuum induced in this way reduces oxygen levels. This in turn might take the edge off mental acuity and potentially cause errors in judgement. Long exposure to reduced oxygen levels leads to people doing dangerous things by mistake.

Hence ensuring any vacuum is of a very short duration is essential to safe operation of the submarine.

This was all extremely hazardous and – adding to the danger – the boat was passing through busy shipping lanes. At night visibility was only a few hundred yards. With driving rain and high seas, it was all quite hairy. To give the crew some respite, Forsyth took the boat deep, planning to come back up in daylight, about six in the morning. It was forecast the storm would have moderated by then, with better visibility.

The weather actually worsened, with storm force 12 winds, even bigger seas and – despite daylight – zero visibility amid the spume and spray. It was now impossible to snort because the submarine was broaching. This meant she would suddenly find herself exposed on the surface, unable to alter course quickly or safely in the shipping lanes.

Forsyth thought one solution might be to try and snort head-on to the run of the sea. This would unfortunately put *Alliance* beam-on to the shipping lanes, with no hope of avoiding collision should her path converge with that of a merchant vessel.

'The problem was snorting in such heavy seas, which meant the engines had to be stopped and then started continuously. Each time an engine had to be restarted, compressed air needed to be fired into the cylinders to move the pistons, initiating engine firing via the fuel injectors. We were now using up air faster than the compressors could restore it. Running the compressors was also further draining an already uncomfortably low battery. We were approaching a situation when there might not be enough air to surface the boat or battery power left for propulsion if we had to go deep to avoid shipping. We were on a downward spiral in which the reserve of safety was rapidly diminishing to the extent that my boat and crew were potentially both in serious jeopardy. At this point, with most of the crew sea sick and many frightened, I had to look calm and confident even though I was seriously worried.'

The words of his Teacher on the Perisher, Cdr Dick Husk, repeated themselves inside Forsyth's head: 'Remember that everyone in the Control Room watches your face in times of stress. Learn to be a poker player.'

He decided to surface and run the boat closed up as if dived and snorting. 'That way I would at least avoid the constant wash over the snort head valve and consequent engine stops.'

This ensured restoration of compressed air in the bottles (needed for the ballast tanks) and also enabled the battery to be recharged. This, though, presented a new danger, for *Alliance* risked being rolled right over by a giant swell. It remained essential for the submarine to keep her head into the sea. In such a mountainous ocean, the boat overcome by waves, the air filled with enormous amounts of spray and lashing rain, nothing was visible via the periscope. Forsyth was blind to any ships that might lunge out of the murk and poleaxe his boat.

'I was very aware the survival of my Ship's Company depended entirely on my judgement and actions. All my training and experience was about to be put to the test.'

Taking a deep breath he gave orders for the boat to turn due west, putting her head to sea.

The moment her course settled he ordered: 'Blow all main ballast.'

This used up almost the last reserves of HP air in the bottles – but took *Alliance* up like a rocket, making everyone brace themselves.

As soon as she broke free, lunging out of the water and settling, Forsyth ordered a turn to the south.

Now *Alliance* was pointing along the shipping lanes. Forsyth prayed they didn't meet anything coming the other way. 'We immediately started rolling, caught violently by enormous seas from the west.'

One moment of extreme danger had been overcome but the boat was still at risk. All but blind – unable to open conning tower hatches to put an officer and lookout on the bridge – she was also finding it difficult to make headway.

'The top of the periscope was now some 45 feet above the water. It was moving so much with roll and pitch that a watch keeper could only spend 15 minutes looking through it at any one time. Even then he needed a bucket within easy reach to be sick into. We could operate radar but, even with its higher elevation, it was so full of "noise" – echoes from waves – as to be almost useless.'

Air was slowly being pumped into bottles and amps restored to the battery. Preparing a meal of sandwiches and soup required the cooks to perform an athletic feat as the boat was rolling 30–40 degrees either side of vertical. Bit by bit the weather gradually improved as the eye of the storm passed through, until it was thought safe to send someone up onto the bridge. Anyone going up there would need safety harnesses so he would not be sucked out and drowned. Such circumstances required men of experience and so the First Lieutenant, Tim Honnor, and a senior seaman were selected. Dressed in full waterproof foul-weather gear and with safety harnesses, they climbed up into the conning tower, and shut the lower lid.

A third man went up with them to shut the upper lid once they had exited. He would thereby operate a water-lock, to prevent it pouring into the submarine itself, with the attendant risk of electrical fires and other flood damage. Forsyth was on the periscope trying to judge when a suitable gap in the enormous waves would give them the best chance of exiting safely.

There would be a perilous few moments as they climbed up through the fin, trying to maintain their balance and keep clipped on to the ladder via their safety harnesses.

Spotting a momentary lull, Forsyth told a sailor to make two taps on the lower lid – the signal for them to go for it.

Inside the conning tower Lt Honnor swung the upper lid open. He and the other man climbed up. The third man shut it and sealed them outside.

They edged up the last few rungs of the ladder to the bridge, unclipping and then clipping their safety harnesses each time, cursing at the water cascading down on them, which numbed their hands.

Inside the Control Room everyone waited tensely, imagining their painfully slow progress, praying their shipmates would not be drowned or swept away. The two volunteers climbed out of the tower and onto the bridge, protected only slightly by its shoulder-high surround. Another moment of peril came as they unclipped themselves from the top rung of the ladder and reached for the safety rail running around the inside. Tense and with adrenaline surging through their veins, freezing water swept over them. It momentarily filled up the inside of the bridge. Safely clipped in, they used a voice pipe to shout down to the Control Room that they had made it. A collective sigh of relief flowed through the submarine. After six hours of fighting the storm, with everybody stood to, exhaustion was setting in. Now part of the crew would be stood down from watch, to try and get some sleep if they could, wedged into their bunks.

It took around two hours for the weather to calm down enough for both hatches in the tower to be opened, allowing the diesels to work full pelt. This charged the batteries more swiftly and increased the flow of fresh air to the crew. Forsyth was invited up to the bridge, so he could make his own assessment. Donning full foul-weather gear and safety harness he ascended.

'When I emerged onto the bridge I saw a wave that I thought would swamp us. As this thing came thundering towards us the First Lieutenant – perhaps with a touch of deliberate irony – yelled that it was much better than it had been two hours earlier. The swell passed by without filling the conning tower with water. As far as we were concerned it was now just a typical rough surface passage requiring seamanlike precautions.'

Gazing across the storm-tossed surface of the sea, Forsyth mused again on his peculiar resistance to seasickness.

Prior to taking command of *Alliance* he had suffered terribly, but it seemed no more. Throughout the remainder of his sea-going career he would remain immune. It convinced him the ailment is all in the mind – as a submarine captain he was simply too busy keeping control of things and maintaining a calm exterior.

Having succeeded in his first command – despite the best efforts of a raging storm to sink his career and the submarine (drowning everyone in her) – by September 1971, it was time for Forsyth to leave *Alliance*.

Following the tradition of unconventional dress code in the diesels, indeed of not wearing what would be regarded as uniform at all, Forsyth's 'steaming gear' had included a tattered old green sweater. It was taken from his 'gardening things' wardrobe. Whenever *Alliance* was carrying out an important mock attack, Forsyth would don the green sweater. It was considered by everyone in the boat to be a talisman of good fortune.

Over time it had become, in its owner's words, 'dirtier and holier'.

Forsyth decided the stinking old thing had come to the end of its life and consigned it to the wardroom bin. The captain's Steward thought this was an undignified end for such an important feature of the boat's life.

Unknown to *Alliance*'s CO, after he had climbed up to the bridge to bring the boat into Plymouth for the last time, a funeral party was assembled.

Looking down, Forsyth was surprised to see a group of his sailors emerge onto the casing for'ard. They were carrying a cardboard box coffin with a White Ensign draped over it. The officiating 'padre' was actually the Navigating Officer dressed accordingly. They assembled solemnly, like any funeral party carrying out a burial at sea. Forsyth was informed that within the coffin, now placed on a plank for tipping over the side, was the infamous green sweater. A few prayers were intoned and, to the shrill blast of the Bosun's pipe, it was sent into the deep. A ship passing at the same time thought it was a real burial, and out of respect for the deceased dipped her ensign.

This was the twilight of the Second World War-era diesel submarines in the Royal Navy and *Alliance* would end her sea-going career in 1973.

The early 1970s saw other changes in the culture of the Navy. Some were not universally welcomed, none more so than the end of the rum ration. In the missile age it was regarded as anachronistic, and even dangerous, to still issue ratings with an eighth of a pint of the black spirit each day. A drunken or even slightly intoxicated sailor could do a lot of damage with a slip of the finger on a firing button, or at the helm of a nuclear submarine.

Doug Littlejohns was among those pleased to see it go.

During his time at sea on breaks from university he'd witnessed the alarming consequences of submariners called to their action stations after downing rum (having believed they would not be needed for some hours).

'I was aboard *Ambush* in the English Channel surrounded by shipping and the fore planesman couldn't keep us on depth – so we couldn't see out the periscope. He kept going deep and the periscope was then pulled under water. It was highly dangerous. The rum ration was manageable if you knew you were going to surface and, or, going back into harbour. If you were dived for 24 hours you had to issue the daily tot as it was the sailors' right to have the rum. The thought of what that could mean in a nuclear boat – the potential consequences – was frightening.'

The last tot was issued on 31 July 1970 and on hearing it was consigned to history Forsyth thought 'good riddance'. He felt that while people played, and drank hard on dry land, at sea in a submarine was no place for 'rum rats'. As the Navy minister, David Owen, explained in the House of Commons the troublesome tot was not a good idea in the era of the 'instant response' naval fleet.

Down in the mouth though some might feel about losing their rum, they did gain a new badge to proudly signify their trade.

In July 1971 British submariners finally won the right to wear their own 'Dolphins' – like a pilot's wings, the visible sign of belonging to an elite.

Littlejohns received his in a car park at Faslane, parading alongside hundreds of other submariners, including those from his first boat as a full-time submarine officer, the O-Class diesel *Onyx*.

'At the signal I turned towards my neighbour and pinned on his Dolphins while he did mine.'

There had been a measure of opposition to the whole idea - the Silent Service took great pride in its covert nature, so some felt it went against the grain. Modest old veterans grumbled: 'We don't need to tell the world what we are.' That soon faded though, when they saw how splendid the Dolphins looked. To this day they are highly coveted and worn with great pride. The sheen was taken off that pride a little in the late summer of 1971 by the discovery that not every sailor who had served in submarines was quite so loyal to his Service or shipmates.

G iving an account of his espionage activities, Sub Lt David Bingham told a Special Branch officer: 'All I can say is thank God it is over.'

The former submariner's relief swiftly turned to abject despair as the full scale of his betrayal and the ruination brought on his family hit home and also became a national scandal.

The day after his arrest a detective interviewing Bingham in the Admiral's Office Block at Portsmouth Naval Base learned from the self-confessed traitor that he had taken 19 painkiller tablets. Though yet to be charged, he also demanded to retract his confession. Bingham was taken to hospital and, having failed to end his life, soon after was transferred to a civilian prison, where he could be more closely monitored.

David Bingham's sorry tale was a counterpoint to the intelligence-gathering activities of the Submarine Service in which he had once served. While British submarine captains used periscope cameras to photograph the latest Soviet naval developments, Bingham snapped secret documents giving away NATO tactics and technology.

Returning unheralded and ignored to port with their latest intelligence scoops, the submariners took silent satisfaction having gained an edge for their country in the shadow war. Meanwhile, David Bingham held covert meetings with a Soviet naval officer in country lanes and on suburban streets to get his espionage instructions and hand over packages of secrets.

The Bingham case capped more than a decade of betrayal by traitors with naval connections. Just as NATO submarines probed Russian waters, Soviet intelligence continued to exploit human flaws, targeting those who had access to secret information on British submarines and sonar technology. At the dawn of the 1960s there was the case of the Portland spies with their *Dreadnought* plans in a shopping basket. There was also George Blake, another former submariner. A Dutchman by birth, but whose father was a naturalised British citizen, he was open to exploitation because, as a teenager living in Cairo, he was indoctrinated by left-wing cousins on the virtues of hardline socialism.

During the Second World War, Blake sought refuge in England. After becoming a Royal Naval Reserve officer he put his name down for Special Service. He hoped to be parachuted into Holland, where he could join the resistance to the Nazis, but also didn't mind serving in destroyers. He was dismayed to end up at HMS *Dolphin*. For him, becoming a submariner was not an attractive proposition.

Even worse, he found himself plunged into training as a diver operating from X-Craft mini-submarines. After learning how to exit the tiny boats during exercises in the 100ft-tall, water-filled escape tower at Gosport, Blake was supposed to head for Scotland to do it for real. Plans changed when he was found to be allergic to enriched oxygen. Removed from X-Craft training, Blake served time as an Officer of the Watch at *Dolphin*, enjoying the company of pretty Wrens (Women's Royal Naval Service), but otherwise finding it all rather tiresome. When offered an opportunity to serve in fast attack craft he eagerly seized it, but in 1944 was diverted into naval intelligence.

After the war, and by then assigned to MI6, Blake worked under diplomatic cover in South Korea. When hostilities broke out he was interned by communist North Korea, from where, in 1951, he sent a note to Russian intelligence offering his services. The former trainee submariner would later maintain he turned traitor out of a sincere conviction that the Soviet cause was just. Released from captivity and embedded in MI6, Blake betrayed hundreds of Western agents working behind the Iron Curtain before he was arrested in April 1961. Pleading guilty to all five charges of breaking the Official Secrets Act, Blake was sentenced to a record-breaking 42 years in jail. In 1966 he escaped from Wormwood Scrubs prison in London and was spirited out of the country to Russia, where he later apologised for causing the deaths of Western agents.

John Vassal was a homosexual Admiralty clerk who, in the early 1950s, was posted to work for the Naval Attaché at the British Embassy in Moscow. He was invited to a party and photographed engaging in various sexual acts at a carefully staged honey-trap orgy. Blackmail, combined with tempting offers of cash for secrets, turned Vassal into a very worthwhile KGB asset.

On returning home, Vassal achieved a senior position on the naval side of the Ministry of Defence. Among the secrets he passed to the Soviets was information on torpedoes and sonar. Brought to trial in 1962, he received a sentence of 18 years in prison but was released on parole a decade later.

And now, in 1970, here was Bingham, in some ways the most shocking of the Royal Navy traitors, for he was a serving officer and had been a submarine rating from January 1958 to February 1963.

Bingham was at one time part of the Malta-based submarine *Talent*'s crew and was an Acting Leading Seaman in the new diesel boat *Oracle*, when she was running in and out of Barrow on sea trials. Bingham also served in submarine depot ships and ashore at *Dolphin*. Taking advantage of the meritocratic policy that allowed lower-deckers to aspire to the wardroom, Bingham became a General Service officer. In 1970, aged 30, he was too old and lacking in command experience and training to become a submarine officer. He joined the surface fleet and specialised in diving and Anti-Submarine Warfare. The highest rank he could reach before retirement was Lieutenant Commander. Promotion, and a bigger salary, would be a long time in coming, if ever, for a father of four children who had big debts. By September 1969, Bingham was serving in his first ship as an officer – the anti-aircraft frigate HMS *Jaguar*, patrolling Asian and Australasian waters.

Despite his rough edges Bingham was popular with fellow officers. He seemed to spend a lot of time in the Operations Room scrutinising manuals and other documents normally kept under lock and key. It was, though, part of his trade to be fully briefed. A character assessment a few years earlier judged Bingham to be well above average and even exceptional, though with a slightly 'apologetic manner'. Bingham was considered 'highly adaptable, utterly obedient and loyal' as well as 'quick and accurate in his work'. In reality, debt was the true master of his destiny and it would lead him into becoming yet another naval traitor.

In a picture dated circa 1901, the crew of the Royal Navy's first submarine, *Holland 1*, gets a welcome breath of fresh air as their boat cruises on the surface.

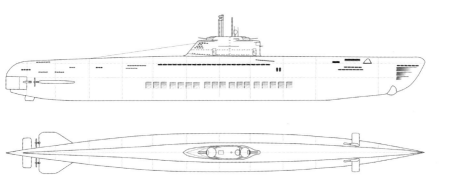

The Nazi-origin Type XXI U-boat, which provided the technological basis for early Cold War submarines used by the British, American and Russian navies.

Tim Hale's first boat, HMS *Subtle*, proceeding up the canal to Brussels in 1955.

The young submariner:
Sub Lieutenant Tim Hale, 1956.

Rob Forsyth as a Midshipman in 1958.

21 October 1960: Britain's first nuclear-powered submarine, HMS *Dreadnought*, slides into the Walney Channel during her launch by Queen Elizabeth II from the Vickers Armstrong yard at Barrow-in-Furness.

HMS *Auriga* sails past the towering skyscrapers of New York in 1963.

A Foxtrot Class diesel submarine of the Soviet Navy on the River Neva in central St. Petersburg (Leningrad in the Cold War). During the Cuban Missile Crisis some Foxtrot submarines were sent into the danger zone armed with nuclear-tipped torpedoes.

The captain of *Auriga* tests the strength of the ice pack as the First Lieutenant watches from the hydroplane.

Tim Hale's accident-prone submarine, HMS *Tiptoe*, pictured in 1967.

Midshipman Dan Conley at sea under training.

Midshipman Littlejohns in his Whites while serving at sea in tropical waters.

HMS *Sealion* – which both Rob Forsyth and Dan Conley served in – pictured with ship's company on her casing at the 1977 Silver Jubilee Fleet Review.

The towering fin of HMS *Warspite*, with officers and ratings on the bridge, possibly including Tim Hale who helped save the SSN from potential destruction in October 1968. *Warspite*'s fin was very badly damaged in the incident.

A Polaris missile blasts into the sky after being fired during a test off of Florida by a submerged British SSBN.

HMS *Resolution*, the first of Britain's Polaris missile submarines on sea trials in 1966.

HMS *Courageous* at speed.

The diesel submarine HMS *Alliance* in dry dock at Devonport in the early 1960s.

Lt Cdr Forsyth on the bridge of his first submarine command, HMS *Alliance*.

May 1970: Sub Lieutenant David Bingham with his wife Maureen. Just under two years later he was sentenced to 21 years in jail after pleading guilty to selling secrets to the Russians.

The frigate HMS *Rothesay*, aboard which Bingham betrayed his country by photographing naval secrets. *Rothesay* is escorting an intruding Soviet Whiskey Class submarine out of NATO waters.

For Britain's navy the early to mid-1970s was an era of tight budgets, a manpower shortage and retreat from East of Suez initiated by the withdrawal from Aden in 1967. Now there were plans to hand over the British naval base at Bahrain to the US Navy. By the end of 1971 Singapore would be relinquished and before the decade closed the Royal Navy would also withdraw from Malta, its last naval bastion in the Mediterranean. The British Empire was truly finished and those ships left in its rapidly declining fleet were often confined to port due to lack of funds for fuel. The Russians seemed determined to fill the vacuum and anything that gave them an edge over the Anglo-American axis at sea was most welcome.

Bingham's offer of naval secrets should also be set against a canvas of alleged corruption and waste in some naval shore establishments, where (for example) the catering arrangements were being abused by certain individuals who 'lost' foodstuffs. In reality they were taken home and sold off.

Wages in the Navy had slipped behind those offered by civilian employers, so graft was not uncommon. Working the system was commonplace among dockyard workers. Aside from sleeping on night shift (much as their comrades did in the car factories of the Midlands), they were adept at taking liberties with ministry property. Some sailors were even working as restaurant waiters, hotel porters and mechanics to make ends meet. With moonlighting common practice, the border between probity and corruption sometimes blurred. It must have seemed a short step across the line to lucrative espionage for the Soviets.

In early 1970 David Bingham lay in a hospital bed at Royal Naval Hospital Haslar getting depressed. His family was £2,000 in debt. There were new uniforms, a civilian suit and an obligation to attend social functions, none of which he could afford. Unable to get married quarters, the Binghams had been forced to buy their own home in Cowplain. His wife, Maureen, was also overly fond of shopping and bingo – another drain on the family finances. One night when she came to visit him they discussed possible solutions. As an officer he had access to various documents the Soviets might be keen to see, so Bingham suggested she make a visit to the Russian Embassy in London. He wrote a note giving details of who he was and his job in the Navy. Bingham later covertly met Lori Kuzmin – Naval Attaché from the Russian Embassy – in a central London apartment. Over vodka and snacks – the volume of a radio turned up to obscure their conversation in case they were being bugged – the two men discussed the practicalities of betrayal. Kuzmin was particularly keen to obtain information on sonar equipment and so Bingham bought a Soviet-funded compact camera to photograph secret documents. On several occasions he drove out into the countryside to drop off packages of films covered in putty to look like rocks. Bingham hid them under an old discarded car door by the side of the road for Kuzmin to pick up later. The Soviet naval officer in turn left packages containing cash and films with just one frame exposed. Bingham processed the films at home, creating prints from the exposed frames so he could read his orders and see sketch maps of drop-off and pick-up locations.

If there is one thing a navy is desperate not to reveal, it is the future destinations of warships. Should a foe know where vessels are going they can be trailed and, in time of war, destroyed.

When Bingham copied details of future warship movements – potentially putting at risk the lives of many fellow Royal Navy sailors – he also committed the deed aboard one of the most illustrious ships in British naval history. In March and April 1971 he was sent on a training course in the old cruiser *Belfast*, anchored at Fareham Creek, in Portsmouth Harbour.

As an officer, Bingham was given a cabin to work in and that was where he photographed secret documents giving the worldwide disposition of the British navy. Sometimes he sneaked documents home and, while Maureen was at the bingo, photographed them in the bedroom. He told his children not to disturb him as he was studying for exams. To get enough light, he put a 500-watt bulb in the overhead fitting, spreading things out on the bed. The Russians began to nag Bingham, complaining in successive notes about his camera technique, or lack of it. Some shots were out of focus, caused by camera shake, making documents hard to read.

They suggested he rested the camera on a hard surface.

On one occasion when driving back to the family home at Cowplain, Bingham was required by Kuzmin to call in at a railway station car park and put a crunched-up cigarette packet in a telephone box. This would signify he had made a drop-off. Bingham found a pale blue Renault with Swiss plates, and with two young men sitting in it, parked nearby. Fearing they would do him harm if he climbed out, he chucked the cigarette packet out of the window and sped off.

To gain access to the relevant Fleet Operational and Tactical Instructions (FOTI) and recent Naval Intelligence Reports (NIRs), Bingham was forced to take the extreme risk of photographing them aboard HMS *Rothesay*, the warship to which he had been drafted.

FOTIs and NIRs were never allowed off the ship but he could take them to his cabin. Even then, photographing them was fraught with risk, not least because he had to put the 500-watt light bulb in the light over his bunk. Someone passing his cabin in the darkened passageway might wonder what was going on. After carefully making double sure the cabin's sliding door was locked, Bingham propped manuals and secret documents up at the far end of the bunk. He squinted through the viewfinder and began clicking off frames, exposing five films in all, prickling with anxiety and fear every time he heard footsteps in the passageway. But Bingham got away with the espionage equivalent of stealing exam papers from the headmaster's study.

To find release from his daily worries Bingham liked to go shooting or fishing. The solitude gave him time to think things through. Each pull on the trigger provided a cathartic explosion.

There comes a time when such distractions will provide no escape.

A decade of a rollercoaster marriage, thwarted ambitions and lack of financial stability had resulted in looming disaster for his family.

He had joined the Navy to serve his country, going to sea as one of a special breed, the Cold War submariner, and now he had betrayed his shipmates and his country.

Bingham's dark night of the soul came when his wife was at a bingo evening. On returning home she found him slumped in the chair with a shotgun close at hand and disgustingly drunk.

She asked him what on earth he was doing, picked up the shotgun and put it away, telling him scornfully: 'You would not have the guts to do it in any case.'

Bingham realised he had to end it another way. On going back aboard HMS *Rothesay* at the end of his summer leave in August 1971, he went in search of the First Lieutenant, who also served as the ship's security officer. Bingham was at last able to unburden himself. Later that day, the captain of *Rothesay* had the unpleasant duty of writing a note informing senior officers ashore that his deputy torpedo officer had confessed 'he was and had been for some years a Soviet Agent'.

Until then the captain believed Bingham to be above average for an officer promoted from the ranks, a happily married family man. Furthermore, the captain's note observed: 'I have found no obvious character defect. His hobbies are country pursuits – shooting and fishing.'

During interrogation Bingham identified Lori Kuzmin as his primary contact and claimed it was he who visited the Soviet Embassy rather than his wife. It was there that the Naval Attaché gave him money for a camera. Later Bingham claimed he didn't go to the embassy.

Bingham said he was told to memorise and destroy all maps but didn't because, since Christmas 1970, it had been on his mind to confess.

The Navy launched an inquiry, quizzing those whom Bingham had encountered in his career to see if they had noticed any odd behaviour. His captain in HMS *Jaguar*, Cdr Michael Clapp, said he felt Bingham found it hard to make the transition from being a senior rating to officer. Clapp was aware Bingham's home life was not a happy one. Bingham's preoccupation with studying manuals in the *Jaguar*'s Operations Room was something that was not unusual in an officer ambitious to further his career.

The one-time submariner claimed there were dozens of other naval officers and ratings operating as Soviet spies in the Navy. This prompted a massive mole hunt, which came up with nothing.

Kuzmin had departed the UK shortly before Bingham confessed, handing over his duties to another operative. He was therefore not among 105 officials expelled from the Soviet Union's embassy in London in 1971 as a penalty for the Bingham case.

Of major concern to the British was the extent to which the highly secret FOTI had been compromised. The potential advantage the Soviets had gained from sight of NIRs was also assessed.

In a secret briefing document, the First Sea Lord and Chief of the Naval Staff, Admiral Sir Michael Pollock, explained FOTI 'spell out the total fighting capability of the Royal Navy and form the basis of Fleet Exercises'.

When it came to the NIRs, the Soviets would not learn anything they did not already know. However, as Pollock explained, 'some articles may provide a new indication of allied [intelligence] collection capabilities and the quality of technical analysis available'. That had to include an insight into the success rate of submarines in the Barents.

The First Sea Lord suggested: 'If an enemy studies this [material] in depth he will be presented with the total fighting capability and, perhaps more importantly, the serious weaknesses (particularly in electronic warfare) of the Royal Navy. The accuracy and extent of our interpretation will be a good guide to the effectiveness of the Soviet security measures, and will almost certainly assist them in concentrating their security and deception activities in the most appropriate directions.'

Pollock saw the FOTIs' exposure as the most serious breach and remarked: 'Unfortunately there is little doubt that important information has been passed to the Soviet authorities who will now be better aware of the strengths and weaknesses of UK and Allied maritime strategy and equipment. Although action is being and will be taken to minimise the effect there is no gainsaying the fact that serious damage seems likely to have been caused.'

Within FOTIs were details on a new system of controlling SSNs from ashore (and from surface warships). Link Ship was a means by which a Fleet boat would operate ahead of a surface task group, utilising sensors to hunt out potential enemy submarines. A deeply flawed idea, it required an SSN to use active sonar, which told both friend and foe where the submarine was.

To make matters worse, communicating information about suspect contacts to the task group would, again, create exposure. The underwater telephone link to the surface warships did not work well anyway. While it was useful for the Soviets to know about Link Ship, the lack of viability and fact that Bingham had given details on it away soon saw it abandoned.

A senior naval intelligence officer provided a concise 'SECRET U.K. EYES ONLY' survey of the Bingham damage. While he believed no individual means of Royal Navy intelligence gathering was 'actually compromised' he did feel 'the Soviets will have received confirmation of the general nature and usefulness to us of one or two sources, especially electronic intelligence'.

The Russians would be able to create a more formidable defence against intruders in the Barents. The naval intelligence officer noted: 'the Soviet Union now has a very good insight into our methods and capabilities in the field of Naval Technical Intelligence generally.'

He finished on a very sombre note: 'Director of Naval Warfare will no doubt be considering what action he can take to reduce the tactical consequences to the Fleet.'

During his trial in March 1972 Bingham ended up pleading guilty to all 12 charges laid against him, receiving a total of 21 years in jail.

Maureen Bingham would soon find herself in the same dock as her husband. The Defence depicted her as a put-upon Mrs Mop – she had been reduced to working as a cleaner. The Prosecution portrayed her as a latter-day Mata Hari. Having denied all three charges laid against her, Maureen Bingham was acquitted of two charges of passing secret material to the Russians, but found guilty of committing an act preparatory to her husband's offences. She was sentenced to two and a half years in prison.

In the aftermath of the trials an officer wrote in the *Naval Review* that the Binghams were to a certain extent betrayed by the Navy, though obviously they had to bear the main responsibility.

Somebody should have spotted they were in financial trouble and that it could lead to something dreadful. There were plenty of warning signs but nobody did anything.

Bingham's actions would make life harder for submariners whom he had at one time served alongside. Despite this, they would still carry the struggle for intelligence-gathering superiority into Russian waters.

At the same time as the former submariner's trial took place at Winchester Crown Court, HMS *Courageous* was preparing for her forthcoming spying mission in Northern waters.

Having set sail on Contractor's Sea Trials in late May 1971 and successfully completed them, she returned to Barrow to be commissioned on 16 October that year. She was already scheduled to pull a Northern patrol in August 1972.

Following further sea trials, weapons firings, and also working up life-support systems, other equipment and machinery to operational pitch, *Courageous* entered an Assisted Maintenance Period at Faslane during February and March 1972. This was when she received most of her Special Fit, making her capable of deep-penetration espionage missions.

The training did not stop even when the boat was alongside in Faslane, for her submariners then used the Attack Teacher, a brand-new simulator that replicated a submarine Control Room.

They also used the attack team trainer at Rothesay, which was still there as a hangover from the days when those waters hosted a depot ship and a squadron of submarines. It was being phased out. The submariners mourned the imminent demise of this facility, as they much preferred a training environment with pubs and a good hotel bar nearby to being confined to a Ministry of Defence establishment.

Among those honing his skills in the Rothesay Attack Teacher, or RAT, as a Plotter was Pitt.k. He found that one of the simulated Control Rooms even revolved on its axis to provide extra stomach-churning authenticity.

Getting to grips with the power and lethality of an SSN was a major challenge, for the Royal Navy was still on a fairly steep learning curve when it came to 'flying' them. Pitt.k was thrilled by the turn of speed and manoeuvrability of *Courageous*, but he was also well aware how easily it could go awry. 'A couple of degrees at high speed on the hydroplanes could bring on some very sharp angles, very quickly. Intensive and frequent training was conducted to ensure that the planesmen were fully competent – we had nearly lost *Valiant* when they had had a planes incident at high speed in the early days. To keep depth you need a good trim, and/or speed. You could overcome a bad trim with speed, but with just slow speed you cannot really do so. You need to have a good trim as much as possible. There are a lot of variables that will alter the trim. You are always making fresh water out of seawater and this will alter the trim if it fills up the fresh-water tanks. When a watch changes you get people moving around. If fifteen people are going aft, that is a ton going aft and that can also radically alter the boat's handling. You take counter-measures to offset that kind of thing.'

While *Courageous* herself was cutting-edge, both her weapons and the torpedo tactical control system were not as modern as the platform or the sonar. The Mk8 torpedoes were the same as *Dreadnought* had been equipped with, yet were still considered more reliable than the Mk23 wire-guided weapon.

Pitt.k was excited by the prospect of 'going North' and took confidence from those around him. 'We still had a good hard core of *Warspite* lads aboard. They were experienced in those sorts of operations and they didn't seem too worried by the prospect of going back up there.'

Pitt.k and the rest were given briefings on what and what not to expect. Ushered into a lecture theatre at Faslane, training staff they had been working with (but who did not have security clearance) were asked to leave. The men of *Courageous* were then briefed on various North-ern patrol matters, including what the average Russian sailor was like. *Know thy enemy, lads.* They learned that some Soviet ratings couldn't even speak the same language as the rest of the crew. *Muscovites regard Kazakhs as aliens.* The *Courageous* submariners were also told about the growing Soviet threat – the Red Navy was sending a new nuclear sub-marine a month down the slipway. *It was astonishing.* The British took years to build a single boat. *Courageous*, for example, was only the sixth British hunter-killer submarine since 1959.

Even though their focus was on putting as many hulls in the water as possible, the Soviets were getting better at building faster, quieter sub-marines, such as the Victor IIs and Deltas.

To make sure the British SSN's crew knew their potential enemy, and could identify intelligence-gathering targets, bulkheads and locker doors in *Courageous* were adorned with photo pages from MoD and NATO ship- and aircraft-recognition journals. Even time spent in the wardroom heads could be used constructively. More recognition posters were posted on the back of the door. Pitt.k and his shipmates also had to learn how to identify the different Soviet radars and sonars, plus general capabilities of Russian warships and their systems.

In addition to the SSN being tested hard to ensure she could handle the forthcoming mission, Pitt.k and the others were subjected to rigorous personal scrutiny. 'Before you went into "the programme" you all had to be Positively Vetted. They would do that to make sure you didn't have a vulnerability that would make you malleable – such as debt, being homosexual, or a drink problem – something the agents of an enemy power could use to get you to work for them. They checked on your parents and your parents' parents to make sure they weren't Russian or of East European origin. You received a thorough interview and had to fill in a massive form, to provide information they would go away and check.' The lessons of the Bingham case were being learned hard and fast.

Right from the start on her first front-line deployment, *Courageous* was in the thick of it, with two promising contacts. The Sound Room identified them as a Yankee Class SSBN and an older (much noisier) boat, most likely one of the Hotel, Echo or November classes (or 'HEN' as they were also known).

Proceeding extremely cautiously at more than 200ft, the British SSN edged closer and raised the thinner, less obtrusive, attack periscope. *There they were, exactly where they were supposed to be* – the product of uncannily accurate bearings produced by the Sound Room – a Yankee and an Echo on the surface.

The Soviets had completed construction of 26 Yankees since 1967, with five more being built across the USSR during 1972. Trailing and capturing the distinctive sound signature of each one was a vital task.

Should it ever come to all-out war, time would be of the essence in eliminating enemy SSBNs. Better not to waste it hunting and killing a HEN when there were Deltas to destroy.

That year a new variant of the SD-N-6 nuclear missile (with a one-megaton warhead), called the Mod 2, entered service, extending the range from 1,300 to 1,600 nautical miles. Greater range meant the Yankee didn't have to be so close to the USA, and would therefore have more ocean to hide in.

Catching one on the surface presented an ideal opportunity to carry out an underwater look. *Courageous* entered Ultra Quiet State, preparing to slide right underneath the Soviet boat, which would have her own sonar operators listening. This was a game changer for *Courageous* – no training exercise in a simulator. A miscalculation here could be very dangerous, as the former *Warspite* ratings in the crew knew only too well.

The aim was to ever so carefully photograph and film every single inch of the Yankee's belly, while recording her distinctive sound signature. The atmosphere in the Control Room of Britain's latest SSN was extremely tense. Then one of the Soviet boats sent a single active sonar ping into the water.

With the captain, Cdr Sam Fry, on the periscope and everyone in the Sound Room finely tuned, there followed the unmistakable sound of vents opening. Both Russian submarines – partially submerged already– rapidly dived right ahead of *Courageous*.

This forced her to swiftly turn starboard, following a wide circle to both take herself out of danger and sweep around, aiming to end up directly astern of the now submerged targets.

The Soviets continued to cruise in close company, subsequently carrying out exercises over the next day and a half. Throughout *Courageous* stayed well in their baffles, totally undetected, gathering all the intelligence she wanted. This mission had not been compromised by whatever Bingham gave to the Russians. It most certainly wasn't helping them right there and then, to better detect a British hunter-killer in their own backyard, doing the business.

33 | TOO CLOSE BY HALF

A miserable April day in 1973; the black casing of the Polaris missile boat HMS *Repulse* glistened with rain as, with tugs in attendance, she eased away from the jetty at Faslane Submarine Base. Mist and low-hanging cloud pressed down on the Gareloch, which rippled turgidly, black as molasses. *Repulse*, her own screw turning quicker, easily pushed the water aside, fizzing as it rippled across her nose, white ribbons of wake gently wafting astern of the great beast. The casing party arranged themselves in a line, the damp chill kept at bay by their chunky submariners' sweaters.

On the bridge in the submarine's big, broad fin Lt Cdr Rob Forsyth, XO of the Starboard Crew, kept an eye on proceedings. By 1973, each SSBN was doing several patrols a year, something that was only possible with two crews per boat, using the Port and Starboard system. Forsyth found this well established pattern required a good rapport between them, for within 48 hours of returning to Faslane an SSBN would be handed from one crew to the other. The Port Crew, which stood by at home while the Starboard Crew operated *Repulse* at sea, would put all the maintenance work in hand. The Starboard Crew would enjoy a couple of days' leave. On returning from leave they would support the other crew preparing for the next patrol. Once the boat had sailed, the men of the off-duty crew would enjoy some long leave and reconnect with their wives and children.

It was now the turn of *Repulse*'s Starboard Crew to take her out on patrol, with Forsyth calmly issuing instructions as the 7,500-ton, 425ft-long nuclear-armed submarine picked up speed and made for the Rhu Narrows, gateway to the Clyde.

Repulse carried out a dive, just off the Isle of Arran, to check her trim was correct, but then surfaced to complete the rest of her transit to deep water. Gliding out of the shallow, sheltered zone, *Repulse* passed between the Mull of Kintyre and Rathlin Island.

Forsyth was stand-in captain – the Commanding Officer, Cdr Tom Green, was indisposed due to a very bad back and confined to his bunk – and so did not stay long on the bridge, as he had business below.

Handing over to the Officer of the Watch (OOW) Forsyth climbed down the ladder inside the fin's inner tower and emerged into the Control Room. Several hours later, off Malin Head – the most northerly headland in Ireland, the OOW buzzed Forsyth on the internal communications network to say there was a fishing vessel nearby. It looked suspiciously like a Soviet spy ship, an Auxiliary Gatherer Intelligence (AGI); these pests recorded the departure and return of the Bombers.

Whenever a SSBN was about to make an appearance, this was their customary loitering spot. It meant they could pick the British submarines up while they were still on the surface. Exactly when *Repulse* would deploy on patrol was never publicly acknowledged.

A dedicated observer concealed on the shores of the Gareloch might earlier have spotted the submarine leaving for, and returning from, a short shake-down cruise designed to make sure everything worked okay.

Another indication was an order placed with the NAAFI butcher and a local baker for fresh meat and bread, around a week before the boat sailed. While it was not revealed which type of submarine, Fleet or Bomber, the amounts of lamb chops and loaves were a bit of a giveaway. Polaris boats had the largest crews of any British boat; more loaves and chops meant bigger submarine.

The internal comms panel in the Control Room buzzed again. It was the OOW saying the AGI was getting closer. Forsyth climbed back up to the bridge. Spray wafting over him, he used a pair of binoculars to scan the Soviet vessel's upper works. Its superstructure was host to a forest of aerials and domes, indicating an ability to scan multiple radio frequencies and also detect and classify radars.

This AGI appeared determined to actually intercept *Repulse* rather than just sucking in intel and standing off as she sailed past. Deciding to go and seek the advice of the captain, Forsyth descended swiftly, squeezed through the crowded Control Room and went along to the CO's cabin. He knocked on the closed door and was invited to enter.

Sliding it shut behind him and pulling across the curtain, Forsyth found the captain gazing at him from his bunk, clearly still in pain.

'Well?'

Forsyth coughed to clear his throat.

'I thought you should know, an AGI is shadowing us rather too closely.'

'Nothing unusual about that ...'

'Yes, but he appears keen to intercept and possibly interfere with us diving.'

The CO looked faintly irritated.

'I am not in a position to advise you – you must decide on the best course of action.'

Nobody minded too much if you dented a diesel boat in an encounter with the Soviets, but this was a different ball game altogether. As a Cold War battleship *Repulse* was of course carrying atomic weapons – 16 missiles, each of which could destroy many thousands of lives and devastate whole cities – as well as being nuclear-propelled. These two factors made whatever decisions Forsyth took in the next few minutes all the more crucial. Not only for his own career prospects but also the UK's national strategic defence, not forgetting NATO's nuclear umbrella. As he went up the ladder to the bridge, he grumbled under his breath: 'Polaris warheads, a nuclear reactor, the lives of 143 people – not much to worry about.'

He found the AGI continuing to close fast.

It took up station only two cables off, on the submarine's port quarter. Deciding to observe pleasantries expected of two vessels in close company on the open ocean, Forsyth ordered a sailor to flash a light signal greeting:

Good afternoon.

There was no response from the Soviet, except for possibly somebody waving back – or was that a rude gesture?

Regardless of her unwelcome companion, *Repulse* held course for waters where she could be sure of at least 50 fathoms to dive in safety. Recognising the British submarine would soon attempt to slip into the deep, the AGI moved even closer, closing down the distance uncomfortably.

The Russian's actions bordered on harassment, the AGI now only one cable directly astern. *Too close by half.*

Scanning the Russian vessel while he weighed up his next move, Forsyth realised this could easily develop into a full-blown diplomatic incident (at best) or even pose a serious threat to *Repulse*. Collision was a real possibility if the British submarine reduced speed or even altered course.

In such a situation the AGI – as overtaking vessel – would be responsible for taking evasive action. Was the Russian captain competent enough to handle such a situation – to harass his British opponent, but avoid anything tantamount to an act of war?

That was the razor's edge they all walked along during close encounters at sea, whether on the surface or in the depths.

Forsyth suspected the Russian didn't give a damn, another of

Gorshkov's bruisers, forbidden to do anything but show aggression in the face of the West. Discussing the situation with the OOW, Forsyth mused: 'If we dive at normal speed, she could easily overrun us and possibly cause damage as our speed slows.'

This was a tricky situation and the light was fading fast, adding to potential risks by further degrading everyone's acuity.

With decision point approaching, as the 50-fathom mark loomed, Forsyth hoped the AGI would not seek to deliberately hit *Repulse*.

The Soviet vessel was built to extremely tough standards and could withstand damage, whereas the submarine could not. Even a minor collision could lead to the deterrent patrol being abandoned.

Forsyth wondered: *Is this the AGI's aim?*

A whole new level of confrontation?

Disappearing into the ocean was fundamental to the success of the whole venture. That *Repulse* had been spotted and trailed by the AGI was embarrassing enough, but the patrol did not start in theory until the boat dived and vanished. Forsyth had some more time, though not much, to shake off the Soviet. Whatever transpired next, nobody would be able to accuse him of not trying hard to avoid a collision.

Forsyth ordered a yeoman rating to send the international light signal requesting: *Give me more sea room.*

The Russian edged even closer.

There was no way a Polaris submarine could outrun an AGI on the surface. The only option left was to shake the shadower off by diving. Forsyth took the precaution of a call to Action Stations, so everybody throughout the boat would be closed up and ready to respond to any event conceivable (or inconceivable).

Descending to the Control Room again, Forsyth picked up the hand mike to brief *Repulse*'s men on what was about to happen: 'We are going to carry out a World War Two style full-ahead crash dive.'

This was definitely not normal practice in Bombers, which had their programmes planned weeks, if not months in advance. On patrol beneath the waves they rarely went above a couple of knots. Ballistic missile boats were notorious for being slow to dive anyway, but Forsyth was not afraid to take a risk. That willingness had, after all, extracted himself and HMS *Alliance* from peril in the Bay of Biscay. He concluded the briefing:

'We need to reach our safe depth of 120ft as fast as possible.'

The moment the echo sounder confirmed sufficiently deep water, Forsyth ordered full speed ahead. *Repulse* put a few vital extra yards between herself and the AGI, which piled on revs to try and catch up. The bridge watch team disappeared from the top of the fin, hatches clanging shut as they climbed down through the tower into the pressure hull.

The last man secured the inner hatch.

Repulse's main vents opened.

Driving forward at 16 knots, the SSBN plunged into the deep.

Spray erupting and water boiling as the ocean covered her massive black hull, last to submerge was the broad fin, carving through the sea like a killer whale's fin. It provided a perfect aiming point for the charging Soviet spy ship. Deck angled down sharply, *Repulse* entered her natural environment.

She levelled off at just below 120ft. Sonar operators in the Sound Room reported the AGI's props close overhead. Forsyth was reminded of his submarine command course when he had been required to take his boat deep, in order to duck under an 'enemy'.

Forsyth was unable to resist a reflexive look up at the Control Room's deckhead, criss-crossed as it was by cables and pipes.

It was almost as if he could see the AGI's bows cutting through the sea overhead, but the seconds ticked by without the sound of anything crunching into *Repulse's* fin. Forsyth felt certain the Soviet vessel had at the last moment altered course to avoid contact.

Repulse soon shook the AGI off, disappearing into the Atlantic, commencing the patrol on time and remaining undetected. Her crash dive may have been the first, and probably only, such manoeuvre ever carried out by an SSBN of the Royal Navy or US Navy.

Although he had come from commanding his own submarine, Forsyth was not at all put out to be second in line aboard *Repulse*. Being XO of a Bomber was a stepping-stone to becoming captain of a Fleet submarine.

It was a responsibility so much greater than a diesel and needed somebody who was an experienced officer to act as second-in-command. Forsyth did have to acquire some new skills by attending Greenwich for six months. A nuclear theory course made use of a low-power reactor in the heart of the historic college on the Thames – despite the local council declaring the borough a nuclear-free zone. That greatly amused Forsyth. While he sometimes found going back to school at the age of 32 a bit tiresome, he did enjoy exploring the many local pubs and visits to West End theatres for hit shows such as *Showboat* and *Hair*.

As XO of *Repulse*, Forsyth was at the other end of the pecking order within the SSBN to Michael Pitkeathly during his earlier deployment in the same boat. Part of the XO's portfolio was to oversee the smooth day-to-day running of the SSBN. To that end, Forsyth took great care to make sure every eventuality was planned well in advance.

'In SSBNs if you hadn't thought about it two weeks beforehand you were late, whereas in SSNs you worked on a basis of instant reaction to events as they unfolded. The whole point of being in an SSBN was that everything would have a plan, leaving nothing to surprise you. We were almost check-list happy. We would spend hours discussing every eventuality and how we would handle it, from a fire, to the risk posed by going to periscope depth when updating the navigation system via a satellite fix.'

The latter had the potential for exposure when the SSBN put the communications mast up. Of the 143 people on board for a patrol – 115 crew and 28 passengers of various sorts, the latter mainly trainees – only two knew where the boat was – the captain and the Navigator.

There were three cardinal rules for any SSBN patrol, which sought to achieve a difficult balance between stealth and being ready to launch missiles:

1. *The submarine must be undected throughout. Surfacing, whether delib-erately or accidentally, would give the Soviets an opportunity to spot the boat, if not with a surface unit – AGI or warship – then via aircraft or submarine. The foe's all-seeing eyes in earth orbit, reconnaissance satel-lites, were also a danger.*
2. *The submarine must remain in constant communication with base, so that intelligence updates could be sent and/or the order to fire missiles received.*
3. *Maintain the submarine at readiness to fire throughout the patrol.*

With a keel depth of 68ft, Sea State had to be very carefully calculated. When it was very high the boat could, potentially, find herself exposed on the surface between the swells/waves.

'The large flat missile deck of *Repulse* could act like a suction pad if you got too close to the surface,' Forsyth explained, 'wave motion is circular and would push/pull you up. Suddenly, you are on the sur-face, from whence it may take several minutes to submerge again. Such a massive *faux pas* would require a full report because it would have breached one of those three cast-iron patrol aims.'

In an attack submarine the captain could react instantaneously and instinctively whenever required but even popping the scope up in an

SSBN was carefully calculated. During *Repulse*'s spring 1973 patrol, for example, there was a deep conversation between the CO and Forsyth about the balance of risks involved in rising to periscope depth. *Repulse* needed to extend the mast to get a satellite navigation fix but had to minimise potential exposure. The risk from broaching in an extreme winter gale was so high they decided not do a satellite navigation fix. Such conditions could persist for weeks.

The Navigator would be involved in these discussions. On this deployment he was a very promising young Lieutenant named Chris Wreford-Brown. He would later find fame as the captain of the SSN *Conqueror* when she sank the Argentinian cruiser *Belgrano* during the 1982 Falklands War.

To avoid detection during a satellite fix attempt, *Repulse* could alternatively rely on a seamount position fix using a discrete echo sounder, which did not make a distinctive ping.

Normal navigation was conducted via SINS, in which Forsyth had every confidence (with a few caveats). 'It would still give you a pretty accurate position after two or three days without an external fix. But to know exactly where you were, and to monitor SINS drift every now and then, you would need to get a navigation fix.' The life of an SSBN might be more sedate than an SSN, but clearly the same need to calculate risks affected every minute of a deployment.

Living as they did, cheek-by-jowl with nuclear-tipped weapons that could destroy every human being – including their own nearest and dearest – it was only natural for the men of *Repulse* to contemplate Armageddon.

Forsyth and others frequently debated whether they would actually launch the missiles if *Repulse* got the signal. 'We thought about it a lot and probably concluded that someone had to be ready to do it. We believed in what we were doing. For us the Cold War really was black and white – we did think the Soviets were going to take over the world, given half a chance. We were playing a role in stopping them doing it. Yes, we would launch missiles, but hoped we wouldn't have to – I don't think we just shrugged our shoulders and thought it was an interesting job. We also jokingly said we would fire only if Radio 2 and Radio 4 were off air. Radio 3 was head-in-the-clouds classical music. Radio 1 never knew what the real world was up to. If Radio 2 and Radio 4 were on air, and there was no mention of an Armageddon-type crisis building up – just the usual radio patter – we might seriously debate whether the fire signal was genuine.'

Joking aside, it was actually a major reason for a patrolling SSBN to regularly tune into radio programmes. Even so, far removed from normal everyday life and events, the submariners rarely heard anything on the radio that was worth mentioning in conversation, or even putting in the *Repulse*'s daily newspaper.

One major topic that had to be discussed, no matter how distasteful, was the best counter-measure if someone went mad and, as Forsyth put it, 'ran amok and tried to launch a missile'.

The solution was brutally simple.

'We did carry side arms, when necessary, but a dived submarine is not a good environment in which to fire live rounds. So we had a large club hanging up by the missile-firing panel – in fact, a US-issue baseball bat – and we would hit them with that. Although of course it was not as simple as someone just pushing a button and launching a missile, as there were so many steps in the process. Technically, you could blast one out of the tube but it would not be activated or targeted.'

Should the order to launch missiles come, the process would unfold via a carefully laid down sequence incorporating many steps. The decision to fire would be issued – from a bunker somewhere in the UK – by the Prime Minister advised by the Chief of the Defence Staff (CDS). The PM would authorise the 'release' of nuclear weapons rather than order: 'Fire.'

Should the PM have been wiped out with the rest of the British political leadership before orders could be issued – there was a hierarchy of cleared ministers – inside a safe within a safe on board each Polaris submarine (bolted to the deck in the CO's cabin) was a letter of last resort. This conveyed the PM's wishes. This would be opened and read by the captain and XO. Forsyth speculated the alternatives had to cover 'hit back', 'don't hit back' or 'some other personal instruction'. To this day writing that letter – whose contents are known only to the writer – is one of the first jobs a newly elected PM must tackle. It is the chilling moment when the terrible responsibility of leading a nuclear-armed state hits home.

In the Cold War, should the order to fire have been issued, a National Fire Control Message (NCM) would have been transmitted to the SSBN. Co-ordinates of the cities or military bases to be destroyed would have been loaded into the missiles. The NCM contained two sets of authentication codes, one each for the CO and XO. These had to match those held aboard *Repulse*. As a further safeguard against a single person losing his mind and trying to initiate the launch system, the codes were kept in two separate safes, their respective combinations known only to each man.

The most crucial steps thereafter were:

1. *Authentication of the firing signal by XO and CO, via bringing the separate codes together to achieve 'unique authentication'.*
2. *'Permission to Fire', given by turning the Captain's Key – also found in one of the safes – in a Control Room panel.*
3. *Completion of the firing circuit by the Weapons Engineer Officer, who was also the Polaris System Officer, via a pistol grip and 'trigger' attached to a wire. This was connected to a control panel in the Missile Control Room.*

After these three stages were completed, the system then took over and automatically progressed through a series of further actions. The moment of firing would come when the submarine rose to launch depth.

Once pressure inside the tubes had been equalised with that outside, the lids would open and the missile (or missiles) would be ejected.

Tons of water a minute were moved by the hovering system, keeping the boat stationary and level, to avoid damaging the surprisingly fragile missiles as they left the tubes and during their short journey to the surface.

With the missile breaking the surface, first-stage ignition would kick in, rocket motors firing. It would roar away into the sky but the crew of an SSBN would not know exactly where the missile was headed. This prevented the perfectly understandable temptation to tell a loved one or friend not to live there. Or, as Forsyth put it, 'in case we had an aunt in Minsk and told her'.

If the Polaris 'birds' ever flew, to whatever destination, it was certain the world the men aboard *Repulse* had left behind when their boat departed Faslane no longer existed.

Discussions of what to do after launch did take place, but such debates were always afflicted with a sense of unreality, of kicking things about just for the hell of it. Forsyth admitted 'it was hard to seriously visualise exactly what post-Armageddon would be like'.

In pure tactical terms *Repulse* would have a far higher chance of surviving than land forces, surface warships or the civilian population – all instantly obliterated or slowly poisoned by radiation. 'We could well find ourselves in an "On the Beach" type scenario,' he felt. 'Whether there would be any form of government able to give us any direction was highly doubtful, albeit there was a very-low-frequency slow-speed communication technique, which might survive and provide some way of contacting us.'

Having launched missiles, there was a chance the enemy might pinpoint *Repulse*'s location. Forsyth thought 'the arrival of missiles in Minsk and other places, from multiple launch platforms – American, other British and possibly the French nuclear *Force de Frappe* – would somewhat disrupt command and control in Russia. Our immediate threat would, therefore, be from surface ships and submarines that detected, possibly visually, our missile launch. Our own sonar and intelligence plot would have given us prior knowledge of them, so realistically our first aim was to be ready for self-defence and/or to counter-attack them.'

Repulse had torpedoes, sonar and a combat system, just like the SSNs, but as a bigger submarine, with a large missile compartment, she was much easier to detect and target in a fight. British SSBNs did practise submarine versus submarine tactics, but opportunities to do so were limited. Forsyth knew his boat was not as sharp as would possibly be required to win such an encounter. Her biggest strength would be to keep slow and very quiet and seek to disappear again.

Heading for Australia or South America was proposed during one discussion – far away from the heart of a NATO versus Warsaw Pact conflict. Society in those parts of the world would probably survive, at least for a time. Ultimately Forsyth found the post-Apocalypse discussions fantasy stuff. 'But, really, we had no plan,' he admitted, 'we just knew that our chances of survival were a lot better than our families' and that was little comfort.' After all, what would be the point of carrying on? Off watch, drifting through the deep, dark ocean, carrying enough explosive power to kill all Mankind, the men of *Repulse* sometimes couldn't help but think about the unthinkable. Most of the time they ignored it.

As her men waited for the dawn of a doomsday they hoped would never arrive, *Repulse* gently cruised along, a sea-going, self-contained community of which Forsyth was *de facto* mayor.

The main foe he had to combat was the tedium of an eight-week routine, which, as Pitt.k had discovered during his SSBN vigils three years earlier, aimed to be as uneventful as possible.

'Once you dived, life on board became extremely quiet and highly organised,' explained Forsyth. 'Excitement was not something you were looking for. A primary aim of the XO was to ensure people were busy and occupied when off watch and not sitting around brooding about what was happening back home.'

Keeping morale up would rely on providing in-house entertainment, such as a Sod's Opera, a movie or games evenings.

If entertainment looked likely to generate noise, an assessment was made on threat level. The intelligence picture would be studied, to check if there were any Soviets potentially lurking nearby to pick up the racket.

Some submariners filled their off-duty hours with studying for degrees. Business Studies, Maths and English were among the popular choices. And then there was model-making, with Forsyth bringing aboard a plastic kit of a capital ship from an earlier era.

'I spent a whole patrol making HMS *Victory* – quite a big task. Even though deodorants and aftershave were considered a potential risk to the carefully controlled artificial atmosphere, we were allowed to use small amounts of glue and paint. Doing the *Victory*'s rigging kept me well occupied.'

There were even model-making competitions and visitors to the wardroom in the wee small hours would find Forsyth bent over the table working away, determined to triumph with his HMS *Victory*.

It was also during the dead of night that Forsyth walked his parish beat, on the lookout for potential trouble, not of a law-breaking variety but in terms of morale. There were people working in small compartments quite some way removed from the heart of things who might start brooding, especially at night.

'I got into the habit of drifting around, listening to what was going on and chatting to watch keepers away from the centre of the boat. Then I would do a bit of model-making, then drift off again to talk to the Officer of the Watch, before returning for more work on *Victory*. I found people would chat more in the middle of the night – all sorts of things would come out about their potential problems that you could talk through and help resolve.'

The *Repulse*'s daily newspaper – mainly containing scurrilous reports and cartoons – made the XO butt of most jokes, but that was fine by Forsyth. The men needed mental diversions to keep them alert and on their game. There was nothing better than some really exciting news about the eccentricities of the newspaper's favourite target.

'On one occasion mid-patrol, I decided to acquire a "dog", by wandering up and down with a piece of string, which had a scrubbing brush at the end. The Ship's Company probably thought I was going off my rocker. Most people chose not to say anything when they went by, other than "Hello, Sir", as I walked my "dog" up and down the main accommodation passageway.'

One brave soul, a Sonar rating, stopped to inquire:

'What are you doing, Sir?'

Forsyth replied: 'Don't be stupid, I'm exercising my scrubbing brush!'

A report on the XO going bonkers – accompanied by a cartoon – eventually ended up in the newspaper, as Forsyth knew it would. It really boosted morale to think the XO was going nuts – such was the perversity of British naval humour. The Doc, Surgeon Lt Jim Powell, realised Forsyth was not actually becoming unhinged. Powell had very little to otherwise keep him occupied, for *Repulse*'s men were all young and fit.

The Doc would listen sympathetically to moans, complaints and imagined illnesses. For the first week of a patrol sailors acquired everyone else's cold but after that they remained infection-free until returning home, when they were liable to catch any virus on the loose.

Like many Medical Officers in the SSBNs Powell had been drafted to *Repulse* from training without any prior service in submarines. In fact the British SSBNs were the first UK submarines to carry a doctor on a permanent basis. He found his new shipmates an interesting bunch, later confessing to Forsyth that he thought them 'mad as hatters'. The Doc realised nothing could ever have prepared him for the strange world of a Polaris submarine. While they were 'a very odd bunch of people', he decided, 'somehow they seemed able to co-exist successfully'. To keep himself occupied Surgeon Lt Powell ran the wardroom wine bar, was the 'schoolmaster' (Education Officer) and also oversaw quiz nights and the bridge school. To give people a sense of night and day, which he believed would be better for their well-being, the Doc agreed with Forsyth that it was a good idea to switch operational and accommodation spaces to red lighting at night.

A feature of life in another British SSBN was a Scalextric track occupying most of the missile compartment. It was artfully arranged around the tubes, known in SSBNs as Sherwood Forest, on account of their tree trunk-like appearance. *Repulse*'s men had a scaled-down version, around just a couple of missile tubes. The boat's technicians adapted the cars to sharpen their performance. They would go faster, took corners better and, most importantly, stuck to the track. Flying off risked dashing a tiny plastic car to smithereens against hard metal.

Whether it was model-making, studying for exams or contemplating the primary reason they were all there, a major thing to be ignored was separation from family, friends and loved ones. In that regard *Repulse*'s submariners were as cloistered as monks who had taken a vow of silence.

It was questionable if the weekly 'familygrams' that maintained a rigid – and minimal – form of personal communication from the UK served any true practical purpose, except for providing psychological support.

'In that way they were of enormous importance to everybody,' conceded Forsyth. 'The off-crew back at Faslane would monitor what was in the familygram before it came to you, so it didn't offer a lot of privacy. They aimed to make sure no difficult or distressing news would get through, such as your wife dying or a child being seriously ill. They wanted to prevent bad news hitting you like a lightning bolt. Anything that would upset the crew at sea was censored out. As reliable information documents the familygrams were, therefore, actually useless, no more worthwhile than greeting cards.'

While separation from family was for some people an ache they preferred to ignore – or not have exacerbated by upsetting news from home they could do nothing about – others were delighted to be out of touch.

Their problems were left behind in the surface world. This could lead to 'patrol happy' syndrome. Some men, unable to face the responsibilities and pressures of family life, were even eager to be at sea. As soon as they got in the front door at home they would yearn for the less complicated life they enjoyed in *Repulse*. Forsyth thought they regarded home as 'confusion and chaos'. He reflected: 'On patrol they were part of a perfectly ordered ant heap. Everybody had a job, they all knew what they were doing and were busy. Their life at sea was a comfort. Sometimes after a boat got back in, people would linger more than they ought to and had to be told to go home.'

The type of person serving in the Bombers varied and not all were volunteers. As had been the case since the beginnings of the Submarine Service, the Royal Navy reserved the right to compel sailors to serve in the boats. Either way they all knuckled down and got used to their strange new existence, a type of job that even mystified some submariners.

Forsyth, who would serve in all kinds of submarine, admitted: 'There were tribal rivalries between the SSN boys and people in the SSBNs – the former were always rude about the Bombers, but it was a job that required a different form of initiative.'

As his first nuclear-powered boat, *Repulse* meant quite a sea change in thinking for Forsyth. 'It drew out of you an organisational ability, rather than gung-ho, whites-of-the-eyes stuff – you went from piracy, in the diesels, to pragmatism. The penalties for getting things wrong were so much higher. Aside from the challenge of raising my game, I certainly enjoyed putting on a clean white shirt and being more organised.'

The normal custom was for the SSBN to cruise at no more than 2–3 knots – walking pace – which was barely moving in such a large vessel. For Forsyth, more used to the constant state of motion in a diesel, it took some getting used to. Yet the tactical challenges were just as demanding.

'At that speed, if there is a threat coming down the line, it will take you most of a day to get off its track, putting a safe 50–60 miles between yourself and whatever it is. Everything had to be quite deliberate. This was to retain stealth but also because you had so much "string" hanging off you.'

The 'string' on an SSBN was the communications aerial – the very-low-frequency (VLF) wire – that *Repulse* trailed all the time. Coming out of the back of the fin, it ran just below the surface. Also trailing off the submarine was another wire, the bathymeter (an instrument for reading salinity, water pressure and temperature), and, on later patrols, a towed array sonar.

A towed array was a means to put a sonar set on the end of a wire, so that its ears (microphones) were removed from the noise generated by the mother vessel, so enhancing the chances of picking up any potential foe.

If *Repulse* wanted high-frequency (HF) radio reception she could rise to periscope depth and raise the Wireless Transmission mast or, from deep, reel out an HF radio buoy.

The process of checking to make sure no Soviets were shadowing *Repulse* had to be conducted very carefully. During a normal period on watch in the Control Room, Forsyth would frequently issue the order: 'Clear stern arcs.' This involved the boat turning back on herself, then waiting until the towed array streamed straight astern again – the sonar in the bows would then seek to detect anything that had been lurking close behind the SSBN.

The submarine's forward momentum was reduced even more during this process, sometimes to only one knot. Forsyth thought it was 'a bit like walking through mud – using a lot of energy but not making much progress'. Managing the course of the boat while trying to give her men a semblance of normal life, in what were uniquely abnormal circumstances, could further complicate matters.

Forsyth's second deterrent patrol was at sea during December 1973 and he was determined the crew should not miss out on the highlight of the month. 'Christmas lunch was planned days ahead, for it was both a tactical and practical decision. On the day a storm was blowing above water and although we were quite deep, at around 300ft, the swell effect reached us and made *Repulse* roll uncomfortably when beam-on to it. I sought permission to steer a certain course – putting the submarine's head into the run of the sea. This enabled us to sit down for the meal without being thrown around. When it came time to serve the meal we had to clear our stern arcs, doing a complete circle. We also looked at intelligence for potential threats. The CO said: "We can have 45 minutes on one course." It was a case of putting the turkey on the table, clear stern arcs and then serve and eat. You don't want to get jumped by a trailing Soviet submarine during Christmas lunch.'

By such means did *Repulse*'s men celebrate the birth of God's son, drifting along in a submarine containing enough explosive power to snuff out all of the Lord's creations.

There was a growing sense of unease in the West.

Russian maritime power was fast evolving into a giant whose intentions were an enigma, providing endless hours of debate for NATO intelligence analysts, but no definitive answers.

By 1973, the Soviet Navy was rapidly gaining on, if not edging ahead of, the Americans. A quarter of its 400 submarines were by now nuclear-powered. The USSR was building up to 15 nukes a year, while the USA could manage only an average of 4.5. It was estimated the Soviets would soon field more SSBNs than the USA.

American submarine construction yards declined while the Russians expanded theirs; the variety of Soviet boats increased rapidly.

They had managed six new designs of nuclear-powered submarine since 1963. The USA had sent only two new types to sea in the same period. Observing all this, a former Royal Navy officer tried to divine exactly why the Soviets were building *so many*. Commander Nicholas Whitestone, who at one time served in the Naval Intelligence Division, suggested there were three possibilities.

- The Soviets were preparing to refight the Battle of the Atlantic. In any war they would send out submarines to sink troop ships and supply vessels, depriving NATO of reinforcements and starving the West's civilian populations.
- They wanted to have enough submarines to match and kill the Polaris boats (and also to attack American and British aircraft carriers).
- The Soviet Navy was a political weapon, to exert pressure on the West. Its burgeoning might was a means of underwriting Russia's diplomatic moves.

The likely answer was that it was a mix of all three – ready to attack shipping, seek out enemy submarines, and intimidate the capitalists with its numbers and growing firepower.

While Whitestone pondered the big picture of the stand-off, other professional analysts scrutinised the boats themselves. What exactly was the Charlie Class cruise missile-armed submarine for? Attacking carriers? Or land targets? How exactly were the Charlie's weapons guided to target? Until the day hostilities erupted, nobody in the West would know for sure, though efforts to provide answers would be made by submarines on intelligence-gathering missions.

The Soviet predilection for continuing investment in submarines that bordered on the obsolete puzzled a former British submarine captain, turned writer, Capt. J. E. Moore; he remarked sarcastically that it showed 'yet again how indifferent the Soviet Union is to heavy arms expenditure ...'

The Soviets were also fielding the Delta II SSBN, with a submerged displacement estimated by Western sources to be 16,000 tons, as large as a small aircraft carrier. Such leviathans were sliding down the slipways in the early 1970s at a rate of seven a year.

Captain Moore issued a warning: 'All these monster ships are being built at the vast complex at Severodvinsk [on the shores of the White Sea], which has a greater construction potential than all the submarine yards in the USA combined. The Deltas are in most respects the most potent warships ever operated.'

When it came to surface ship killers, by 1973 there were 15 Echo IIs in the Northern Fleet alone. While unsophisticated, they had their uses. Like other Soviet submarines that did not pass the West's quality test, the Echos offered Admiral Gorshkov the benefit of decoying NATO away from the key units, such as SSBNs. Each Echo II would, he hoped, require thinly stretched NATO forces to exert themselves on the hunt. The most feared of the Soviet hunter-killers (at this time) was the Victor.

Around 20 of them were in service by the mid-1970s – thought to be capable of at least 33 knots dived. With their eight 21-inch tubes, a submerged displacement of 4,200 tons and a length of 285ft, it was reckoned their torpedoes were equal to Western tinfish.

The Achilles heel of the Victors, despite a highly streamlined, broad hull – indicating deep diving ability – was free flood holes in the outer casing. Water constantly flowing through them made a Victor much noisier than NATO hunter-killers, particularly when it became a burbling rush at speed. Still, Capt. Moore pointed out, 'they are extremely fast and dangerous craft, able to sink virtually any kind of surface vessel'.

Across the Atlantic, Admiral Hyman Rickover, father of the US Navy's nuclear submarine force, reckoned the West had a lot to be worried about.

He believed the Soviets were creating other types of boats that were faster, could dive deeper and were quieter than ever. In 1969 the CIA received intelligence from what it described as 'strollers' who had spotted an intriguing new super-streamlined submarine taking shape in Leningrad, at the Sudomekh Yard on the banks of the River Neva.

American naval attachés twice made forays into forbidden areas around the shipyard. Somehow they managed to retrieve material, which they would later claim fell off the back of a lorry. It was sneaked back to laboratories in the USA for analysis.

Ironically, the most tantalising clue would ultimately be retrieved on American soil. A naval analyst working for the CIA teamed up with a US Navy researcher to call on a scrapyard in Pennsylvania that specialised in purchasing unusual scrap metals from the Soviet Union. After painstakingly examining every potentially relevant item on the site, the two men discovered a piece that seemed promising.

Etched into it was a series of numbers that began '705'. To expert eyes this was something very intriguing indeed. Analysis of the machined metal soon revealed it to be titanium and, as would subsequently be discovered, the mystery boat was known in the Soviet Navy as the Project 705 Lira.

At first, it was believed to be a new form of diesel boat.

A senior US Naval Intelligence submarine analyst named Herb Lord suggested, after studying photographs and other data, that it was a radically new form of SSN.

Lord maintained it was a 'super submarine' made from titanium.

With advanced weaponry and sensors, it could pose a serious threat to Western naval operations. He told colleagues and superiors the Soviets had – at least in this case – abandoned their cautious approach to submarine design – the incremental, career-preserving way of doing things. *This boat was different.*

Lord's claims did not immediately take root. According to a recently declassified CIA case study, the sceptics in US naval intelligence circles maintained 'the shaping and welding of heavy titanium hull sections, especially in the generally "dirty" shipyard atmosphere, was impractical, if not impossible'.

The idea of creating whole sections of a titanium submarine in the open air was too ridiculous – usually when titanium was welded it had to be carried out in specially enclosed areas filled with fire-retardant argon gas.

Nothing this big could be made from it, they said.

An entire submarine hull made from titanium?

Impossible.

Regardless of its powerplant or hull composition, a single unit of what would be labelled the Alfa Class by NATO was completed in 1970. What was *her* precise role?

Anti-shipping?

Anti-submarine?

It took several more years for Herb Lord's analysis to prevail over the sceptics – and he actually retired before his views became accepted. The CIA analyst Gerhardt Thamm ultimately took up Lord's cause and he confessed: 'it became my mission to convince the US Navy that the Soviets were building high-threat submarines using advanced construction technology'.

While Rickover's team believed the Soviets were improving submarine construction they, and others in the USA, remained very dubious about the Alfa being an SSN. They refused to believe it would be anything more than a dead-end experiment, whatever it was.

In reality one of the most revolutionary submarines ever constructed, the Alfa spotted moored at a fitting-out quay on the banks of the Neva in 1969 was merely a one-off prototype. There would ultimately be a class of six commissioned examples, whose capabilities chilled the blood of NATO commanders. The fastest and deepest-diving attack submarine the world had ever seen, the first Alfa was a rare and mysterious beast.

She was a product of the most brilliant minds in the Soviet submarine design world. Latter-day Norse gods had applied their knowledge of metallurgy to try and secure mastery of inner space for the Kremlin. Russian naval architects, scientists and mathematicians were brilliant, their products simply amazing.

With the Alfa – because they were hoping to achieve a massive leap ahead of the West – the Russians took their time about pushing the prototype to the limits. The roots of what would become the Alfa programme went back to the early 1960s, when the Holy Grail was the so-called Interceptor submarine.

A type of hunter-killer tailored to the flash-bang nature of any likely war, it would be able to hit hard and fast, then disappear. The new Delta Class SSBNs, armed with the SS-N-8 (Sawfly) missile, could bombard America from the comparative safety of the Greenland and Norwegian Seas. Any hunter-killer riding shotgun would not need long endurance, for the Bombers would be relatively close to home.

Such a fast deep-diving submarine could make quick forays in the hunt for surface and submerged targets. The Interceptor submarine could be small, with a modest crew, and also a minimal fit for sonar. Detection abilities of Maritime Patrol Aircraft and helicopters, or other elements of detection equipment (including seabed sensors), would aid the mission.

Generally the reason nuclear-powered submarines were so much bigger than diesels was the need for complex and extremely powerful machinery and powerplant. That in turn increased weight, which decreased speed. The answer was to keep the propulsion plant as small as possible while constructing the boat from lightweight material. The Soviet solution was a liquid-metal reactor while using titanium for the boat's hull.

Titanium offers huge advantages, for not only is it much lighter than steel, but it is also extremely strong. It has a very low magnetic signature and is not so vulnerable to corrosion. Hard to obtain, and expensive, it does not have the same give as steel. This lack of elasticity under the extreme pressures experienced by deep-diving submarines meant it could crack more easily. Aluminium and manganese alloys were introduced to try and restore elasticity. Titanium was also difficult to bend into the radical, streamlined shape the Soviet naval architects devised for the space age Alfa. With an ultra-streamlined exaggerated hump for a fin, she looked like something conjured up by Arthur C. Clarke.

One Russian submarine officer who saw an Alfa under construction thought her lines stunningly beautiful. She was a work of art rather than a product of industry. On joining the Alfa's crew, composed of the best and brightest the Soviet Navy could assemble, he was overcome with pride. He exulted: 'I felt as if I had just discarded my tractor and boarded a spaceship.'

With six tubes and packing a maximum of 18 ASW missiles or torpedoes, the acceleration of the new wonder submarine was incredible. It could go from 6 to 42 knots in just 120 seconds. The Alfa had a remarkably small crew of just 45. Thanks to high levels of automation, it could be reduced to as few as 31.

The use of liquid metal for reactor coolant was extremely radical – and very dangerous. The US Navy had commissioned USS *Seawolf* in 1957 with a liquid-metal reactor. Not much more than a year later she was brought into a dockyard to have it removed and replaced with a pressurised-water reactor.

A major challenge was ensuring the liquid metal did not actually solidify, bringing the system crashing to a halt.

The Alfa had two compact reactors to offset that annoying tendency.

A major advantage of using liquid metal was that it did not become radioactive, so it wasn't necessary for the steam-generating machinery it passed through to be clad in heavy (bulky) and expensive radiation shields.

The top turn of speed achieved by the Alfa with a five-bladed screw was phenomenal – up to 45 knots. Maximum diving depth was 2,460ft. This was more than twice any other contemporary Western or Soviet boat. The problem with such a high turn of speed – the fastest ever achieved by an SSN – was the noise, which was likened to a jet engine roar.

The prototype was worked hard, frequently clocking up those impressive high speeds, under huge pressure at great depth. There were several problems with hull cracking and reactor 'freezes'. Pipework, torpedo launch equipment and even the compressed-air system were subjected to extreme stress. In 1974 the exhausted prototype was cut to pieces, allowing a full autopsy. The results were studied and adjustments made to both design and construction methods before a limited production run went ahead.

Admiral Gorshkov lavished attention and money on the Alfas – so expensive but highly capable, they were dubbed 'golden fish'. They were the elite of Russia's submarine force. No wonder, for the Alfas appeared to offer *technological* parity and even superiority over the West.

The CIA's Gerhardt Thamm eventually won his battle to convince the US Navy the titanium SSN was reality, confirming that Herb Lord (who had passed away in the meantime) was right. Thamm felt he proved 'that the Soviets had indeed built a submarine that was "better than good enough"'. Despite huge costs, 'the Soviets continued the Alfa project with tenacity unmatched by Western navies'.

The Americans were working on their 688 Class attack submarines (also known as Los Angeles Class). The first of these would be launched in 1974 and enter service in 1976, with another 37 commissioned by June 1989.

A major part of Britain's attempt to respond would depend on safely proving and bringing into service another brand-new kind of SSN.

The Royal Navy opted for quality rather than quantity as Britain's withered defence-industrial base and sickly economy could never hope to compete with Russian or American output.

The heavy responsibility of taking the first of a new Swiftsure Class of SSNs through trials and into service would ultimately fall on the shoulders of the 36-year-old Cdr Tim Hale.

It was late in the summer of 1971 that he was told his next appointment would be *Swiftsure*, in command, building at Barrow. She would be deep-diving and incorporating all that had been learned from earlier Royal Navy SSNs. Hale was keenly aware of the enormous challenges involved in taking a new submarine out of build, having also experienced that process in *Dreadnought* and *Warspite*, except now *he* was the captain.

The success or failure of the new SSN was down to him.

On 6 September 1971, the day before *Swiftsure* was launched at Barrow, Vickers laid on a private train from Euston to the Lake District for VIPs.

Hale got an extra-special treat as he was allowed to ride on the footplate from Oxenholme to Windermere, so fulfilling a boyhood dream of being an engine driver. With the wind in his hair, smuts and smoke in the air, he was captain of a steam-powered machine on his way to take charge of a steam-propelled hunter-killer. Except, in *Swiftsure*, the heat source was a nuclear reactor rather than a coal-fired boiler.

Later, looking at *Swiftsure*'s massive bulk on the slipway waiting to go into the water, Hale was struck by not only how far he had come, but also the Submarine Service.

'Sixteen years after joining my first submarine – an old Second World War-era S-boat of 600 tons – here I was, the Commanding Officer of the first of the new Swiftsure Class nuclear-powered submarines, which displaced 5,000 tons dived, was more than 270 feet long and with a breadth of 32ft. *Swiftsure* represented an enormous shift in technology, a major increase in the size, endurance and capabilities.'

Work creating Britain's new, deep-diving SSN had started way back at the beginning of the 1960s when the Admiralty set down requirements and began the process of detailed design. With a delay of several years caused by diversion of people and resources into creating Polaris SSBNs, the process of taking *Swiftsure* from drawing board to reality culminated in April 1969 with commencement of construction. She was the only new Royal Navy vessel ordered in the 1967–68 session of Parliament.

Originally known as SSNoX, the workers at Barrow soon realised she would be a 'super boat' – a kind of Fleet submarine not seen before. Not only would this second generation of British attack boats be faster than their predecessors, but stealth was important and they would be deeper-diving.

Admiral Sir Peter Herbert, who would become Flag Officer Submarines in the early 1980s, described the Swiftsures as 'particularly quiet', also conceding 'their diving depth is classified but is known to be great. The published speed [submerged] is in excess of 30 knots …'

Though 13ft shorter than the Improved Valiants – such as *Courageous* – the hull did not taper so much towards the stern. A major flaw in predecessor SSNs was cramming too much machinery into the aft ends. This new boat would be more elongated in shape, with extra room aft. The fin was shorter and fatter – this reduced a propensity for the boat to roll inordinately at high rates of turn when dived. Its strength also helped the SSN to break through ice. Later Swiftsure Class boats would eventually have a revolutionary pump jet propulsor employing a ducted multi-blade propeller.

Far quieter than a conventional screw – creating less cavitation – the pump-jet propulsor looked like a giant lampshade.

With the blades shielded there would also be less chance of any towed array sonar having its wire cut or becoming twisted around the boat's stern. *Swiftsure* did not start out with the propulsor though, as at the time of her construction it was still being trialled on the Valiant Class boat HMS *Churchill*. Some experts in submarine warfare speculated the next step would be to dispense with the propeller – a major generator of noise as it churned the sea – and use a pure water jet. The Russians were rumoured to be working on their own variant of the pump-jet propulsor, though they were thought to lag at least a decade behind the West.

Reflecting the push for a quieter SSN were retractable foreplanes on the bows of the boat. These could each be withdrawn inside a noise-absorbing compartment. The fact that they did not have exposed hydraulic ram mountings allowed a smoother flow of water over the hull.

A major enabler of deeper diving was a design that possessed fewer points via which the dreaded fingers of pressure at depth could gain purchase. A simpler and stronger hull – not as long as the Valiants but with increased internal volume – achieved this and fitting seawater-cooled equipment required fewer inlets. The heat signature was also reduced – fewer inlets meant fewer outlets for warmth to escape through and be picked up by infrared sensors on satellites.

The pressure hull was not waisted, like *Dreadnought* and the Valiants. *Swiftsure* was more of a big fat cylinder, with caps at either end. With a safe diving depth of more than 1,000ft, *Swiftsure* had a much deeper crush depth.

The PWR1 reactor was a new all-British design by Rolls-Royce Associates. It provided more power output for fewer revs per knot on the shaft (about 100 rpm maximum, as against *Dreadnought*'s 200 rpm). This gave *Swiftsure* a top speed of 30 knots dived. Lower rate of turn on the blade meant less chance of cavitation. Combined with a multi-bladed screw, less noise was created for greater speed, while – with more astern power – the boat was safer to handle. Or at least that was the theory and the job of proving it all against operational reality was down to Tim Hale.

Creating the crew of an S-boat was, no less than *Dreadnought*, a matter of assembling the brightest and the best, with the most junior officer in *Swiftsure*'s wardroom destined originally to be Doug Littlejohns.

Having won his Dolphins aboard the diesel HMS *Onyx*, serving as her torpedo and navigating officer, Lt Littlejohns saw that boat into refit at Portsmouth in December 1971. He was appointed for a short time to the staff of SM3 and after Christmas was meant to take the nuclear course at Greenwich and then go to *Swiftsure*.

A mystery ailment intervened. 'I was struck down by some unknown viral infection which kept me in the Royal Naval Hospital Haslar for two months of tests.' This was a bitter blow for someone so keen to graduate into nuclear submarines, but Littlejohns's morale was boosted by a visit from his future boss. 'I had never met Tim before but I was deeply touched by the fact that he took time out of his busy schedule to come and see an unknown junior Lieutenant who was about to take on one of the lowliest jobs in his wardroom.' By the time Littlejohns was discharged, the job in *Swiftsure* had gone to somebody else. Instead, after a period at Faslane, he spent six months in HMS *Oberon* before finally being sent to take the Greenwich nuclear course.

*

Swiftsure's first port of call following Contractor's Sea Trials (CST) was Faslane, on 30 September 1972. Hale deftly put the SSN on the sea wall in just four engine movements – no need for tugs to assist at all, and he felt it proved the brakes performed well.

'I rather fancied this as my best-ever alongside, and therefore was smiling smugly as I welcomed on board Captain SM3, who was Martin La Touche Wemyss. He proceeded to give me one of the biggest bollockings of my life, because ahead of us was *Repulse*, then the next Bomber due on patrol. If we had hit her (and damaged *Repulse*'s) propeller, national deterrent cover would have been breached. So I learned again that, as soon as you become cocky, something comes along and kicks you in the goolies.'

As would be expected in any cutting-edge vessel, there were a few teething problems during *Swiftsure*'s sea trials. These served to remind Cdr Hale that life was a process of constant education.

'As she was not my first SSN, I thought I knew it all. However, before leaving the basin in Barrow for the first time in September 1972, I found that she wouldn't turn as I expected and I was forced to take assistance from a tug. Eventually two feet were added to the lower rudder, so that she would steer properly while on the surface.'

Hale also didn't reckon on a clumsy Vickers worker giving everyone a fright. It happened during one of the *Swiftsure*'s early dives, on 16 October 1972, at 400ft down in an exercise area off the Clyde. The boat was operating on single main engine drive, with one of the turbines connected and a single turbo generator, when the Vickers man stood on a flood alarm in the diesel generator room.

Treating it as if for real – which must be the case when any alarm goes off in a submarine – Hale ordered: 'Full ahead, 20 degrees up. Blow main ballast tanks. Surface!'

It was four years and one week since *Warspite*'s emergency surface in the Barents. Looking at the digital depth gauge in the Control Room, Hale thought it seemed to be counting down rather slowly for a submarine hurtling up at a steep angle. He decided to lessen the angle of ascent.

'Ease angle from 20 to five degrees,' he told the planesman as *Swiftsure* hit 15 knots. Feeling the submarine breaking the surface, Hale instructed: 'Slow ahead.' The digital depth gauge still read 235ft.

Had they continued at the original speed and angle of climb, *Swiftsure* would have leapt out of the water and flopped back, probably plunging deeper than she had been originally. That was not something you wanted with a potential leak aboard; nor would it be easy to recover control.

Nerve-racking though it was, the captain's prompt actions and instinct for something not being right had proven to his sailors that he was a safe pair of hands. Hale did his utmost to remain attuned at all times to any looming problems, whether in the shiny new equipment or the men who operated it. Every single submariner was a vital cog in the war machine.

'On a quiet evening I might go around *Swiftsure* with a cigar, though I didn't smoke them very often. I would talk to the boys and they gave me good answers. They all knew how the boat worked. In a submarine everyone had to know their job, as any one man could sink the ship. As the CO you know the level of responsibility and it is high. You take the decisions and you have to live with them. Therefore, you better know your boat and your men. It's a team game.'

Swiftsure was commissioned on 17 April 1973, exactly ten years to the day that Britain's first Fleet submarine, *Dreadnought*, passed the same milestone. Hale's instinct for looming trouble asserted itself again when *Swiftsure* was returning to Faslane from a two-week shakedown cruise that had included a very deep dive, to around three times the deepest diving depth of a Second World War-era submarine. This feat was followed by the new SSN passing a safety inspection on 11 July 1973.

On the night of 12 July, north of Ireland, it was very dark, an overcast sky preventing starlight. The sea was rough and visibility poor. Leaving the boat in the very capable hands of the ship control team, Cdr Hale retired to his cabin to snatch some sleep. About two hours later he suddenly snapped awake and thought: *Something is wrong.*

Swinging his legs over the side of the bunk – glancing at the clock, which read 03.37 – he went into the Control Room.

On entry, he heard the Officer of the Watch say over the intercom from the bridge: 'Full astern ... Starboard 30.'

Seeing the search periscope was up, Hale grabbed the handles and pressed his eyes to the cups, finding a small cargo vessel looming out of the filthy night, about 50ft away. *Swiftsure* pivoted and the ship slid past with just feet to spare. The Perisher submarine command course had taught Hale to act by instinct, but this was something else.

'Perisher is a process of making sure a guy is safe in command. It gives him a driving licence. What kind of submarine captain he ultimately becomes is defined by his personality, his style of command and also the essence of something mysterious – a kind of magic – that nobody can break down into a scientific formula.'

On a stormy night just hours from home, via some innate sixth sense, Hale had been suddenly aware, even when asleep, that disaster loomed. Like some animal in the wild, attuned to even slight variations in its environment, he sensed things were not right.

The incident had all the ingredients for a disaster: bad weather, past three in the morning, everybody tired and on the way home, with a junior officer on watch. The Officer of the Watch did extremely well on this occasion. The team did not fail.

In March 1973 Doug Littlejohns had headed south from *Oberon* at Faslane to Barrow, where he joined the second S-boat, *Sovereign*. Laid down in September 1970, she was launched in February 1973 and was fitting out within sight of Tim Hale's new SSN, following completion of the latter's Contractor's Sea Trials. 'I watched Tim take *Swiftsure* to sea for the first time after commissioning. It was a moving experience for me, as all I could see in *Sovereign* was a large lump of metal, which had yet to become a vibrant SSN.'

Sovereign was destined for completion in the summer of 1974, but Littlejohns would not be with her. Not long after *Swiftsure* departed Barrow, he also made his own exit. Receiving a new appointment with no warning – known in the Navy as a pier-head jump – Littlejohns headed back to Faslane to join the diesel boat HMS *Otter* as her Navigator and First Lieutenant.

She was a submarine with a roguish reputation. Maybe it was the Scottish love of a dram or two to relieve the stresses and strains of life, but the boat absorbed a hard-drinking reputation during the course of her three-decade career. Completed in August 1962, by Scotts shipyard on the banks of the Clyde, in March 1964 *Otter* joined the older Porpoise Class boat *Narwhal* to carry out a Northern patrol. This was partly under Arctic ice, with all the familiar, nerve-shredding hazards. Finding a polynya, the two boats surfaced and submariners from *Otter* played cricket on the ice against the men of *Narwhal*. In 1966 she took part in Exercise Quick Pursuit with not only *Dreadnought* but also four other British diesels. Working alongside a dozen NATO submarines and aircraft from alliance nations, Quick Pursuit took place north of the Faroes and between Iceland and Norway. A rehearsal for intercepting Soviet submarines attempting to break out into the Atlantic, *Dreadnought* played both friend and foe for the diesels. She emphatically demonstrated the sheer speed and submerged endurance of SSNs.

Joining *Otter* seven years later, after a lot more patrols and exercises under her belt, Littlejohns was not unaware of the boat's work hard, play hard tradition. 'All ships and boats have a reputation, which normally starts in the building yard. For *Otter* we used to joke that a fresh-faced young man would get on the overnight sleeper train from London to join the submarine in Faslane and arrive in Glasgow with horns and a tail. But, while the crew was a challenge in harbour, at sea they were excellent.' *Otter* had failed the navigation part of operational work-up, which was why Littlejohns was appointed to her.

The boat soon provided an opportunity for Littlejohns to demonstrate his talent for unconventional solutions to unusual tactical problems. Some bright spark had come up with the idea of placing Mars bars, Kit Kats and other energy-giving 'nutty' inside a deactivated Mk9 mine, which would be laid by a submarine off a hostile shore. Special Forces teams subsequently landed were supposed to haul the mine out of the water, prise it open and offload its cargo of sweeties. Energy levels suitably boosted they would then sweep all before them while causing raiding mayhem. Anyway, that was the idea. The task of carrying out a trial run fell to *Otter*. She dropped the sweets-laden mine successfully in Loch Ewe, just a few hundred yards off the beach, between an island and a naval fuel jetty. Next up was landing the Special Forces, who would simulate a beach reconnaissance mission. Littlejohns scrutinised the charts and assessed it would be very risky taking *Otter* into such shallow waters at night, especially if there was no moon. To solve this problem, prior to *Otter* departing Faslane, one of her submariners acquired a small, oil-burning, yellow-painted road lamp. After laying the Mk9 mine, *Otter* surfaced behind the island, hidden from any observers at the jetty. Her Leading Radio Operator rowed ashore in a dinghy, tied the borrowed lamp to a pole, lit it and withdrew.

When *Otter* came in that night she carried not only the Special Forces team, to be landed once the submarine surfaced between the island and jetty, but also the the Flag Officer Submarines Navigator. He was assessing Littlejohns's skills to ensure he was up to the job.

The plan was executed perfectly. *Otter*'s CO, Lt Cdr Pat Burke, spotting the light through the periscope and gained an excellent bearing so the submarine could move in perfect safety to the drop-off point.

Oblivious to this trickery the FOSM Navigator pronounced Littlejohns had passed the test. While *Otter*'s mission had proved a success, and the Special Forces managed to haul the mine ashore, the Navy ultimately decided it was an awful lot of effort just to provide some nutty to the troops.

Beyond such messing about with half-cocked concepts, the deadly submarine construction competition continued unabated. This was

despite America and Russia negotiating Strategic Arms Limitation
Treaty I (SALT I), which was signed in 1972.

It was meant to help establish détente – the easing of strained political
relations between the two power blocs. With *The Basic Principles of Relations* as its foundation, it was devised to bind the USA and USSR into
doing 'their utmost to avoid military confrontations and to prevent the
outbreak of nuclear war'. The Americans – weary of Vietnam and with
an ailing economy – wanted to lock the Soviets into agreements limiting
their rapidly expanding military might. The Soviets regarded SALT as
setting the seal on their rise to superpower status. *If the Americans felt
obliged to negotiate, they must be in fear of Russia's power.*

The process of negotiating SALT had begun in 1969, shortly after
President Richard Nixon was elected. Four years earlier the Americans
possessed 464 Submarine-Launched Ballistic Missiles (SLBMs), while
the Soviets could offer only 107 (with shorter-range and less powerful
warheads).

By 1969 the Soviets were catching up, fielding a more effective SLBM,
with the potential to put 240 at sea, compared with the American
arsenal of 656 SLBMs. There were thousands more nuclear weapons in
land-based silos and carried by aircraft.

The advent of Multiple Independently Targetable Re-entry Vehicles
(MIRVs) meant each missile could actually deploy several warheads,
carrying them aloft like passengers in a bus before disgorging them over
targets.

The Russians, who had traditionally built bigger rockets because of
their inability to pack a big enough explosive yield into previous models
of smaller warheads, now had the advantage of being able to fit more
MIRVs to each missile than the Americans.

In an analysis marked 'Top Secret' the US State Department (under
the direction of Dr Henry Kissinger) estimated that by 1978 – without
some form of arms limitation agreement – the Soviets would be able to
strike first and kill 139 million Americans. If the USA struck first, then
87 million Americans would be killed in the subsequent retaliation (the
enemy having fewer missiles to fire back). This was the chilling mathematics of Mutually Assured Destruction (or MADness). Of particular
concern to the Americans was the Soviet Union's development of Anti-
Ballistic Missile (ABM) systems, which threatened to neuter Polaris
and Intercontinental Ballistic Missiles, removing the West's advantage
in potential killing power. The Americans developed the new Poseidon missile system and made plans for an even more advanced weapon

named Trident. In Britain the government decided it was cheaper, and politically easier, to upgrade Polaris. The Royal Navy pointed out the Super Antelope modification would make Polaris missiles heavier – reducing range – requiring that SSBNs operate closer to the Soviet Union. This would probably expose them to greater risk of detection by Russian submarines and surface vessels. An agreement between the USA and USSR in 1972 saw limitations placed on ABMs, but in conditions of great secrecy the UK administration gave the green light to Chevaline (as Super Antelope became known). Options for replacing Polaris altogether by the 1990s were also studied.

In October 1973 the Yom Kippur War saw a massive ground assault by Syria and Egypt – without explicit Soviet backing – against Israel. In the eastern Mediterranean each side's missile craft engaged in battle. It provoked increased tension at sea between the Russians and the US–British axis, with American nuclear forces put at Defense Condition 3 (DEFCON 3), an alert status just one step down from that declared during the Cuban Missile Crisis. The Soviets surged dozens of surface warships and 25 of their submarines into the Mediterranean via the Strait of Gibraltar.

The Soviets suffered a merchant vessel sunk and authorised their warships to fire on Israeli naval vessels and aircraft (leading to some minor clashes). As Egyptian troops and tanks mounted a formidable thrust across the Suez Canal and deep into the Sinai – with Syrian armour also swarming over the Golan Heights – some in Israel's high command advocated using covertly developed battlefield nuclear weapons. Egypt asked Moscow to intervene militarily. Alarmed, the Americans said they would step in on the side of the Israelis if Russia did that. Both superpowers mounted a massive air shipment of conventional arms.

In the UK Vulcan nuclear-armed bombers were ordered to take off and fly to their loitering stations. At sea British and American Polaris submarines were advised of the increase in tensions.

Having reached boiling point again, the Cold War simmered down. Both Moscow and Washington were scared by where the Yom Kippur clash might lead. Much to everyone's relief, the latest of several ceasefires finally held.

As the Yom Kippur War had raged 24-year-old Lt Dan Conley made his way to Faslane to join *Swiftsure*, in which he was to be Sonar Officer. Conley had actually first set eyes on the new SSN when he sailed into Barrow aboard *Oberon*, returning home from the Far East in early 1972, to receive a short refit at the Cumbrian yard. Conley had done his apprenticeship in the diesels and was now graduating into the nuclear-powered Submarine Service.

A change in working uniform was one obvious manifestation of his transformation. 'It was back to a different ball game altogether,' he realised. 'A number of officers appointed to nuclear submarines had to make a radical transition from service in the Far East. Out there, in an "End of the Empire"-style scenario they had enjoyed dinners of lobster thermidor and cold beer in the Officers' Club. Now, with the withdrawal from East of Suez, it was back home and serving in cutting-edge submarines. It was time to get down to the real Cold War business after our time in the sun. In a diesel I typically wore a short-sleeved shirt or a fisherman's jersey and a pair of lightweight slacks. Other crew members dressed in what was most comfortable for them. It could lead to an eccentric and eclectic mix. In the engine room you might find crew dressed in Arab garb or as French onion sellers.' Now it was proper naval uniforms.

Conley went to Greenwich, for tailored courses to prepare – like Hale, Forsyth and Littlejohns before him – for service in the cutting-edge, modern Navy. They included a nine-week nuclear-engineering course – ten months shorter than Hale's because Conley wasn't qualifying as a nuclear reactor watch keeper – and also further training in sonar operation. Joining *Swiftsure*, Conley found Cdr Hale well aware of the make-or-break nature of his responsibility. The captain rode through his doubts and Conley was impressed with the CO's 'supreme self-confidence'. He felt Hale's 'nuclear engineering qualifications ideally suited him to the job of a taking a first-of-class boat into service'.

The XO by this time was Lt Cdr Geoffrey Biggs. He and Tim Hale had been friends since the early 1960s, when they were both hard-living young submarine officers. Conley had encountered Biggs in *Sealion*, appreciating his help during tough times.

Now Hale was delighted to have Biggs as his second-in-command.

For a start they shared a love of horse racing. *Swiftsure*'s new XO – who had recently commanded the diesel boat *Orpheus* – was said to have been 'the only naval officer to have his own box at Ascot'.

The son of Admiral Sir Hilary Worthington Biggs, he joined the Royal Navy in 1956, passing out from Dartmouth two years later and becoming a submariner in 1960.

Although at Charterhouse School his nickname was 'Shag', relating to his invariably scruffy manner of dress, Biggs was known in the Navy as 'Beastie'. A lover of good living and the ladies, Biggs enjoyed his time at Greenwich enormously, as it opened up the capital for nocturnal exploration.

Despite Biggs's reputation as a bon viveur, Hale recognised that his XO was a highly professional submarine officer. 'His normally scruffy appearance belied a thoroughly organised approach to running a brand-new, first-of-class SSN. Geoff's seamanship and technical knowledge, his ship-handling both surfaced and dived, meant that I could, and did, hand over command to him on operations. This was the whole point of having a command-qualified CO in SSNs and SSBNs.'

Lieutenant Conley found *Swiftsure* herself 'a tremendous machine, of that there was no doubt'. Yet to prove that she could deliver the promised performance, *Swiftsure* would, he realised, be required to push the envelope, during a series of trials 'that had a degree of risk'.

It was better to push the performance envelope of the boat – and her weapons – in controlled conditions, away from the foe, than to find something did not work during an encounter with a Soviet submarine.

In October 1973, Hale took HMS *Swiftsure* south, stopped off briefly at Devonport, then set course for Gibraltar. His SSN was destined for torpedo-firing trials on ranges off the Rock, deeper than any British submarine had ever tried before. The aim was to prove both Mk23 and Mk24 'Tigerfish' wire-guided torpedoes could be fired on the move, at certain speeds and particular depths. It was the first time out of UK waters for the submarine. Cold War submarine crews – aware they lived life on the edge – were especially ready for the unexpected during sea trials in a totally new submarine. Firing torpedoes at speed was always a tricky prospect and extreme depths made it an even more hazardous enterprise – it was a process replete with risk, as Hale freely admits.

'It is no exaggeration to say the first torpedo firings with *Swiftsure* at 1,000ft were very hairy. Having a bow cap open at that depth creates a hole in the hull 21 inches in diameter, so the full sea pressure is on the rear door of the torpedo tube.'

Hale was pleased the weapon discharged okay but *Swiftsure* was limited to 6 knots when, instead of disconnecting, the outboard dispenser hung off the front of the boat. It required the bowcap to stay open. At that speed it takes a long time to surface from 1,000ft, with extreme pressure on the torpedo tube rear door. When such a technical limitation presents itself, the focus narrows to the safety of the boat and her men rather than proceeding with any further trials.

As *Swiftsure* finally approached periscope depth Lt Conley was charged with overseeing a sonar check to make sure the coast was clear – in some of the busiest shipping lanes in the world. Fortunately there were no other vessels about and *Swiftsure* surfaced safely.

A maximum diving depth of 1,000ft was average among the sort of submarines Swiftsure Class boats faced in the Cold War. It is no secret the maximum depth achieved by the US Navy's Los Angeles Class SSNs was in excess of 1,400ft. For the Royal Navy it was essential to have a submarine capable of launching a torpedo that deep, and a weapon that could both hunt and kill in those zones.

By 1973 there were high hopes the sophisticated Mk24 Tigerfish could replace the less than awesome Mk23, giving Britain a one-shot, one-kill decisive edge. Precise details of its capabilities were top-secret, but it was likely Tigerfish could sustain 50 knots for 10 miles.

The potential of Tigerfish was awesome, which was probably why it was so hard to get it right. Eventually the favoured tactic would be to fire two, no more than 20 seconds apart, with one assigned by the onboard combat system to attack and the other held in reserve.

The operators on board the launching submarine – each watching a small screen with the relative positions of both weapon and target displayed – would steer them on parallel courses. Both Tigerfish would run at high speed until they got close to the target, when a signal to reduce speed would pulse along their wires. Slower speed reduced propulsion noise and made them harder to detect. It also made it easier for the Tigerfish sonar to scan for the target and lock on. Use of the torpedo's own active sonar would, though, be avoided if possible because active pinging was a giveaway. If possible the controllers would guide each weapon almost to impact, using the SSN's own passive sonar and combat system.

When a Tigerfish sent a signal back along the wire to indicate it had acquired a target, the Weapons Control Officer could opt to either let it guide itself or retain control. The torpedo would be fitted with either an impact fuse, requiring it to actually hit the target, or a proximity fuse. In the latter case the sheer force of the explosion – creating a large gas bubble that lifted and violently flexed the target – would it was hoped be enough to break the back of the enemy submarine (or surface warship).

The Navy claimed that Tigerfish could be left in a flooded-up tube for a year, without any need for maintenance, and still be ready to fire. A Tigerfish reload – and 20 reloads were carried by *Swiftsure* – could, according to a head of the Submarine Service, be accomplished in the extraordinary time of 15 seconds. But, as Admiral Sir Peter Herbert acknowledged, 'it is unlikely, with modern weapons such as wire-guided Tigerfish, that rapid reloading would be necessary ...'

Those who had to operate the machinery and carry out the potentially dangerous task of reloading might dispute that it could be done in 15 seconds. It was a complex process, even with a good, well worked-up team. The tube would have to be drained, a very heavy torpedo moved from its rack and inserted into the tube. If it was a Tigerfish – rather than a Mk8 – the guidance wire would have to be attached.

In combat the boat would, anyway, withdraw after firing a torpedo to acquire stealth before attacking again.

Submarine versus submarine encounters would, it was thought, take place at ranges beyond a couple of miles. The chances of success with a free-running weapon at that distance – even with a homing capability – were next to zero. Wire-guidance was essential though it was felt the Soviets – who had also developed wire-guided weapons – might try to close the range and fire a salvo of unguided torpedoes. Some might pass close enough to acquire and home in on the target.

Tigerfish was the answer but its troubled development would vex many a British submarine captain hoping he could match his superb boat with an equally deadly weapon.

While the requirement for Tigerfish was issued in 1961, one submariner noted with barely suppressed incredulity: 'It took more than 20 years to appear on the scene in anything approaching a reliable or effective form.' Trouble with the wire dispenser, as discovered by *Swiftsure* in October 1973, was but one step on the long road to getting it right.

If the British could stray into the Barents Sea to spy on new naval vessels conducting trials and weapons tests, it was only to be expected the Soviets would attempt to repay the disfavour.

During *Swiftsure*'s torpedo firings off Gibraltar in October 1973, she was dogged persistently on three days by a Kashin Class destroyer carrying out sonar sweeps. Hale managed to lose the interloper quite swiftly on day one but on day two the Soviet warship was more persistent.

Swiftsure's CO scrutinised his shadow via the attack periscope, finding the Kashin had taken station on the port beam about 1,500 yards off, with a Kanin Class destroyer also lurking at two miles' distance.

'I could see the Kashin was a very tidy ship, well handled, with better station keeping than our designated Royal Navy escort frigate. I wondered why our escort warship couldn't run theirs off.'

Hale lowered the periscope, went deep and ran at speed, losing the Kashin. After a sonar check to make sure the Soviet was not directly overhead, *Swiftsure* surfaced. On day three, during a period when *Swiftsure* was surfaced, the Kashin came charging up fast from astern, but then drew off to a respectable distance. On the bridge to get a look at her, Cdr Hale told the signalman to send an Aldis lamp message using International Code.

'Follow me into harbour.'

The Kashin replied, also by lamp: 'No, you follow me.'

Hale sent back: 'Farewell.'

Swiftsure's captain felt he would have enjoyed meeting the CO of the Kashin for he was 'clearly a good ship handler, behaved decorously, and was very competent'.

Otter needed to be tough in order to handle the role of target submarine and was specially built to take hits from practice torpedoes. She was unique among the Oberon Class in having a steel casing rather than one made of glass fibre laminate or aluminium.

That was why in early 1974 she made an Atlantic crossing, heading for duty on a firing range off Andros Island in the Bahamas.

Although the island was located in the British-administered Bahamas, the Americans were permitted to establish and develop the Atlantic Undersea Test and Evaluation Center (AUTEC) under a US–UK agreement (rubber-stamped by the Bahamian government) in the early 1960s.

The centrepiece of the facility was the Tongue of the Ocean (TOTO), a trench between 700 and 1,100 fathoms deep, 110 nautical miles long and around 20 nautical miles broad.

Shielded from large swells and almost current-free, TOTO also possessed minimal background noise due to lack of surface traffic. In short, it offered perfect conditions for testing submarine sonar and torpedoes, and also a safe environment for manoeuvring at speed.

For *Otter* the assignment to AUTEC was not a particularly well-timed deployment. A Faslane-based submarine with Scottish crew, she was to depart on 1 January. Littlejohns ordered all her men to be aboard by 14.00 – a deliberate ploy to sober them up. It was no mean feat, given the Scots' love of a few drinks to bring the New Year in.

On their return *Otter*'s submariners were ordered to get their heads down to sleep off the booze. This was followed by a restorative meal, before the boat sailed in foul weather. Littlejohns saw *Otter*'s men were still not happy but, regardless of hangovers and queasy stomachs, they sailed out into the teeth of a force 10 gale. Unfortunately, she could not seek relief from the raging ocean by diving and going deep. *Otter* was required to make the passage on the surface, not only because it was faster to do so – 10–11 knots surfaced compared to 6 knots dived – but also as part of water space management. This would ensure she did not trespass submerged into areas where friendly boats were operating.

The bridge watch keepers were continuously drenched and it was impossible to cook safely in the galley or to sit down and eat in civilised fashion. *Otter*'s crew lived on boiled eggs for a fortnight, supplemented by a traditional rough-weather dish: Pot Mess.

This had many variations, but all the ingredients – typically stewed steak, spuds, chopped tomatoes, veg, baked beans and spaghetti – came from a can. Best of all, it could be eaten from a mug.

Regardless of the prohibition on diving, an engine defect – requiring a cylinder head removal – could only be tackled with better stability. That wasn't possible on the surface. *Otter* submerged to carry out repairs – despite not being cleared to dive – and stayed down for six hours. During this time Littlejohns was not impressed by Soviet stealth (or rather lack of it).

'We detected two Soviet submarines – an Echo II and a possible Yankee Class boat, which went past at very close range. The Atlantic is a huge ocean and we shouldn't have heard them with our sonar set, but the Russians were noisy because they were both making quite high speeds.'

As he had now been in submarines for some years, the ethos of the Silent Service was firmly embedded in Littlejohns, its way both of working and of living. Above all, he was attuned to its people and their psychology.

'Officers, if seaman branch, wanted to be submarine captains. A bigger salary motivated some ratings, but most enjoyed the relaxed attitude in boats compared to the more rigid approach of surface ships. Submariners are, though, definitely a different breed. Officers and ratings alike, they love the adrenalin, the action, and informality. Underpinning it all is quite a rigid system of procedures and command. It is the iron fist inside the velvet glove. Submariners are responsive to good leadership. They take pride in their work. In the surface navy the pressure of work is different, less intense. There is great pride in the fact that there are no passengers in a submarine.'

Otter's work hard, play hard mentality was always a useful valve to let off steam. When the British boat's men were on a break from target boat duties in April 1974, they were guests of honour for a Diesel Boats Forever Association party at a mansion in Fort Lauderdale, Florida. Because the Americans by then operated an all nuclear-powered submarine force they loved entertaining British diesel boat submariners. As the party became more boisterous, Littlejohns assessed that pre-emptive action was required.

'The boys were getting a bit rowdy, so I told them to fall in and show the locals what we were made of, with me leading the crew of *Otter* into the swimming pool fully dressed. We all got wet but they cooled down and it only cost me a pair of Prince of Wales check trousers.'

In January 1974, *Swiftsure* followed *Otter* across the Atlantic, like the diesel boat also operating out of Cape Canaveral, Florida. Her objective was not to try and hit *Otter* with torpedoes but to use AUTEC for sonar and manoeuvring trials. After some maintenance courtesy of the US Navy, in January and February Cdr Hale put *Swiftsure* through her paces. The SSN dived to depths in excess of 1,000ft and clocked up speeds of between 5 and 28 knots, depending on the manoeuvre being executed. It was a hell of a rollercoaster and along for the ride was a team of boffins from the Admiralty Experimental Works (AEW). They were asking Hale and his team to perform certain evolutions, but the captain of the submarine remained very much the boss. Hale was not going to let their desire to push things fatally screw the boat up.

'You cannot blindly let the trials team dictate what manoeuvres are carried out, as they will destroy the ship. We did fast runs with increasing amounts of port then starboard rudder to see what rate of turn could be achieved and what ship attitude occurred – for example, did she adopt bow up or down? We discovered that starboard rudder caused bigger bow-up angle than port rudder, which was different to predictions by the naval architects. Also, starboard pulled off more speed. It seemed starboard wheel would be useful in pulling out of steep bow-down angle in an emergency. At speed, we also got significant snap roll.' This last quality was the equivalent of an aircraft banking into a turn.

For Hale, *Swiftsure*'s Bahamas roller coaster reinforced salient truths about seamanship in a nuclear-powered submarine. 'The crew of an SSN or SSBN does have to possess great technical knowledge – of the nuclear power plant, hydrodynamics, sensors and weapons – but their high-tech vehicle is also a ship at sea, and it operates in three dimensions. If it goes to all stop, a surface ship will, in normal circumstances, float. Not so in a submarine or aircraft. You have to keep the thing moving and put it on the interface of the fluids – water and air – in order to achieve stability. The need for awareness and competence is thus paramount in order to stay alive.'

AUTEC might have offered perfect test conditions in a comparatively benign environment compared with the Barents, but it didn't means things couldn't go badly wrong. As *Swiftsure* headed out into the trench to see how far the performance envelope could be stretched,

Hale thought of himself as a test pilot, flying a large complex vehicle and reflected: *If it goes tits up the buck will stop with me.*

During earlier sea trials it was discovered too much rudder, with snap roll, potentially caused the SSN's two turbo generators (TGs) to trip out on low lube oil pressure. If the boat was in full power state, at high speed, with Fast Main Coolant Pumps operating, loss of the TGs simultaneously would cause total loss of coolant flow in the reactor. There would be an automatic shutdown, followed by emergency cooling from which recovery of the reactor system would be very difficult. Avoiding such a disaster was uppermost in Hale's mind as he took *Swiftsure* deep and wound up the speed. He accepted that the only way of demonstrating the risk was in controlled conditions, levelling off at 500ft to permit depth excursions in both directions – manoeuvre room above and below. 'When the trials team wanted high-speed turns with over 20 degrees rudder, I agreed to do it, but with key people closed up on the planes and in the Manoeuvring Room. They were all warned what we could expect. We did the turns in three-quarters power state – slow pumps maintaining the flow of coolant through the reactor. After the snap roll had steadied, into the turn, which was to port, the starboard TG tripped out. This was shortly followed by the port TG tripping out. But we were by then 2S/2S – two slow pumps on each loop – and were therefore system safe. The reactor stayed on line and we got the TGs back on. I had already taken the ship up to 200ft and levelled off at slower speed so we could put her on the roof if necessary.'

After the previous sea trials, baffles had been put in the lube oil sumps to limit the free surface effect – which led to loss of lubrication from the TGs – but it appeared snap roll alone was not the cause. The AEW team leader, Bob Charlesworth, and Hale reckoned it must also be the high rate of turn. It was an operational limitation, which Hale later explained very carefully to Flag Officer Submarines. *Swiftsure* would be operated bearing that potential problem in mind, with her crew ready to take action during similar manoeuvres. It was overcome in due course, ensuring the Swiftsure Class could operate to their full potential speed and manoeuvring, which would be essential in any contest against an opponent.

While *Swiftsure* – a brand-new kind of boat still feeling her way – was restricted in the main to sea trials and exercises, there were occasional operational forays. One of these saw her sent in early August 1974 to find and trail the notorious 'West of Ireland Whiskey'. The elderly diesel-electric boat, which traditionally lurked in the UK's North West Approaches, occasionally trespassed into the Irish Sea itself.

Aside from acting as a waypoint for Soviet nuclear submarines breaking out into the Atlantic, this old hand from the Baltic Fleet was also used to train new submarine captains how to operate in enemy waters.

As Sonar Officer, Dan Conley felt *Swiftsure*'s mission was a useful early test for equipment and the submariners operating it. Despite her age, when dived and cruising on her battery, Conley found, the Soviet boat was 'very difficult to detect'.

'We did achieve a contact, partly by chance, and we held on to her for half an hour in the Shetland–Orkney gap.'

The British SSN had also received some prior information from a passing Maritime Patrol Aircraft on where to look. 'I had seen this lad before,' recalled Hale. 'The Soviets ran N–S on longitude 13 degrees west, and so we plotted his approach, went to look and found him on active sonar at 18 miles.' While *Swiftsure* soon lost the contact, Conley felt the Whiskey was probably later detected 'snorting somewhere to the west of the Outer Hebrides'.

Hale believed in full disclosure on board, frequently telling his sailors what was going on. Should *Swiftsure* engage in the tense business of shadowing a Soviet submarine they needed to be sharp. In such an instance he would tell them via a broadcast: 'We are going to do a trail. Those of you who need to get your heads down then do so.'

Having experienced the insidious effects of fatigue during trails of Soviet submarines in Northern waters – and also watch-keeping on long-distance submerged transits by *Dreadnought* and *Warspite* – Hale was acutely aware of the fine line between admirable stamina and foolish risk-taking.

'I can remember one occasion in particular when we had been in the trail for four or five days. I knew I was tired and I thought that the rest of the crew would also be very tired, too. I said: "We are going to pull off and go deep so we can sleep."'

Aside from taking *Swiftsure* through sea trials – running risks while proving her systems – and occasionally searching out Russian submarines, Hale also tried her out on underwater looks.

He would be on the periscope as he took the SSN under warships, giving instructions that required nerves of steel not only on his part but also on the planesman's. There was no room for error. It was a daring, precision dance, the captain of the SSN relying entirely on his highly trained team while the sailors put their faith in his fine judgement.

'You are doing, let's say, 8-10 knots, with the big search scope up, going in the wake of the target vessel. The guys have done it before, so know what you are doing. So you are saying, for example: "Left two degrees, right two degrees. Take half a knot off." It is rather like a delicately executed arabesque – the Control Room team is the dance troupe, their timing, their reliance on one another, is absolute. *The underwater look is very precise.* Let's say the target vessel was doing 10 knots. You would do 10.5, run under his keel to his sonar dome, take pics, then come back to 9.5 knots, let him slide past you, between four and six feet above. Occasionally you might do it on a submarine, but have to be careful as he might dive on you.

'In such circumstances you would have 5,000 tons of SSN to keep at depth within six inches of variation. Then you have got a ship on top of you that will go up and down depending on the sea state. You might – at some stages – have just two or three inches of clearance.

'Even so, it is all done quite fast, speed controlled by revs. The man on the throttle has to be extremely good – maintain the boat at exactly the right speed. Planes must be right, hydraulics right. It is a good game; a dangerous game. Focus is complete. No time for nerves. You see the air bubbles, sonar dome, the target's screws or some other protrusion sliding past your periscope.' A key part of the underwater look was that the target – whether Soviet or NATO vessel during an exercise – should not know. With the former, evidence of success would soon be logged in an intelligence database. With the latter, submariners always delighted in presenting an unsuspecting friendly frigate captain with evidence, in the form of a still image taken just inches from his warship's screws.

*

Having successfully taken *Swiftsure* through sea trials, and commissioned her into service, Cdr Hale departed to take up an appointment as Flotilla Operations Officer for Flag Officer Submarines. His shore-based workplace was Fort Blockhouse at Gosport, the Submarine Service headquarters, overseeing global missions for the RN's submarines. Being the captain of a brand-new type of SSN was the pinnacle of Hale's career so far. Reflecting on his time in command of her, Hale felt *Swiftsure* was 'a brilliant design, a world-beater, but she could be a prima donna and required sensitive handling. I was a tired man when I left after two years and eight months in command.'

Dan Conley continued to serve in *Swiftsure*, under a fresh captain, Cdr Keith Pitt. As the most cutting-edge, silent, deepest diving and fastest SSN in the British fleet, *Swiftsure* was designated to perform intelligence gathering missions in the Soviet backyard. Between August 1974 and summer 1975, Cdr Pitt put all his efforts into training himself and his men to ensure the boat was fully capable. He was relentless, trying to think of all the angles, applying anything that might reduce the chances of being caught in the Barents.

A potential vulnerability was the Electronic Support Measures (ESM) mast – the primary means of sucking in electronic intelligence – being shorter than the periscopes.

'He was worried about showing too much periscope when it [the ESM mast] was up,' said Conley, 'which it would be for the majority of our time on station. Pitt came up with the idea of sitting on a box on castors at deck level, to look through the main periscope.'

This meant *Swiftsure* could maintain the scope at the same height as the ESM mast. It aimed to ensure the risk of counter-detection was reduced but did not necessarily make for effective periscope watch-keeping. 'If the submarine was rolling,' Conley explained, 'the box-on-castors would skitter about all over the place. It was very hard for anyone using the periscope to retain control.'

Even so, Conley witnessed *Swiftsure*'s watch keepers becoming 'an awful lot sharper with working the ESM/periscope combo'. Much to his chagrin, he didn't get to go on the boat's first Barents patrol.

He was not *that* annoyed to be leaving because he was going off to the submarine command course, although he did regret not doing at least one trip up North beforehand. Within the Submarine Service, talent was spotted early and nurtured. While Pitt and Biggs put forward Conley for Perisher, it was Capt. R. R. 'Tubby' Squires, CO of SM3, and first captain of *Warspite* back in the early 1960s, who recommended

Littlejohns for the course, which he would take in early 1975 – just three years and 11 months after he qualified as a submariner. Conley followed a few months later. It was Rob Forsyth, fresh from being XO of *Repulse*, who would decide whether or not they had the Right Stuff to become submarine captains.

In the nick of time, just as the warship's bows were about to crush it, the periscope disappeared under the water.

From his chair on the frigate's bridge – silhouetted by the stark light flooding in through its big windows – the captain gave orders for the helm to go hard over, bringing his ship around in a tight circle.

The lookouts spotted a swirl of water indicating where the submarine had been while the captain used binoculars to scrutinise the rapidly dispersing disturbance. He ignored a voice in his head urging caution, to avoid damaging his own ship. Ordering full ahead, he aimed straight for the spot where the target most likely lurked.

In the Control Room of the submarine, a young officer held the mental image of where he anticipated the warship would be.

Surely his opponent would now be at a safe enough distance to risk coming back up to periscope depth? The scope slid up from its well and he snapped the handles down, twirling it to where he expected to see his quarry. A gigantic, creaming bow wave filled his entire view through the scope. *It appeared he would be the killed rather than the killer.*

The warship was seconds away from ramming, but a wiser head saved him, diesel submarine *Onyx* and the lives of all 75 men aboard.

Even as the eager young buck stared into the jaws of disaster the boat's planesmen had been ordered to take her to a safer depth. The NATO frigate passed safely overhead, missing *Onyx*'s fin by only a few feet.

Rob Forsyth had left it to the last moment, but his confidence in the highly experienced submarine crew coping with a narrow margin of error had been total. He took the trainee submarine captain to one side and told him: 'If you come up again too early, then you are dead – literally and figuratively.'

It was all part of the Royal Navy's notorious Perisher submarine command course. As 'Teacher' at the beginning of each week Cdr Forsyth visited warships playing targets, briefing their Commanding Officers to head for the periscope of the Perisher boat, without hesitation or deviation.

'It is safer if you try and hit it,' Forsyth explained, adding for extra emphasis, 'just go straight for the scope.' Prior to the recent attack run

Forsyth had called the frigate captain on the radio. 'Do you recall the briefing I gave you?' he asked, hearing an affirmative response.

'I want you to be extra compliant on the next one. Put the wheel hard over, make a tighter turn than normal and head for where you think we might be.' Warship captains always needed extra reassurance that they would not cause any harm to the submarine no matter how hard they charged. This time the safety margin was cut extra fine, to teach a hard lesson.

The aspiring submarine captain in question had developed the bad habit of coming up too quickly, without prior checks using his sonar to ensure the 'enemy' really was at a safe distance.

Forsyth felt that in all other respects he was competent and also safe. 'But he does need to be frightened at some stage,' he thought, 'so that he knows his limits.'

Shock delivered, the student submarine commander believed it was all over for him, that he had failed and would soon be ordered off the course.

Over the next few weeks it became evident he had learned his lesson. He went to the other end of the spectrum, with Forsyth finding he must now encourage him to bring the boat back up. In the end, related Forsyth, 'he passed Perisher with flying colours and was a better and wiser man for the experience'.

The Royal Navy still required a new breed of hunter-killers who could strike hard and fast, getting away to fight another day. There could be no fair-weather sailors in their ranks. They were selected or rejected with utter ruthless efficiency. The Royal Navy was by 1975 running two Perisher courses per year, using a pair of boats, with half a dozen prospective submarine commanders aboard each, under the tutelage of a highly experienced officer. Cdr Forsyth was one of two Teachers – the other was Cdr Toby Frere, who had also been at sea during the Cuban Missile Crisis.

Forsyth had come up through the Submarine Service at a time when the majority of boats were not nuclear-powered. His period in command of the diesel boat *Alliance* and in *Repulse* as XO fully demonstrated his fitness to become Teacher. Those appointed to the role were considered by their Submarine Service peers to be above average. Others might be more aggressive or supremely ambitious, but those qualities were not necessarily what Teacher needed.

Forsyth was unruffled in the face of danger. Professional, with an eye for detail and understanding of submariner psychology, he could be empathetic when needed but would not hesitate to weed out those who could not handle command. It was an enormous accolade to be Teacher – driving an SSN or being Teacher were *the* two top jobs in the Submarine Service. Forsyth hoped that if he could put in a successful term he would get an SSN command.

On his maiden attack run as Teacher, Forsyth found he was as tense as the student. By the end of day one each student had completed three or four attacks, while Forsyth's tally was 20.

The Perisher consisted of four parts. The first sought to broaden the horizons of the participants beyond the world of the submarine. They learned how their boat fitted into the bigger picture, operating with (and against) surface units, also in co-operation with Shackleton and Nimrod MPAs. Such missions served the higher tactical and strategic purpose in Anti-Submarine Warfare and other combat disciplines. The 'Perishers' – as the students were also known – visited surface warships and flew in the RAF aircraft.

Ashore in HMS *Dolphin* and at Faslane were full-size simulations of submarine control rooms – attack team trainers – used during Part Two to teach the basic skills of commanding a submarine during an attack. Mistakes could be made in a safe environment before plunging into the decisive Part Three (at sea). After each session in the trainer, a student was required to evaluate how well he had performed, writing it up in a log, which Teacher would examine. It was important the Perishers learned how to be self-critical, because that faculty was considered vital in submarine command. Forsyth thought any man who believed he made no mistakes was dangerous.

Each night there would be lectures by Teacher. Topics ranged from how a captain should deal with a sailor arrested during a run ashore in a foreign port, to writing a confidential report on a subordinate officer who deserved to be sacked. Mundane matters, such as how to conduct a cleanliness inspection of a boat, were also discussed.

Part Three, also known as the Periscope Course, was the maker or breaker of careers. It involved the Perishers facing an increasingly complex range of attack scenarios.

It was quite a journey and, for Rob Forsyth, delivering a new batch of command-qualified submarine officers would be a supreme achievement – as well as guarantee his career would have a future, too.

There might be a few bumps along the way and in the days when diesel boats were the training vessels, rather than expensive nuclear-powered submarines, a certain amount of damage was permitted. Flag Officer Submarines in 1975 was Vice Admiral Sir Iwan Raikes, who, as a Second World War veteran, was no stranger to risky exploits.

Briefing Forsyth on what was required of Teacher, Raikes remarked: 'Try not to hit anything but if you do I will back you up.'

It helped that submarines selected as Perisher platforms were well-run vessels and to prepare for the honour had received extra training to constantly operate on the edge.

Going aboard *Onyx* – whose captain was Lt Cdr Dickie Jones, an Australian who had transferred to the RN – Cdr Forsyth had already decided on an incremental approach. Starting off at the lower end of the risk scale, he would slide up to the higher end when sure the submarine crew could handle it. He had willing partners in *Onyx's* Ship's Company, as they wanted to prove theirs was the best submarine attack team in the Service.

The day before the Perisher began, Forsyth mustered *Onyx's* hands in the boat's torpedo spaces while she was alongside at Faslane.

'I am going to borrow your boat from your captain,' he told them. 'I am always going to look after you – you must always look after me, even when I ask you to do odd things. You will depend on me; I will depend on you.' It seemed to do the trick. When Forsyth went aboard the following day he sensed an air of eager anticipation. The fully seasoned submariners of *Onyx* would be swift to judge whom they might want as future captains, and who should definitely *not* be allowed to command a boat. They soon had their own sweepstake running on which Perishers they thought would make it. Seasoned crews were rarely wrong in their assessment.

No sailor wanted somebody who could not do the job getting through, as their lives might one day depend on that person. Teacher didn't want to know the betting odds, though, as he had to objectively assess the Perishers.

During attack team trainer sessions ashore he had already begun to understand them a little better, so he had a rough idea of their capabilities.

One man whom it was very important for Cdr Forsyth to keep on side was *Onyx's* captain. He had to hand his boat over to Teacher during each attack, so mutual trust was vital. In theory Teacher would not put the submarine into a hazardous situation, but in reality the whole point was to do just that. Dodging hard-charging frigates in mock attacks was the only way to test the students properly. Forsyth reflected that even he would be required to operate at the limit of his ability, in order to stretch them.

For the first week at sea, during each attack run *Onyx*'s captain hung around in the background of the Control Room, looking on like a concerned parent watching his children in the care of another adult. Lieutenant Commander Jones trusted Teacher, but, even so, it was *his* boat, *his* crew. Satisfied Forsyth knew what he was doing, the CO retired to his cabin and stayed out of the way, busying himself with paperwork. Even then he would have an ear cocked to what was going on in the Control Room.

At sea each student assumed the role of captain in attacks on a single ship, four times daily, with two before lunch and two in the afternoon. The other students did not stand idly by, for they were expected to perform useful roles alongside the boat's crew. They plotted targets, calculated firing solutions and produced the settings for simulated torpedoes, to ensure the phantom weapons 'hit' the target. This coalface teamwork showed how to cope with a stressed captain and reinforced the need to help him out. If they failed the student on the scope, why should he work hard for them when it was their turn?

While the student took the attack periscope, Forsyth was behind him on the larger search scope. The latter would sometimes be left raised, enabling lookouts and radar operators in the frigate to fix exactly where the submarine was. In their early attacks the students were often so fiercely intent on maintaining their focus they had no idea Teacher's periscope remained up to provide a marker.

Pressure ramped up steadily, expressed by the number of ships students were taking on. After a single ship in Week 1, the challenge escalated in logical fashion, through two, three to four warships and, for the last couple of days, a tanker as well. The main challenge by then was evading the attention of warships, dipping under them to get a clear 'shot' at the tanker.

While in the heat of an attack there was no direct communication between Teacher and surface vessels, during brief breaks there would be consultations. Quite often the assigned frigate was not British, coming from another NATO nation instead. This could present added pressure via a potential language barrier. In one Danish frigate only the captain spoke good enough English for emergency situations. Rather than risk his ship – or sink a submarine by accident – that particular Commanding Officer virtually lived on the bridge, handling all radio communications with *Onyx*. Forsyth's own skill as a submarine captain was the best failsafe to ensure neither submarine nor warship came to grief. This belief in his own powers was not a product of arrogance, but of training and experience. Extra hazards intruded via fishing boats deliberately venturing into clearly marked submarine exercise areas off the Clyde. It was suspected some disregarded warnings to stay out in order to catch themselves a submarine periscope and obtain some tasty compensation for damaged nets.

If the student thought he might get some help to avoid these pests, indeed any sympathy at all, then he was mistaken. Forsyth considered it 'part of the fun ... the trick was to be able to evade the fishing boats early and get to a spot of relatively open water to conduct the attack'.

The only assistance a student could expect was Teacher drawing his attention to the presence of fishing vessels. Teacher would also watch carefully to see if the student was observant enough to spot them on his own (and was always ready to take over if he didn't).

Aside from hopes of a submarine command being at stake, in such circumstances lives were also at risk, both in fishing boats and in the submarines. Should either be snared disaster could follow.

Evading that eventuality was a superb test of nerve and command potential. As he watched the students working their way through the gauntlet, Forsyth made further calculations on who had the right stuff and who did not. 'Some people have naturally got what it takes to make a good CO. It will be someone who can have a quick look through the periscope, and then hold the tactical picture in his head, making rapid decisions on what to do next. There were students who, at first, you thought would be fine. Perisher put them under pressure, took them out of their comfort zone – so you had to keep them in there to see what really lay beneath. Being a submarine CO is all about handling severe pressure, sometimes for days – or even weeks – at a time. In the first week you begin to get an idea who can handle it calmly – there is a lot to learn – but you can already see who is getting sweaty in a tight corner.'

By the end of Week 3, or at least the beginning of Week 4, Teacher knew who was *definitely not* going to pass. It was important to draw a dividing line between slow learners and those who would never get the required spatial awareness. They had to know what was going on outside while also keeping track of events inside the boat.

The best way for a student to ensure he had a handle on what was happening – before putting the periscope up – was to do Control Room Rounds, to visually check everything, and everyone, was in place.

Teacher also threw a few spanners in the works. Forsyth might order some members of the team out of the Control Room – with the exception of those responsible for safe operation of the boat – to see if a student on the attack scope noticed. Once was forgivable, but fail twice and the man in question would be gone. There would, conversely, be serious question marks against anyone who was overly distracted by happenings in the boat while on the scope. Failing to take the submarine deep early enough to avoid collision with a surface vessel was the blackest of black marks. Committing that error in Week 1 or Week 2 of the at-sea phase was not terminal, as every student would experience one or two occasions where Teacher took over. If it happened more than once in Week 3 or Week 4, then it was, as Forsyth termed it, rather drily, 'very bad news'.

Having received his summons to Perisher while serving in HMS *Otter*, Doug Littlejohns departed for some well-earned leave, then set about girding his loins for the rigorous test of mettle that lay ahead.

He would take his tilt at qualifying for submarine command on the course run from January to June 1975. Littlejohns did not know Forsyth but had seen him in the wardroom at Faslane, though they did not actually converse until Perisher. Forsyth had heard of Littlejohns as a highly competent, ambitious young officer who – no doubt – would be a handful.

He was determined to remain the boss.

To help prepare for Perisher, Littlejohns obtained a set of ship models. While he sat in an armchair watching television his wife would call to him from the sofa, holding one of them aloft.

Was the ship coming at him? Showing him its stern?

Or beam on? What type was it?

Warship or merchant vessel?

Frigate or destroyer?

Angle on the bow? This was the most important – he had to get that within 5–10 degrees. This would give the course of target, from which other things could be calculated – the torpedo track angle in particular.

It was a good way of training to make instant, and hopefully accurate, assessments of targets through the periscope.

His fellow Perishers were an Israeli, two Canadians, a Dutchman, two Australians and six Britons, split down into A and B sections, each of them running in parallel aboard their respective boats.

Aboard *Onyx* Littlejohns found sailors had some unusual ways of showing their confidence, or otherwise, in the would-be submarine captain at the helm. A cook, whose normal working environment was the galley, at Action Stations took care of an attack plot. This man possessed the rare talent of being able to write backwards with a chinagraph pencil on the vertical, transparent track display. As Littlejohns made his way to the attack scope – full of eagerness and anxiety – he noticed the cook was wearing a leather flying helmet. As he would later discover, the cook pulled it on whenever a particularly aggressive student took control.

Littlejohns was not the kind of man to appreciate command being taken off him at *any* stage, considering it 'an insult to have the plug pulled on me ... and a matter for much grumpiness if I thought that Forsyth had done it just to make a point'.

Plenty of pranks were unleashed on the students to test the envelope of their tolerance. Just as one was trying to keep the periscope crosshairs on a frigate, a voice called out: 'Fire! Fire! Fire!'

Two sailors lugging a hose came lumbering through the Control Room, while people yelled contradictory instructions about where the fire might be. This apparently confused the hose carriers so much they chased round and round the attack periscope, binding the student tightly to it.

Littlejohns, who was on the chart table as the attack navigator, watched it all unfold, less than amused. He had seen these sorts of antics before, having served in four submarines acting as the Perisher boat.

As the process of weeding out progressed, Littlejohns found he was even more in his element. With fewer Perishers, he was able to do more attack runs, which he found most thrilling, especially when it came to Week 4. Faced with a quartet of warships to evade while attempting to nail the tanker was very exciting.

'One frigate goes one side and then a frigate comes at you straight on. Another is coming around behind you. You are on and off the periscope like a yo-yo, having a look every five seconds and then realise you will have to dive under a fourth frigate to get at the tanker. It would either make you or break you.' As he went through the Perisher wringer, Littlejohns recognised that *Onyx*'s men were coolly assessing him. As he looked around he wondered if he had passed their test ...

In HMS *Otter*, when she was the Perisher boat, he used to find out how the tote was going on who would pass and who would fail. He now wondered what the odds in *Onyx* were on him passing.

As Littlejohns progressed through the Week 1 and Week 2 attack runs, Forsyth judged here was a young officer who had a very firm grip on what was needed. His scope work was excellent, but was there perhaps a danger of over-confidence? It was time to shake things up. Forsyth asked two of the submarine's stewards, at that moment not troubled with catering for officers in the wardroom, to have a pretend fistfight. He told them to stage it in a passageway leading off the Control Room. They enthusiastically complied, with much swearing and mock punches thrown. Aware of the disturbance, but in the middle of completing an attack, Littlejohns asked one of his fellow students, a Dutch officer named Driekus Heij – filling in as XO – to go and quieten things down.

'Knock their heads together,' Littlejohns suggested.

The Dutchman did better than that.

He knocked one of the 'brawlers' out, abruptly bringing the 'scrap' to a halt. Nursing their bruises the stewards vowed never to be drawn into Perisher play-acting again. Teacher was pleased to see Littlejohns had not tried to ignore the incident.

He had delegated immediately and achieved a result, but Forsyth felt Littlejohns was still rather too fond of using the periscope.

Someone who does that makes it easier for a potential enemy to spot he's there. In the middle of the next attack, Forsyth decided to deploy a dramatic means of illustrating it was not necessary. He told Littlejohns to go aft and ask a sailor the date of his birthday. Littlejohns complied, but found it nerve-racking. 'He made his point very well and I had no desire to make that run to the aft end of the boat and back again – EVER.'

Some people took themselves out of the course. At the end of Week 1 one aspiring submarine captain quit. In Week 3 two 'perished'. The Canadian student looked like Forsyth might also axe him, because of his over-reliance on a notebook rather than using his initiative. Warned off, he made an effort to mend his ways and survived.

To make attack runs as realistic as possible, the Perisher boat did actually fire practice torpedoes at frigates. Their warheads were full of water rather than explosive and they were set to run at least 20ft under the target. Despite these precautions, unleashing torpedoes, even during an exercise, could be fraught with danger. In one instance torpedoes meant to run under actually ran on the surface, forcing a tanker to take urgent evasive action. The aim was not to make all the torpedoes run directly under the target, but to achieve a spread, sending some astern and some ahead. This would ensure whichever course the vessel took it would stand a good chance of encountering at least one. Having them all too close meant if you missed with one then you missed with all. It was usual to fire two or three torpedoes. Each Perisher student was, though, given an opportunity to fire a salvo of six. The torpedoes themselves were recovered (as they floated at the end of their run) by a specially assigned craft – the Torpedo Recovery Vehicle – standing by to pluck them from the water.

When somebody was clearly destined to 'perish' it was, by necessity, a cold, ruthless process. The student in question would embark on his latest attack, unaware Teacher had already made up his mind. The purpose of this final run was to ram home – for the young officer, his fellow students and everybody in the boat – that submarine command was not really the job for him. It served to buck up those who were still in the game. It reassured *Onyx*'s sailors – and by extension the Submarine Service and Navy as a whole – that only the best of the best were allowed to become submarine captains.

Teacher devised the run to ensure he failed again. He created such a close-quarters exercise the already jittery student inevitably became flustered and lost focus on the picture in his head, rendering the situation unsafe.

Forsyth immediately gave the orders for going deep in an emergency: 'Full ahead together. Flood Q. Keep 90 feet.'

Flooding the Q tank accelerated the speed and momentum of going deep by adding a large volume of water well for'ard. This tipped the bow down and made the submarine heavier. On hearing the dreaded words 'Flood Q', the student knew it would at least cost him a brandy at the bar that night. If it happened too often he would fail the course.

Everyone knew what was coming. Nobody caught the failed student's eye as he relinquished the attack periscope – the last time he would ever use one. He filed out of the Control Room with the other Perishers and went to the wardroom. The boat was returned to her regular crew, while the students had a coffee or tea. His fellow Perishers conspicuously avoided talking about the student's blatant fail as they poured the milk and spooned in sugar. Forsyth had headed for the CO's cabin, from where he sent word for the doomed man to come and join him. As the student made his exit nobody said anything, or met his eye. Forsyth recognised it was best to make it a swift knife job rather than shilly-shally around. It was, he felt, a necessarily ruthless process and 'psychologically the best way and a proven system over many years'. He invited the student to sit down. Looking him square in the eye, Forsyth said: 'There is no point in going on with something you can't do.'

Far from being crestfallen, the student let out a sigh of relief. He knew it was never going to happen for him. He just wanted his part in Perisher to be over. The wardroom steward was in the officers' bunk space packing the failed man's bag.

Forsyth had earlier asked the submarine's CO to radio for the transfer boat. *Onyx* broke the surface, hatches clanging open. The student emerged onto the outer casing and stepped across to the other craft. His bag was passed over by the steward. The transfer boat backed away, the failed student took one last look at the submarine where his career in the Silent Service had perished. *Onyx*'s casing party had already disappeared. The boat moved away, slowly driving herself back under. Water frothed and bubbled. She was gone. He will never again step aboard a submarine. If he wishes, the Perished one may carry on serving in some other part of the Navy but is no longer part of the brotherhood of submariners. It is less than 30 minutes since his failed attack run. In the wheelhouse, the skipper of the transfer boat nudges him, and without a word presses a glass of whisky into his hand.

Below the waves *Onyx* is immediately handed back to Forsyth and his students for another attack run. The remaining Perishers will have no time to dwell on what has just happened.

By the conclusion of the periscope phase those students that remained were considered safe and competent in managing an attack. They received grades that went from 'Good' to 'Excellent' – all depending on the skill levels each displayed. The surviving students travelled from Scotland to HMS *Dryad,* the Maritime Operations School near Portsmouth, for advanced tactical training. In the bucolic surroundings of a country house, where Generals Eisenhower and Montgomery planned D-Day, the future submarine captains learned about the complexities of joint operations with land and air forces, as well as NATO allies. It gave the students a break, with a slightly more relaxed routine, before going back to sea with the Teachers.

While they could justifiably feel good about having made it through to the last two weeks at sea, the students could still fail.

Littlejohns ignored that troubling notion.

'You always have the thought at the back of your mind: is he going to "get" me? But, in the main, I felt I could do it.'

Most people lost weight during Perisher, but not Littlejohns, who suffered at the hands of the modern sailor's traditional dietary nemesis.

'I put on weight, as I ate a lot of chips.'

For the final fortnight at sea the submarine was HMS *Rorqual*, a Porpoise Class diesel. In the first week of this final phase she moved out into the open ocean for the students to carry out submarine versus submarine tactics, working with aircraft and 'attacking' ships. The aim was to allow the students to develop their broader skills. Teacher applied a lighter touch, letting the Perishers run things on their own as much as possible.

The objective in the final week was to train in landing Special Forces, lay mines and carry out other close inshore work by both day and night.

It was during one such inshore exercise off the west coast of Scotland that Forsyth seized an opportunity to severely test Littlejohns's nerve. How cool would this supremely confident and aggressive officer remain the closer he got to the shore?

Forsyth selected the very restricted and shallow waters of Kilbrannan Sound, a stretch of sea separating the Kintyre Peninsula from the Isle of Arran. Teacher was determined to ensure Littlejohns was not again addicted to periscope looks.

How well would he cope without any at all?

The submarine wasn't going fast and Forsyth thought the worst that could happen was touching the bottom, which was gently shelving soft sand and shale. It wasn't the sort of thing you would do in a nuclear-powered boat, but the risk was acceptable in a diesel.

Forsyth might have been asked to explain a slightly dented boat, but for Littlejohns a collision or crunch of any kind would represent career termination.

'I realised what was going on, and was determined not to let Forsyth see that my knees were knocking.'

As Littlejohns took *Rorqual* in, he realised Forsyth was keeping him down for far longer than other Perishers. *Teaching another lesson about periscopes, was he?*

'You are going to end up in Glasgow,' *Rorqual*'s Navigator remarked, a mischievous glint in his eye.

Littlejohns growled back: 'I am not hitting anything!'

Adding to his irritation, a Port Auxiliary Service craft was following and keeping track of the dived submarine. Littlejohns knew it was there from sonar readings and was infuriated by his inability to shake it off by evasive manoeuvring. He had no idea *Rorqual* was leaving a smoke trail. Teacher had ordered flares to be ejected from the submarine every few minutes.

Forsyth felt the point of what was known as PROWLEX resided in its ability to push people further and further, so they would be on the edge of their capabilities. They would discover their personal limits and be comfortable. It was important for a submarine captain to know what his limits were so he could pull back from a situation that threatened to slip from his grasp.

In the end Littlejohns neither crashed the boat nor sank his career, surfacing safely in Inchmarnock Water.

Shortly afterwards, off Lamlash on the Isle of Arran, came another test of nerve and skill. It involved taking on board Special Boat Service (SBS) commandos waiting in a pair of canoes for the submarine to come and pick them up. *Rorqual* would approach submerged, periscope up, snagging a rope extended between the canoes. Further complicating the challenge, Littlejohns was required to recover the SBS men at night.

Once the periscope snagged the rope, the canoes would be gently towed out to deeper water, *Rorqual* surfacing close by. 'Only in James Bond movies do you surface underneath the canoes,' observed Littlejohns. 'That would have been too dangerous as the canoes could so easily capsize.'

To spice things up Teacher decided to inject some surprises into the scenario. Forsyth had spoken to the SBS raiding party boss earlier, requesting that he and his men pretend to be drunk and make life awkward. When he put his periscope up to get a visual fix on the canoes, Littlejohns found the commandos hurling empty beer cans in his direction.

They couldn't be pissed, could they?

Eventually, having landed a few glancing blows on the scope, they gave up and Littlejohns was able to snag the rope. An extra challenge was presented by a lack of power.

Forsyth had deliberately prevented anyone from recharging the submarine's battery during the day. Manoeuvring under the SBS craft required a careful application of revs, plus a light touch on the hydroplanes.

It consumed remaining battery life at a rapid rate.

As they saw the submarine's fin emerging, the SBS men paddled for all they were worth, in order to be alongside the foreplanes – so they could grab them to climb on board. The torpedo loading hatch was just by the foreplanes, the submarine surfacing just enough for it to be opened. Pulling canoes aboard and collapsing them, they disappeared into the boat. After picking the SBS group up, to successfully complete the scenario Littlejohns must also make a dived exit, to preserve the covert nature of the mission.

Having towed the two canoes further out from the shore – *big tick* – and surfaced close by them – *another tick in the box* – without capsizing them or drowning anyone – *huge plus points* – Littlejohns also showed his command of the situation by giving the SBS men a bollocking for mucking about – *as a submarine captain was well within his rights to do.* 'I spoke to them when they came aft to the Control Room – you don't shout abuse on the surface when operating off a hostile coast and you stay in the Control Room in case you have to dive suddenly.'

To apply an extra layer of stress, Forsyth had one more trick up his sleeve. Littlejohns was on the scope and alarmed to see a fast-moving craft emerge from behind a shadowy headland. Searchlight traversing wildly from left to right, this thing was seeking him out. *Another typical Forsyth dirty trick.*

If that bloody searchlight picked up *Rorqual's* shiny black hull, Little-johns could be on his way to a fail, right at the end, just as he feared. *All those chips, the weight gain, would have been a dead loss ...*

Issuing a few curses under his breath, he ordered a crash dive, piling on the revs, which further drained the power. The lights flickered from white to a dirty brown, the classic sign of a submarine's batteries near-ing exhaustion. Glancing around, Littlejohns saw *Rorqual's* Weapons Engineer Officer turn a 'whiter shade of pale'. Diving at speed with the battery about to conk out was not advised – *Rorqual* could find herself crashing to the bottom with no power left for the critical systems to work, such as weapons, lights and radio communications.

But of course this was Perisher, and the oncoming surface craft with the searchlight knew the submarine's approximate position.

If he wanted to pass Perisher, Littlejohns had to do the right thing *in the context of the exercise.* That required instant action to extract *Rorqual* from the path of the oncoming 'enemy'. As soon as *Rorqual* was under, Teacher ordered Littlejohns to turn over command to the boat's regu-lar Commanding Officer, Lt Cdr Jonathan Cooke. He took her away swiftly, and above all safely, surfacing as soon as possible to charge batteries.

This was the end of the course.

Heading back to the Clyde, *Rorqual* paused for a moment in Lamlash Bay and it was open bar in the wardroom.

Called to the CO's cabin about 00.30 Littlejohns parted the curtains to enter and found a beaming Forsyth offering him a glass of champagne.

'Well done, Doug, you've passed. You have command of *Osiris*.'

The next student came in to be told the good news, and so on before they were all together in the submarine's wardroom, knocking back celebratory drinks and congratulating each other.

Littlejohns felt fantastic. 'I was full of confidence in my abilities and ready for anything.'

It was the crowning moment of his career – so far – and a memorable time for other reasons, too. 'After *Rorqual* returned to Faslane, I got off the boat, my wife met me and I saw my son Andrew walk for the first time, from the car to my arms. It was a fantastic time.'

The chaotic rush-hour traffic of Paris was for Dan Conley the perfect preparatory training ground for his Periscope Course.

He had married Linda, an officer and communications specialist in the Women's Royal Naval Service, in March 1975. A pause in Perisher following the ashore phase enabled them to enjoy a summer holiday travelling around France, including forays into the capital.

The at-sea segment of Perisher would see Conley stretching his mental arithmetic capabilities to the limit – calculating time between periscope looks, target solutions and working out settings for the torpedoes. He decided to learn his times-tables up to 19, arming Linda with a submarine attack calculation slide-rule so she could fire mind-bending questions at him from the passenger seat as he navigated Paris traffic.

'The height of the target's mast is 8oft and the periscope reading on it is 17 minutes of arc,' she proposed. 'What is the range of the target and when do you next need to look at it? Given a speed of 15 knots and angle on the bow of 60 degrees what would the torpedo deflection angle be?'

Changing through the gears as his car squeezed between lines of traffic on the roundabout at the Arc de Triomphe, Conley churned out answers. 'Range of the target 4,600 yards, need to look next in 2 minutes and 50 seconds, torpedo deflection angle 16 degrees.'

Passing the Parisian version of Perisher gave Conley confidence that he had gone a long way towards limbering up his mental muscles.

For the real thing he was entrusted to the care of Cdr Forsyth, whom he had previously encountered six years earlier, during his trying times in *Sealion*. Conley joined *Finwhale* in Scotland after the usual attack team trainer work ashore at Gosport.

He thought there was too much time spent on periscope work.

Surely sonar skills were more important in facing down the Soviets?

And he was also not entirely convinced about the theatrics staged by Forsyth. These included a rating running into the control room with a knife while he was on the scope. 'Here we go again,' thought Conley, ignoring the melodrama while maintaining his focus on the target.

It never got so bad Conley thought he would fail but he did make a serious error during Week 4, failing to pay enough attention to a frigate loitering on the flanks.

'I should have looked at the ship 1.5 minutes after the last look, but I left it to 2.5 minutes, and he could have been right on top of us during that vital delay.'

Aside from calculating periscope intervals, he also tried to determine where he stood in the rankings of Perishers.

'If others on the course are evidently doing worse and you are still holding your own, then you speculate you are not for the chop. This is especially so if Teacher is giving other students special test runs to build up their confidence. They are the barometer for how you might be doing, too.'

It was unsettling to adjourn to the hotel at Rothesay where students stayed and find one or two faces missing at dinner. Conley held his nerve, deciding he must treat it like a school exam, and worry less about all the periscope work. In the end he did enough to get through, and of six Perishers in *Finwhale* Forsyth cut only one, a Norwegian.

After five weeks ashore learning about joint warfare with the rest of the Navy and the other two armed forces, Conley worried that having worked himself up to a high pitch – passing the most gruelling part of the Perisher – he might cock it up in the final phase.

He was to join *Onslaught* at Devonport in early November, with Linda driving him down there from their home near Portsmouth. There was a slight mishap that did not bode well. 'Our Irish Setter was in the back of the car and unfortunately crapped all over my charts, which had been prepared for various scenarios such as mine lays, photo recces etc. I cleaned the charts off as best I could and marked the resultant brown stains with the annotation "Dog Shit".'

Onslaught sailed out into the South West Approaches, where things started off with a major joint exercise, the boat then moving north to the Clyde for the inshore phase. Running the gamut of the usual test exercises, each Perisher taking it in turns to command the boat for a day, Conley found when his time came he was being over-cautious. Forsyth took him to one side for a reassuring word.

'You have proved safe on the periscope, you can take and handle risks – now you can relax.'

Trying his best not to let caution get in the way, Conley proceeded with laying mines, landing marines for raids and using the periscope to carry out reconnaissance. All the time he had to evade ASW helicopters and surface craft. Course concluded, *Onslaught* headed for Faslane, with Conley called into the captain's cabin to hear his fate. He found a smiling Forsyth, who told him: 'Congratulations, Dan, you are the new captain of *Otter*.'

Perisher was a mix of formalised procedure and intense pressure, leavened with occasional outrageous twists courtesy of Teacher, all designed to push students to their limits.

For Littlejohns it was 'highly emotional and draining but I enjoyed it because I could do it'.

Forsyth found being Teacher as exacting as Perisher.

Of course for those who 'perished' it was grim. Not only would they not be submariners any more, but failing Perisher was not a good reference for a future job, even in the surface navy. As the 1970s wore on, it was realised this might be a waste of good naval officers. Some of those who fell at the submarine command course hurdle would eventually captain surface warships.

'At the time I was Teacher, the Perisher was a career wrecker or maker,' admitted Forsyth. 'It was indeed like getting the black spot in *Treasure Island*. Of those who failed, sometimes it was a case of poor selection or the guy didn't want to do it in reality, but he wouldn't admit it. There were some who refused to even do it. They asked to leave the Submarine Service and went back out to General Service.'

Passing Perisher was the key to joining an exclusive club, an elite within the navies of the world. It was understandable if the men who passed felt themselves to be young Gods, or at the very least afflicted with an easy arrogance that suffuses those who have faced the toughest of tests and triumphed. This was not Muhammad Ali-style bombast, but iron self-belief, forged in the fire of the world's toughest submarine command course. Submariners in a dicey situation – whether diesel boat or SSN – would not want to entrust their fate to some shrinking violet who required a focus group meeting every time he needed to take a life-or-death decision.

Forsyth conceded the periscope course was artificial, but the anti-ship role would be of equal importance to the anti-submarine mission in a shooting war. The point of the Perisher in the 1970s was not to teach actual submarine versus submarine tactics, but rather to see who had the personality and grit to handle the pressures of command. The periscope phase checked they could safely operate a submarine under extreme pressure. The Perisher and the processes it subjected would-be submarine captains to were fundamental to fielding an effective submarine force.

Perisher was the gold standard for submarine crews. They knew that if their captain had passed it they were, quite simply, entrusting their lives to a safe pair of hands. For Britain it meant the captains of its highly valuable – and scarce – submarines were the best men for the job

During the time Forsyth took Littlejohns through Perisher, the Ministry of Defence made an attempt to get to the bottom of what enabled one man to pass the course while another failed. If a formula could be arrived at, then perhaps they could avoid wasting time, and money (as well as ruining careers of otherwise decent officers) by sending the wrong people to Perisher. A female psychologist was sent down to HMS *Dolphin* and then to Faslane, to assess what made a submarine captain tick. She interviewed the Perishers during their time in the command team trainers as they geared up for the at-sea phase. The idea was that she would later interview the same men again, to try and assess what led to failure. During an interview with Littlejohns she asked if he could say why he responded to a given situation in a simulated attack. Littlejohns weighed up the question carefully, but the best he could offer was: 'I don't know ... it felt right.'

Telling a civilian the secrets of his trade was not something Littlejohns could do with ease. Perish the thought.

'I had no idea what the secret was – it was second nature!'

In the end, the psychologist was defeated, giving up on her attempt to distil the secrets of becoming a successful submarine captain into a fixed formula.

It was ludicrous to even try.

It was not a mechanistic process.

Submarine captains were, after all, human beings, not robots. Littlejohns regarded it as an intuitive art form.

In July 1975, more than 100 miles above the Earth an American Apollo spacecraft and a Soviet Soyuz docked. An astronaut from each nation shook hands in the docking tunnel.

Over the next two days their crews carried out a series of joint experiments, swapped jokes and shared meals, the apogee of détente. Surely it was a firm sign the standoff between East and West might soon come to an end? Not long after the joined spacecraft slid across the heavens far above, in waters off Dorset the real state of affairs underneath the PR gloss on historic space liaisons was somewhat less warm-spirited.

Lieutenant Doug Littlejohns, in command of the diesel boat HMS *Osiris*, was more than a little annoyed by the antics of Russian deep-sea trawlers. The only catch some of them were after was intelligence and inflicting as much interference as possible on Royal Navy warfare training.

The relatively shallow waters off Portland were not suitable for Soviet nuclear-powered submarines to stooge around and even their diesel boats would soon be flushed out. The spying job therefore fell to AGIs and, as *Osiris* shuttled back and forth beneath the waves, a dozen Russian 'trawlers' intruded. All of the Soviet vessels had nets over the side to reinforce their cover, but, in compartments aboard, English-language operators were listening in on wireless transmissions between British surface warships. Cameras with high-powered long lenses captured the latest modifications to weapons and sensors while aerials arrayed on their superstructures sucked in communications traffic.

Hovering on the edge of the training areas was one thing, but actually invading them was another, and Littlejohns was reaching the end of his patience. The 'trawlers' were passing through not only from north to south, but also east to west.

Normally a Soviet AGI would stand no chance of finding a submerged NATO boat, but *Osiris* was tasked with being the so-called 'clockwork mouse', executing set runs, to train surface warship sonar operators and lookouts.

Osiris regularly fired smoke grenades to indicate where she was (white smoke) and also when she would be commencing a mock attack (green). Taking their cue from these, the AGIs were following the British submarine's track, one of them managing to snag *Osiris* in its nets. As his boat was tipped 20 degrees up, Littlejohns cursed volubly:

'What's the f'ing fool doing? Trying to kill us?'

Decisive action was needed or the boat and all her men could be lost. Littlejohns ordered full power – 18 knots maximum speed – *Osiris* surging through the net, ripping it apart. Pieces of the submarine's fibreglass casing and fin broke off. With *Osiris* free, the net's cables whipped aboard the trawler, sending Russian seamen running for their lives to avoid being decapitated.

Should anyone spot the damage to *Osiris* from the Portsmouth shoreline and contact the press, it could blow up into a major story. Littlejohns decided he would bring his boat back in under cover of darkness. He was not looking forward to explaining the damage.

The pressure of commanding a submarine had not initially been a comfortable one for Littlejohns. 'The first nine months in command I think I was hard to please, because I was unsure of myself. I thought: "Can't let the crew know." Underneath it all I had learned a lot about myself. I experienced a blinding flash of light, realising that I wasn't doing it right. I was volcanic – too much like a Roman candle firework. So, I learned to relax and let the submariners do their job.'

Littlejohns grew into his own skin, retaining a firm grip, yet enjoying the job more. Keenly aware that there was no point in being hesitant in a fight with another submarine – should that day ever come – Littlejohns wielded his boat aggressively. The sailors created a cartoon depicting him at the periscope dressed as legendary stunt motorcyclist Evel Knievel. In a speech bubble he declares: 'Full dive ... Loop the loop.'

The new, more relaxed, Littlejohns was very amused. There was no smile on his face when he brought *Osiris* alongside *Dolphin* and took the long walk to the squadron commander's office. Fortunately, Capt. Hugh Oliphant, a Second World War veteran who won the Distinguished Service Cross for his exploits, understood what it was like to be in a tight spot.

As their discussion began, Oliphant handed Littlejohns a tumbler of whisky on the rocks, arming himself with one, too.

If the boss needs a stiff drink, surely that can't be a good sign?

The young submarine captain was invited to explain what had happened. Coming to the end of his account, Littlejohns took a sip of whisky and concluded it by saying: 'They were deliberately interfering with us and endangering the lives of everyone in my boat. They were a serious threat and they meant to be.' Oliphant agreed. Relieved that he had the backing of the boss, Littlejohns glanced up and spotted a plaque on the wall, which read: *A collision at sea can spoil your whole day.*

Fortunately, the Admiralty took the view that such encounters were bound to happen when Soviet trawlers did something stupid.

Another irritating AGI soon found itself receiving attention from Littlejohns, in the same waters off Scotland where a similar vessel caused trouble for Rob Forsyth in *Repulse*.

Littlejohns was tasked with taking *Osiris* out to keep the Soviet intelligence gatherer busy while a Polaris SSBN slipped out to deep water. His orders were to show his own periscope, and act in 'a foolish submariner manner', keeping and holding the AGI's attention for a while. Littlejohns thought it would be a rather good idea to start by taking an underwater look at the Soviet vessel. NATO might obtain some good photos of her rudder and prop to assist in detection and identification at a future date. A more important objective was to find out whether she was fitted with sonar and torpedo tubes.

Raising the periscope and pressing his eyes against the lens cups, Littlejohns gently took *Osiris* in under the AGI, which was hove to but riding a fairly frisky swell. What he saw was the biggest, and best, intelligence-gathering auxiliary the Soviets fielded – one of half a dozen Primorye Class vessels, each displacing 5,000 tons. Larger than many frigates and based on fish-processing factory ship hulls, they often hung around at the exit points from the Clyde, trying to intercept both RN and USN submarines. Snugly underneath the Soviet ship, and with perfect neutral buoyancy, Littlejohns ordered *Osiris* to slow right down, almost to a halt.

There were just a few feet between the periscope and the weed-fouled, barnacle-encrusted underside of the AGI.

She disappeared from the view, taken up by the swell, while *Osiris* stayed in place, not moving an inch. The AGI duly came crashing down. Littlejohns was alarmed to see her hull miss his periscope by a couple of inches. Realising this was a game not worth pursuing, he ordered an increase in speed and told the planesman to take *Osiris* deeper. Extracted from underneath the Primorye and pulling away, Littlejohns put into effect the 'foolish submariner' ploy. Bringing the boat back up and again raising the periscope, he ordered the helmsman to zigzag *Osiris* to and fro. Lookouts aboard the Soviet ship duly spotted the scope shuttling back and forth; the captain of the AGI decided to give chase. Elsewhere, the Polaris boat slipped out to sea and dived without interference. Score: one minor victory for NATO.

Primoryes were not the only vessels Littlejohns was asked to keep an eye on during his early days in command of *Osiris*. He was also tasked with supporting efforts to help the Army and Royal Ulster Constabulary contain 'The Troubles', as the civil unrest in Northern Ireland was known. Vessels were being used on gun-running trips between Scotland and the strife-torn province.

'This had us sitting on the bottom in a bay about 200 yards from the beach and main road using special optics on the periscope at night. All went well on the first night, and we helped to nail a couple of craft. As the sun set on the second a Royal Naval Reserve minesweeper came into the bay and dropped anchor very close to where we were lying. He had not been cleared to know about the operation and I was concerned that he would collide with us as the tide turned. His draught was deeper than the top of our fin. I eased the boat off the bottom as soon as I could and crept out to sea with only a few feet beneath the keel. I sent my first-ever stroppy signal to Flag Officer Scotland and Northern Ireland, for not keeping the minesweeper away, and got an immediate apology.'

As a welcome break from seeking out terrorist arms shipments across the Irish Sea, the Fifth Hand, Lieutenant Tim McClement, managed to organise a visit to the boat's 'twin town' of Ilkley in the scenic West Riding of Yorkshire. Ilkley's association with the RN stretched back to the previous holder of the name *Osiris*, a Second World War submarine, its citizens having raised money for her crew's welfare.

Littlejohns and 30 of his submariners travelled by train up from Plymouth, where the boat was in dry dock, changing into their smartest uniforms at Leeds. Met at the Ilkley train station by a brass band and the mayor, they marched through the streets to the town hall, for a reception in their honour. 'The lads were billeted around the town and had a ball. Nearby Bradford got jealous of the publicity, so we were invited to a lunch in their Town Hall and I had to give a speech. I remembered that a Bradford boy, Richard Dunn, was about to fight for the world heavyweight title and so proposed a toast to his success. That earned us another dinner in the original Harry Ramsden fish and chips restaurant. Unfortunately, Dunn would be beaten to a pulp by Muhammad Ali.'

Aggressive actions by AGIs off Scotland, and in waters within sight of Dorset, indicated an increasingly confident, even arrogant, Soviet Navy. As recently as May 1975, the West had shuddered at the sight of a massive global deployment. Out they came, ship after ship, submarine followed by submarine – from Murmansk in the far North to Vladivostok in Soviet Asia – a ceaseless surge of Russian naval power, streaming out onto the high seas.

The Kremlin's maritime forces were regularly deploying to the Caribbean, the Indian Ocean, and off the west and east coasts of Africa.

By the mid-1970s many in the USA felt the West was losing strategic parity with the Russians. The defeat in Vietnam was coupled with increasing Soviet and Cuban influence in Africa, including Angola, where a Marxist regime would win power after a bitter civil war. It all came amid an economic crisis in the West with oil prices rocketing and a stock market crash. The Hawks thought détente was the West gone soft, their mood of doom and gloom increased by the Helsinki Treaties putting human rights at the top of the USA's foreign policy agenda.

The major worldwide exercise that drew the Soviets out of their bases in 1975 saw 200 surface ships and an estimated 100 submarines deployed simultaneously around the globe.

This was gunboat diplomacy on an epic scale.

And the West trembled, for Russia was no longer a giant imprisoned by lack of open access to the sea or a decent navy.

The hardline head of the Soviet Navy himself, Admiral Sergei Gorshkov, expounded the virtue of deploying his force as a political instrument to reshape the world. He had secured overseas naval bases and anchorages from Cuba to Syria and from Vietnam to North Africa. Gorshkov thundered: 'The Soviet Navy is a powerful factor in the creation of favourable conditions for the building of Socialism and Communism, for the active defence of peace and for strengthening international security.'

By that, Gorshkov meant using his navy as a counterpoint to Western maritime hegemony, for leaders of his generation still feared the Soviet Union being surrounded and invaded from all sides. Russian naval forces were breaking the stranglehold of Western maritime powers. They could no longer lock the Soviet fleets into the Black Sea, the Baltic and the Barents, while the new surface warships and submarines expressed Gorshkov's global ambitions. Even as Britain and other Western nations plunged into economic crisis – some not having enough money to send their ships to sea very often – the centrally controlled communist superpower could pour hundreds of billions of roubles into its military might. It constructed the new jump jet carrier *Kiev* and Delta Class ballistic missile submarines every bit as good as anything the USA and UK could create. It was quite simply awesome; one American naval officer in a warship shadowing part of the Russian fleet openly expressed his wonder:

'What they've done in ten years is absolutely fantastic. From almost nothing they've built up a first-rate navy, and it's an imposing threat.'

Off the Azores a low-flying P-3 Orion MPA swooped over a Kara Class cruiser, a new warship rated among the world's most formidable missile platforms. With their motor drives whirring, the Orion's cameras snapped away. Eavesdropping tech sucked up signals traffic for all it was worth yet the Russians didn't care. In fact, they were openly boasting over the airwaves – broadcasting orders between groups of warships in plain language on easily accessible channels.

With Gorshkov's iron hand on the tiller it seemed that nothing could deflect the triumphant, globe-girdling course of Soviet naval power.

In early May 1975, the US-based news magazine *Time* reported that not only had Kara Class missiles cruisers been spotted off the Azores, but North African and Syrian ports were simultaneously host to Soviet vessels.

A Russian naval presence was detected in the Pacific, off the Philippines and even in the Sea of Japan. Moscow dubbed the global deployment 'Spring', while to the West it was 'Okean 1975', a back reference to the NATO codeword used for a similar, but more modest, surge mounted by the Soviets in 1970.

Gorshkov had a master plan to deliver a devastating blow against the West should war ever be necessary. It would show his masters in the Kremlin their investment in a trans-oceanic navy was not a wasteful distraction from the Central Front in continental Europe.

Should hot war erupt on land, the Warsaw Pact would soon overwhelm NATO with tanks and mechanised infantry. Things would swiftly turn nuclear on the battlefield as the West's armies struggled to hold back the Red tide.

Any major war in Europe would last a few weeks at most and Okean

1975 was a dress rehearsal for global Armageddon. The Russians claimed to have created command and control networks – utilising satellites – that enabled Gorshkov to transmit the 'go' signal for first strikes around the world. His orders would pulse across high and low frequencies that even penetrated the deep ocean to Soviet submarines. Combined Russian naval combat units would allegedly deliver Gorshkov's 'first salvo' within a 90-second time frame, no matter where they were.

With Special Fit SSNs occupied round the corner in the far North, Littlejohns and *Osiris* would be tasked with spying on the Soviets in their new playgrounds of the Mediterranean and Indian Ocean.

Helping in this endeavour was an experimental narrow-band sonar, which was far better than the broadband versions used previously.

To try out the new sonar, *Osiris* engaged in a game of hide and seek with HMS *Valiant* west of the Bay of Biscay. Lying in wait, taking advantage of the diesel's innate advantage in stealth – batteries being quieter than nuclear propulsion plant – Littlejohns let the SSN get really close. While the diesel boat successfully detected *Valiant*, she did not have the speed or stamina to hold and chase her. Even so, Tim Hale – in his new job as Flotilla Operations Officer for FOSM – had pushed to have narrow-band sonar introduced for the O-boats. Hale was delighted when he received news of Littlejohns's *Valiant* detection.

Osiris was next tasked by Hale to chase down a contact that looked like a Soviet diesel.

During the course of pursuing this task Littlejohns brought *Osiris* to periscope depth for a good all-round look. As he swept around, he caught sight of another periscope and realised 'someone else was doing the same, just 200 yards away on the starboard beam'.

Snapping the handles up and sending the periscope down into its well, Littlejohns ordered the planesman to take the submarine deeper. In the Sound Room the sonar operators devoted their efforts to sound signature identification. The other submarine – a Juliett Class boat – appeared to have come up from the deep to snort. Would she have detected *Osiris*?

Judging by her movements, the answer was no.

Littlejohns's boat was now given the go-ahead to call at Gibraltar for a short break before participating in some warfare training. On board for the trip was an officer Littlejohns assumed was a Chilean submariner. Vickers was building O-boats for the South American nation and *Osiris* was being asked to provide some worthwhile sea time for the future First

Lieutenant of one. Except, on talking to the man, Littlejohns discovered he was 'an army officer whose last job was interrogating dissidents'.

Slightly taken aback, he hoped sincerely that the Chileans also had some properly trained submariners to operate their new boats.

'The Chilean was not cleared to any level of security, so we had to run two navigation charts – one in the Control Room and one in my cabin. And he was not allowed in the Sound Room for the *Valiant* exercise or the Juliett detection, nor was he given the periscope during the latter period.'

With the run ashore at Gib concluded, *Osiris* was involved in a course that aimed to teach the Principal Warfare Officers (PWO) of the surface fleet the art of Anti-Submarine Warfare. For Littlejohns this was an opportunity to show what he could do in an attacking situation, especially as Capt. Oliphant had joined the boat. 'Three Leander Class frigates were scheduled to come out past the Gib breakwater and turn south in line ahead. *Osiris* was told to attack them. We were given a huge amount of water to manoeuvre in, which was ideal. I realised they would have to exit by Europa Point, so I positioned the submarine in waters only a few hundred yards off the lighthouse and torpedoed them one by one like ducks in a shooting gallery at the fair. I heard afterwards that the PWOs were still having breakfast when the green grenades went off – during that kind of exercise a submarine fires smoke grenades to provide a sign on the surface that a torpedo attack has been made. They had decided that I wouldn't be anywhere near the Rock, so were not expecting my attack. Basically they were applying peacetime thinking. Oliphant was thrilled and decided he wanted to see the green smoke and discomfited frigates. I had great difficulty in persuading him to give me back the attack periscope – he just loved watching the targets go by at 200-yard intervals all nicely lined up. By the time the PWOs in the frigates got their acts together – to try and find and attack us – we were doing 18 knots to the east. They never found us. I would have loved to be a fly on the wall for the course officer's debrief.'

Osiris sailed back to Gosport feeling the glow of a successful trip and Littlejohns received congratulations from none other than Tim Hale, who, as Flotilla Operations Officer, always took time out to deliver credit where credit was due.

Having first encountered each other back in 1972 when Hale came to visit a poorly Littlejohns in the naval hospital next door to *Dolphin*, the two men sometimes met in the wardroom bar at the submarine base.

They also occasionally engaged in a game that perfectly embodied the cheerful competition via which boisterous young submarine officers blew off steam. Evenly matched in height and build, Littlejohns and Hale were each given two empty Coca-Cola bottles – mixers of the classic waisted variety made from thick glass, as was common in the 1970s.

The objective – cheered, clapped and roared on by their fellow officers, who were all suitably loosened by alcohol and enjoying the fun – was to place their toes on a line and then see how far out each one could stretch using a bottle in each hand for support. The victor was the man who left one of the bottles furthest away and then managed to get his contorted body back over the line without touching the floor. An older and wiser Littlejohns would concur that such after dinner high jinks were probably not altogether safe. 'I think Tim and I were honours even on that game. When I reflect on it now, if at any stage one of those bottles had broken, it would probably have sliced through our hands, straight into our chests and finished us off at the end of a lively evening.'

The headline tasking for Littlejohns and *Osiris* as she headed out East of Suez in September 1976 was an exercise off Karachi with a British naval task group (led by the guided-missile destroyer HMS *Hampshire*) and working with the Pakistan Navy. For good measure, the planners in the command cell running submarine operations at Fleet HQ – responding to a request for intelligence on Soviet Navy operations – sent a signal asking *Osiris* to have a look at two anchorages. First call was waters off Kithera, one of the smaller Ionian Islands, and an anchorage just outside territorial waters. The Soviets kept a gaggle of forward-based auxiliary ships there to support surface combatants and submarines passing through. The task at hand – photographing the undersides of major Soviet Navy warships at anchor – was not one for which Littlejohns had received any training, but he had absorbed reports by people who had mastered the skill.

'It was a daunting prospect, but at least Kithera had properly charted soundings. Taking photos of a Moskva Class helicopter cruiser and a couple of frigates at anchor is not like doing it on a moving ship, even going at one knot. They didn't have a very long anchor cable, but I could see it and hear it clanging.'

Littlejohns relied on his instinct – drawing on years of experience navigating submarines – and a good memory for what his predecessors had said of previous such exploits. He threaded his 2,410-ton, 295ft-long, black-painted submarine around the anchor cables of Soviet ships in the shallow, sparkling clear waters of the Med. It was the submarining equivalent of a camel going through the eye of a needle, but for Little-johns it was all in a day's work – and explained in a matter-of-fact fashion.

'The deep-water anchorage at Kithera is about 135ft deep. A Moskva draws about 25ft of water and the bottom of my keel to the top of my periscope is 70ft. The gap between the top of periscope and underside of the target vessel is 10ft and we are 30ft off the bottom. That's not a lot of room for manoeuvre, but we did it.'

After this brief nose around Kithera – totally undetected by the Soviet ships she spied on – *Osiris* headed south to go through the Suez Canal, a pause at Alexandria providing an opportunity for further espionage. Littlejohns admired his boys' efforts.

'We saw old Soviet-built Whiskeys and Romeo diesel boats, my lads taking photos like mini-James Bonds. One of the Romeos was even in dry dock. Not vital intelligence, as they were elderly vessels, but worth having. It was interesting that during a cocktail party in Alex the senior Egyptian officers of Commander and above – who had been trained in Britain before Nasser took control – drank gin and tonic or brandy and dry ginger. The juniors, who had been trained in Russia, drank vodka.'

While she was at Alex, *Osiris* received a signal confirming that Little-johns had been promoted to Lieutenant Commander and the newly promoted captain now took her through the Canal. The first British submarine to do the transit since 1956, she was not entirely welcomed by the Egyptians. They were perhaps making a point about the fashion in which British forces had last visited Suez.

'They put us at the back of the convoy, not the front where warships traditionally go, but we did some overtaking to avoid being late out of the transit. My assigned canal pilot, a retired Egyptian Rear Admiral, nearly had several babies while we were overtaking other vessels, but in the end he was quite complimentary. All the way down the canal the search periscope was taking pictures of the massive army camps and weapon emplacements, which all went back to London.'

Once into the Red Sea the boat dived – to check the trim in different water conditions. Surfacing, after a short period *Osiris* again submerged, this time for some time, not surfacing again until approaching Karachi. On the way there she called at the island of Socotra. In the Cold War it was firmly in the Soviet orbit, but Littlejohns would prove it was far from being a no-go zone.

In recent times the US Department of Defense has expressed a desire to use an airfield and port on the island of Socotra, which is around 150 miles east of Somalia and 240 miles into the Indian Ocean from the shores of Arabia. The Russian Navy has stated it might also contemplate a return to its old base. In the twenty-first century both nations are interested in combating piracy emanating from the failed state of Somalia and also countering terrorism across the wider Indian Ocean. In the 1970s Socotra was under the sway of the People's Democratic Republic of Yemen, which had gone decisively over to the Russian side in the Cold War. From 1971 onwards Socotra was a very useful anchorage for Soviet warships and *Osiris* would pay them a visit to see if there was anything worth photographing. Littlejohns reckoned conducting a recce at periscope depth in such clear and shallow waters was not going to be easy. The boat could hit the bottom and might accidentally surface. Someone might attack the intruder but Littlejohns thought the element of surprise was probably his most reliable defence. 'If we had inadvertently surfaced I would have just piled on the revs and dived again to exit the area. I doubt if any onlookers would have recognised us as a Royal Navy boat so far from home.'

Studying the Admiralty chart for Socotra was not exactly reassuring, for it appeared to have been surveyed back in the 1700s by a contemporary of Captain James Cook.

It offered very few soundings and, worst of all, there were little stick people inked on it and a caption declaring: 'Here be natives.' The oath Littlejohns uttered on seeing that could not be repeated in polite society.

The charts may have been next to useless, but his submariners had faith in the CO of *Osiris*. While he ran the boat along tightly disciplined lines, Littlejohns still held faith with the piratical spirit that gave them all a buzz. It would see them through safely.

There were bound to be some 'targets' at Socotra as the Russians had few other places to seek shelter in those waters. With sea conditions benign, the sea tranquil – an oily, gently undulating swell – Littlejohns took the boat in at very slow speed, around 2 knots. It would need precision on the trim and the hydroplanes to keep the absolute minimum amount of periscope showing above the surface. As he inspected the warships and auxiliaries at anchor, Littlejohns saw one or two slumbering forms littered around the boiling upper decks, under awnings. *There were no sharp-eyed lookouts aboard this lot.*

Everybody else must have been below decks in the air-conditioned interiors, if indeed the Soviets were efficient enough to have those systems working. Littlejohns kept up a running commentary as he moved the submarine cautiously around the anchorage firing off the camera. He was enjoying himself; he relished the *Boys' Own* nature of the escapade. Should someone stir from a vodka-induced slumber aboard a Soviet ship, by the time their befuddled brains realised they had seen a submarine periscope, *Osiris* would have headed for the exit and be well away.

Osiris surfaced on the other side of the Arabian Sea, where setting course for Karachi was fairly easy – she just navigated by the smog on the horizon. The paint had come off the fin, possibly as a result of warm water and increased salinity. It was hanging down like six-foot-wide strips of wallpaper. The *Osiris* submariners scraped it off as best they could, the boat entering Karachi looking like a zebra. Scrounging some paint from the Pakistani Navy, the submarine was soon made to look more presentable.

Heading home, on the way back up through the Suez Canal, Littlejohns decided to depart *Osiris* temporarily at the Great Bitter Lake. The First Lieutenant, Robin Oliphant – no relation to Capt. Oliphant, the squadron commander – took the boat on.

Climbing into a Land Cruiser with the Marine Engineer Officer, Frank Muscroft, they headed for the pyramids. Littlejohns had wanted to see them since boyhood when he was an ace Classics scholar. And it was surely appropriate for the captain of a submarine named after the Ancient Egyptian god of the afterlife and underworld to take a look. Once there the two British naval officers couldn't resist climbing a pyramid, until halted by the gun-toting local police who called them back down.

The two tourists rejoined *Osiris* at Port Said just before Littlejohns welcomed back on board an important visitor, in the person of the submarine squadron boss, Capt. Oliphant. This would be a testing time as Oliphant was giving *Osiris* the first phase of an inspection on the way to Piraeus, Athens. He was checking the boat was being run efficiently and performing properly on a long-distance deployment.

Not far from the Greek islands, Oliphant asked Lt Cdr Littlejohns to do a make-believe minelaying mission and also 'attack' a frigate (an unsuspecting ferry). Picking the exercise areas he remarked that during the Second World War his boat had been stuck on the bottom in the same spot, suffering the ordeal of being depth-charged. He didn't mind telling Littlejohns that he spent his time hiding under the wardroom table.

There was a tricky moment after the minelaying exercise. As the submarine conducted a deep dive, one of the hull valves in the Engine Room sprang a leak, at around 550ft. Littlejohns immediately ordered *Osiris* to surface. It was the sort of express elevator ride that pleased Oliphant. He was delighted to see decisive action to ensure the safety of one of his squadron's boats and her crew. On returning to the UK in December the deployment was pronounced a great success for a variety of reasons that Littlejohns listed with pride. 'We had made some good diplomatic moves, fired up the Egyptians about how good our boat was compared with theirs, did some clockwork-mousing – playing a submarine target – for the Pakistan and Greek navies before attacking them back. We contributed some good intelligence and had shown that we could still operate a long way from any home base. We had mended several big leaks and rebuilt a Barr and Stroud periscope. We even rebuilt the main diesel engine exhaust deflectors without which we couldn't run the engines. For that we used empty tins that had once contained the Three Nuns tobacco I smoked in my pipe.'

And it was also well worth it judging by the reaction of the boys in the Defence Intelligence Service after the results of the Socotra mission were delivered. A message of grateful thanks was sent to Lt Cdr Littlejohns, who proudly conveyed the news to his sailors.

Dan Conley's first command, the diesel submarine *Otter*, had just pulled into Rosyth Naval Base, across the Forth from Edinburgh, following a major exercise. He was working on papers in his cabin, when there was a knock at the door. A sailor poked his head through the curtain announcing that the second-in-command of SM3, the boat's parent unit at Faslane, was coming aboard. Conley was not expecting any visits from senior officers and wondered what it could be about.

Welcoming the Commander into his cabin, Conley enquired why he was enjoying the pleasure of his company.

The answer hit him like a bolt of thunder.

'I am here to warn you that an embarrassing story is about to hit the papers,' revealed the submarine squadron emissary.

The Ministry of Defence press office had been receiving inquiries from journalists on the *Evening Standard* and the national papers about an alleged incident aboard *Otter*. Apparently it involved Mary Millington, the star of numerous 'adult' films.

The colour drained from Conley's face, as he had no idea what the other man was talking about.

And it had all been going so well.

At the beginning of December 1975 Conley had joined *Otter* in Faslane as her new captain. In the New Year he took the boat to sea, getting to know the vessel's foibles and those of her crew. As the submarine's Navigator and then First Lieutenant, from April 1973 to November 1974, Littlejohns had certainly been challenged to strike a happy balance in *Otter*'s work hard, play hard approach to life. Now it was Conley's turn to find out how much of a handful *Otter*'s men could be.

The submarine's first operational voyage with Conley as captain involved another transatlantic crossing to AUTEC. For several weeks the boat would act as a target for SSNs, rehearsing their submarine versus submarine tactics while also working with surface ships and helicopters to hone their ASW skills. To protect her from potential exercise torpedo hits, *Otter*'s ballast tanks and vents received additional protective cladding.

It was a good deployment with some wonderfully hospitable ports of call, including Bermuda, Charlestown, Cape Canaveral, Fort Lauderdale and Nassau in the Bahamas. Conley found he was on a steep learning curve but it wasn't anything he couldn't handle.

'We were "hunted" by frigates and the Swiftsure Class boat *Sovereign*. On one occasion a practice wire-guided Tigerfish torpedo hit *Otter* inadvertently. It made a loud noise as it struck our bows. We surfaced and put a diver over the side, who reported one of the torpedo tube shutters stoved in. Bits of torpedo were now embedded in it.'

Nothing was more hazardous, though, than *Otter*'s encounter with Mary Millington. She had been starring in European hardcore porn movies since the early 1970s, while also occasionally turning tricks as a call girl, all of which was not exactly on Conley's warning radar.

The 'it' girl of Britain's cheesy and seedy porn movie industry, Millington was on holiday in the Bahamas. She just happened to be staying in the Britannia Beach Hotel, Nassau, where some of *Otter*'s sailors were also residing as part of the usual custom of not staying aboard the boat while in port.

Conley's wife, Linda, had flown out to join him while the submarine continued her duty as AUTEC target. The afternoon Mary Millington was invited on board *Otter* – fortunately, as it would turn out, entirely without the captain's permission or knowledge – Lt Cdr and Mrs Conley were having lunch with the British High Commissioner.

According to legend, once aboard – and away from the prying eyes of officers or senior ratings – Millington shed her clothes, handing her camera to a sailor while she struck some poses with his shipmates. It would be claimed she even had sex with one or more submariners aboard *Otter*, although this was later denied. Millington also featured in porn magazines, such as *Whitehouse* and *Ladybirds* (for instance). Describing her as its 'editor', the latter published a pictorial report on her visit to *Otter*. One of the more sedate images showed Millington on the casing in front of the fin, clad in skimpy bikini, wearing a sailor's cap and with an arm draped around a delighted submariner. In another photo a lifebelt with 'H.M.S. Otter' and the boat's crest emblazoned on it was helpfully placed in the foreground. The saucy report remarked, by way of introducing a picture essay: 'Mary, sexually unattended since she left London a week previously, was feeling the itch – as was the crew of H.M.S. *Otter*.'

It went on in the same risqué vein, depicting Millington as invited on board *Otter* for drinks and dinner. Furthermore, it claimed 'Mary and the boys' were 'too drunk and randy to even think about dinner'. It even had the effrontery to ask primly: 'Does the Navy only bother with security during times of war?'

Feeling fury bubbling in the wake of having his collar felt by the submarine squadron troubleshooter, Conley ordered an investigation. Yes, the Officer of the Day knew she had been on board, but he had no idea she had allegedly gone naked. As for the contents of the so-called porn magazine report, it was all a pack of lies. Conley was worried he might follow in the footsteps of an American submarine captain whose career had been wrecked by a similarly racy episode. In July 1975, the CO of the US Navy nuclear-powered attack submarine USS *Finback* had been relieved of command for permitting a topless go-go dancer to do a routine aboard his boat. Perched on one of the SSN's sail-mounted planes, she shook her stuff as the boat proceeded out to sea. That story made the front page of the *Washington Post* and even an item in *Time* magazine. The US Navy took a dim view of such antics and the *Finback*'s CO was relieved of his command. While *Otter* and Mary Millington also made national headlines it was a storm Conley managed to weather. 'I was not in the least complicit, nor at the time was I aware of the incident, and possessed the perfect alibi of being at lunch with the High Commissioner. It was, though, a difficult time for me as, apart from all the publicity, questions were even asked in Parliament.'

The rest of the Navy found it hilarious and did not miss any opportunity to mock. 'Meeting other vessels at sea they sometimes signalled us, enquiring: "Is Mary Millington on board?" It did not do *Otter*'s morale any good and, at the time, it was most certainly a blemish on my professional career. The responsibility for the incident was ultimately mine.'

Conley survived to command another day. Departing *Otter* in April 1977, to oversee evaluations of the new Tigerfish torpedo, he made the traditional call on Flag Officer Submarines, at the time Rear Admiral John Fieldhouse. Referring to the incident, the admiral remarked drily:

'If you can survive that, you can survive anything.'

Tim Hale looked at the piece of paper in his hands and sighed.

The message typed on it read: 'From James Bond film unit to HMS *Fearless*. Many thanks for a good shoot. A highly eventful week when many were stirred but none were shaken. Signed 007.'

He handed the signal around his fellow officers in the wardroom. Grabbing his horse's neck, the ice cubes clinking in the glass, Hale let out a harsh laugh. 'Shaken not stirred!? Sod off!'

He immediately felt bad – they meant well, and it was nice to know the movie people had been happy, but he was in such a jaundiced mood.

Just a few months ago, as FOO, he'd been sending submarines on many dangerous missions that gave the West an edge against the dastardly Soviet foe. Signals placed on the communications network conveying congratulations were not uncommon after an SSN or a diesel had pulled off a successful spying mission. But that was then and this was now and he was XO of the amphibious assault ship HMS *Fearless*.

In early November 1976 the ship sent one of her Wessex helicopters to Malta, where it picked up a film crew.

The Bond movie production company was borrowing *Fearless* to shoot the final scenes of *The Spy Who Loved Me*.

There had been hopes Roger Moore, the latest incarnation of Cdr James Bond, and Barbara Bach, playing sexy KGB agent Triple X, would visit *Fearless* for filming. In the end all they got was a second unit shooting the ship with a space age escape capsule bobbing about in her wake. Shots of it actually being brought into the assault vessel's stern dock were created on a mock-up at Pinewood Studios. In the completed scenes shocked British and Soviet intelligence chiefs get an eyeful of Bond and Triple X making love inside the recovered capsule. When asked what he is doing, Cdr Bond responds: 'Keeping the British end up, Sir.'

Real drama had intervened just as the film unit was about to begin its work at sea, when *Fearless* sailed to the rescue of a 6,500-ton Greek-flagged freighter, which was on fire five miles to the north-east of Malta. The blaze was so bad her crew were in the process of abandoning ship, fearing immolation once flames reached the cargo of lighter fuel, paint, oxidising acid and benzine. Despite this, *Fearless* went alongside the *Nostros Vasso Athene*, with valiant naval fire-fighting teams soon bringing the situation under control.

Fearless arranged for the smouldering freighter to be towed to safe harbour at Malta before returning to sea for the film crew to complete its work ... or rather, as Hale recalls, try to. 'We had to go back in the next day and send across a small craft with the fire-fighting team – the fire (aboard the freighter) had relit ... they put it out again, this time permanently.'

Bravery awards were later presented to some of the fire-fighters and salvage money was also forthcoming.

The Bond people made up for not sending out their stars to film in *Fearless* by inviting Hale and others to the London premiere of the movie in July 1977. Commander and Mrs Hale got to meet the legendary producer Cubby Broccoli. Hale was delighted to discover the movie mogul was very pro-Navy and such a good host the former SSN captain could forgive the many cheesy inaccuracies in submarine operations in *The Spy Who Loved Me*.

It opens with a tense sequence in which a British SSBN disappears, shortly followed by a Russian equivalent. There is even an *avant garde* British submarine operations centre. It features in a sequence during which the cinematic equivalent of Hale (as FOO) remarks, rather ashen-faced: 'We've lost one of our nuclear submarines ...'

'How bloody careless,' thought Hale with a chuckle as he watched the action unfold on the silver screen.

At one point 007 visits Faslane in uniform, dropping in by Sea King helicopter. In a Polaris Operations Authority building, Bond is introduced to Flag Officer Submarines, among others, and receives a briefing.

The Bond series boffin Q steps forward to shock everybody by revealing someone has devised a fiendish 'wake tracking system'. It allegedly enables potential foes to easily trail submarines with pinpoint accuracy. Much of the subsequent story revolves around a mad shipping magnate using the system and one of his supertankers to swallow British, Russian and American nuclear-powered submarines. Seizing control of their nuclear weapons, the villain's aim is to launch simultaneous strikes on Moscow and New York. Leading a mass breakout of imprisoned submariners Cdr Bond ultimately defeats the evil scheme. During a visit to Pinewood as a guest of Cubby Broccoli, the sight of life-size fake submarines created inside a gigantic sound stage impressed Hale.

Introduced to Roger Moore and Barbara Bach, the actor asked Cdr Hale what he reckoned to it all. The naval officer thought it would turn 007's hair white if he knew the reality of Cold War submarine operations.

Hale contented himself with remarking: 'It's all good stuff.'

Unfortunately he couldn't say the same for his time in the surface navy. His sense of humour and tolerance had been sorely tested. While they meant well and did their best, his shipmates in *Fearless* – spending their time ferrying around Royal Marines and training cadets from Dartmouth – just didn't have the same war-fighting edge or outlook on life as submariners.

'I had come from the life-or-death ethos of the Submarine Service and it just wasn't the same, not as rewarding or thrilling as my previous existence. I was neither shaken nor stirred. Many submarine officers did make the transfer successfully, but for me it was not the way I wanted to spend the rest of my working life. In the aftermath of the Greek freighter incident, *Fearless* was visited by lawyers and other City boys. One of them was an old friend of mine, Mike Allen, ex-Swiftsure, who was working for Mike Cooper, who had been my First Liuetenant in Tiptoe back in the late 1960s.'

Cooper was now a top man with a London-based maritime law firm.

Hale revealed he was fed up with the surface navy and Cooper proposed: 'Why don't you come and join us?'

Hale was 41 years old and if he was going to have a second career he had to make his move now – stay in the Navy and command a surface ship, or leave and become a lawyer?

He liked a challenge and working as a lawyer in the City seemed more enticing than anything the Navy could offer and, moreover, a long-term proposition. What he wanted most of all was a second career that was, in its own way, as rewarding and satisfying as his life in submarines.

If anyone embodied the mystical black magic of submarine command – the indefinable intuition that defied statistical analysis – it was Beastie Biggs.

Having served as XO to Hale in *Swiftsure*, acting as mentor to Conley as a young Sonar Officer in the same boat, he was appointed Teacher in succession to Rob Forsyth. Doing well in that job paved the way for command of an SSN, which was HMS *Superb*. The previous ship to hold the name was a Second World War-era cruiser, decommissioned in 1957. Back then her nickname was 'Super B' but it was changed to 'Super Bee' in the submarine's lifetime.

Arriving a week before Biggs travelled down to Devonport to take command was Lt Cdr Doug Littlejohns, who experienced a dramatic start to his time in the Swiftsure Class submarine.

A fire broke out in the boat's No. 1 Main Ballast Tank 15 minutes after the SSN was signed over to the new XO's temporary command. Dockyard workers using a welding torch had set fire to wooden staging. Submariners are trained to tackle all manner of fires inside their submarine all the time, but could never have imagined such an occurrence. A ballast tank was usually full of water or empty. Fortunately the blaze caused only minor damage and was easily extinguished by submariners wielding fire hoses.

As the newest SSN in the fleet, *Superb* was the pride of the submarine flotilla, in June 1977 starring in the massive Silver Jubilee Fleet Review off Spithead. Flying FOSM's flag she was just one of 170 ships on show, 97 of them crewed by the Royal Navy. The £60m SSN had been launched at Barrow in late November 1974 and commissioned in November 1976, the same month as sister vessel *Sceptre* was launched. *Superb* was the 304th submarine constructed by Vickers, the government blaming her protracted build on strife in the British shipbuilding work force.

With older vessels paying off, including a quarter of the diesel submarine force (under the 1975–76 Defence White Paper), there was a need to get the yards moving more quickly. Proposals for the construction of frigates, destroyers and other naval vessels were axed, but not SSNs.

In early 1977, as *Superb* worked her way up to becoming fully operational, the Secretary of State for Defence, Patrick Duffy, revealed unsettling figures for warship orders placed in the previous ten years. Out of six vessels ordered in 1966–67, two were SSNs (*Conqueror* and *Courageous*), in 1967–68 just one (HMS *Swiftsure*). There wasn't another submarine order until *Sovereign* (1969–70), but the only other vessel ordered that year was a minesweeper. HMS *Superb* was ordered in 1970–71, the other three vessels that year being Amazon Class frigates. Ten vessels were ordered in 1971–72 and just one of these was an SSN (*Sceptre*), whose construction would also be protracted. The only naval vessel ordered in 1972–73 was *Spartan*, and thereafter in 1976–77 just one more SSN (*Splendid*). This was pathetically slow compared with Soviet submarine construction rates. For example, seven Victor II SSNs were built between 1972 and 1978, while 23 of the even more stealthy and faster Victor IIIs would be completed between 1978 and 1988.

The charismatic Biggs would run *Superb* with considerable élan, displaying more than a dash of cavalier spirit, which was appropriate for a boat carrying the motto 'With Sword and Courage'.

A seasoned *Superb* hand by this time was Michael Pitkeathly, who had joined her in October 1974 while she was still in build. After several patrols in *Courageous*, he had completed his RP1 (Radar Plotter) course and was promoted Petty Officer after being drafted to the new SSN along with quite a few of his old shipmates. The reason for this was simple: *Superb* was to be the Special Fit boat, destined for adventures in the North. She needed experienced players.

Knowing this was the kind of mission that lay ahead, *Superb*'s men were keen to play their part in the Biggs–Littlejohns dynamic.

The new command team was regarded highly, one rating from the time remarking: 'Biggs was well known – he was excellent – and Littlejohns had a bit of a reputation.' For his part, Pitt.k recognised that it was often a case of 'appointers matching a Commander with an XO they think will together make a good team'.

The new XO was dynamic and ambitious but above all he was highly competent and Super Bee's men liked that. When it came to officers there were some you wanted to be with and others that you wouldn't want to take you into tricky situations. These two fitted the bill perfectly and while Biggs was well known for not suffering fools gladly, he would deliver rebukes with care not to humiliate people in front of others, or belittle them.

For Lt Cdr Littlejohns, who left command of *Osiris* in December 1976, the path to becoming XO of *Superb* lay via an appointment as Staff Warfare Officer in the Second Submarine Squadron (SM2), the parent unit of submarines operating from Devonport. It would be the first of several jobs that immersed Littlejohns in the arts of submarine warfare. In this instance it encompassed responsibility for assessing the war-fighting capability of each boat, making sure they were able to handle the missions that would come their way. As further preparation for being second-in-command of *Superb*, Littlejohns was next appointed to *Swiftsure* as a FOSM rider for a patrol in the far North.

Whereas in the past Special Fit submarines going into the Barents might have carried a third command-qualified officer who was an American, that custom had lapsed. Now the third man was British, usually someone destined to be the XO or CO of an SSN. That was how Littlejohns made his first foray into the Russian Navy's home waters, working with the resident XO to draft the patrol report, which was a work in progress. Littlejohns was able to take some of the pressure off both him and the CO by taking his turn in command. Learning about the practical reality of being XO of a SSN was a bonus. By the time he reached *Superb*, Littlejohns had picked up some useful tips, but Biggs was something else, as he soon discovered.

'Some COs could cultivate a cavalier attitude that was deceptive and Biggs was one of them. He could be in his cabin just by the Control Room reading a pulp fiction novel – and he was a voracious reader of anything – but he always had one ear keeping track of the sonar contacts.'

After listening to the Sonar Operators calling out a contact, via the speakers in his cabin, Biggs would wander into the Control Room, cigarette burning in his hand. He told them it was the same suspected Soviet detected six hours earlier. Littlejohns was awestruck. 'Biggs was the most intuitive submarine captain I ever met. He was almost mystical.'

It didn't take long for Biggs to feel confident he could let Littlejohns take charge. He told his young XO: 'You are fitter, younger and brighter than me – you drive the submarine. If you get it right then I will take the credit but if you get it wrong I will carry the can.'

In the following months Biggs proved true to his word and Littlejohns relished the challenge of driving an SSN. It wasn't ever a one-man show, for he understood 'a ship is nothing without the crew and doing Special Fit was much more crew melding than anything. Once you could show the crew that they were better than the Soviets it made life very enjoyable. Let's say you are a rating and you have heard about the 'enemy" Soviets, but never encountered them for real. Then your team trails a Soviet submarine and fires an imaginary torpedo – you would do a simulated firing rather than using a water shot because of the noise. The boat gets away undetected by the foe and you feel that your hard work helping to plot a firing solution has paid off.'

On such important and dangerous missions – with no room for error – nobody wanted to be the weak link in the chain, especially when the boat was stretching the parameters of the performance envelope.

Pitt.k was a Petty Officer of the Watch in *Superb* when she was on the surface, which involved assisting with navigation. When the SSN was dived he became heavily involved in fire-control solutions and drawing on his plotting skills, though he wasn't sure he wanted to get involved in ship control. 'I was a planesman in *Courageous* and had done my fair share, but on joining *Superb* I kept very quiet about it because I didn't want to do it again.'

Littlejohns had other ideas. As part of the process of getting to know *Superb*'s crew, he had been reading people's career reports and decided Pitt.k had more to offer.

'You have been on the planes before, haven't you?' he asked, ordering Pitt.k into the hot seat. Taking advantage of deep water in the Atlantic Littlejohns put *Superb* through some high-speed manoeuvres, which Pitt.k appeared to handle with aplomb. 'You are obviously a born planesman,' Littlejohns told him.

And so, much to his disgust, Pitt.k knuckled down to more sessions as planesman. It was, potentially, a very stressful job. Responsibility for the fate of both the submarine and her crew would, literally, be in Pitt.k's hands. He was only too well aware of the pressure.

'To physically keep depth and steer a course is very hard work, for you have to be very precise. It is mentally demanding. You would probably only do two hours in the seat. In general, when on patrol, the submarine used an autopilot for both steering and maintaining depth, but the Command didn't have full confidence in it. Hence the need for someone in the seat at all times.' A planesman would work in tight partnership with the Ship Control Officer of the Watch (SCOOW) who was also doing the trim. The SCOOW would relay the orders of the Captain, XO or Watch Leader, keenly aware they must not take the boat beyond the performance envelope.

This had been defined for each type of submarine in the Navy by Admiralty boffins. They used models in a massive water tank, plus computer simulations and other means of experimentation, to explore and define safe operating parameters.

The Manoeuvring Envelope was outlined on a board that used several graphs to provide a visual guidance on what sort of plane angle – and speed – could be used. It was, in effect, a large slide rule. Prominently displayed in the Control Room, at a glance the SCOOW and others involved in ship control could check they were within the envelope, or at least not busting it open to a dangerous degree. Top of the fear list was after planes jamming on dive or ascent during a manoeuvre, the submarine hurtling at high speed ever deeper until she imploded, or leaping uncontrollably out of the water.

For Littlejohns and other aggressive submarine captains observing operational parameters religiously could be as dangerous as flouting them. 'If you wanted to be ultra-cautious then you would stay within the envelope,' said Littlejohns, 'but you wouldn't be a very effective captain.'

The enemy would of course also have his own operating envelope and it might not match yours – to beat him you might have to push the edges of your own.

It was a matter of common sense – intuitive understanding based on experience and instinct about what the submarine could, and could not, handle. For the planesman, executing the orders of the SCOOW, it was also about gaining a feel for the boat. At 4 knots you would require big movements on the control column, but at speed everything had to be more subtle – and careful.

Throughout the Cold War the Russians would constantly switch surface units between their various fleets – a highway of frigates, destroyers and cruisers between the Arctic, Baltic and Black Sea. They were perfect prey for the sleek black sharks of the Silent Service. If *Superb* was on exercises to the north-west of Ireland and a Soviet surface warship was detected heading south or north, she might break off to go and have a look at any new fittings and how the target operated. The Russian vessels were often steaming at low speed anyway, possibly to preserve fuel, making it easier to get some photographs of what lay below their waterline.

Pitt.k didn't do the famed underwater look on the planes of *Superb*, for he was required to plot a target's track. But he had done it while serving in *Courageous*, so he knew how utterly exhausting it was for the planesman.

'During an underwater look a boat was at a high state of readiness – it was a different atmosphere from usual running. The planesman was very focused, to ensure precisely the right depth and course, with constant adjustments, for the target ship often wouldn't be following a completely straight course. The SSN would speed up to get underneath, then slow down, and you have to be very wary of depth separation. Other factors include the swell and the estimated keel depth, with a little bit of extra room if the submarine is a new build, for safety. You have to know the height of the periscopes – both search and attack will be up, one with stills camera and the other shooting video – and your own boat's keel depth. Always add some room for error. It is hard work being the planesman in such circumstances. You clear your mind and work entirely as one with the captain, who is on the scope, responding to what he's saying. He will be saying left or right one or two degrees, up or down one foot or two.'

There was no margin for error with the tip of the submarine's scope a matter of feet away from spinning screws or with the hull of a vessel riding a strong swell.

Sometimes – though it was a very rare occurrence – a target might react. Pitt.k's most heart-stopping underwater look came in *Courageous*, when the target appeared to take particular exception.

'We were off North-West Ireland and giving a Kresta Class ASW cruiser the once-over. It seemed they knew we were there because they dropped three charges – not depth charges, more like small exercise charges – so we disengaged rapidly.'

The Soviet warship had possibly switched on an echo sounder and was aggravated to discover a rather large contact directly underneath. For, as Littlejohns pointed out, 'unless the target was pencil-thin people on board the Soviet ship could not actually see what was underneath. The wake created by a ship also helps obscure you – they are not going to see you down there – after all, a ship is wider than a submarine.'

Visual detection was also made more unlikely by refraction, dirty water, sunlight glinting on the waves, although a submarine at periscope depth might be seen from an aeroplane.

For Littlejohns and other command-qualified officers, the most thrilling underwater look was on a Soviet submarine. As Alfie Roake had found with his snooping around in a diesel boat 'up North', subjecting the foe to close-up scrutiny was fraught with risks.

With Soviet submarines trimmed down while on the surface, it made them much faster to dive than Western boats. This meant whoever was doing an underwater look had to be particularly vigilant. After taking an educated guess on the trimmed-down Soviet's draft he would ease underneath. The Sound Room would be on a knife-edge for any signs of ballast tank vents opening to indicate the target was about to dive. For cool customers Biggs and Littlejohns in *Superb*, this would be no cause for undue stress – she was so close to the Soviet a move of a few feet to port or starboard took her out of harm's way.

Should the underwater look be prolonged, the planesman would get seriously tired and the captain might order the submarine to pull away and do it again some other time. In *Superb*, they were swift workers, the whole look lasting no more than 30 minutes before vanishing, leaving the Soviets in blissful ignorance. It wasn't just the Russians that *Superb* liked to play tricks on. The occasion of a visit by Rear Admiral Martin La Touche Wemyss – the man who had bollocked Tim Hale for bringing *Swiftsure* alongside too close to *Repulse* – provided an excuse for an amusing prank. Wemyss was at the time Flag Officer Flotilla 2, with his flag flying on the large guided-missile destroyer HMS *London*. In a previous life he had been a diesel submarine captain, also served in the Russian section of Naval Intelligence and had played a part in bringing the Polaris programme to fruition.

As an old friend, Cdr Biggs invited him to lunch aboard *Superb*. Having never served in a nuclear-powered submarine, or one of the newer diesels, Wemyss had not been below 400ft. Before sitting down to eat, Biggs asked the SCOOW and Trim Officer to gradually, with no fuss but great care, take the boat very deep. Once the agreed depth was achieved, over the speakers in the wardroom came a flat calm voice reporting the submarine was at a depth of 1,000ft, provoking Wemyss to almost choke on his lunch. He hadn't noticed a thing. With a twinkle in his eye, he told Biggs off for playing silly buggers. Commander Biggs responded with a laugh that such were the marvels of modern submarines – so very far removed from the old diesels.

One aspect of the Silent Service that was a painful and convoluted process was perfecting a torpedo that could fulfil its potential to catch and kill fast, deep-diving Soviet submarines.

Such is the way with cutting-edge technology, and it was especially the case in the Cold War when East and West were competing so intensely to achieve military superiority.

The development of submarines has over the decades seen its share of mishaps as result of malfunctioning technology, but it is only through a process of trial and error that glitches can be ironed out.

The troublesome wire-guided Mk23 and the Mk24 Tigerfish, which

Hale's brand-new *Swiftsure* had test-fired off Gibraltar in 1974 – with very mixed results – were still a problem four years later.

Following his time in command of *Otter*, in April 1977 Dan Conley, who had been *Swiftsure*'s Sonar Officer during those earlier trials, got to work intensively on Tigerfish teething problems. He was appointed to lead a group ensuring submarine crews were certified to use them.

Conley was well aware of the recent chequered history of British submarine weapons development.

'The first post-war Royal Navy anti-submarine torpedo was the Mk20, with its wire-guided version – the Mk23 – introduced into service in the early 1960s. The Mk23 was both unreliable and it had severe performance shortfalls.'

Now the saga of Tigerfsh was in full swing, with Conley and his team frequently embarked in submarines, both diesel and nuclear-powered, to conduct certification firings. These took place in two locations: the British Underwater Test and Evaluation Centre range off Kyle of Lochalsh, in the Western Highlands, and AUTEC, the latter for deep-water evaluation tests of Tigerfish.

In addition to certifying the submarines for the whole process – from handling and firing to controlling the Tigerfish – Conley and his men studied how the weapon itself ran, measuring the failure trends, assessing where weaknesses lay.

British submariners wanted a torpedo that was as good as their submarines. One serious problem, in both the Mk23 and Tigerfish, which vexed Conley was the guidance wire breaking shortly after launch. This rendered it useless, as it was not yet armed.

'At least in the case of the US Navy's Mk48 if the wire broke, it was automatically armed. For a submarine captain, indeed his crew, the prospect that your main weapon system might fail would be a terrifying prospect in war, especially in a situation where you might have to take on a Soviet nuclear submarine.'

The Mk23 had a passive homing capability, using its own sonar to detect a target, but this was limited by only being able to 'listen' downwards for very-high-frequency noise.

Conley's verdict was that its 'target-acquisition range in most situations was very constrained. With a maximum speed of 18 knots and maximum effective depth of 800ft it would have been utterly useless against a nuclear submarine. It was just about OK against a noisy diesel boat snorting.'

That was a serious set of handicaps, as the Mk23 was the only ASW weapon the Silent Service had from the early 1960s to the mid-1970s, when Tigerfish started on its long road to effectiveness. When the pea in the peashooter didn't work – and the Mk23 offered at best only a 30 per cent chance of performing as expected – the Royal Navy still resorted to the short-range Mk8 torpedo. This was a point-and-shoot (unguided) weapon, which, Conley felt, 'could only be used against submarines that were at periscope depth'. In the quest for something better Conley's team oversaw 100 firings of Tigerfish, so he became acquainted with the reliability of the new weapon and developed tactics on how to get the best out of it. Eventually there would be improvements, which would raise its reliability. Conley was keen on the use of realistic, moving targets rather than static ones, which he felt 'could mask a host of problems, both weapon and operator'. His assessment was that Tigerfish would succeed, provided reliability problems – wire breaks and poor components, including suspect batteries – could be overcome.

All his work with Tigerfish led to some deep thinking on Conley's part about tactics for modern submarine warfare. It was so radically different from the Second World War model of the periscope (or even surfaced) attack against warships and submarines.

'The nuclear submarine has the speed and endurance to make long-range interceptions on other submarines or surface forces,' he explained. 'High-speed sprints need to be followed by periods at slower speed to regain the target and to assess his range and movement. As the picture builds up then the final approach phase should be conducted to minimise your own risk of counter-detection, achieving a good firing position. This optimises weapon capability and effectiveness. This takes quite a bit of skill and experience. If a submarine target is detected at huge range, injudicious use of high speed to get into a firing position – increasing your own noise generation – could result in counter-detection and attack. The idea is to assess where he is at long range, maintain contact, but stay beyond his sonar counter-detection range. You do a very carefully planned approach using bursts of speed as appropriate, until in a good firing position and poised for the right moment to strike.'

HMS *Superb* would apply similar skills when she went North on her first foray in search of the intelligence prize, but first she would play a predator on the prowl in home waters.

In late 1977, with several weeks below the surface of the sea – cut off from the rest of humanity – lying ahead, *Superb* made a visit to Zeebrugge. Her mission was to allow the lads to let off steam. Britain was also keen to display its latest SSN, so she would also welcome aboard politicians who sat on NATO's Military Committee.

Next on the agenda was a work-out where a dozen frigates of various NATO nations were on exercise. *Superb* would be a wolf among the surface-fleet sheep, approaching waters off Dorset as if she were close to Russia. The planners and other staff in the operations centre at Portland were deliberately kept in the dark and only Flag Officer Sea Training himself knew. Littlejohns enjoyed it all enormously. 'This had never been done before – putting an SSN in the Portland exercise areas – and our job was not to be caught. We had a lovely time. It was the Thursday War – the big exercise held at the end of each week. At a prearranged time the admiral announced there was an intruder and he scrambled all warships. They came out pinging away, because they thought it was a Russian.'

Superb had been told to loiter in a particular location, to give the NATO warships a chance of detecting her, but it never happened. The exercise areas off Portland were, like the Barents, comparatively shallow so provided an excellent familiarisation for the environment *Superb* would soon be entering.

The SSN let one of the surface vessels achieve a one-sonar-ping hit. This ship would think the intruder was a Soviet diesel, capable of 6 knots submerged at most. They would never dream it was a nuclear-powered Fleet boat capable of at least four times that speed. The obvious thing for a submarine to do in exiting the Portland exercise areas was head west towards deeper water. But, as Littlejohns explained, 'we went east at quite high speed for five miles. Then we put up periscope, put up the intel mast and caught the whole thing. They never found the intruder and never knew what it was.'

That was just an appetiser for what lay ahead and throughout the boat adrenaline levels were rising.

A sure sign of imminent deployment to the far North was embarkation of the usual intelligence-gathering specialists who would operate the Special Fit equipment. They were also put through their paces.

Their presence made the cramped interior of the boat even tighter – the total number of people was 125 with riders, but *Superb* was never designed for that many. She had 98 fitted bunk spaces, so it inevitably led to disgruntled senior ratings giving up theirs and being ejected into the junior rates mess and down into the Weapons Stowage Compartment (Torpedo Room). Even so, the Communications Technicians (CTs) were tolerated with a certain amount of respect, especially as some of them were ex-submariners.

Tolerance was key to everything running smoothly – everybody had a job to do and the CTs would be working six hours on and six hours off, adapting themselves quite quickly to living and working in a submarine.

'A great many of them were highly experienced,' said Pitt.k, 'and had several trips up North under their belts. They knew what the score was.'

Acoustic Intelligence specialists – two officers – each had a perch in the Sound Room while the CTs had their own little areas stuffed with equipment, including the radar office on three-deck with their gear inside it.

Pitt.k contemplated the forthcoming mission with a mixture of eager anticipation and borderline anxiety. 'I knew it was going to be a long haul, but exciting and interesting. There was still some trepidation be-cause it was my first time as the RP1 in the boat, but we had a good command team and were very well worked up.'

Littlejohns recognised that Pitt.k's team would be fundamental to the success of the mission ahead. 'They had to be good. It was Pitt.k's boys operating the plots, charts and DCA – the boat's Action Information System – so they had to be top-notch. If they weren't they could have given the captain bad information.'

There was no room for flawed input in a zone where life-or-death decisions were part of the daily routine.

For the back afties, the Marine Engineers in charge of the reactor and other vital life-support systems – who worked in a shift pattern whether at sea or alongside – the geographic location of *Superb* made no differ-ence to the essence of their job. Pitt.k's, on the other hand, in the heart of the Control Room action, revolved around knowing where any po-tential threat might be lurking on an hourly, if not a minute-by-minute, basis. The pace and nature of his routine could change by the second. The different nature of their job didn't mean the back afties were not in-terested and they showed a very keen interest in how *Superb* was doing.

Like everyone else in the crew they were able to see exactly where the SSN was at any given moment, courtesy of a prominently posted chart. During quiet periods an officer would go back and brief the engineers on where they were. Some of the engineers pretended indifference to their shipmates in the for'ard part of the boat. Pitt.k sometimes got the impression that 'basically a lot of people back aft were quite happy not to know where we were going or what was going on – quite happy to run their machinery so those at the fore end could do their job'.

During pre-deployment training, and later on the long haul around the top of Norway, off-duty hours were often enlivened by the nightly movie, though Cdr Biggs displayed monotonous taste.

Among the stock of films taken aboard HMS *Superb* was the recently released *ABBA: The Movie*, which the captain demanded to watch almost every night in the wardroom. The only break from the ordeal came when showing it might create noise that could be picked up by a nearby Soviet submarine. 'Goodness know what they would make of that,' Littlejohns growled to himself.

The cheesy tale of a journalist's frustrating odyssey across Australia in search of an interview with the Swedish supergroup was more than Littlejohns, or any other officer, could bear. If they never heard 'Mamma Mia' or 'Money, Money, Money' again it would be too soon. In one scene a journalist asks an Australian man with a large moustache: 'Are you an ABBA fan?' The man responds: 'Not particularly ... I hate 'em.'

As each successive showing ground them down, *Superb*'s much put-upon officers joined in with ever greater glee: 'We hate 'em!'

Their protestation started off as a low murmur but got louder even as Biggs waved an ABBA flag made out of a small paper rubbish sack.

Littlejohns pondered the CO's infatuation with the Swedish group and concluded: 'Biggs was deeply in love with the blonde female. It became a big joke, which he took mainly in good part.'

As president of the mess, with power to over rule the captain in cer-tain matters, Littlejohns banned any further showings. Unfortunately for the junior ratings Cdr Biggs imediately took the film reels to their mess, forcing them to show it on their projector. They had just started *The Spy Who Loved Me* (which at least featured submarines and sub-mariners in action) and groaned inwardly as it was replaced.

On the whole Biggs got on very well with the wardroom. As was the tradition, the captain had breakfast in his cabin – so officers who were grumpy in the morning could moan in private about his love for ABBA

etc. – but he sat down to lunch and dinner with them. He could otherwise come and go as he pleased to have a coffee or two, and a chat.

Biggs was a mad-keen cribbage player. He would often loiter in the
wardroom of an evening, awaiting the Marine Engineers coming off
watch – who had to pass through to reach their bunks – intent on nab-
bing them for an hour or so of crib. Their brother officers introduced all
sorts of ploys to distract the CO – such as raising important matters for
the following day's programme – just so the poor old engineers could
get out of their overalls and into bed. Sometimes, though, it was all to
no avail. Biggs was not beyond turfing someone out of his bunk for a
game of crib.

'The Golden Fleece was to get a new asset,' observed one experienced
British submariner who went on several Cold War missions into dangerous waters, 'to photograph and record a new warship type.'

There was plenty to see in the early to mid-1970s and *Superb*'s predecessors on missions into the Barents had witnessed extraordinary things,
bringing home substantial useful intelligence.

For example, *Swiftsure* – Hale's old boat – after his time in command once notched up four patrols in 1976–77, with the usual five-week
maintenance period for the boat (plus leave and training for the submariners) between each one. On such patrols the senior ratings in the
Sound Room worked very closely with the captain or XO, identifying
promising-looking targets, while the junior ratings were very willing to
learn their craft.

There was a constant discourse on contacts between the Sound Room
and Control Room. Occasionally there could be strong disagreements.

If the senior rating in charge of the Sound Room passionately felt the
captain was getting it wrong he might not hide it.

'Don't tell me that contact isn't a fucking submarine, Sir.'

And of course it was. The good captains took it well, while the more
authoritarian ones were not so pleased.

There were very few occasions when a CO would not take advice
from the senior rating of the Sound Room about contact analysis.

A key skill was to identify the exact bearing of a contact, so the periscope could be put up for the minimum amount of time.

In one incident a British SSN picked up what appeared to be a Yankee
Class SSBN preparing to test-fire missiles. The Soviet submarine was
making a rendezvous with an escorting vessel. The British SSN heard
Soviet submariners talking to this craft on the underwater telephone.

Provided with an excellent set of bearings after 15 hours on the trail, to cover all angles it was agreed the XO would use the attack periscope to look down the bearing where the Sound Room said the Yankee was.

He caught the moment of missile launch on both moving and still film as it disappeared down range.

Another time a British SSN picked up an interesting 'rattle' that it warily closed on. It was the chain of a moored barge that was to be the target of conventional surface missile firings. With this alarming realisation the SSN pulled out of the impact zone, to avoid being hit by one of the incoming Russian projectiles. Sometimes not even the Sound Room was needed to detect and then analyse the weapons firing, for the explosions were so close they echoed through the boat's hull. While there were clearly risks to British submarines in such situations, the Russians might also suffer. One Royal Navy SSN witnessed a Soviet surface warship getting walloped. A Kresta II Class cruiser was acting as the co-ordinating vessel for an anti-shipping missile test firing by a Charlie Class submarine. Missing the target barge, the missile hit the cruiser, causing an explosion.

Now it was *Superb*'s turn to head off into the North and she would experience a very busy time. There were so many sound signatures, rocket firings and new types of vessel to record and photograph that days tended to merge – six weeks of endless, round-the-clock intelligence gathering.

Towards the end of the patrol, when people loosened up slightly, morale improved at the thought of heading home. Then came crushing news.

The Americans needed the British cousins to stay on station for an extra week as the US Navy SSN allocated to take over was delayed. Grumble though they might the men put up with it.

Having pulled ten weeks up North, the *Superb* returned to Plymouth in April 1978, for the boat to receive some much-needed maintenance and her crew to be rewarded with some well-earned leave.

Their rest and recuperation period was almost immediately interrupted by a visit from the Prime Minister, James Callaghan, to open the brand-new submarine support base at Devonport. It was decided he should also inspect the nation's newest SSN. The reaction among *Superb*'s men was predictably grumpy.

Instead of being at home with their families, the submariners were forced to get their boat clean, and she was far from pristine. *Superb*'s men then put on their Number One uniforms and paraded like a bunch of stuffed dummies on the boat's casing. Callaghan gave a speech, declaring the new base, named HMS *Defiance*, formally open.

Callaghan had a quick walk through the submarine. Had the PM enquired about the submariners' welfare he would have received short shrift. Not only had he interrupted their leave at home, but dreadful levels of pay meant many of *Superb*'s men were so badly off their wives were claiming social security payments. Flat broke was a suitable description of their financial status. *And the nation, too.*

These were strange times indeed, and management of the nation's finances was replete with arcane Byzantine practices.

The Navy was the smallest it had been for 80 years, yet there were tens of millions of pounds in its shipbuilding allocation unspent, as shipyards were not completing warships swiftly enough.

Conversely, if they speeded up to get the vessels completed ahead of time, the government was forced to pay out crippling bonuses. That would wipe out the underspend and put the naval shipbuilding budget into the red. Yet this money could not be carried over to the following year or diverted to improve naval conditions of service. Many Royal Navy sailors would have appreciated a pay rise. For example, 30 per cent of newly commissioned officers were so poor they couldn't afford to complete their professional training and resigned.

The Navy minister, Patrick Duffy, visiting a vessel on deployment in the Middle East, bluntly rebuffed demoralised ratings who asked if there was any chance of a bigger pay packet. 'Speaking as an economist I wouldn't pay you another ha'penny,' he told them. Yet Duffy, who had seen service in the Fleet Air Arm during the Second World War, was very much for the nuclear Navy. On the right wing of the Labour Party, he opposed any proposals for the UK to unilaterally abandon nuclear weapons.

Under his stewardship as Navy minister, between 1976 and 1979, the Swiftsure Class programme at least continued. That any British nuclear-powered submarines were being built was a miracle and new surface combatants were a rarity.

In the USSR construction of Kiev Class Large Anti-Submarine Cruisers (*Bol'shoy Protivolodochny Kreyser*, or BPKR) far outstripped anything Britain's ailing industrial base could produce, in terms of both size and capability. On 18 July 1976, a new BPKR named *Kiev* slid through the Turkish Straits bound for her first front-line cruise in the Mediterranean.

Built at a shipyard in the Ukraine, in reality *Kiev* (laid down in September 1970, commissioned in May 1975) was an aircraft carrier. She could embark 18 Ka-25 Hormone ASW helicopters and a dozen Yak-38

Forger jump jets. International law forbade the operation of carriers in the Black Sea, and their passage through the Straits, hence the 'cruiser' label.

A sister vessel named *Minsk* had been launched in May 1975, with construction of a third Kiev Class initiated that October.

As Soviet maritime aviation grew, the British were discarding theirs. *Ark Royal* – last big strike carrier of the Royal Navy – was being decommissioned without replacement.

There had been deep unhappiness in Parliament at her demise. During a Defence debate as *Kiev*'s commissioning into service loomed, the Conservative MP for Tynemouth, Neville Trotter, suggested with deep sarcasm that 'it might be fitting ... to arrange for a photograph to be taken of the two ships passing each other – the *Ark Royal* going to the scrap yard and the *Kiev* ... proceeding to the high seas'.

The Soviets realised maritime-based strike power in international waters – whether Kievs or missile-armed submarines – was a go anywhere, attack any time capability. There were also Russian naval bases at Alexandria and Mersa Matruh in Egypt. In Libya Colonel Muammar Gaddafi was keen to be the USSR's best friend in the Arab world. He signed a treaty allowing the Soviets to use his country as a base for naval and air forces. There were hundreds of Russian 'military technicians' flooding into North Africa.

Propelled by alarm at the Soviet Navy's carriers – along with nuclear submarines the true mark of any front-rank global fleet – the British were building a new class of 'through-deck cruisers'. They were described as such because cost-averse politicians were afraid of the term 'aircraft carrier'. The first, *Invincible*, showed the new type of ship was configured more to combat the upsurge in Soviet submarines than to project power. She would host eight Sea King ASW helicopters and half a dozen Sea Harrier fleet defence and reconnaissance jets. Construction of *Invincible* was characteristically slow thanks to a scarcity of funds and continuing doubts over her relevance. Laid down in July 1973, she was not launched at Barrow-in-Furness for another four years and finally commissioned in 1980. A second British 'through-deck cruiser' was laid down at Swan Hunter on the Tyne in October 1976. Construction of the future *Illustrious* would be equally lacklustre.

In the meantime, what could be done to counter the rising menace *Kiev* and her sisters posed? That job would fall to Rob Forsyth in a new hunter-killer submarine, for HMS *Sceptre* was close to her first front-line mission.

A torpedo in one of *Courageous*'s tubes.

A starboard bow view of a Russian spy vessel observing NATO ships. A vessel similar to this one caused trouble for Doug Littlejohns when he was captain of *Osiris*. Background, left, is a Russian warship.

HMS *Swiftsure* on sea trials in October 1972.

Both Kashin Class and Kanin Class ASW destroyers of the Soviet Navy shadowed HMS *Swiftsure* during her sea trials. This Kanin Class ship was captured (via the periscope camera) while in pursuit of the British SSN.

A torpedo track (right of image) as a practice weapon heads towards a NATO frigate taking part in a Perisher course.

After successfully passing the Perisher, Lt Littlejohns at the periscope of his first submarine command, HMS *Osiris*.

(*below*) Tim Hale in February 1977, during a moustache-growing competition, when XO of the amphibious assault ship HMS *Fearless*. Hale is wearing a US Navy Pea Coat, with a badge featuring the USS *Nathan Hale* crest and also that of the USN's Submarine Development Group 2 (DEVGRU 2). The USS *Nathan Hale* was named in honour of one of Tim Hale's American forebears.

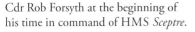

Cdr Rob Forsyth at the beginning of his time in command of HMS *Sceptre*.

HMS *Sceptre* on the surface during sea trials in 1978, carrying out a transfer of personnel via winching up to a Sea King helicopter. Forsyth is on the SSN's bridge (middle of three officers).

An aerial view of a Soviet Victor II Class nuclear-powered attack submarine underway.

Dan Conley while XO of HMS *Spartan* in the late 1970s.

The British SSN HMS *Conqueror* returns to Faslane from the Falklands War, flying the Jolly Roger to indicate a successful war patrol (including sinking the cruiser *Belgrano*).

A gigantic Typhoon Class ballistic missile submarine of the Soviet Navy.

Cdr Littlejohns in his Volvo lorry driver's chair at the heart of the action in HMS *Sceptre*'s Control Room.

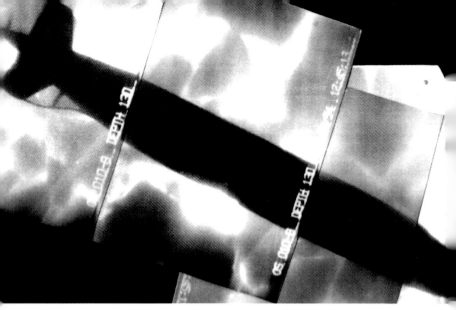

A composite created from an underwater look on a NATO submarine surfaced in a polynya. Taken by a British SSN using the periscope camera, it is a mosaic of four images – an impressive example of the famed underwater look.

A British sailor from HMS *London* and a Soviet Navy rating at Murmansk, August 1991, parading together in remembrance of the joint British-Russian sacrifice during the Second World War, but also signifying the end of the Cold War.

Return of the last of the Cold War warriors: in May 2010, after a career lasting 32 years, the Swiftsure Class submarine HMS *Sceptre* returns for a final time to Devonport. She would be decommissioned in December the same year.

The first of a new generation of British hunter-killer submarines, *Astute*, is rolled out at Barrow-in-Furness, summer 2007.

Built in the Cold War, Sierra Class SSNs of the Russian Navy like this one are active again today off the coast of the USA. They have been attempting to spy on American naval units, including aircraft carriers.

The remarkable sight of what appears to be a full-scale submarine on dry land, which is in fact the Cold War Submarine Memorial at Patriots Point, Charleston, South Carolina. Aside from commemorating the endeavours of US Navy submariners, it also salutes those of the Royal Navy whom it calls 'reliable friends and loyal comrades always – who were standing against a common threat throughout the Cold War.'

The process of taking the latest Swiftsure Class SSN from build to operating against the Soviets was complex and gradual, involving sea trials that were not without risk. With such an investment of scarce funds in just a few – yet highly capable – submarines, the *Sceptre*'s captain and his men had to be at their peak.

For Rob Forsyth, command of *Sceptre* was a reward for being a successful Teacher on the Perisher. She had been launched at Barrow-in-Furness in late 1976. Her future captain and his family were there to watch her go in the water. Forsyth had never seen a hunter-killer boat on the stocks of a construction yard.

It was rather daunting.

'My overwhelming thought was just how big she was. I was going to be wholly responsible for the safety of what amounted to an underwater block of flats with rounded corners, and six storeys high.'

Sceptre hit the water on a dull, overcast November day, with everyone chilled to the bone, especially sailors in their thin Number One uniforms. Lady Audrey White, wife of Admiral Sir Peter White, the presiding Chief of Fleet Support, performed the honours. As *Sceptre* was destined to be a Plymouth-based submarine she was christened with a bottle of West Country cider rather than wine. This caused Lady White some anxiety, as of course scrumpy bottles had thicker glass – would it break as required when she pulled the launch lever?

Seafarers are a superstitious bunch and the failure of a christening bottle to smash is always seen as an omen of bad luck.

On the end of a long ribbon, the bottle swung across the space between the platform on which Lady White stood and the nose of the boat, thankfully shattering on contact.

Forsyth only had eyes for his new submarine, totally oblivious to everything except *Sceptre* sliding down the slipway. 'As she settled into the water and floated for the first time I instantly felt an enormously deep-rooted affinity with her, not that dissimilar from parenthood.'

This was to be *his* boat.

It would be another ten months before *Sceptre* was ready to sail on sea trials, for everything in a submarine has to be correct for that first voyage. If anything goes wrong it can mean the loss of the boat and her entire crew.

Commander Forsyth presided over a precisely calibrated process: 'The pace of events during that period – from taking the reactor critical for the first time to the final spit and polish for Admiral's inspection – was very carefully scheduled. The biggest challenge was to wean the growing Ship's Company off the comfort of Barrow-in-Furness bed-and-breakfast lodgings and bring them together as a trained team. The accessibility of the Lake District was good for character-building climbing and walking expeditions. We also did a lot of equipment training, using simulators in Faslane – but nothing really prepares you better for the reality than reality itself.'

For *Sceptre* the first voyage was north to Scottish waters, in late September 1977, heading for Faslane on the surface. It provided an opportunity to see how she handled and gave her machinery a work-out.

The weather was pretty uninspiring – drizzle and fog deteriorating to a force 8–9 gale – making for a miserable, but relatively safe, passage to Faslane.

Remaining in Scotland, the moment of truth approached – the submarine's first dive. *Sceptre* sailed at 7.00 a.m. on 3 October 1977, a dull day with rain, but seas reasonably calm. She headed for Clyde Exercise Area Quebec, a box of water cleared of all other submarine activity (unless it was the Russians). It was where all British submarines did their first dive after leaving Faslane.

Forsyth and his crew were by then confident in the boat's capabilities and safe operation. Having sailed her on the surface and completed all sorts of training and equipment trials both at sea and ashore, they were well acquainted. They had also been through the process for diving a Swiftsure Class boat while in harbour, so knew the moves instinctively.

The prospect of a first *real dive* gave an extra edge to proceedings.

The success of previous Swiftsure Class submarines, while providing confidence the basic design worked, could not predict the individual characteristics of a boat. To that end a Safety Vessel was on hand; just in case the submarine got into trouble and a rescue operation was required.

Sceptre waited until the Safety Vessel was in position before beginning the process of diving.

Weather on the surface was a factor but wind force 4, rain and visibility of less than three miles would not stop the dive.

Happy to proceed, at 12.50. Forsyth gave the order.

Unlike the movies, there were no blaring klaxons, nor did everybody dash around yelling at each other.

All the valves were opened up and calmly checked, the various compartments reported in using matter-of-fact tones and the XO reported to the CO: 'Submarine opened up for diving, Sir.'

Everybody and everything was in its correct place.

All systems were ready to go.

Forsyth ordered the Officer of the Watch, who was on the bridge: 'Come down below. Shut the upper lid.'

He turned to the Trim Officer and instructed: 'Dive the submarine.'

The Trim Officer in turn ordered: 'Open main vents.'

SSNs take a comparatively long time to submerge, with a forward momentum of around 4–5 knots, settling slowly into the water. Today's dive was to be even slower because it was the first ever.

Spray shot out the top of the ballast tanks, water poured into the bottom, as the boat finally disappeared under the surface 20 minutes later.

Throughout there was extra watchfulness to make sure everything went safely but no anxiety per se. These were procedures they had rehearsed many times alongside, but they were still poised for any emergency.

The things that could malfunction ranged from a simple dial in the Control Room, such as a pressure gauge, to leaky hull glands. The latter were seals around pipes penetrating the inner pressure hull, into the free-flood area between it and the outer casing. In the alongside rehearsals for diving, the air pressure in the boat had been reduced incrementally, to simulate the increase in external pressure as the submarine slipped deeper.

Now, though, it was water pressure during a real dive.

Would the sea squeeze its way in around the gland?

The most difficult thing to get right was the trim – too light and the boat would take *a very long time* to go down. Too heavy and she would sink like a stone – *too fast*.

As soon as a depth of 58ft was achieved, the periscope was raised. Forsyth scanned the surrounding area, finding no problems in the scope's operation, nor water penetrating its seals. Next, having received 'all systems watertight' reports from all compartments, Forsyth ordered *Sceptre* down to 150ft. After checking for leaks and confirming all equipment was, so far, performing as expected, the submarine was gently put through her paces. Over the next five hours she performed well.

Diving, banking and rising – no worries.

The key equipment was checked in a carefully calibrated sequence, including hydroplanes and propulsor, ticking them off one by one.

Other than a few fishing vessels and their nets to avoid, there were no navigation problems. After surfacing to switch a rider – one of the team from the Faslane-based submarine training team overseeing trials – Forsyth took *Sceptre* back down. This time he felt a lot more confident and noted in his trials diary: '2nd dive nicely controlled and felt more like "my" submarine.'

The weather was not something he could gain mastery over and it deteriorated to a severe degree, staying bad during the next four weeks of sea trials. The time came for *Sceptre*'s return to Barrow for further work on ironing out significant defects exposed by the sea trials. It would be no easy passage. Cruising on the surface as the boat emerged from the shelter of the Clyde areas – one moment in relative calm, the next battered by stormy seas – risked serious consequences for the bridge watch team if nothing else.

A few years earlier, in Hebridean waters further to the north-west, the *Courageous* had lost a sailor, sucked out of the fin during a watch handover as he tried to connect his safety harness.

He was never seen again.

Forsyth didn't want anyone lost at sea. His boat dived as soon as she had emerged from the Clyde and was in deep water, but eventually *Sceptre* would have to surface on approaching Barrow. That moment came on 11 November, the weather getting even worse, with 40-knot winds.

These would make it very difficult to thread the SSN through the treacherous Walney Channel and dock gates at the Vickers yard. Forsyth had no illusions about the performance qualities of *Sceptre*, which were no different from any other large submarine in such circumstances.

'On the surface an SSN or an SSBN is a big lump of pig iron and, while you have the main propulsor turning, it is behind the rudder and gives thrust ahead, not much manoeuvrability on the surface to port or starboard. For that we had the Secondary Propulsion Motor – also called the "egg beater" – a pod with a prop, which was lowered through the hull. It could manage a couple of knots at most and only gave a minimal ability to manoeuvre the stern. That was why nuclear-powered submarines were always escorted by tugs. They did the real business of moving you sideways.'

Weather conditions prevalent in early November 1977 were not conducive – even with the assistance of tugs – to squeezing an SSN through the narrow Walney Channel and into the dock.

Rather than risk getting her hull crunched, *Sceptre* diverted to a sheltered anchorage off the island of Anglesey. Here she found a large number of other vessels taking shelter, her sleek black hull and killer whale lines a stark contrast to their rust-streaked paintwork and cluttered superstructures.

The following morning *Sceptre* weighed anchor, but the gale was still blowing force 8–9 from the south-west. Contact with Barrow revealed that it would still be too dangerous to try and slide the boat into the dock there.

Forsyth's diary noted glumly: 'Entry cancelled again.'

The boat headed north on the surface to drop anchor in a sheltered bay off the Isle of Man. A passing local fishing boat hailed *Sceptre*, its skipper shouting across an offer to take the submarine's mail ashore in return for some cigarettes.

There had not been a lot of letter writing going on in the submarine, but the fisherman would be able to buy newspapers, which would help to relieve the tedium of waiting for the weather to ease. In return for the papers, he got his ciggies while *Sceptre* also took up his offer of some freshly caught fish. Having to stay at anchor waiting for the storm to pass through – exiled aboard their boat in a lonely anchorage – was agonising for submariners who just wanted to get back to their families and loved ones.

They were consigned to twiddling their thumbs, watching movies or playing cards. Listening to the radio provided a distraction, while the sailors' favourite pursuit of moaning about things in general – which they did with intense black humour – was also prevalent.

Submariners were meant to be deep below the surface of the ocean, away from the storms and troubles of the outside world.

Bobbing around on the surface was just not natural.

A big beast like *Sceptre* in such rough weather close to the shore also offered the hazard of her anchor dragging as it lost its purchase on the seabed. Without tug boats and only the 'egg beater' this could be very tricky. The trouble with using too much power from the propulsor in shallow water was energy ending up going into the seabed, digging up sand and shale instead of providing the boat with momentum and control. Even assessing whether or not the anchor was fully retracted into its well in the bottom of the submarine was problematic.

Whereas in a surface warship the status of the anchor could be checked with the naked eye as it emerged from the water, with a submarine the only way of knowing it was safely home was a loud thunk. Further troubling Forsyth was his most peculiar position, charged with commanding his Ship's Company in a vessel not yet technically owned by the Navy.

Sceptre still belonged to the shipbuilders, not the Ministry of Defence. They were therefore entirely responsible for her safety. Vickers would have its own pilot on board a surface warship to conduct sea trials. However, they did not have qualified submarine pilots, so the Commanding Officer – as remains the custom in such situations to this day – was employed by the shipbuilders to be their pilot when the boat was at sea. He was paid the princely sum of a guinea (£1.05 in decimal currency).

For the Walney Channel there was a local pilot who would come aboard and act in an advisory capacity, so even then the ultimate responsibility was Forsyth's. Faced with tricky sea states and seeking refuge from a storm, he was responsible for taking a £60m submarine in and out of (sometimes) unfamiliar harbours. They might not have been surveyed for a while. It all required the utmost concentration and navigational judgement.

Then there was the matter of getting a large submarine through Barrow's narrow dock entrance at the end of the voyage. In his diary entry for 12 November Forsyth confessed: 'Not sure that a guinea is appropriate payment for pilotage responsibility!'

Assisting him in weighing up the piloting and navigational factors was the Bracknell Weather Centre, to which he spoke via radio on a regular basis to find out the latest forecast.

At 5.55 a.m. on 13 November 1977, after speaking to the Barrow Pilot's office, Forsyth climbed up through the fin to the bridge. He scanned the skies and studied the sea state, judging things were definitely improving.

The wind had moderated to force 4 and conditions were finally okay to safely navigate the Walney Channel. Forsyth was warned that it was a temporary window of comparative calm.

The Barrow Pilot told him on the radio: 'If you are going to do it, then do it now.'

By noon that day the boat was snugly back home at Barrow without incident – and just ahead of further bad weather. Forsyth noted with relief: 'Secured in the dock. Forecast storm force 10! Phew!'

Over the next four months *Sceptre* was subjected to a series of demanding basin trials and defect rectification work. The whole point of these was to find potential problems before the submarine was officially handed over to the Royal Navy. They would be put right at no extra cost and by the same team that constructed her.

In the first phase of *Sceptre*'s sea trials almost a hundred defects were found, including a malfunctioning 'garbage ejector'. This compressed rubbish and ejected it from the boat. For obvious sanitary reasons it had to work. Sealed inside 3ft tall cans, the garbage would be removed from the boat and sink, rather than float to the surface providing traces that could be picked up by the Soviets.

Also in need of attention was the 'egg beater' propulsion pod. Aside from helping out when berthing it was needed in case the reactor shut down or the main propulsion shaft failed. With the pod popped out – power provided by an auxiliary diesel engine – fumes would be vented via a snort mast, also sucking in fresh air.

An indicator displaying what way the pod was pointing – and hence in which direction the boat was being assisted – seemed to be wired up wrongly. When it showed 'port' it was pointing starboard and vice versa. Vickers worked hard on solving that glitch (and others), for the submarine had to be ready for her official commissioning on 14 February 1978. The next milestone would be successful completion of a training package to raise both boat and crew to fighting efficiency.

The weather on 10 March 1978, the day scheduled for *Sceptre* to make her final exit from Barrow, was another miserable one. A thick fog rolled in as the SSN prepared to transit through the lock gates. While the ceremonial band playing just a few yards away on the quayside could be heard, it could not be seen. On the bridge Cdr Forsyth held a quick discussion with shipyard representatives and a sea rider from Captain Submarine Sea Training at Faslane. They agreed it would be wise to postpone departure for a day. Nobody wanted to take unnecessary risks with such an expensive and rare beast.

Once *Sceptre* made it into the Irish Sea there was a deep dive to 500ft and a submerged full-power trial at 300ft.

This would be her first night dived since the previous set of sea trials. Step one was to 'catch the trim' – another tense moment etched in Cdr Forsyth's memory. 'The most difficult thing to get right post-build is the calculation of overall weight of the boat. My diary tersely records: "7,000 gallons light. Took long time to go down." It also records that by midnight we had done our first trip below periscope depth, to 300 feet. Fortunately, we were watertight.'

Speed was increased gradually.

If a nuclear submarine went from stop to maximum speed then it would be very noticeable and people might feel the stern dig in a bit.

In this instance speed was raised gradually, with checks carried out to make sure there were no leaks or other problems. Then another increase, all the way from 20 revolutions on the shaft to 110.

All very calmly done and barely noticeable.

Deep-diving and full-power tests over the following day brought to a close Cdr Forsyth's time as *Sceptre*'s 'one-guinea pilot'. It was now his duty, on behalf of the MoD, to sign a certificate declaring trials successfully completed. This milestone event came at 4.07 p.m. on 12 March 1978, the boat on the surface in the Irish Sea.

Sceptre's captain felt it was 'a sobering signature moment'.

With three S-boats already in service – *Swiftsure, Sovereign* and *Superb* – *Sceptre* was radically different from her sisters in one major way. This in turn opened up the door for another first in naval history, the new SSN breaking with the tradition of having men-only at sea in warships. *Sceptre* was the first British submarine to be fitted with a fully computerised Action Information and Fire Control System, known as Type DCB. Its primary objective was to do away with allegedly old-fashioned hand plots – plotting the course, speed and range of a target on paper. DCB was a successor to an earlier system named DCA, which had been fitted to the three previous Swiftsure Class boats. According to Dan Conley, who saw this earlier incarnation at work in *Swiftsure*, it could 'store up to 64 contact tracks, calculating range, course and speed from exclusively passive sensor systems. At the time it was state of the art, albeit with a minuscule computing capacity in today's terms.'

DCB was less of a giant leap for mankind and more a baby step forward for British submarines. By inputting information such as the target's propeller revolutions – providing a good idea of speed – or the range at which sonar had detected it, the DCB could use Kalman algorithms to produce a 'best fit' for the speed and range of each contact. As the situation evolved, inputting further data picked up from the submarine's sensors enabled the 'best fit' to slowly become even more accurate. The DCB constantly ironed out myriad small variations in track to produce a true position and course. It could also supply target speed and heading on a large number of contacts simultaneously. The overall aim was to speed up the process of hunting down and killing the enemy – *you could do it to him before he could do it to you.*

DCB provided very good fire control but it was difficult to have confidence in the computed solution, unless you had further input – via sonar or periscope – that concurred with what it was pumping out. For someone like Forsyth, who had been Teacher on Perisher, visual confirmation was a reassuring failsafe.

'If you were at a depth of 180ft, with possibly 30 contacts, how good were the solutions provided by DCB? The solutions were more often wrong than right. Sometimes, coming to periscope depth to assess surface targets, you would be surprised to see how off the DCB was.'

DCA had been solely utilised as an Action Information Organiser – used for plotting targets and keeping track of them. DCB's big ambition was to actually provide an integrated fire-control capability – constantly and precisely keeping track of multiple targets and then firing the weapons to destroy them. It did not in its early years live up to that potential.

With DCA there still needed to be a weapons operator – looking at a screen and using left and right buttons to control a wire-guided torpedo's track to target. The idea with DCB, and the new Tigerfish torpedo, was that the computer would fire it and then send impulses along the wire to convey information, tweaking it to stay on course. The DCB could also input target data to the (non-wire-guided) Mk8 torpedo. Once launched from the tube that tried and tested Second World War-era weapon ran of its own accord. You hoped the firing solution made before it left the boat held true.

A major problem with DCB was the lack of a shore trainer for *Sceptre*'s crew to test its efficacy prior to using it at sea. This, Forsyth reflected rather sarcastically, was 'all in the name of cost savings'. It created considerable training problems. These were only solved partially with the help of a small team of female sailors from the Women's Royal Naval Service. The Wrens, as they were known, were not meant to be sea-going. While women had been to sea in British warships for centuries, they were more likely to have been wives, sweethearts or passengers, rather than members of the uniformed service. They were rarely allowed to spend the night aboard a warship at sea (and never in submarines). Women sailors have since 1990 been a fully integrated part of the fighting fleet, serving in surface ships and combat aircraft of the Royal Navy. A decision to finally allow women to serve at sea in British submarines was taken in 2011. Back in 1978 it was a brave group of Wrens from Faslane who cheerfully volunteered to help solve *Sceptre*'s DCB difficulties, spending a few days and nights at sea wielding handheld computers.

It was, Forsyth mused, entirely against all regulations at the time – and done without any higher-up approval – but 'they generated target data for our DCB, so we at least knew what the answer was meant to be. Their input was, literally, vital.'

Ground-breaking though it may have been, and appreciated though the efforts of the Wrens were, DCB still proved to be insufficiently re-liable without the extra data. Periscope checks on the multiple targets it claimed to be tracking revealed its 'best fit' firing solutions were often unfit for use without the prescribed assistance.

It would take a long time to put right. DCB's imperfections were, though, not a handicap for an experienced team of Cold War warriors.

Sceptre successfully completed sea trials and work-up to prove the boat ready for front-line service. Combining the flawed DCB with tried and tested paper plotting of potential targets – using brains and instinct to supply the rest – the SSN's submariners embarked on their first missions to find and track the Soviets.

Reliably lurking in the old stamping ground where previous submar-ines (including Hale's *Swiftsure)* had found her was the notorious West of Ireland Whiskey. She was snooping on NATO activities with a raised Electronic Intelligence (ELINT) mast. Forsyth's sonar team picked up the Soviet boat quite easily – a chronic noise problem made her sound 'like a steam train'. Forsyth wondered – as did Hale before him – if the Whiskey was some form of clocking-out gate for other Russian submar-ines breaking into the Atlantic.

He felt 'the Whiskey's sonar wouldn't detect an SSBN or SSN unless she ran into it', but that didn't mean relaxing vigilance. Even an old crock could spring surprises on a state-of-the-art hunter-killer. 'I was at periscope depth one day west of Ireland when she rose up from the depths, and started snorting, literally right alongside us, only a couple of cables [around 350 metres] away.' Pulling back as silently as possible, *Sceptre* tracked the Russian for several days, both at depth and while she snorted.

As an intelligence target she had little new to offer to the British submarine's ELINT team but did give them and the sonar operators some practice. Here was a live Soviet boat rather than some simulation. It enabled Forsyth to apply another layer of operational preparation.

'As commissioning CO I had to make sure *Sceptre* was able to float, move and fight – this was an early opportunity to train the intelligence-gathering team.' Everybody would need to present their best game when *Sceptre* went in search of serious prey.

Nuclear-powered submarines – both NATO and Soviet – would take advantage of the stealth offered by hiding among bottom contours, such as undersea canyons – or trenches. They could use them to make fast transits. Taking a high-speed passage down one of these rat runs was an exciting business.

And potentially very dangerous.

One suitable trench can be found down the centre of the Sea of the Hebrides. Some 70 fathoms deep, it is only a couple of miles wide in its narrower parts – a good fit for a Swiftsure Class boat, so long as her captain kept a cool head.

Having cleared shoals off the Shiant Isles, north-west Scotland, at periscope depth, before going deep Forsyth ensured he knew precisely where *Sceptre* was. He used the scope to take a navigational fix of Vaternish Point on the north-west corner of Skye. From then on he would rely on Dead Reckoning – the boat's position deduced by the SINS.

This kept track of direction of travel and distance from the last positive fix. The SSN descended into the trench, clocking up a sea mile every two minutes – 50ft a second or 28 knots. That's fast for any craft under the water.

The Hebrides trench has a tricky left-hand bend about 10 nautical miles and 20 minutes after the start of the run. It was vital to get course and speed of approach right. Hitting the canyon wall was not advised. *Sceptre* also had to be dead centre, because the next 10nm (20 mins) were through the canyon's neck. On each side there would be less than a mile between the submarine and walls. Rather close in a 272ft-long SSN.

There are no cross-currents in a trench, so Forsyth could be confident that particular variable – a characteristic of the open ocean – would not cause any deviation in track. It would also allow him to maintain a precise Speed of Advance (the average speed along the chosen track).

Placing himself centre stage in the Control Room – holding a mental image of the canyon through which his sizeable submarine was passing – Forsyth absorbed verbal input from the Navigating Officer, who was keeping the track chart. The helmsman and planesman at their controls, ensuring the boat maintained correct course and depth, also called out readings.

Forsyth kept a watchful eye on things, pacing around the Control Room, so he could look at the track charts and ship control system operators. In particular, he studied the faces of the hydroplane and helm operators – the instant any lack of focus showed, or a sign of nerves, that man would be replaced. They must respond to orders instantly while keeping control of themselves and the submarine.

Drawing on all his reserves of mental acuity, Forsyth could visualise the sides of the canyon rushing past.

'You definitely don't want to time the turn wrong; so some form of confidence check is *absolutely* necessary.'

That was provided by the bow-mounted Type 2001 sonar, which had to be used with care. The timing of the single ping was critical. Get it right and only one was necessary before making the turn. Find yourself forced to ping twice, or even more, and there would be no point in trying to hide in the trench. There would be a massive signpost saying where *Sceptre* was.

Do that in a hot war and the SSN might be found and killed.

With just over two miles to go before the sharp bend, Forsyth was being watched intensely by the Control Room team. Each one of them suppressed the natural anxiety of those whose lives are in the hands of one man. They trusted him completely, but still …

Forsyth judged the time was right. Walking across to the sonar display he ordered its operator: 'Transmit.'

A short, sharp pulse of sonar … a rapier thrust into the darkness.

Its bat squeak reverberated through the hull.

Forsyth started two stopwatches hung on cords around his neck.

Two were needed in case one stopped unexpectedly.

He had to know *to the second* how long it was until the turn.

Leaning over the shoulder of *Sceptre*'s sonar console operator watching the screen, he saw the ping's reflection. The sailor reported: 'Echo range 4,000 yards.' The display briefly showed the contours of the canyon wall and the bend ahead before fading.

Forsyth used this information to confirm his calculation. The boat's Navigating Officer, bent over the track chart, also computed a solution. The two of them verbally agreed.

Moving back into the centre of the Control Room, noting the elapsed time, Forsyth tapped into what he called 'the Perisher spirit'. Wearing what he hoped was an encouraging smile, Forsyth calmly uttered one of his favourite Teacher axioms:

'Time is exact.'

It was all calculated to instil confidence in his team

They need not worry.

All is well.

He had a handle on the situation – at exactly the right second he would act. They would see that their run down the trench was fun.

Possibly the best rollercoaster in the world.

Should he get it wrong, it could be a ride to oblivion.

If too much rudder was used in a fast-moving SSN, it would cause the boat to do a very fast snap roll and the stern to sink. *Sceptre's* course might suddenly digress from plan with dreadful results.

Everyone and anything not tied down would go flying, so the most experienced helmsman and planesman aboard had been placed behind the controls. Moving over to stand behind them, Forsyth ordered the turn.

'Port 5 – Steer 180'

The helmsman carefully moved the rudder five degrees to port but no more. The boat swung onto a new course.

This was not an occasion to miscalculate.

They were aiming to shoot the boat through the neck of a bottle.

The canyon sides came down in giant steps, the Outer Hebrides to starboard and Inner Hebrides to port.

Safely around the bend, *Sceptre* entered the narrowest part of the trench. Everyone concentrated just that little bit harder.

As the boat still hurtled along at 28 knots, ten more miles were eaten up. Now people could relax momentarily, for the trench widened to a couple of miles each side, but Forsyth recognised this was 'still very narrow for a high-speed submarine'.

With a slight tweak to the course, the tension eased for the next two hours but everyone knew there was one final hazard and it loomed large in Forsyth's mind.

'At the end of this leg lies Stanton Banks; a 10-mile-wide underwater rock castle – with steep cliffs crenellated by towering pinnacles. You cannot go over it, you have to go round it. Once again, it is vital to check position before a final sharp left-hand bend to the south-east.'

Sceptre had now been dived and on Dead Reckoning for more than three hours. Errors might well have crept in.

As a safeguard, Forsyth and the Navigating Officer reluctantly agreed to using another sonar ping to determine their position. Two pings were to be avoided, but sometimes the tactical risk was worth it. Anybody who had managed to pick the first ping up would have been left behind long ago.

Forsyth and the Navigating Officer picked their reference point for the second ping – a large pinnacle on the north side of the trench, with the Stanton Banks arrayed behind. If their Dead Reckoning was still correct, the sonar reflection should give a range of 4,000 yards to the pinnacle (plenty of room) but if it was less something had gone awry.

There might be a need for radical action.

This time their Dead Reckoning was bang on.

Having determined where the boat was, Forsyth and the Navigator started stopwatches, agreeing distance and time to the next turn.

This took *Sceptre* safely through a gap and skirting the Inner Hebrides – homeward bound to Faslane. The echo sounder indicated shoaling water as they crossed the 50-fathom line. Eventually, on Forsyth's command, the boat's speed was reduced, *Sceptre* slowly coming to periscope depth.

He did an all-round look to check for surface traffic, plotting any contacts on the chart and using DCB to keep track of them. The boat took avoiding action to skirt around busy areas on her way back to Faslane, finally surfacing off Arran.

The year concluded with a deployment to an area off the Azores designed to test the *Sceptre*'s capabilities in various submarine versus submarine engagements. This required a memorable high-speed dash for a couple of days, which provided one of Forsyth's career milestones.

'We marked midnight New Year's Eve by ringing "full ahead" on the telegraphs, 16 bells on the ships bell and photographed the log as it exceeded 31 knots; thereby setting an underwater speed record.'

At such moments the automatic hydroplane system came into play, but every hour the helmsmen – who had to sit in and monitor the system anyway – took over to control the submarine manually, in order to remain sharp.

'At the speed we were travelling, an error by a tired human watch keeper might have caused an inadvertent steep dive. At 30 knots and from an initial depth of 300ft if a submarine achieves a 30 degrees bow-down angle it will exceed safe depth in well under a minute. That could be fatal.'

Sceptre was to act primarily as a target for NATO submarines, to see if they could track Britain's increasingly feared stealthy Swiftsures. The cat-and-mouse games saw boats circling at reasonably close distances but with depth separation to prevent accidents. Sonar operators in each submarine tried to detect the opposition and then there would be feverish activity using the DCB – with assistance from the sensors – to plot a firing solution. One promising contact turned out to be an amorous whale. Mistaking *Sceptre* for a potential mate it tried to cuddle up and get affectionate.

Having shaken off the whale, and completed the submarine versus submarine exercises somewhat later than scheduled, *Sceptre* set course from the Azores to Bermuda. Again, this was to see how the boat performed, but also with the enticing prospect of a run ashore in tropical climes.

Forsyth noted in his diary that the exercise concluded at 13.45 on 9 January 1979 and by 14.00 *Sceptre* was clocking up '28 knots for Bermuda'.

As a new boat, there was plenty of power to draw on, Forsyth taking full advantage. 'This was early on in the reactor core life and no restrictions on usage were in force. Submarines had yet to be clad with rubber tiles, which made them much more silent – but much slower! Happy days. We surfaced seven miles from St David's Light, at 07.30 on 12 January, having carried out the passage at very high speed. We only slowed down twice a day to stream the communications buoy to pick up signals.'

Commander Forsyth was delighted that *Sceptre* was proving to be 'very fast – the fastest in fact'. He exulted in commanding 'a deep-diving submarine at a time when the Cold War was at its technical height'.

He realised his job was to take on the 'ever-improving Russian ships and submarines that were appearing every year'. The British SSN's crew would apply themselves religiously to understanding the opposition, in order to counter their tactics if things ever turned nasty.

In February 1979 *Sceptre* was getting ready to meet that growing menace via intelligence-gathering patrols. There was to be a deployment in the Mediterranean, which was at the time host to large numbers of Soviet surface warships and submarines.

It was the cockpit of hot conflict during the 1970s, for civil war raged in the Lebanon while Turkey, a NATO nation, even invaded Cyprus to protect its ethnic minority population in the north of the island. Arab–Israeli wars erupted every now and then while the British retreated from a major presence in a region where they had once injected stability via their navy.

In March 1979 Colonel Gaddafi would even visit Malta to gloat over the Royal Navy's withdrawal from the island fortress. The Americans, though, remained in force to contest the Soviet Union's determined attempt to colonise the Mediterranean. The US Navy's 6th Fleet held the line, with support from the much-diminished Royal Navy whenever it could manage.

Sceptre's primary target during her Mediterranean foray was no less than the carrier *Kiev*. Forsyth received orders to find the Soviet warship, trail her, photograph her and record the carrier's distinctive sound signature.

A task that would once have involved a whole fleet of warships was now assigned to a single SSN. *Sceptre* possessed the supreme advantage of absolute stealth – no funnel smoke or tell-tale silhouette on the surface to give her away. Yet, even for a nuclear-powered submarine it was no easy task. Deployment of *Kiev* was the manifestation of Admiral Gorshkov's global ambition. *Sceptre* would try to puncture Gorshkov's hubris and she was well placed to act. 'We were lying alongside in Gibraltar enjoying a run ashore when intelligence from a Maritime Patrol Aircraft reported *Kiev* was in the eastern Med. We were hurriedly tasked and sailed immediately.'

Her propulsor churning up water, *Sceptre* moved away from the sea wall, tugs in attendance. Heading out into the Bay of Gibraltar, Soviet agents based in Spain undoubtedly had their binoculars tightly focused on the SSN. She was soon lost to vision, sliding beneath the surface in a flurry of spray. Unfortunately, it wasn't long before a noise problem forced Forsyth to expose his boat again, attracting the unwelcome attentions of a Soviet 'trawler'.

'On first diving at 10.30 we detected a rattle in the casing – something not secured tightly? – and for the next three hours alternately surfaced to look for it and dived to check it out. At 14.00, still on the surface, we were closed by the Soviet Mirny Class intelligence-gathering ship *Vertikal*. She might even have been sent to find us. I decided to return to Gib on the surface to fix the rattle, so that we could do it without being pestered by *Vertikal*'s close surveillance. The Soviet vessel would not dare pursue us into Gibraltar's territorial waters.'

The small, 850-ton converted trawler could only manage a top speed of 15 knots, enough to stick close to *Sceptre* on the surface. No way would she be fast enough to catch and hold a submerged SSN, but by the time *Sceptre* got clearance to dive going west she could be back in Gib.

The behaviour of the AGI was most curious.

'*Vertikal* criss-crossed our stern wake continuously. We wondered whether she was fitted with a wake detection type of equipment and had seized the opportunity to check it out.'

Sceptre dropped anchor in Gibraltar harbour at 18.00, leaving the Soviet spy vessel loitering at a distance. A thorough investigation beneath the casing found a securing bracket for ropes had corroded and broken loose. Weighing anchor after fixing the problem, *Sceptre* made her way back out to sea. Diving the boat at 23.00, Cdr Forsyth ordered the ship control team to set a course east. For most of the following day, *Sceptre* crept slowly forward, awaiting vital intelligence on *Kiev*'s suspected location from Commander Task Force 69 (CTF 69), the command cell for NATO attack submarines operating in the Mediterranean. At 17.00 CTF 69 transmitted instructions, suggesting an increase in SOA to 15 knots. It says something for *Sceptre*'s legs – her high turn of sustained speed while remaining covert – that anyone would even dream of ordering her to steam around 2,000 miles in pursuit of *Kiev*.

The most a Second World War submarine could manage submerged was an SOA of about 3 or 4 knots. The strategic advantages of nuclear propulsion were abundantly clear. Not only did *Sceptre* cut like a knife through the deep, but she would not pause in order to recharge batteries or take in air. In terms of capability, *Sceptre's* Med foray was a world removed from the exploits of *Taciturn* and *Turpin* in Arctic waters during the 1950s. Her ability to remain fully submerged for weeks at a time gave the Royal Navy a terrible swift sword to wield on globe-spanning missions.

There was excellent vision for periscope observation. It also meant good conditions for surveillance aircraft seeking to detect submarine masts by radar or visually. This presented the familiar dilemma of trying to gather intelligence while not giving the foe opportunities. Eyes pressed to the cups of the scope, Forsyth twisted the handles to pitch the lens upwards.

He scanned for traces of surveillance aircraft operating without detectable radar. In naval slang he was 'using the MkI eyeball'.

Twisting the handles again, he brought the lens level, turning the scope from side to side. Forsyth had studied intelligence photos of the *Kiev*. She had a huge, tiered island superstructure topped off with massive radar arrays, hopefully making her easy to see and identify.

There was nothing matching that description to be seen.

And what of the escorts?

A Kara or Kresta cruiser, possibly both. He had memorised their silhouettes, too: tall, jagged outlines with the same distinctive radars.

There was no sign of them.

Even after night fell either Forsyth or one of his watch keepers would still use the scope to maintain a lookout for traces of the *Kiev*.

Night-vision periscopes were in their infancy at the end of the 1970s and *Sceptre* was fitted with a prototype. In Forsyth's view it overcame some potentially lethal problems presented by using earlier periscopes: 'Imagine a pitch-black night with the periscope being washed over by waves from four to eight feet high, the submarine gently rolling at periscope depth, and there is no starlight. You cannot see the horizon and have nothing to focus on. You are not sure if you are looking at sea or sky.

'If there is anything out there – such as a Soviet warship – you will only see it from two or three miles away, as an intermittent light or not even that. Making matters worse, whatever the vessel might be it will probably not be carrying lights, as would be the case in wartime. That

leaves barely time to carry out an attack or take avoiding action, whichever is required.

'The periscope watch keeper rotates the scope round and round in the
hope that if he keeps doing so, and if there is something there, he may
see it. Switch in night vision – in my time image intensifiers fitted to the
existing scope – and suddenly you can see the sea and horizon, a faint
light becoming a globe of greeny yellow light. You cannot tell a red port-
side light from a green starboard light as such devices are colour-blind.
As you can see the outlines of the ship, or land mass or whatever, this
does not matter.'

On the third day of the hunt, *Sceptre*'s sonar operators picked up the
sound of an elderly Juliett Class diesel – a type packing four nuclear-
tipped Shaddock cruise missiles.

Snorting air to recharge her battery, the Soviet boat was somewhere
to the south. *Sceptre* briefly settled into a trail as the Juliett moved away
at low speed – snorting still in progress. The Juliett stood little, if any,
chance of detecting *Sceptre*. The Soviet submarine was old, while the
SSN was new.

Sceptre sped east leaving the diesel far in her wake.

To aid in the hunt for *Kiev*, the British SSN needed to uplink to
NATO's signals network. By doing this she would tap into specially
encrypted messages detailing the latest intelligence on Soviet Navy
movements. These were broadcast at certain times of the day. To connect, *Sceptre* had to slow down and wait at certain depths. The SSN had
various options.

She could receive signals via a low-frequency trailing wire, which
enabled her to stay deep and avoid detection, but Forsyth felt it was
painfully slow. 'Or you could communicate via a buoy on the end of a
wire. The latter avoided the need to go to periscope depth. Because the
buoy was streamed like a kite, at the end of a reelable wire just below
the surface, with depth-keeping an uncertainty, it could pop up to the
surface. This presented a detection opportunity for anybody looking for
you. Or you could come to periscope depth, and use omni-directional
"loops" in the fin to pick up the broadcasts. This also posed a detection
risk – because you had to use your periscope for safety. With the top of
the boat's fin around 15 feet below the surface there was a real danger
that you could be run down by merchant ships. A vessel wouldn't need
much draught to hit you at that depth, so it was best to keep an eye open
for danger. You could, though, use your electronic listening equipment
to warn of approaching radars etc. On balance, the loops were the best

option. You were more aware and in control of the threat environment.'

The morning of 3 February was a bad one. *Sceptre* tried three times to synchronise with the NATO broadcast without success. Tired of slowing down to try and tap into the signal, Forsyth decided not to even bother with the next scheduled broadcast. When the fifth opportunity came around the SSN slowed and came to periscope depth. This time she managed to successfully pick up the intel. Forsyth noted in his private diary: 'Our position now 20 miles East of Hammamet [an anchorage used by Soviet Navy units on the Tunisian coast]. Target is 500 miles east of me. We will have to move like hell.'

A high-speed submerged dash took *Sceptre* to the south and well past Malta, right over to waters west of Cyprus – just in case *Kiev* pulled into the Soviet forward naval base at Tartus in Syria. On the morning of 4 February – the fifth day of the pursuit – *Sceptre* took in another intelligence report. Forsyth read a sheet of paper torn from the printer with some irritation. It was bad news. *Kiev* was actually some way to the south-west. He gave a frustrated groan and muttered: 'Now they tell me …'

The intel report – from a NATO Maritime Patrol Aircraft on the lookout – revealed *Kiev* and her escorts had headed for an anchorage in the Gulf of Sollum, off Egypt. They were not especially welcome, for President Anwar Sadat had recently ejected the Soviet Navy from Egyptian bases.

However, the Sollum anchorage lay *outside* the territorial limit – and therefore *within* international waters. Technically there was nothing the Egyptians could do about it. Eager to curry the favour of the West, and in particular the USA, Sadat authorised his navy to carry out live firing of weapons in the Gulf of Sollum. This made life decidedly uncomfortable for Soviet ships at anchor.

Forsyth ordered the boat around, *Sceptre* speeding west while trying to tap into more intel signals. Reliable signals synchronisation remained elusive.

Sceptre withdrew to waters off Crete, where there was a strong NATO naval presence, so she could relax her routine. That evening attempts were made again to pick up signals but with no success.

The following day – 6 February, the seventh day of the hunt – *Sceptre* moved in, until she was maintaining a distance off the Egyptian coast of between 100 and 150 miles, mainly at periscope depth and occasionally deeper. At that distance an SSN could swiftly close with the North

African coast; Forsyth's tactic was to position his boat within range of not only Sollum but also the Gulf of Bomba off Libya.

Might the *Kiev* now be a guest of Gaddafi?

This would enable *Sceptre* to make a high-speed run to intercept the *Kiev* in either direction. There would be plenty of deep water too, hopefully allowing speed without detection.

At 21.00 *Sceptre* came to periscope depth. Using the new (UHF) NESTOR secure voice communications system, she was able to talk to a passing NATO Maritime Patrol Aircraft without fear of Soviet eavesdropping. Forsyth asked for a message about communications problems to be passed back to CTF 69. For the next five days, 7–11 February, the British SSN prowled south of Crete, settling into an unexciting routine of waiting for *Kiev* to poke her nose into the open ocean. Two of her escort ships, a Riga Class destroyer and a Kresta Class cruiser, made a break for it and Forsyth was dismayed to not hear of this until it was 12 hours too late. On the afternoon of 12 February there were promising signs, picked up by an MPA, which had identified *Kiev* at Sollum.

Its sensors detected heat around *Kiev*'s funnels and increasing amounts of steam. She appeared about to set sail.

Though displacing 43,000 tons fully loaded, the Soviet carrier could still manage 32 knots thanks to four propellers driven by eight turbo-pressurised boilers. *Kiev* used this power to make a clean getaway, leaving Forsyth fuming. 'Actionable intelligence from sources beyond the submarine always came a bit late, because we lacked the soon-to-be-standard satellite communications fit that all surveillance SSNs received. *Kiev* got a head start on us before we received the signal and so evaded our attentions. We returned to Gib.'

It was deeply annoying, underscoring the need for SSNs tasked with surveillance to have a better communications outfit. The old HF broadcast system was not up to it. More reliable uplink to intel was the only way to make best use of a nuclear submarine's considerable tactical advantage.

'It was a stern lesson to their Lordships,' thought Forsyth, 'that if you couldn't compete in the Soviet numbers game – choosing to have fewer, but immensely more powerful submarines – you better have the ability to put them in the right place at the right time.'

As the latest kind of Fleet submarine, *Sceptre* was a supreme hunter-killer, but if the quarry could not be found it could not be trailed, or killed. If a shooting war broke out, the ability, or lack of it, to get timely information could mean the difference between victory and defeat.

Sceptre and her sister S-boats represented a great leap forward for the Submarine Service. Several upgrades would ultimately give her, and other NATO nuclear-powered boats, an even keener edge. It was the advent of satellite communications that provided a game changer, proving to be a double-edged sword.

With satcoms, according to Forsyth, 'you could download a whole series of signals, including intelligence reports, in seconds. It was a case of put the satcoms mast up, suck in the data burst then mast down and away you go. Of course, it also meant people ashore became less careful about not sending signals to you. It was the beginning of the end for total independence. Nelson would not have liked radio signals, as they would have given other people an ability to interfere with his on-the-spot decision-making. Nor do submariners, really. The upside is better intelligence; the downside is today's tight political control of operations straight into the Captain's cabin.' That ability of headquarters in the UK to direct – some would say interfere with – submarine operations would come to fruition during the Falklands War just a few years after *Sceptre*'s frustrating pursuit of *Kiev*.

There were other workouts *Sceptre* could take advantage of should she get the opportunity, again demonstrating Forsyth had the nerve and steady hand to bring everyone safely home. Under his cool-headed command *Sceptre* proved equally adept at the famed underwater look. Forsyth did not underestimate the challenges of bringing off such an amazing feat with a 5,000-ton nuclear-powered submarine in shallow waters. It was a task that British boats deployed to the Mediterranean were often called on to do – Littlejohns, for example, in *Osiris* in 1976 – but whether or not Sceptre did it in 1979 is something Forsyth is not prepared to be specific about.

'It truly was one of the more challenging tasks asked of surveillance submarines,' he will admit. 'Of course, it was the easiest way to check on the hull design, screws and sonar of a Soviet surface warship. At least it would not change depth – unlike a submarine. When your periscope is only a few feet below the target it's nice to know the target can't dive deeper!

'If the ship you are looking at is at anchor then this adds its own dimension. It's stationary, so you have to be almost stopped in what could be quite clear water, especially in the Mediterranean. There is also the small matter of the ship's anchor chain to avoid and probably insufficient water to pass underneath, so you need to do two passes – one each side. Those who grumbled about all the periscope work on the Perisher course might have wondered what the pressure was being applied for. During an underwater look it was quite apparent.'

When it came time for passing on command of *Sceptre* in March 1979, Forsyth – whose next job was as a desk officer in the Ministry of Defence at Whitehall – felt somewhat proprietorial handing the keys of *his boat* over to Cdr Barry Carr. He consoled himself with the thought that *Sceptre* and her men would be in good hands.

In late 1979 the Russians did something extraordinary that foreshadowed a famous spy novel. They published information it was claimed could only have come from material passed to them by the ex-submariner turned Soviet agent David Bingham. The headline of the story in *The News*, Portsmouth, screamed: 'SUBS SECRETS SURFACE'.

Despite some experts suggesting it might all be guesswork, other sources said the material was so secret it could only have come from documents photographed by Bingham and sold to Russia.

The former Sub Lieutenant had been released from prison that October and was on parole but he was saying nothing.

The Moscow gambit included a publication featuring a diagram that, according to *The News*, allegedly showed 'in considerable detail the areas Western submarines would patrol to intercept Russian submarines trying to enter the Atlantic'. Information on how NATO would protect convoys in time of war was also published. The Russians even provided details on what depths NATO mines could allegedly be laid at on the seabed in the Greenland–Iceland–UK Gap (GIUK) – again to prevent Soviet submarines entering the Atlantic. Making public such sensitive information was an interesting ploy, for it tempted the West to deny its accuracy and inadvertently give the game away. In his novel *The Russia House*, published in 1989, John le Carré tells the story of a Soviet weapons scientist code-named Goethe who works on the USSR's ballistic missile programmes among other things. Goethe – real name Yakov – produces a detailed handwritten manuscript on how inept and incapable the Soviet military machine really is. He tries to send it covertly to Barley Blair, a jazz-loving, alcohol-soaked Russophile publisher based in London. Yakov asks Blair to publish it in order to dismantle the MAD-ness of the East–West confrontation. The British and American intelligence services get involved and agonise over whether or not it is an elaborate plot run by the Scientific Disinformation Section of the KGB.

They argue over the authenticity of Yakov's material …

It was worthless.

It was pure gold.
It was smoke.

Did it show 'the Soviet nuclear sword had rusted in its scabbard'?

Or was it just 'a fiendish plot'?

Barley is trained as a spy and sent to Moscow with a 'shopping list' of questions to confirm the scientist's work, but by telling the Soviets what they need to know, the Americans and British might just indicate their vulnerabilities. Publication of material allegedly obtained via Bingham's espionage exploits in the early 1970s was possibly a real-life precursor to le Carré's own yarn. When news of the Moscow gambit broke in 1979 the Royal Navy and UK security services declined to make any comment at all. By doing this they wisely denied the Soviets any insights into whether or not Bingham's material was still useful eight years after it had been obtained.

As for the former submariner turned spy, after changing his name to Brough he ran a hotel in Bournemouth and at one stage was a vice-president of a local Conservative Club (where nobody was aware of his past as a Soviet agent). Divorced from his wife in 1975 while still in prison – she had been released after serving 30 months – 'Brough' later ran an alternative-healing centre in Stratford-upon-Avon. He died in February 1997, at the age of 56, when his Volvo car was in collision with a tree during gales and caught fire. A Leamington Spa coroner ruled his death accidental.

There was a feeling during 1979 that the nuclear-armed face-off was escalating and hardening. It prompted a Cassandra-like speech from the senior naval officer who was perhaps more responsible than anyone else for equipping Britain with nuclear-powered (and armed) submarines.

The last British naval vessel visited by Admiral of the Fleet Lord Mountbatten of Burma was HMS *Superb*, in May 1979, five months before his assassination at the hands of the IRA. Mountbatten was not unfamiliar with submarines, having served for a short time in the steam-powered *K-3* more than half a century earlier. The same month as his *Superb* visit, Mountbatten made it clear he favoured a halt on all sides to the escalating nuclear arms race. For a man who had brought the *Dreadnought* into service and paved the way for Polaris it was a remarkable speech – shocking even, coming as it did from a former First Sea Lord and Chief of the Defence Staff. 'The world now stands on the brink of the final Abyss,' warned Mountbatten. 'Let us all resolve to take all possible practicable steps to ensure that we do not, through our own folly, go over the edge.'

He was not advocating unilateral disarmament, but calling for a sane balanced reduction on all sides and pleading for the USA and USSR to redouble their strategic-arms reduction efforts. He felt Britain was the nation least likely to press the red button. Mountbatten's speech went largely unremarked in the newspapers or on television and was ignored by most contemporary politicians.

President Jimmy Carter – a former command-qualified submarine officer who had worked with Admiral Rickover in the US Navy's nuclear submarine programme – echoed Mountbatten's fears. Carter leavened them with optimism. 'Nuclear weapons are an expression of one side of our human character,' said Carter in his farewell address to the nation as he left office in January 1981. 'But there is another side. The same rocket technology that delivers nuclear warheads has also taken us peacefully into space. From that perspective, we see our Earth as it really is – a small and fragile and beautiful blue globe, the only home we have. We see no barriers of race or religion or country. We see the essential unity of our species and our planet; and with faith and common sense, that bright vision will ultimately prevail.'

The Strategic Arms Limitation Treaty II (SALT II), which like its predecessor sought to limit strategic nuclear weapons, had been agreed by Carter and the Soviet leader, Leonid Brezhnev, at Vienna in the summer of 1979. It was not ratified by the US Senate due to the Soviet invasion of Afghanistan at the end of that year.

For the USSR enemies stretched from NATO in the West to China in the Far East. Thirty-four years since the end of the Second World War the Kremlin was still intent on ensuring the Soviet Union would never again be invaded from all sides.

This meant land, sea and air bases, from the Baltic to the Arctic and Asia, also sustaining the scar of the Iron Curtain that ran across the centre of Europe. Four fleets were operated by Russia throughout the Cold War, with the most important remaining the Northern Fleet, followed by the Pacific Fleet. A lot of the supporting infrastructure on the shores of the Kola and also in Kamchatka and around Vladivostok remained remote. It was expensive to construct and maintain, never mind creating suitably formidable submarines and surface ships to make use of it. Defence projects were predominant in Soviet heavy industry and also science, with the majority of resources, and the best scientists, assigned to them (none more demanding than submarine forces). Twenty-five per cent of the USSR's gross domestic product was poured into defence but it was not productive in terms of the wider economy. That stagnated during the late 1970s, a period when the West was emerging from recession and starting to boom.

Détente had offered a boost in superpower status but it wasn't doing much for trade, which created wealth and jobs. The vast majority of Soviet citizens had to deal with food shortages and shoddy goods, not forgetting a lack of civil rights and other personal freedoms enjoyed in the West.

Could the Kremlin gamble on a war with the West to lift the Communist Bloc out of its stagnation? Dare it take by force the industrial resources, capture markets for Soviet goods, pluck the bounty of the West from its tree? Could it establish hegemony over Europe that the USA and Britain would never dare to challenge? The Warsaw Pact had massive superiority in ground forces on the Central Front – a red tide could easily sweep across the North European Plain to the English Channel.

In the event of any war, the majority of NATO reinforcements would have to come across the Atlantic from the USA. That's why a major Western priority was preventing Soviet attack submarines from surging through the GIUK Gap. The Russians, though, planned for any land war to be short, so there might not be any campaign with decisive effect at sea. It would all be over long before fresh American troops could reach Europe, possibly with battlefield nuclear weapons exchanged. Therefore, the Soviet Navy would fight a protective war.

And the dawn of a new decade saw a dangerous escalation, with both sides playing increasingly high-stakes poker. The Soviets viewed things with brutal simplicity – they would seek to tie the American Gulliver down on the one hand, while on the other finding a different means of gaining nuclear superiority. Though the USSR sought to shackle the USA's strategic nuclear weapons capabilities via SALT II, from late summer 1976 it also fielded the SS-20 intermediate-range nuclear missile. As it was not an intercontinental weapon, the SS-20 was not barred under SALT. Mobile and poised behind the massed tank divisions of the Central Front, it possessed precise targeting – a capability its cruder predecessors lacked. With a range of more than 3,000 miles, the SS-20 could hide itself in the vast interior of the Soviet Union west of the Urals, all but invulnerable to detection and destruction. SS-20s – each one carrying three MIRVs – could, for instance, take out port and dockyard facilities in Southampton, Liverpool, Glasgow, Faslane,

Portsmouth, Chatham and Plymouth. This would make it very difficult for American reinforcements and supplies to come ashore even if they did make it across the Atlantic in time of war. Royal Navy ships and submarines would have no home bases left. Airbases, barracks and entire cities could also be destroyed while millions of civilians and military personnel would be dead or dying.

The Americans would provide a response to the SS-20 that neutered the threat and actually increased Moscow's vulnerability. The USA decided in late 1979 to soon deploy mobile land-based Pershing II and Gryphon Ground-Launched Cruise Missiles (GLCMs) that were also very difficult to destroy (and they possessed even better accuracy than SS-20).

The Pershing IIs and GLCMs would by the early 1980s threaten the western USSR, including Moscow. Should Armageddon ever dawn the Kremlin would receive little or no warning of their imminent impact.

And then there was the forthcoming Trident missile system, which would be carried to sea by the USA's Ohio Class SSBNs and possibly in a new generation of British submarines.

With a range of 4,600 miles Trident enabled the West's primary SSBNs to hide in a far greater arc of ocean, making it even more difficult for the Russians to find them.

While the West might have been awed by the 'Okean' exercises and terrified by the SS-20, Russia's ballistic missile submarines remained its ace card and provoked much fear in NATO capitals. The Delta IIIs were being succeeded by a truly awesome class of SSBNs, the Typhoons, the first of which, *TK-208*, was launched in September 1980. There would be six Typhoons in all, and gaining firm details on their capabilities was a key NATO goal. Possessing a submerged displacement of 26,000 tons, a Typhoon was 558ft long – with a beam of 79ft and draught of 43ft. In terms of sheer bulk that exceeded anything the West could offer. Powered by two reactors, the Typhoons packed 20 Sturgeon ballistic missiles.

The advent of the Typhoons, and later Deltas armed with ballistic missiles with a range of several thousand miles, meant they could launch from the Norwegian Sea and Barents Sea.

Traditionally for ballistic missile submarines – both Soviet and Western – the operational areas had to be off the continental shelf, beyond the 100-fathom line and well clear of merchant traffic. They lurked beyond sea lanes and within range of the targets, such as Washington or Moscow.

The Bastion concept, though, was a bid to break that habit.

The later Deltas and Typhoons could avoid exposing themselves to SOSUS and predatory NATO hunter-killers by adopting it. From the Kola and White Sea they could head straight out under the ice rather than risk a breakout into the Atlantic.

Big bruisers with double hulls, they could bash their way through and launch all missiles in a single salvo, each bird carrying MIRVs. For NATO it was a nightmare scenario – the Russians could place their SSBNs on the top of the world and reach anywhere they wanted – particularly with Victor IIIs acting as their guardians. Hidden, safe and undetectable, the only way to get them might be to send an SSN under the ice.

The British, despite their experiences with the A-boats and occasional ventures by SSNs to the North Pole (sometimes working with the Americans), did not really have much of a doctrine for finding and killing Soviet SSBNs under the ice. With the advent of the Bastion concept they had to get into the business. Littlejohns had experienced the first faltering steps towards evolving a doctrine. An SSN he served in was tasked with trailing a Delta and a search was made for material that might give some advice on tactics.

'All we found was an old Arctic operations manual from the Admiralty,' he recalled, 'and it said if you ate the liver of a polar bear for more than a few days it would kill you. One meal would not, though.'

This was not terribly useful knowledge when it came to hunting the Soviets *under ice*. It was not on the whole a comfortable experience.

The SSN trailed the target for some time but on losing contact in the strange sonar conditions – which none of the crew had experienced before – she withdrew. Littlejohns reflected: 'If we are going to go under the ice we need to be better prepared.'

Relevant tactics were not unknown altogether. In his time as an SSN captain and running submarine operations for Flag Officer Submarines, Tim Hale made a study of the Marginal Ice Zone (MIZ) and also tactical opportunities where the cold Labrador current meets the warm Gulf Stream.

Icebergs melting formed the Grand Banks off Newfoundland, with the dirt they carried falling to the seabed. The confluence of the warm current and the shallower water over the banks also created ideal fish feeding and breeding grounds. 'If you want to hide a boat you go in where the fish feed,' thought Hale, 'the noise they create helps hide you, while the ice limit also provides cover. If you slide your submarine under the ice and lurk in there, it is like someone sitting in a darkened room of a house and looking out onto a lit street at the traffic going by, in this case Soviet submarines. The SSN can also be likened to a pike waiting under a river bank for passing prey.'

There were still Soviet SSBNs that needed to venture out into the Atlantic – the earlier Deltas and the Yankees – to place themselves within missile range of their targets.

'You would think that trade routes could provide useful cover for the Russian SSBNs seeking to break out,' mused Hale, 'because of all the ships running up and down creating plenty of noise. The Russian SSBNs did not use the trade routes as, of course, the noise of traffic also prevented them hearing if they were being trailed. They would come out via the Iceland–Faroes Gap, use a seamount to get a fix then transit down to the Bermuda area, and areas around the Virginia Capes. We had to track them on the way out and also when in their patrol areas.'

When it came to the much-vaunted Typhoon, Littlejohns first sighted that particular quarry on the surface, during a quick periscope look.

It perplexed him.

He thought: 'Is that really going to go under water?'

Littljohns realised Typhoons were reasonably quiet as the big double hull kept the noise-generating machinery a long way from the water.

'They did cause a stir,' he said, 'but they were logical if that was what politicians wanted.'

For the business of nuclear deterrence is not about decisions made by the military – it is the politicians who decide what the money should be spent on and also give the order to fire missiles. Littlejohns thought the Typhoon was 'the ultimate expression of the will of the Kremlin to build it bigger, meatier, make it all more terrifying'.

For all their impressive size and attempts at reducing noise, the Typhoons were soon being tracked.

The US Navy was also deploying a huge new ballistic missile submarine, for USS *Ohio* was lead vessel in a class that would ultimately number 18. Displacing nearly 19,000 tons submerged, with a length of 560ft, a beam of 42ft and a draft of just over 36ft, each *Ohio* carried 24 Trident missiles. Having embarked on summer sea trials, *Ohio* herself would be handed over to the USN at the end of 1981.

A year before she entered service the Russians had obtained details of sonar systems being fitted to *Ohio*. Moscow published them for the world to read, in that way hitting back at NATO attempts to counter the Bastion concept. It sought to neutralise the Ohios by exposing their secrets.

In the UK, the requirement to construct a successor for the Polaris boats was threatening a financial and political storm, particularly at a time when significant other parts of the Royal Navy might be discarded by a cost-cutting government. In the meantime, during February 1981, Dan Conley would be among those tasked with trying to find and track the Soviet submarine menace in the latest S-boat.

Spartan found her quarry well out into the Atlantic to the west of the British Isles. She had been directed by Northwood HQ to loiter in a box of water on the anticipated track of a Victor Class SSN returning to northern Russia from a foray into the Mediterranean.

Like a salmon migrating back upriver the Victor was heading home, though not to spawn but rather regenerate at her base in the Kola Peninsula. Settling into the trail, the Swiftsure Class boat's captain was Cdr James Taylor with Lt Cdr Conley as XO. It was the British SSN's second Northern patrol since commissioning in late September 1979. *Spartan* soon recorded the Soviet boat's distinctive noise signature and operational habits.

A problem loomed, though: the merging of the warm Gulf Stream and colder Norwegian Sea would make it difficult to maintain contact.

The velocity of sound would vary dramatically, even being reflected by the temperature boundary layers. These were also fishing grounds thick with noise-generating trawlers, their props creating noise mixed in with whale calls and shrimp claws clicking.

As suspected, contact with the Victor was lost and Conley suggested to Taylor it might be best to make a high-speed dash to lie in wait on the anticipated track in the Norwegian Sea. It would offer better sonar conditions and contact was soon renewed. This time *Spartan* maintained it.

So far, so as predicted: a Victor heading home to the Kola.

Conley was surprised by what happened next.

'We reached a point about one hundred miles to the south-east of Bear Island when the Soviet's behaviour changed and it was quickly apparent he had moved into a search mode. *Spartan* remained cautiously observing and listening at a distance of some miles beyond the Victor's sonar counter-detection range. It was clear the target was frequently checking baffles – turning sharply to take a look astern at her blind spot. The Sound Room reported an intriguing pattern of manoeuvres, the Victor executing several sharp turns around one focal point. This suggested she was working with another submarine and, as we carefully edged a bit closer, the noise signature of that other boat – a Delta Class SSBN – was picked up.'

Before a Soviet nuclear missile submarine departed on a patrol, one of the better variants of SSN might be ordered to perform a 'delousing' manoeuvre, which entailed checking the surrounding sea for any NATO 'vermin'. Like a pilot fish seeking out and eliminating ectoparasites from the skin of a much bigger shark the 6,000-ton Victor sniffed around the 13,000-ton Delta.

Conley listened in to the Sound Room reports and studied the Local Operations Plot, thinking the Victor's delousing was 'very evidently ineffective', or *Spartan* would have been detected.

With the Victor fully occupied, Cdr Taylor felt this provided an opportunity to move even closer, but *Spartan* had to be careful not to startle the Russian. Any response was likely to be highly aggressive.

There were three submarines operating in very close proximity, and it was in such situations that terrible accidents could happen. *Warspite* had her crunch not too far away, while since October 1968 there had been at least two collisions in the Barents between American and Russian submarines. There was a further suspected bump with a US Navy SSBN in waters off Scotland, with at least a further three reportedly between American and Russian submarines in waters off Petropavlovsk, one of the key Soviet naval bases in the Far East of the USSR.

As the Victor finished delousing, an interesting dilemma was presented to *Spartan*. The Combined Task Force 311 (CTF 311) submarine operations command cell at the NATO Headquarters in Northwood expected her to continue trailing the Victor all the way home. Sufficient water space had been cleared of all other NATO submarines for *Spartan* to follow that course.

The coalface reality was that in the scheme of things a Delta SSBN beginning a patrol – a target Northwood was completely unaware of as it had not been picked up by SOSUS – was far more important. Yet *Spartan* could not give away her position by sending a message to Northwood. There was cleared water space northwards too, all the way to the edge of the ice, though Taylor did not know how much longer he would be allowed room for manoeuvre. Northwood would expect his moving haven to go south-east, not north.

Having done what her captain must have regarded to be a good job of sanitising the area around the Delta, the Victor headed off to the south-east and home. Conley sensed 'a great buzz throughout *Spartan* with the appreciation that we had just undertaken a very unique piece of intelligence gathering of a Soviet SSN sanitising a deploying SSBN'.

Spartan trailed the Delta, which was doing around 5 knots, the British SSN on her port quarter, the SSBN heading north-west

Conley was to take duty command of *Spartan* that evening, so went to the wardroom for an early evening meal. On returning to take over, giving Cdr Taylor a break, he was disappointed to find contact with the SSBN had been lost. Conley quickly estimated where the SSBN target was likely to have gone and contact was duly re-established.

A few hours later – shortly before midnight – confusion crept in. The towed array appeared to be producing contradictory data – exactly what bearing was the contact on?

It seemed to be switching from one side to the other. 'Are we on the Delta's port quarter,' pondered Conley, 'or her starboard quarter?'

Commander Taylor had retired to his cabin, to get some sleep, content to let his XO carry on, knowing Conley's expertise in manoeuvring a boat to squeeze the most out of towed array.

As *Spartan* closed down the distance, the sonar picture sharpened, Conley reporting to Cdr Taylor they had contact with not one but two Deltas. As they headed into the Greenland Sea, getting ever closer to the MIZ, there was a gap of around ten miles between the SSBNs

The Delta was one of the most formidable, and silent, of the Russian SSBNs at the time so to get two of them together was an absolutely amazing catch. Packed with up to 16 SS-N-18 nuclear-tipped Stingray missiles each, they represented an awesome gathering of potential destructive power in one spot of ocean. That the USSR could deploy a pair of such powerful boats simultaneously was a fearsome demonstration of how the Soviet submarine expansion continued. In 1981 it included two Delta IIIs either being built or fitting out to undertake sea trials, an Oscar cruise missile submarine under construction, a pair of Alfas, and even three Victor III Class SSNs. The USSR was completing a Delta III every year. During the final two decades of the Cold War it would build a total of 36 Deltas, culminating in the Delta IV.

There was plenty of demand for intelligence on what all these new boats looked and sounded like, together with weapons and sensor capabilities. Despite the massive disparity between NATO and Warsaw Pact force levels of all kinds – land, sea and air – there was still a need to ensure that, should the terrible day ever dawn, the West would be quicker on the draw than the East. Conley and other NATO submariners hoped High Noon would never come – but by putting *Spartan* deep into the foe's territory the Royal Navy was attempting to retain a winning edge.

*

The Deltas carried on sailing in close proximity, *Spartan* maintaining her trail into the next evening, acquiring intelligence that Taylor later described as 'pure gold'.

As the submarines approached the oceanic front between the Barents and the Greenland Sea, background noise increased, something caused by a spike in marine biological activity. The water temperatures had dropped dramatically by now and Conley noticed exposed internal surfaces of *Spartan*'s hull were gathering frost.

He recognised it was a venture into uncertain waters, with risk factors rising: 'Owing to the absence of a navigational fix for several days, not very detailed charts, and lack of knowledge of where the ice edge started, and appreciating that HQ had no idea where we were, we were somewhat venturing into the unknown. Since we were not fitted with satcom we had no secure method of radioing for extra water space as any HF transmission could easily be intercepted and *Spartan*'s presence given away. Approaching the edge of our allocated areas, we had to break off the trail and headed south away from the Marginal Ice Zone.'

Spartan was soon re-tasked to meet a Charlie Class cruise missile-armed submarine headed back to base. The British SSN pulled away to head for the Norwegian Sea and await the arrival of the Soviet boat. After a few days of trailing the new target, *Spartan* headed back to the UK.

A relatively new submarine, *Spartan* had proved the stealth of the Swiftsures again, and also the professionalism and precision of the Royal Navy's submariners. Appointed her XO in September 1978, Conley had joined *Spartan* while she was still in build. The previous ship of the name, a cruiser sunk off Anzio in 1944, had also been constructed at Barrow by Vickers and at 5,770 tons did not displace much more than her successor.

During *Spartan*'s Contractor's Sea Trials Conley's pay was boosted by four shillings from Vickers – 20 pence in decimal money – for taking command. The captain was poorly and ashore with mumps. Conley was alarmed to find more sickness aboard the SSN.

'No sooner had the captain departed than a serious problem emerged in that many members of the crew became ill with violent stomach ache and dizziness. Fortunately the symptoms, although very unpleasant, were short-lived, and the cause was determined as fresh-water contamination. This compounded the challenges of undertaking machinery trials in the Irish Sea working up to full power when dived. These were achieved travelling up and down a bottom feature known as the Beaufort's Dyke. A relatively deep trench of water – about 30 miles long – it is just over two miles wide. Working up to top speed, executing a sharp reversal of course at either end only a few hundred feet off the bottom, with a rather green crew was very tense. On reaching the boat's maximum 30 knots, a fifty pence piece was successfully balanced on its edge on the wardroom table: there was virtually no vibration – an excellent example of British engineering at its best.'

Commissioned and worked up as a front-line unit, *Spartan* had fulfilled Conley's long-frustrated ambition to go up against Soviet submarines on a Northern patrol. Her first was, though, not as successful as the second with the Victor and Deltas trailed. During the earlier operational deployment it was a question of having the technology but not the skills to exploit it fully. 'The bottom line was that while we were fitted with a towed array for the first Northern patrol we were not trained in its use. Tactical procedures were not in place and we made a mess of a long-range approach on a Soviet submarine. I took lessons away from it. How could we do the next one better, figuring out: "Where did we go wrong?" It was about this time that I started my crusade of using information from the towed array more effectively, in order to get a boat into a better approach and firing position. This was called Towed Array Target Motion Analysis.'

That second patrol in the North, with Cdr Taylor as captain, was Conley's swan song in *Spartan*. His next job would see him crossing the Atlantic on secondment with a crack US Navy squadron to work on submarine versus submarine tactics.

The *Spartan's* home base at Devonport was by then also a major refitting dockyard for nuclear-powered submarines, a function recently assumed, with Chatham doing less of such work. Rosyth was the other submarine refit centre, handling both SSBNs and Fleet boats. Creating a nuclear submarine force and possessing such infrastructure was a massive investment that only a front-rank nation could manage and Devonport's new Submarine Refit Centre had only been opened in May 1980.

It came at a time when the Conservative government was cutting other parts of the Navy and its support bases. The defence budget was in trouble, having overspent itself by around £700m. The Treasury was insisting economies should be made.

Despite assurances from the Prime Minister, Margaret Thatcher, that

Britain would pursue a maritime-based defence strategy, the Secretary of State for Defence, John Nott, a former Army infantry officer, decided most pain should be borne by the Navy. Since Mrs Thatcher came to power in May 1979 construction of only one nuclear-powered submarine and a handful of mine-hunters and patrol ships had been ordered. By May 1981, it was rumoured, Nott meant to cut the destroyer and frigate force by 27 ships, selling off one of the three new Invincible Class carriers, putting the other two into mothballs. He would get rid of the fleet's amphibious warfare flotilla and the Royal Marines, with three naval dockyards shut.

Nott was at least a fan of submarines. A Polaris submarine had been continuously maintained on patrol for 12 years and he intended Britain should press on with a new generation of SSBNs. The proposed Trident boats would carry 16 missiles, offering 128 independently targeted warheads.

Nott said that would put at risk targets across 'a vast area of the Soviet Union'. He was also determined to increase the number of SSNs from 12 to 17 by 1990. The new Sub Harpoon Anti-Shipping Missile (ASM) would give them a boosted anti-surface role.

In explaining his intentions, Nott was careful to stress he had ordered another Trafalgar Class hunter-killer boat at a cost of £177m and the diesel submarine force would be renewed.

The Spearfish heavyweight torpedo – which was to prove as temperamental during its early days as the (now reliable) Tigerfish – would be introduced as the main conventional strike weapon of Britain's submarines.

In a 'Secret and Personal' note to Mrs Thatcher the First Sea Lord, Admiral Sir Henry Leach, warned the Navy was sharing an unfair burden of proposed defence cuts amounting to '62 per cent of the total reduction contemplated for Defence ...' It was, he claimed, nothing less than a 'proposition to dismantle the Navy'. The First Sea Lord warned the USA would react with alarm, which might affect 'successful negotiation of the Trident project so important to our country'.

Why should the Americans give the Trident nuclear missile system to the UK in order to replace Polaris if the USN's plans to match the Soviet build-up were derailed by Nott's devastating cuts? They would cause gaps the USN would be hard pressed to fill.

As part of his job in the Directorate of Naval Operations Requirements Underwater/sonar, or DNOR(UW sonar) – *a heck of a mouthful* – Rob

Forsyth was tasked with playing a role in developing the next-generation diesel submarine for the Royal Navy.

Known as the Type 2400, and looking like a mini-Fleet boat, it would eventually be known as the Upholder Class, in honour of the remarkable submarine that Wanklyn won his Victoria Cross in during the Second World War. Commander Forsyth's job was to help write up the requirement for a new sonar system that would place the Type 2400 on the cutting edge.

Benefiting from the stealth of a diesel, though naturally not with the endurance and range of an SSN (49 days was quoted as the maximum length of deployment), the Type 2400 aimed to be state-of-the-art.

As well-armed as an SSN in terms of weaponry – with Tigerfish or Spearfish torpedoes and Harpoon missiles – the new diesel would be capable of diving to more than 600 feet (with a high submerged speed of 20 knots). For the Type 2400, Forsyth also worked on defining the requirement for a successor to the notorious DCB Action Information and Fire Control System that would be fitted to the new boat and called, sensibly enough, DCC.

The Upholders' job if the Cold War turned hot would be to cover the GIUK. They were meant to replace the Oberons from around 1990, although only eight would in the end be proposed (and even that was halved, with just four built and commissioned into service).

Working on such an ambitious diesel was interesting enough, but it didn't really float Forsyth's boat. By 1981 he was 41 years old, had achieved his ambition of commanding an SSN and had mastered the challenge of being Teacher, too. It had been a good career and somehow he had managed to spend the majority of it at sea.

Forsyth might get his own warship, but the last time he had been part of the surface fleet he felt like a square peg in a round hole. Still, it might be better as the captain, rather than a junior officer. It was not to be. 'I was fretting to get back to sea but then the government of the time carried out its Defence review and it appeared the surface ships would be savagely slashed. As the Navy seemed about to go into decline my chances of further sea command were reducing. I was too old to get another submarine command, so I decided to opt out before the Navy was emasculated. In January 1981 I stepped "ashore" for the last time as a serving officer.' Forsyth's second career would take him into the realms of top-level management in the defence industry. While he would experience a tinge of regret – and possibly envy? – when he saw some contemporaries command surface warships in the Falklands War, he always felt that he had been right to quit while ahead. Forsyth instead relished new challenges and broader horizons.

In the end Nott decided two carriers were to be kept in service, though *Invincible* herself was to be sold, probably to the Australians. The Royal Marines escaped disbandment and amphibious warfare ships were retained. Plans to cut the number of frigates and destroyers – the older ones, more expensive to maintain – and to shut Chatham and scale back Portsmouth, remained. The dockyard in Gibraltar would close in the near future. Devonport and Rosyth would be the only two major British naval dockyards. Investment in new surface ships and diesel submarines was to be slowed.

Nott regarded the Navy's function as primarily to provide the nuclear deterrent, with other units devoted to supporting that mission. In terms of 'general warfare' he felt that should be spearheaded by a 'powerful submarine force', in order to exploit the UK's strategic position 'on the flank of the Soviet Navy's main exit to the Atlantic'.

By April 1991 Nott felt the Navy should have four SSBNs, 17 SSNs and eight diesel patrol submarines (SSKs), compared with four, 12 and 16 respectively in 1981. Desmond Wettern, eminent naval correspondent of the *Daily Telegraph*, pointed out that there was a lethal confusion in the mind of British politicians. They saw Polaris and Trident as maritime weaponry, but the SSBNs were a national strategic asset, not a naval capability. They were of no practical use in waging war at sea, or in deterring the conventional threat. For that you needed more SSNs and SSKs. The British build rate just wasn't high enough to come anywhere near matching the Russians or playing a bigger role alongside the Americans in the most crucial contest. In such a situation every single SSN was a priceless asset – even one that had been badly chewed by a Soviet submarine's screws.

*'I wish to have no connection with any ship that does
not sail fast; for I intend to go in harm's way.'*

John Paul Jones

The undersea shadow boxing once again yielded a coming together
that could easily have sent men to their doom. The submariners'
dread fear of drowning and being crushed to death was for a few moments more than just Franklin D. Roosevelt's 'nameless unreasoning
unjustified terror' but actual, tangible and justified. The Soviet Delta
III ballistic missile boat *K-211*, a new SSBN only declared operational
in 1980, was cruising at 9 knots, with a depth of 150ft. On 23 May 1981
she had conducted exercises close to the edge of the Arctic ice and was
heading home. The Russian boat's captain was keen to check his baffles
were clear. Performing a look behind, *K-211*'s sonar operators listened intently for any giveaway traces of a shadower. After a double-check sonar
sweep, the verdict was: *All clear.*

Twenty-one minutes later, at 19.51, the Soviet SSBN juddered as she
sustained three short glancing impacts astern and from below, each lasting only a few seconds.

Immediately ordering the boat to periscope depth, the Delta III's
sonar team detected propeller noise on a bearing of 127 degrees. The
contact was judged to be a submarine.

Having ascended to achieve separation, *K-211* also turned to starboard, but the contact was lost within a couple of minutes. Surfacing for
an external damage check, *K-211*'s bridge team found no sign of a Western submarine. The Soviets suspected they had been in collision with a
Sturgeon Class SSN, a type of boat frequently sent into the Barents by
the US Navy.

K-211 sustained minor damage to her rubber coating, caused by
the other submarine scraping along the hull. The three short impacts
felt inside the Delta III were actually one of her screws eating into the
NATO boat. The Delta's starboard screw was damaged, as was an aft
hydroplane, and the Soviet boat also allegedly suffered punctures in
her stern ballast tanks. Occurring almost 13 years after *Warspite*'s near

disaster, the other party in the collision was not an American SSN but HMS *Sceptre*.

To this day the Ministry of Defence will not admit the truth, though a MP would a few years later suggest in the House of Commons that *Sceptre* had experienced a dangerous brush.

The defence minister responsible for responding to the Woolwich MP John Cartwright's claim skilfully evaded either confirming or denying there had been a collision involving *Sceptre* or, for that matter, any other British submarine. He made no comment on whether or not they even operated in the Barents. Dissatisfied with the response, the MP made a salient point about attendant risk. 'Those in our attack submarines, who have the vital task of tracking Soviet ballistic missile submarines, also carry out an important task on our behalf. It is vital to be sure that we are not asking our submariners to undertake unreasonable risks.'

Much of *Sceptre*'s forward outer casing was torn away – a terrifying level of damage. Russian accounts maintain the NATO boat was ascending from a deeper depth than the Delta III, possibly turning across the SSBN's stern. If they are to be believed, *Sceptre* must have been pushed down violently by the force of the collision, one of the Delta's five-bladed screws chewing along her side. The propeller of the Russian boat even cut into the pressure hull by a few, potentially lethal, centimetres, ripping away the front of *Sceptre*'s fin as it raked across the SSN's casing.

One officer in *Sceptre*'s crew – the only person to ever speak openly of the incident – later described 'a huge noise'. He said everyone aboard 'went white'. Fortunately, as was the case with *Warspite*, the Battle Short was used to ensure the British boat did not lose her reactor power. The back afties again had the presence of mind to prevent calamity. Once she had slipped away to a safe distance, an urgent check on *Sceptre*'s watertight integrity revealed the pressure hull had not yielded.

Sceptre then surfaced and how perilously close to disaster she had come was abundantly clear.

It was possible to climb up the tower and see straight out the front of the fin – the bridge was simply no longer there, while the Soviet submarine even left behind pieces of her screw.

There was great concern the damage would be exposed when the boat returned to Faslane, so a disguise was required. A broadcast was made for the smoke curtains and any other suitable fabric available to be stripped and then painted black. The boat did not actually have any black paint, so *Sceptre*'s sailors made a substitute with grease and graphite.

When they tried to put their carefully stitched together shroud over the 23ft-long hole in the hull casing it got sucked inside. A similar attempt to cover the damage to the fin with black 'painted' panelling also failed. The boat would have to be brought into the Gareloch under cover of darkness. Once a temporary disguise was successfully created on the Clyde, *Sceptre* headed south to Devonport.

It was, after *Warspite's* collision, the most serious incident of its kind involving a British nuclear submarine during the Cold War.

Once the press caught a sniff of it, the iceberg collision cover was again trotted out. The *Sunday Independent* newspaper, published in *Sceptre's* home port of Plymouth, ran a headline screaming 'KILLER SUB HITS ICE FIELD'. The accompanying report observed, without irony, that the 'North Polar icecap is a favourite place for the big nukes to carry out training in the deadly business of shadowing the stream of Russian missile submarines coming down from their bases in the Barents Sea.' Apparently ice had broken off the pack and had been in collision with '*Sceptre's* huge conning tower ...'

At the time there were far more sensational stories in the pages of the UK's newspapers. Nobody was killed, no nuclear disaster had unfolded; the incident rapidly faded from public awareness.

The Cold War was becoming old hat – people had learned to live with it. No longer did it loom so large in their minds on a daily basis. The contest had become so deeply immersed in technological rivalry the human risks – an enduring, and indeed growing, threat to mankind – were simply *too big* for ordinary men and women to comprehend. In two decades the world had gone from terrifying itself at the cinema with *On the Beach* and *Dr Strangelove* to seeking a more entertaining take on East–West rivalry.

The Cold War seemed to have lost its hard edge. James Bond as portrayed by the suave (but hammy) Roger Moore was bordering on parody. In *For Your Eyes Only*, the tenth-highest-grossing movie of 1981, Bond was ordered to retrieve a stolen Automatic Targeting Attack Co-ordinator (ATAC) via which the Soviets could allegedly order the Royal Navy's SSBNs to launch Polaris missiles *against Western targets*. Having wiped out the villains who stole the ATAC in order to sell it to the Soviets – and destroyed the device itself – Cdr Bond shares a joke with a genial KGB agent. 'Détente, comrade,' quips Bond. 'You don't have it; I don't have it.'

In fact détente ended a few years earlier, but the wider world did not yet know it. There were growing indications of a new, more dangerous, phase. If overt clashes did happen, they seemed very regional and far away from the NATO versus Warsaw Pact fault line.

At the beginning of June 1981 the Israeli Air Force mounted a daring strike on Iraq's Osirak reactor, to prevent Saddam Hussein from acquiring nuclear weapons. In August South African troops invaded Angola.

And who cared about yet another round of conferences at Geneva to try and reduce the stock of nuclear weapons? The East–West equilibrium seemed settled, no longer a balance of terror but of tedium. The world was living with the Cold War as normal. The face-off that had defined everybody's lives for 36 years was part of the furniture.

The UK's submariners did not share this lack of urgency, for they continued to live on the edge. They *always* operated at war pitch.

For one young submarine officer, keen to secure his first SSN command and get back to sea, *Sceptre*'s accident had unexpected consequences.

Doug Littlejohns swung his car into a space beside 11 Dock at Devonport to be confronted by a worried-looking sailor.

'You can't park there,' the youngster told Littlejohns as he climbed out. 'That space is reserved for the captain of *Sceptre*.'

Fixing the rating with a steely look, Littlejohns pulled on his cap and replied: 'I am about to be the captain of *Sceptre*.'

The rating saluted and stood aside as his new boss strode past. Standing on the edge of the capacious dry dock, Littlejohns was shocked by what he found. To his eyes 'the submarine looked like a gutted, beached whale'. Furthermore, he was shocked to see, 'almost all the outer casing forward of the fin had gone. There was mile upon mile of cables everywhere. The front and top of the fin was missing. What remained was twisted and bent.' Littlejohns went down stone steps to a security gate on the side of the dock. The sailor who greeted him was already on the phone warning of the new CO's imminent arrival. Passing across the gangway, Littlejohns could see people dashing here and there, like a disturbed ants' nest. As he stepped onto the casing the current captain, Coxswain and Officer of the Watch emerged to welcome him aboard.

'We went down to the captain's cabin. He was shell-shocked and had known since Friday – three days earlier – but told only one or two people. I could see everybody looking at us as we passed through the boat. In his cabin he handed over the submarine to me, signing a statement saying there were no confidential books missing and the accounts were square. His heart wasn't in it and nor was mine. I am sure he wanted to get off as soon as possible. Acknowledging that I had command of the boat we shook hands.'

The former captain left the submarine for the last time with the minimum of fuss.

The previous Thursday Littlejohns had been contemplating several more months at Northwood driving a desk.

Then he received a call asking him to come and see Vice Admiral Squires – Flag Officer Submarines himself. Littlejohns anticipated receiving congratulations on a paper he had written laying out the justification for purchasing new Electronic Support Measures. The current ESM fitted to British submarines were, in his view, 'old and knackered', with a limited ability to detect enemy radar emissions – though he used more diplomatic language to deliver his carefully composed analysis.

Instead of big thanks for the ESM paper, Littlejohns was surprised to be given command of *Sceptre*. As a well-connected Commander on FOSM's staff he had already worked out that he was nicely positioned to get an SSN command. This was not the boat he expected and it was also far sooner than he imagined.

'I worked alongside people running the submarine programmes, such as the officer overseeing Flotilla Operations and Programmes, a powerful and influential guy. I got to know him and worked out that *Splendid*, which had been launched at Barrow in October 1979, was now being completed and would probably be commissioned in 1981. I realised *Splendid* would be looking for a captain about the same time I came up for my next job.'

With a lot more boats in service, Littlejohns hoped the Navy – which was working on raising the profile of the Submarine Service – could be persuaded to let him take the newest SSN on a flag-flying world tour.

Then *Sceptre* had her 'iceberg' crash.

While CTF-311, the cell running SSN operations against the Soviets in northern waters from Northwood, was secretive and played things very close to its chest, things inevitably filtered out to be discussed in hushed tones.

As he shared an office with the Flotilla Warfare Officer, a man deeply involved in operational tasking of submarines, Littlejohns soon knew about the *Sceptre* 'iceberg'. He thought: 'Poor buggers, I expect the CO is probably toast.' As he was less than halfway through his assignment to Northwood, it never crossed Littlejohns's mind that he would end up captain of the crippled submarine. 'You could have knocked me down with a feather when I was picked. I think I was just in the right place at the right time, with the relevant experience.'

He had commanded a diesel boat at the age of 29 and was a command-qualified XO of the SSN *Superb* at the age of 32 (promoted to Commander at 33, which was early). Now, as Littlejohns reached the ripe old age of 35, he was catapulted into command of *Sceptre*. As he entered FOSM's office at noon on the Thursday, 'Tubby' Squires looked over his half-moon glasses and proposed: 'Doug, I want to give you a bit of a challenge.'

A pause.

'You know what has happened to *Sceptre*?'

'Yes, Sir.'

'I want you to take over command on Monday morning.'

Littlejohns was immediately excited by the prospect, but it wasn't the ideal way to receive command of an SSN.

'Does the current captain know?' he asked.

Squires replied: 'No, I am telling him tomorrow.'

Littlejohns went back to his office, didn't even go back to his digs, just threw everything in a car and drove to the family home at Alverstoke, near Gosport. He spent the Friday evening and Saturday at home with his family, explained what was happening and drove to Plymouth on the Sunday. Booking himself into the wardroom at HMS *Drake* overnight, in the bar Lt Cdr David Russell came across and introduced himself. 'I am your new XO,' he revealed.

Littlejohns would join *Sceptre* at 10.30 a.m. on Monday, 21 September 1981, and Russell at noon. Shortly after going aboard, her new captain went down to talk to the senior rates in their mess.

He had given up smoking but on entering and taking a seat, declared: 'What I really need is a pint and a fag.'

He counted on the Submarine Service being a small world, assuming correctly that they would have heard of him as XO of *Superb*. Littlejohns clearly knew what running an SSN was all about. He told them he would put the boat together again, give them back their confidence and restore the submarine to the front-line flotilla. There wasn't much of a response. Littlejohns suspected they were still in shock at the rapidity of events.

He realised he would have to get a grip on it soon, that he had to identify their 'g spot' – what made them tick. Littlejohns had yet to connect with them, but intended to do so over the next few days.

He was *determined* to do so.

Next on his 'to do' list was a thorough inspection of the submarine, both inside and out, grabbing the Marine Engineer Officer (MEO) to go with him. There was a tangled mess of wires where the sonar should have been in the bows, and even gashes in the pressure hull. These looked to be more than one and a half inches deep.

The pressure hull was only four inches thick.

Scary, thought Littlejohns, *they were very lucky.*

There were bits of phosphor bronze lodged in the gashes and also similar debris in what remained of the fin. This was a bit odd if *Sceptre* had collided with an iceberg. Fragments of material and the forward indicator buoy – usually released to indicate where a submarine is stuck on the bottom – had also gone through the propulsor, causing further harm. Climbing down into the bottom of the dock, he scrambled underneath.

Thousands of tons rested only on a slim, but extremely stout, line of wooden blocks on the hull's centreline. It felt a little weird with the huge bulk of the submarine suspended just above his head, but he was relieved to find *Sceptre* wasn't damaged down there. Emerging and craning his head back to take in the SSN's huge bulk towering above him, Littlejohns muttered, somewhat sardonically: 'No problem.'

Like a bloody beached whale, he thought again.

Climbing back up the tiered side of the massive dock, he crossed the gangway, and went back aboard.

Gathering his Heads of Department in the wardroom, scanning their expectant faces, Littlejohns asked: 'What are we doing to rehabilitate this lot?'

To her new captain *Sceptre*'s men were no longer submariners as he would recognise them. Littlejohns faced the same challenge of restoring them psychologically and spiritually as Sandy Woodward had in *Warspite* a dozen years earlier.

He felt they were 'not cheeky chappies' and vowed to restore their spirit. The cure prescribed was to rotate *Sceptre*'s men through a spell of leave, then get them back into regular training and ensure they were all fully qualified for sea. It had been a very tough regime under the previous CO, which had made the crew brittle, so Littlejohns devised other activities to raise the general bonhomie among his sailors.

To bond them together again and pierce any private traumas they might be suffering, he introduced more sporting activities – *Sceptre* formed both a rugby and a cricket team.

Littlejohns also spent a lot of time talking to people, getting to know them. He concluded that more responsibility on an individual basis would help rebuild the *Sceptre* team's confidence.

'In diesel boats the CO was the only one who knew what was going on completely – he was a one-man band, because the rest of the officers were so inexperienced on the tactical side. Some people couldn't make the transformation to the new business model. In SSNs it is more collegiate. Your officers are much more experienced. The second-in-command, for instance, has passed Perisher – and might have had a diesel submarine command already. For example, in *Sceptre*, the two watch leaders – representatives of the CO in the Control Room on watch – Paul Boissier and Paul Lambert, ended up as Vice Admirals. They were experienced watch officers. You had degree-qualified nuclear engineers looking after the reactors and two graduate weapons officers. You cannot be a one-man band in an SSN, as I found out during my trip in *Swiftsure*. As XO in *Superb* with Geoffrey Biggs it was different again. A revelation.'

As repairs progressed and with the cycle of leave concluding, the focus switched to sharpening tactical skills in an attack team trainer ashore.

'They were pretty good at that,' decided Littlejohns, 'and I gelled well with David Russell. The big test, though, would be taking *Sceptre* to sea.'

That she had suffered a major amount of damage was beyond a doubt.

To those unfamiliar with just how much punishment an SSN can take, it might have seemed not worth repairing her at all. Mending *Sceptre* would cost a lot less than building a new SSN. It would be quicker. There was also a pressing need for her services. There was never any doubt that *Sceptre* was going back to sea.

In the normal course of things a new submarine would make a trim dive in the dock at Barrow-in-Furness – a tightly controlled artificial situation where nothing fatal can happen. The trim dive at Barrow was used to work out the boat's basic characteristics.

After a commissioned submarine comes out of a refit or some other lengthy period alongside, the first dive is a tense situation, but at least the boat is in good working order and well run in.

Sceptre, though, was a dangerous hybrid – a substantially rebuilt submarine without the benefit of a suitable dock to do a trim dive. Devonport did not have a deep enough one with the right monitoring equipment. Hopefully, the first dive at sea would not reveal any unsuspected problems and the rebuild would prove successful. The figures from *Sceptre*'s completion back in 1978 did not necessarily still hold true. Littlejohns got his crew to work out a trim while the boat was still alongside the sea wall. Fortunately the draught marks were still within an inch of where they should be. When they took her out in December 1981, the first destination was to find at least 300ft of water to see how well *Sceptre* held up.

The main vents were opened.

Everybody's fingers were crossed.

Sceptre dived successfully, Littlejohns relieved to see she did not drop like a stone and retained good trim.

During all this Littlejohns was also on trial, for *Sceptre*'s men were watching their new boss to see how he performed. It all added up to a fair bit of pressure, but Littlejohns could handle it.

'I wasn't nervous – I was never nervous. It is like standing in front of a dog and being scared – you mustn't show it. It wouldn't have engendered confidence.'

With that milestone passed, the next one would be a dive in deep water. Remaining submerged, *Sceptre* crossing the 100-fathom line. Littlejohns wanted as much room as possible, for he intended putting on some radical angles and dangles.

Aggressive manoeuvring would shake out any remaining niggles from the rebuild. It was also a means to restore his crew's confidence in their boat.

Taking it in easy stages, *Sceptre* descended to maximum diving depth.

Prior to departing Devonport, the crew had closed up at diving stations and conducted a simulated voyage (in naval parlance a Fast Cruise). Her crew was at watch-keeping stations, the reactor up and running.

A variety of drills, including fire-fighting, were carried out, to get everybody in the right frame of mind.

Now, back at sea, the real test was about to happen.

Littlejohns was in his chair at the centre of the Control Room.

He needed to be able to place himself at the core of the action for extended periods. To that end – like a number of SSN captains – he'd acquired a sturdy, comfy chair. In his case it came from a Volvo lorry. Tied down, it was secured on the port side of the Control Room next to the DCB panel.

Installed in the chair, Littlejohns was the calm centre – surrounded by a sea of suppressed anxiety – as *Sceptre* went ever deeper.

There are an awful lot of white faces in here, he thought, *but I suppose that's because last time they were under the water there was a fucking great big bang.*

Everybody was praying that the hull held.

The MEO, Peter Hurford, made a pipe: 'Free of leaks.' There was a palpable release of breath. Littlejohns was pleased to see the faces around him looking less pale.

Satisfied *Sceptre*'s structure could handle deep diving and his crew had the strength of mind, Littlejohns decided to increase the tempo.

He ordered 20 degrees bows up and a depth of 200ft. The unflappable Coxswain on the planes reported back: 'Twenty degrees up.'

Littlejohns increased the speed from 7 knots to 20. As they ascended – most submarines would come up at 10 degrees, not 20 degrees – people hung on to pipes or pieces of equipment. Littlejohns braced himself in his chair. The submarine rose through several hundred feet in the kind of steep climb that would have put a jet fighter to shame.

Littlejohns was gratified to hear it shaking things up.

The sound of breaking crockery brought a grim smile to his lips. *Obviously poorly secured at diving stations, so it deserved to get smashed.*

Having brought *Sceptre* up rapidly from the depths, Littlejohns ordered the planes reversed to 20 degrees down at high speed. They didn't go to maximum depth, the Coxswain pretty soon pulling her up.

Littlejohns shook all their cobwebs out with some real flying under water, the boat climbing, diving, banking and turning ever tighter.

There was plenty of room to play with, or rather within.

'You are allocated a box of water, by the CTF in Northwood, and I had requested one west of Ireland because it was quiet in terms of shipping. Having made sure I had the water allocation I didn't need to have particular permission for what I did within that box.'

It still took considerable force of personality, not to mention nerves of steel, to convey confidence and hurl a nuclear-powered submarine around.

'I carried on like that for an hour or so at ever higher speeds, tighter turns and bigger angles and dangles until the crew realised that this was how it was going to be from now on.'

With a rudder the size of an average house, high speeds enabled the hydrodynamically perfect *Sceptre* to really manoeuvre hard under water.

She was very responsive. 'I started to corkscrew her up – ordered the rudder full over – 35 degrees – so when she turned, *Sceptre* leaned into it like an aircraft. The Valiant Class would do that snap roll they were prone to – their large fin would act like an aileron on an aircraft. The Swiftsure Class, with a smaller fin, would keep much more upright. When the rudder is hard over, it drops the stern; the boat would heel over ten degrees, banking. I just treated it as a roller coaster – this was fun. There wasn't any more crockery to smash by the time we'd finished.'

Littlejohns's reputation as a hard charger had gone before him of course, so *Sceptre*'s men weren't entirely unprepared for what happened.

The sonar team was meanwhile vigilant for potential Soviet submarine activity just in case non-NATO visitors made things awkward.

The Littlejohns method was to reassure people *Sceptre* was an utterly responsive weapon of war. That readiness for war also applied to the sailors.

He felt it was a simple rationale. 'We had to do these things, or we would be dead. It can't be armchair comfortable.'

If things turned hot there would be no time to learn cardinal life-or-death rules. Littlejohns would ensure *Sceptre* was ready.

There was a fine line between daring and calculated risk; between pushing against and taking things beyond the parameters of the envelope. It was an awesome weight of responsibility – 5,000 tons of hunter-killer heavy metal 272ft long, hurtling around at high speed, containing more than 100 men who placed their entire faith in their captain not screwing up and killing everyone. Littlejohns handled it all with a smile, regarding

Sceptre as 'a joy to command – my underwater Maserati. You felt that you were in a Formula One car rather than driving a Ford Prefect.'

All his training and experiences had schooled him and prepared him for *this job*. Perisher had confirmed he could handle it.

What was to doubt?

'Human beings are adaptable,' was his statement of faith.

He had no choice but to place himself in their hands, and vice versa. There had to be mutual trust in everybody's abilities.

After a couple of days' and nights' energetic shake-down cruising, Littlejohns was sitting in his cabin reading a paperback when there was a knock on the frame of the open sliding door. The weapons officer, Lt Cdr Andrew Leask, put his head through the curtain. He told his new CO: 'I just wanted to say thanks for giving me my job back.'

He was thanking Littlejohns for having faith in him to do his job without being micromanaged. 'I didn't interfere in the day-to-day running of his department or experiment with new settings on the sonar without telling him.'

It was 2.45 a.m. one morning when the Sonar Officer, Lt Paul Lambert, also called on Littlejohns's cabin, revealing he had performed sonar checks to make sure the surface was clear.

The boat was ready to return to periscope depth, to take in the communications broadcast from Northwood.

Instead of being told the captain would be along in a second, Littlejohns merely responded: 'Okay, do it.'

Most COs take boats to periscope depth themselves, as it is one of the most dangerous times in a submariner's day – because you might get it wrong and come up under a bloody great ship – so to let Lambert take the lead was a definitive statement of confidence. The young officer's reaction was a picture and Littlejohns was most amused.

'He looked at me as if I had just pole-axed him. Then he grinned. I did go out, but stood back in the Control Room. I merely watched Lambert take the boat up to periscope depth. I wanted to train them to take decisions.

It was the first time he had been in control of anything. It made him feel several inches taller. In later years Paul told me that he would never forget that moment.

By the time we came back from a week at sea, *Sceptre* was a fully functioning submarine again and they were submariners.'

Observing the Littlejohns effect was 25-year-old Leading Seaman (Tactical Systems) Keith Sapsed, only five years into his naval career but having already served with *Sceptre*'s captain in HMS *Superb*.

Sapsed joined the Navy at Croydon recruiting office in late October 1976, a week before his twentieth birthday. What with the three-day working week and British industry being on its knees, he felt he might find a more viable future serving his country.

Excelling in his training as a Radio Operator, finishing in the top three of his class, Sapsed was asked if he fancied being a submariner. The incentive of extra money was mentioned.

'So that's what I decided to do,' he said of this pivotal moment in his life, 'and I never had a single regret over the next 21 years.'

On arriving in *Superb* as a Radio Operator 1st Class, Sapsed was involved in Radio Ops and also Tactical Ops. He and the Electronic Warfare equipment operator worked with the Communications Technicians intercepting radar transmissions. The intelligence they gleaned was passed to the submarine's command team, along with any early warnings of detection and possible counter-detection by the Soviets. Sapsed worked closely with Littlejohns.

'He was extremely firm, but very fair. He was already showing signs of being a great tactician and he was actually liked by nearly everyone on board, which for a First Lieutenant was some achievement.'

By the time he joined *Sceptre* at the end of 1981, Sapsed was a Leading Seaman Tactical Systems Submarines (LS TS [SM]). This meant he was part of the command team, where his talents were put to good use analysing sonar contact information. It allowed compilation of an accurate picture of other units in the vicinity and where they might be headed. This was essential to creating a fire-control solution should one be necessary. Such practices were the essence of the Cold War knife-edge under the sea. When tracking a 'contact of interest' both sides cultivated a readiness to switch over to combat at any moment. *Sceptre* had to be ready to defend herself whenever a threat developed, whether by evasion, deploying counter-measures or firing torpedoes. For Sapsed it was apparent Littlejohns would succeed.

'He loved the boat, and I think his men equally, and showed that during his time on board. Like most submarine commanders that have the respect of their crew, he earned it and did not take anything for granted.' Sapsed saw Littlejohns's excellent grasp of tactics at work again. 'Tactically he remained first-class, but I could say that about a number of COs. As a man manager he was very good. I trusted him to always do the right thing, which is extremely important when you are living in a steel tube for weeks on end.'

*

Devonport Dockyard rectified defects identified during her trip to sea and then the SSN set sail again, heading north to Faslane to be worked up for the front line by Captain Submarine Sea Training sea riders. There was also a phase of special preparations for the boat's future intelligence-gathering missions.

Fears about their submarine – the world in which they lived or died, its security and stability – had been pushed to the back of the submariners' minds. Their new captain's radical prescription had worked.

Yet, somewhere deeply embedded in some would always be the memory of that terrifying collision, and there would be triggers. In the case of one young submariner, it was the sound of Soviets.

Littlejohns was sitting in his lorry driver's chair as *Sceptre* trailed a Soviet boat and there was quite loud underwater telephone activity from the target. Over his left shoulder he noticed the young rating operating the hydrophone stepping back, yanking the lead of his headphones out of the panel and shaking, white-faced.

The youngster must have heard something that threw him.

The hydrophone operator was on the same frequency he had been monitoring when *Sceptre* hit the 'iceberg'. He was listening again to what was being said by the Soviets on their underwater telephone. As a Russian voice filled his earphones he had been spooked.

Littlejohns turned around and patted him on the shoulder.

'Don't worry, son, I know what I'm doing.'

Promoted to Petty Officer several months later, the same Leading Seaman came to the captain's cabin to say his goodbyes, shedding tears as he told Littlejohns he didn't want to leave *Sceptre*.

Completing work-up in February 1982, *Sceptre* was qualified for front-line operations. She possessed one critical handicap that had to be allowed for whenever operating in close contact with the foe. Prior to her collision *Sceptre* was quieter – thanks to her revolutionary propulsor – than even the US Navy's Los Angeles Class attack boats. Now she was noisier than she had been before. 'There was no doubt *Sceptre* had a distinctive noise, dependent on speed,' noted Littlejohns. 'This had been caused by all the metal and other rubbish that had gone through the propulsor. After the iceberg incident, at a particular speed SOSUS always knew it was us. It took a long time to find that out, and the Americans were not going to give away the fact that they knew. They seemed to work on the principle with friends that they would only respond to direct questions – the old mantra of knowledge is power. This was despite the best efforts of all concerned to make *Sceptre* as quiet at speed as she had been prior to the accident.'

During one exercise even sister S-boat *Spartan* was able to detect *Sceptre* doing a high-speed dash, but SOSUS could still not pick her up at low speed. Once he had discovered the exact speed at which she generated such a racket, Littlejohns avoided it. Defective technology aside, it was men that made the difference and *Sceptre*'s captain believed they were back in the swing of things. 'The esprit de corps was excellent and we felt we were on the cutting edge of the Cold War.'

Littlejohns knew *Sceptre*'s crew had recovered from the 'iceberg' incident when there was a leak. On 3 April 1982, the SSN was off the west coast of Ireland on her way to take up close surveillance of the Soviets in the far North when one of the hull valves malfunctioned.

Even though it was not close to maximum diving depth, pressure was still pushing water into the submarine's engine room at an alarming rate.

Littlejohns immediately ordered an emergency surface, taking *Sceptre* up at 25 degrees, her men hanging on to whatever they could find.

No time to waste on sonar checks, or periscope looks – it was a pretty empty spot of ocean. There was a one in a million chance anything would be there but a higher certainty of lives lost if the SSN remained dived.

The boat leapt out of the sea like a killer whale, water streaming off her gleaming black casing, slamming back down into the water with a gigantic splash. The engineers had fortunately isolated the problem on the way up, but still it was a pretty alarming moment. Their captain thought the crew handled it well. 'You have to do something to stop it all becoming a huge drama,' observed Littlejohns, 'and you are worried if you don't immediately do something, you will die.'

Sceptre's men were 'remarkable, but, because we had practised for every kind of eventuality, they were quite matter-of-fact about it all'. Clearly, though, the dodgy hull valve was something that would need to be sorted out before *Sceptre* went North. The SSN set course on the surface for Faslane where she found highly unusual activity centred on two SSNs already alongside, *Conqueror* and *Splendid*.

Torpedoes were being loaded aboard, with boxes of stores passed along human chains to disappear down below.

Sensing something big was afoot Littlejohns was ashore as soon as a gangway was put across to *Sceptre*. He headed for the office of Capt. Andrew Buchanan, boss of SM3, to find out what all the fuss was about.

It transpired that, after years of sabre rattling and bellyaching about the Falklands being theirs, the Argentinians had actually invaded the islands and also South Georgia, an outlying British dependency. A British military response was likely.

All this was an unwelcome distraction, for the number one priority in the big league of submarine operations was keeping up the West's guard against the Soviets. Nevertheless, with a fully armed SSN and an eager crew, Littlejohns thought it worth pointing out he could easily switch from a Cold War mission in the Arctic to the potential hot war in the South Atlantic. Never shy about coming forward, *Sceptre*'s thrusting CO told Capt. Buchanan: 'I am ready to go.'

As his boat was deploying into the Soviet danger zone, *Sceptre* was already loaded with war-shot torpedoes and all the stores she would need for several months.

Captain Buchanan said that wasn't going to happen. After several minutes of heated conversation – in which Littlejohns explained why his boat was the one to send south, not the others – he was told to wind his neck in. The decision to keep *Sceptre* on the Northern job was, anyway, well above the squadron commander's pay grade. The US Defense Secretary, Casper Weinberger, and John Nott had discussed how Britain would meet on going joint US–UK missions. It was made clear to the British that failing to honour their commitment to patrols in the North was not acceptable. The Americans did not have a submarine available to fill the gap if *Sceptre* was sent to the South Atlantic. For the Americans the Falklands was a sideshow. Much to his chagrin, Littlejohns had to get his boat up on the roof of the world within six days to take over from a US Navy SSN.

Keith Sapsed thought it was a shame *Sceptre*'s crew didn't get an opportunity to show the 'powers that be' how professional they were.

Fortunately, as he willingly conceded, there were other highly trained submariners in equally proficient submarines that could be sent.

The British ultimately diverted five nuclear-powered attack submarines – *Spartan*, *Splendid*, *Conqueror*, *Courageous* and *Valiant* – as well as one diesel-electric boat, *Onyx*, away from their Cold War missions. Conley's old boat *Spartan*, still commanded by Cdr James Taylor, was the first major British war vessel to reach waters off the islands.

She was ordered to enforce a 200-mile Total Exclusion Zone (TEZ) and observe Argentinian efforts to mine Stanley Harbour, but not to take offensive action.

That would have alerted the enemy to the presence of an SSN and the British were keen to lure out the Argentinian carrier *25 de Mayo*.

Four days after *Spartan* started prowling off the Falklands, *Conqueror* arrived and it was she who found and stalked the Argentinian cruiser *Belgrano*. The *Conqueror*'s captain was the 36-year-old Cdr Chris Wreford-Brown, like most of his Ship's Company a seasoned veteran of patrols in Northern waters against the Soviets. He had also been Navigator of *Repulse* when Forsyth was XO. Now, less than a decade later, he was the captain of an SSN, regarding *Conqueror* as 'a good submarine, with a good crew'. The SSN's experienced XO was Lt Cdr Tim McClement, who had been one of Doug Littlejohns's officers in *Osiris* several years earlier.

The submarine herself was a veteran of at least one close encounter with the Soviets. In 1972 *Conqueror* was sent to confront a Victor Class SSN that had the audacity to sneak into the Clyde itself.

Conqueror had earlier been deployed at short notice to hunt down a small vessel suspected of smuggling arms across the Irish Sea to the IRA. SOSUS picked up the Russian submarine approaching the west coast of Scotland, so *Conqueror* was pulled off that assignment. Detecting a British SSN moving in to expel his boat from the Clyde Channel, the Russian captain did not withdraw gracefully. He brought his submarine right around in a Crazy Ivan, charging straight at *Conqueror*. A collision was only narrowly avoided, the two boats passing with only around 500 yards separation.

Conqueror departed Faslane on 4 April 1982. On the 8,000-mile voyage south McClement put the submarine's men through constant drills to prepare for action, including torpedo evasion and damage-control exercises.

The foe might not be the Russians but it would be a mistake to underestimate the Argentinians. The Cold War mindset must temporarily be set to one side. McClement regarded the contest with the Russians as 'either peace or the end of the world' but now *Conqueror* was cruising into a regional war fought entirely by conventionally armed forces.

After operations off South Georgia, *Conqueror* took up position south of the Falklands – with *Spartan* to her north-east and *Splendid* to the north-west. The primary mission now was to stop an Argentinian naval pincer movement on the task force. On reading the text of the UK's TEZ declaration Wreford-Brown noticed that it said 'any *approaching* Argentine military vessel which could amount to a threat would encounter the appropriate response'. Positioning the submarine as directed between the Burdwood Bank, south of the islands, and the Isla de los Estados, south-east of Argentina, Wreford-Brown searched for traces of enemy vessels on the edges of the TEZ.

He first found *Belgrano* filling his periscope on 1 May, as together with her escorting destroyers *Hipolito Bouchard* and *Piedro Bueno* she received fuel on the move from a replenishment ship.

One by one the Argentinian ships went alongside the tanker *Puerto Rosales*, big hoses conveying oil hauled across and connected. A warship is extremely vulnerable when conducting Replenishment at Sea, so they were in no position to defend themselves if *Conqueror* attacked.

Meanwhile, *Splendid* found an Argentinian Type 42 destroyer and three A-69 corvettes operating to the west of the Falklands. Those vessels were possibly working with the Argentinian carrier *25 de Mayo* – though the enemy flagship herself was not spotted. The feared pincer movement appeared to be shaping up, though *Belgrano*'s group was not at that precise moment threatening the TEZ.

To sink her would not play well in diplomatic circles.

Conqueror therefore began a trail of three surface vessels nobody aboard would ever have imagined shadowing with a view to a kill. Wreford-Brown fired a quick signal to Northwood via the satellite link. He wanted them to know where he was and what he was doing. The SSN then went deep. The sonar operators found the enemy easy to track, and regular signals to Northwood kept the British naval HQ in the picture.

In the meantime intelligence suggested the *25 de Mayo* was at sea and heading south-east, though contact was never made by *Splendid*.

Fleet Headquarters at Northwood was by the early 1980s a hub for NATO submarine operations and co-ordinating centre for all British war vessels on missions around the world. Enclosed within a high-security fence patrolled by elite Royal Marine commandos and deep under the soil of a well-to-do north London suburb was a nuclear blast-proof bunker. Top security clearance was needed to gain entry, not least because indicated on a massive chart occupying a wall over banks of computers were the locations of globally deployed warships.

Above ground were some rather unattractive, typically utilitarian, 1950s-era buildings housing the staff of Commander-in-Chief Fleet and, since 1978, Flag Officer Submarines and his staff. They were analysing *Conqueror*'s signals, assessing her position and that of *Belgrano*.

Because she was loitering just outside the TEZ, it appeared *Belgrano* and her escorts believed they would not be attacked. The *Belgrano* was armed with fifteen 6-inch guns while her destroyers possessed Exocet Anti-Shipping Missiles (ASMs). The group trailed by *Splendid* (commanded by Cdr Roger Lane-Nott) also included the French-origin missile in its array of weapons. With a quick change of direction either force could swiftly put itself in a position to sink British ships. The *Belgrano* group stuck close to the Burdwood Bank, as the cruiser's command team thought its shallow waters might provide some measure of protection from big nuclear-powered submarines. Should the cruiser feel it necessary to seek extra security, she would dash over there and hope an SSN would not follow. It was also the main avenue of attack should *Belgrano* lunge for the British task force.

During the subsequent 30-hour trail, sometimes McClement took command, giving Wreford-Brown a rest. *Conqueror*'s captain retired to his bunk. He tried to get some sleep but found his mind was running at fever pitch. *The Belgrano group must not be allowed to endanger the task force – they had to be attacked to prevent that happening, but how would he conduct it?*

The cruiser had to be the primary target.

He would get close – inside 2,000 yards.

Just like Perisher, except with real torpedoes, against a real target.

On the beam – fire spread right at the middle.

Which weapon, though?

The wire-guided Tigerfish was a long-range anti-submarine weapon but also capable of sinking modern, thinly protected surface warships – but it had well known reliability problems.

Belgrano was a Second World War cruiser, very robustly built – she had armour and special compartments outside her hull to absorb the power of an explosion. To put her down needed a reliable, big punch, and that had to be the unguided Mk8.

But then *Belgrano* and her escorts turned around and headed west.

Away from the TEZ.

What now?

That control of *Conqueror* and the other two SSNs at the time operating in the South Atlantic resided with Northwood irritated Carrier Group Commander Sandy Woodward.

As a veteran Cold War submarine officer – who drove *Warspite* after her 'iceberg' collision – he knew all three SSN captains well. Wreford-Brown, for example, had also been a junior officer under his command in *Warspite*. Rear Admiral Woodward was champing at the bit to wield nuclear-powered attack boats to best effect in conjunction with his surface and air units. He could see the point of central control in the northern Atlantic, when co-ordinating efforts with the Americans.

Strictly regulating the boxes in which SSNs and SSBNs worked was absolutely essential – to deconflict NATO boats from the potential foe. The South Atlantic was a different matter – relatively naked of submarines, except for a few diesels. Any nation except Argentina would surely ensure its boats stayed in port while war raged in the south?

Woodward knew how responsive and powerful his SSNs could be in neutralising the enemy naval threat but Northwood had insisted on retaining control.

Wreford-Brown was even more determined to ensure the enemy cruiser force did not suddenly make an attack run across the TEZ. Of *Belgrano* and her group he reflected with grim determination: 'They won't make it.'

Behind the scenes Woodward had exerted pressure on Northwood by lodging his own orders for *Conqueror* on the satellite net, ending with the definitive instruction: 'Attack *Belgrano* group.'

This was a calculated piece of insubordination, as Woodward knew his old captain from his days in HMS *Valiant* – Flag Officer Submarines, Vice Admiral Sir Peter Herbert – would recognise urgent action was required. The order was removed from the satellite transmission system, to prevent *Conqueror* accessing it. Within hours the Prime Minister and War Cabinet had authorised the necessary modified Rules of Engagement (ROE).

Conqueror received them early in the afternoon of 2 May. They permitted Wreford-Brown to attack any enemy warship outside Argentinian territorial waters.

Utilising skills perfected against the Soviets, the British submarine's crew maintained their constant watch on *Belgrano* both visually, via periscope, and on sonar. *Conqueror* trailed her while between 200ft and periscope depth, often five miles behind. The Argentinians remained oblivious, carving out lazy zig-zags, still not using sonar to try and pick up any would-be stalkers.

Wreford-Brown later explained his tactics: 'In World War Two a submarine would have attacked from around 1,000 yards, but a nuclear-powered hunter-killer is a big beast and the closest we could get was 1,400 yards – any nearer and we would have been at risk ourselves.'

Conqueror was in the perfect kill position – at right angles to *Belgrano* on her port beam, the two destroyers positioned on her starboard side.

Wreford-Brown realised they feared a lethal threat from the north, but he was to the south. Using the attack scope, its narrow head cut through the surface as he conducted an attack of the kind he had mastered on Perisher.

The fire-control solution was good.

He would fire a spread of three Mk8s – which he had worked out with McClement – hoping to hit with at least one.

Eyes pressed to the cups of the scope, Wreford-Brown waited for his moment. He calmly ordered: 'Fire.'

There was a groan and thunk as the hydraulic water ram acted to eject the torpedoes, the submarine vibrating as they sped out of the tubes.

The underwater telephone had been switched to loudspeaker. Momentarily pulling down the scope, like everybody else in *Conqueror* Wreford-Brown listened intently as the fish ran towards the target at more than 40 knots. Counting down the anticipated time to impact – an estimated 47 seconds – he put the periscope back up just before they hit. The first made an orange fireball and some smoke, hitting just aft of the bows. *Conqueror's* crew both felt and heard the explosion. He watched the second hit – water leapt up, debris flew through the air. More smoke. It exploded inside an aft machinery compartment. The third torpedo ran on and hit the *Hipolito Bouchard* – another Second World War-era ex-US Navy vessel – but did not explode, still causing damage to her sonar and engines.

The sound of torpedoes detonating provoked cheers in *Conqueror's* Control Room. They were soon replaced by a sombre contemplative silence in which the submariners thought about the poor souls now struggling for their lives in the enemy warship.

Regardless of whether or not *Belgrano* was heading away or into the TEZ at the time of the attack, *Conqueror's* men were pleased they had removed a threat to the task force. McClement believed it 'saved a huge number of lives'. It occurred to Wreford-Brown that, had they been in an attack team trainer exercise everybody would now adjourn for a coffee, but they were at war, so he gave orders for *Conqueror* to go deep.

She headed east at high speed, leaving behind what sounded like explosions as *Belgrano's* frightened destroyers dropped depth charges in the wrong place.

As *Belgrano* was claimed by the sea, the sailors aboard *Conqueror* heard the old cruiser breaking up but, contrary to speculation at the time, they did not hear the screams of sailors drowning.

Frozen by shock as much as the cold, the surviving men of *Belgrano* watched as their proud old warship slid beneath the waves.

The survivors would drift on hostile Antarctic seas for 36 hours. Of her 1,093-strong crew, 201 went down with the ship. Many of them were killed in the initial explosion and fire storm due to hatches and doors being left upon and unclipped. A further 120 died of exposure in the rafts.

Conqueror now went in search of the Argentinian destroyer escort group. Northwood HQ had stressed in more than one signal vessels rescuing survivors were not to be attacked.

It was not something they needed to tell Wreford-Brown or his men to do. They felt offended that Northwood felt the urge to do so. Over the next few days signals and radio intercepts provided reports of the sinking, with a wide variety of casualty figures quoted.

The submarine's men realised with regret that more than 300 fellow mariners had been killed by their actions. 'None of us had a hatred of the Argentinian sailors,' Wreford-Brown would reflect.

The *Conqueror* stayed in the area for two days, her Sound Room listening to the Argentinian search and rescue ships plying back and forth.

In the aftermath of *Conqueror*'s attack on the Argentinian cruiser, Wreford-Brown found he had lost his aggressive edge and certainly didn't want to go looking for trouble.

He was not an abrasive captain, certainly not in man-management terms, but he did like to wield his boat aggressively. After turning it all over in his mind for a few days, he rationalised that this was war and there were bound to be losers and winners.

The Argentinians had committed an act of aggression against Britain that could not be allowed to stand.

The attacking edge cultivated by Perisher – the consummate skills on the periscope inculcated by the command course – had been applied to lethal effect in the South Atlantic.

Wreford-Brown did not relish the idea of attacking and sinking other Argentinian ships but if the opportunity came to do so, he would not hesitate. The power and utility of the SSN in a hot war had been proved.

A pincer attack on the British task force had been averted, with the lives of 2,000 or so men in the primary targets of *Hermes* and *Invincible* safeguarded. The Argentinian main fleet retreated to its home ports and did not venture out again. That removed a major threat to vulnerable troop ships packed with thousands more marines and soldiers. Those vessels would soon be required to move in close to the Falklands and conduct an amphibious landing. An air attack on the destroyer HMS *Sheffield* three days after *Belgrano*'s sinking, and the British ship's subsequent loss, provided a shock. This contest with the Argentinians was not Cold War shadow boxing. The attack on *Belgrano* had proved that, but somehow for many on the British side it took the loss of *Sheffield* – with 20 men killed and 26 injured – to truly ram home reality. Both parties were landing real blows; blood of brave men was staining the South Atlantic.

Conqueror's attack on *Belgrano* was the first time since the Second World War that a Royal Navy submarine had attacked and sunk an enemy warship. At the time of writing it also remains the only occasion that an SSN has done so in the history of naval warfare.

For the Russians – who had dogged UK naval operations with their spy trawlers and allegedly passed intelligence to Argentina via Cuba – it demonstrated the British would, when pushed, fight.

Margaret Thatcher thought that was one of the key aspects of the conflict, making it enormously significant. It halted a British foreign policy of retreat stretching all the way back to Suez in 1956. She believed: 'We had come to be seen by both friends and enemies as a nation which lacked the will and the capability to defend its interests in peace, let alone war. Victory in the Falklands changed that.'

Britain suddenly regained some standing in the world. A Russian general had even told Mrs Thatcher the Kremlin believed Britain would not fight for the Falklands and if it did, then it would be beaten.

'We proved them wrong on both counts,' she remarked with satisfaction, 'and they did not forget the fact.'

Sandy Woodward, who had undertaken his share of undersea jousts with the Soviets, believed the war 'demonstrated to the Eastern Bloc that the West, if seriously challenged, was not in any way as decadent as they thought. The South Atlantic showed that we would fight fiercely under bloody conditions, take losses of men and equipment, and come back fighting.'

The Soviets were certainly very keen to gain insights into the technology that helped the British win. Captain Anatoly Zotov, Naval Attaché at the Russian Embassy in London, decided on a brief holiday trip to Plymouth in company with the embassy's Air Attaché, Major Serge Smirnov.

Shadowed by police officers from Special Branch the pair enjoyed a pleasure cruise on waters off Devonport Naval Base and dockyard, taking photographs of nuclear submarines and warships.

Next they headed for the Naval Studies Section of the Plymouth City

Library, where they asked to see books about submarines and photo-copied an article from the *Naval Review*.

Zotov did not hide that he was a Soviet Naval Attaché and this natur-ally astonished the library staff, some of whom had served in the Royal Navy. The Russians approached drinkers in a local pub where Zotov introduced himself to patrons of the establishment and suggested they might like to spy for the Soviet Union.

This all proved too much for the British authorities who had become increasingly concerned about Zotov's attempts to set up a spy network. After interrogating various people in Plymouth that the Russians had encountered, the security services delivered a dossier of evidence to the government. Zotov was ordered out of the country.

On ITN News, David Owen, MP for Devonport and a former Navy minister, gave the interviewer, Trevor McDonald, insights into the mo-tives of the British security services.

'They must have thought Soviet spying activity was becoming too flagrant,' he said. 'They must have had some concrete evidence that this was going beyond the bounds of what is acceptable.'

Special Branch had monitored Zotov's terraced home in London for some months. On the day of his deportation Zotov left in civilian clothes, a rictus grin on his face as he walked to a light-coloured Ford Cortina. His wife Nina had already flown back to Moscow. A few days earlier Zotov had mixed with British royalty during a diplomatic recep-tion in Buckingham Palace, enjoying canapés and aperitifs at the UK taxpayer's expense.

At the airport Zotov changed into full naval uniform with rows of medals jingling on his chest and even displaying a submarine service badge. The 53-year-old Soviet Naval Attaché made a good show of main-taining his innocence amid the accusations.

He declared to a gaggle of newspaper and television reporters gath-ered around him: 'I have been a sailor all my life!'

Zotov thundered that the charges made against him were invented.

'I can only repeat what has been said against me is fiction,' he pro-tested, as he awaited his Aeroflot flight home.

He added that he had been 'proud and honoured, as a sailor of the Russian Navy' to represent his service in London.

UK government sources claimed such denials were nonsense, as Zotov had been trying to build a spy network since January 1981 on his arrival in Britain. Some intelligence insiders said a primary objective of Zotov's efforts was to determine how effective the British and Americans were at finding and trailing Russian submarines as they passed through the GIUK.

The British security services were adamant he had failed utterly.

They scoffed that Zotov was 'amateur and ham-fisted'. Some press reports claimed he had been more successful than was being admitted, piggy-backing his efforts on those of a Libyan espionage network.

The month after Zotov was chucked out, Vladimir Chernov, who had been employed by the International Wheat Council to translate English documents for transmission to Russia, was also expelled on suspicion of spying. He too denied the offence. It provoked a tit-for-tat expulsion of British Embassy staff from Moscow, including the Naval Attaché, Capt. Bruce Richardson. A former Commanding Officer of the Type 21 frigate HMS *Amazon*, Richardson returned home to be appointed boss of the 4th Frigate Squadron, and also captain of HMS *Avenger*. He would later command a NATO naval task group. The Moscow embassy's loss was the front-line fleet's gain.

The Falklands War was an accidental demonstration of latent British resolve to meet force with force. At the time of the Argentinian invasion Britain was singularly unprepared to properly defend the islands, with a handful of Royal Marines as their garrison, and only an elderly ice patrol ship deployed nearby. Crucially, there had been no SSN in the South Atlantic – operations against the Soviets were the main effort. Worse, the proposed Nott cuts gave a clear signal – at least in the mind of the Buenos Aires junta – that the Royal Navy was to be shorn of the very capabilities (carriers, amphibious ships, frigates and destroyers) that later proved crucial to retaking the Falklands.

Even after such a demonstration of essential naval power and reach, the Thatcher government carried on cutting, though not as savagely, while its commitment to nuclear-powered submarines remained.

Diesels still had their uses, too, which had also been proven during the war. Trespassing into rocky inshore waters off the Falklands was *Onyx* – Perisher platform for Forsyth when he put Littlejohns through the mill.

Conducting a marathon 116-day patrol, unsupported 8,000 miles from the UK, she sailed to the conflict zone under the command of Lt Cdr A. P. Johnson. Throughout the entire deployment he managed 'a proper wash' just three times, his ablutions mainly being of the 'dip in a bucket' variety. The voyage there and back was agonisingly slow. With

16 'additional personnel' (Special Forces) levered into the boat alongside the regular crew of 68, it was a tight squeeze.

Though Lt Cdr Johnson has never commented in detail on the nature of his submarine's mission, it is believed *Onyx* landed SBS troops on various raids.

Her captain would have used periscope and shallow-water navigation skills he had honed on Perisher. They did not fail him, or his crew. On her return to Gosport, every ship in Portsmouth Harbour sounded sirens and hundreds of sailors cheered the tired old *Onyx* home.

For submariners who did not go south, the confrontation with the Cold War foe had continued of course, and very much away from the glare of publicity. As dramatic events unfolded off the Falklands, many thousands of miles north Doug Littlejohns was taking *Sceptre* up against the Soviets.

Sceptre's men were kept updated on events in the South Atlantic, but for several weeks it was far from certain it would come to war, so they were glad not to be off on what could be a wild goose chase.

That didn't stop the news-hungry media from giving *Sceptre* some glory that she did not deserve. Littlejohns received a signal in early May from Northwood HQ telling him: 'You will be amused to know that they have reported in the *Daily Express* that *Sceptre* sank the *Belgrano*.'

After some amusement the mood aboard *Sceptre* changed. Wives and girlfriends back home might be less than amused. Thinking their husbands and boyfriends were off somewhere in the North Atlantic, suddenly they imagined they were in the middle of a hot war potentially under attack from vengeful Argentinians. Just as well they didn't know about what British submarines did in Soviet waters either, but that was a secret more easily kept as no ships were actually sunk.

The loss of life in the *Belgrano* was not something any sane sailor would celebrate, knowing that he could easily share the same fate. The men of *Sceptre* were no different. Having trained so hard for years, they would have appreciated the challenge of hunting the enemy with a view to a kill. But, as Littlejohns later reflected: 'We don't want to make war – submariners are among the people that least want to make war.'

When Doug Littlejohns was 12 years old, the world was electrified by a signal from the top of the world announcing 'Nautilus 90 North.' Hailed as one of man's greatest triumphs, it announced inner space had yielded one more marvel. The world's first-ever nuclear-powered submarine, USS *Nautilus*, slipped through the black ocean, her precisely calibrated instruments indicating she was on the brink of making history.

Containing just over 100 souls, *Nautilus* was hovering in freezing waters under pack ice.

The submarine's men listened to the captain, Cdr William R. Anderson, explain over the broadcast system: 'In a few moments *Nautilus* will realise a goal long a dream of mankind – the attainment by ship of the North Geographic Pole.'

He added for good measure, as if that wasn't epoch-making enough: 'With continued Godspeed, in less than two days we will record an even more significant historic first: the completion of a rapid transpolar voyage from the Pacific to the Atlantic Ocean.'

The onboard jukebox was switched off to ensure there was absolute silence as the sonar pings probed the ice and dark waters. Picking up his mike, Cdr Anderson told his men: 'Stand by.'

He then counted off the seconds to history being made: '10 ... 8 ... 6 ... 4 ... 3 ... 2 ... 1 ... Mark! August 3, 1958. Time 2315. For the United States and the United States Navy, the North Pole.'

Cheers erupted in the sailor's mess where those off duty had listened breathlessly. In the Control Room there was satisfied silence and smiles.

Anderson was awestruck. Finally the famed north-west passage had been achieved. It was a dream that had driven many mariners insane, claiming the lives of quite a few.

The destination of the American submarine at the end of her ground-breaking voyage was Portland on the south coast of England, where her men were given some well-earned shore leave. She then broke the record for the fastest submerged crossing between the UK and New York.

That *Nautilus* chose to head for a British naval base at the end of her trans-polar voyage was significant. The head of the RN's Submarine Service at the time, Rear Admiral G. B. H. Fawkes, observed not long after: 'There is a brotherhood between submariners of all nations, but none so firm as that between the American and British submariners.'

More than 20 years later, Doug Littlejohns nurtured another dream: to successfully complete the *Nautilus* voyage in reverse – from the Atlantic into the Pacific directly under the North Pole.

Anticipating he would be appointed captain of *Splendid* in early 1981, Littlejohns had worked hard on what he dubbed 'the reverse *Nautilus* plan', intending to take the submarine around the world after making a north-west passage. Ice did feature in his immediate future, but not quite the way he anticipated – *Sceptre* then hit the 'iceberg' and he ended up her captain at short notice. 'So, that's the end of Plan A,' he reflected ruefully.

Never one to give up a good idea easily, he then wondered if *Sceptre* might possibly be the vessel to fulfil his dream. He put Plan B to Admiral Fieldhouse, the Commander-in-Chief Fleet (CINC Fleet), who gave it a very sympathetic hearing. Littlejohns explained his idea during the official meeting each submarine and surface vessel CO has with CINC Fleet at the beginning of a new command.

'My plan, Sir, is that *Sceptre* does her autumn Northern trip as programmed, but rather than come back to the UK in September or October, we go under the Pole and finish in San Diego.'

A submariner himself, the admiral liked the idea, but the Falklands crisis exploded and Littlejohns's Plan B was among the casualties. All future plans were scrapped.

And so, in April 1982, *Sceptre* went North, and after returning entered a period of maintenance, leave and training for her submariners.

There was now a rolling programme of deployments to the South Atlantic to guard against any resurgence of the Argentinian threat.

The long reach of satellite communications had been proved during the recent war, with *Conqueror*'s hunting and killing of the *Belgrano*. Less than a year later, in January 1983, as *Sceptre* headed south, a tendency for back-seat driving presented itself. It was an unwelcome development for an experienced operator like Littlejohns.

'We had a "new" Satphone, which cost the earth, apparently. On my first trip to periscope depth en route south, there was this senior staff officer from Northwood suddenly on the line telling me what to do. This was entirely contrary to the traditions and habits of the Submarine Service, where the CO is given the broad parameters of a task and then left to deploy his own judgement.' For the rest of the patrol the Satphone was mysteriously out of order. Being given helm orders by some person ensconced in a bunker in north London was never going to be a good idea as far as *Sceptre*'s captain was concerned.

As *Sceptre* approached the Equator there came about one of those magic moments that very few people experience.

Littlejohns couldn't resist giving in to his unrealised ambition to become an aviator and so – also living up to his Evel Knievel nickname from *Osiris* – he decided his SSN should 'loop the loop' around the line of the Equator. It sounds impossible, but as Littlejohns explains, it was simply done.

'We passed underneath it, surfaced and transited back to the north.'

Seeking to make the most of it, Littlejohns got on the mike, announcing permission to get some fresh air and relax – plus enjoy a can of beer – on the casing. Leaving the duty watch in charge of the submarine, whoever felt inclined climbed out to enjoy a stunning sunset at Latitude Zero. Their boat was all alone and majestic in her solitude in the vast Atlantic.

Dispensing with the usual 'crossing the line' high jinks, Littlejohns and his sailors took a few snaps to record it for the album. Some of the submariners joked they could actually see the line of the Equator.

For Keith Sapsed and other ratings in the crew it was the perfect piece of light relief. 'We were apprehensive at first, about what might happen on a South Atlantic patrol, but then excited and ready to get down there. Then, because of the long transit, at times we were bored. The Equator crossing was an experience I enjoyed and I think it brought the whole crew together as a unit.' Drawing things to a close and getting back to business, Littlejohns dived *Sceptre*, took her deep and headed south.

He put the crew through training for torpedo-evasion manoeuvres, just in case the Argentinians had the nerve to send one of their German-built diesels out to try and gain revenge.

Evading torpedoes would involve throwing the submarine around like a fighter jet trying to shake a Sidewinder off its tail, deploying counter-measures to distract the weapon away. The angles and dangles executed by *Sceptre* were not likely to be within the normal operating envelope. *Sceptre*'s crew was fortunately by now accustomed to the kinds of manoeuvres beloved of Littlejohns. Even so, there was always an added edge to such rehearsals, for making a good job of them in practice could save their lives if things ever turned nasty.

Littlejohns also had a chat with his MEO. 'It is a big deal, and you don't want to do it for laughs, but I gave him carte blanche to "make the battle short switch" if we were under attack and evading.'

Losing the reactor in such circumstances would be a death sentence, so it was essential to keep on line. That was of course why nuclear submarines had the ability to over ride the usual peacetime precautions. It had saved Hale and everyone else in *Warspite* more than 14 years earlier.

Having arrived off the Falklands and been briefed by the Commander British Forces Falkland Islands, *Sceptre* was tasked with patrolling off the Argentinian coast. As it was so quiet Littlejohns left the SSN in the capable hands of his XO and went off on 'weekend leave'. Changing into civvies he went aft to a workshop in the machinery spaces, and used a lathe to begin making a pair of brass candlesticks for the dining room at home.

Littlejohns had other means to relax and keep himself sharp when not on duty, by every day using a rowing machine he brought aboard and put in the sonar cabinet space. 'I had imported it on our first patrol, up North. Many of the crew asked to use it as well and I was happy to let them. On the next patrol we had two rowing machines and a bike. There were competitions on miles rowed or cycled. That helped to keep my crew alert, as did the regular showering and shaving that were essential to maintaining standards – and morale.'

Mental and physical fitness was one thing, but you can't beat a genuine emergency in a dived submarine for a sudden rush of adrenaline to quicken the pulse. *Sceptre* suffered an extremely serious leak in the primary coolant circuit of the reactor after only a few days on station in waters off the Argentinian air base at Rio Gallegos.

The SSN was gathering intelligence on the air force activities of the recently vanquished foe. That duty had to be immediately suspended.

'We pulled back, further out to sea,' explained Littlejohns, 'where we had to Scram – shut down – the reactor several times to put the MEO and helpers in to ensure that no damage was done to the reactor instrumentation, due to steam jetting out all over them.'

This situation effectively ended *Sceptre*'s time on station and she set course for home, leaving HMS *Warspite*, the other British SSN on picket duty in the Falklands, to pick up the baton.

Warspite's captain was Cdr Jonathan Cooke, who had commanded *Rorqual* for the final phase of Littlejohns's Perisher. The *Warspite*'s 1983 Falklands patrol would be for a record-breaking 112 days, with 88 of them dived. Returning to Faslane in March 1983, *Warspite* had only three herrings left in her deep freeze and – on the fresh fruit side – a couple of lemons. The crew was living off tinned tomatoes and steak and kidney pudding.

Commander Cooke was late for his wedding day by four days.

After a period of leave for her sailors and repairs to the reactor leak – making sure she remained restored to operational status – Littlejohns took *Sceptre* to sea again. It included training in waters off the west coast of Scotland. She called in at Faslane to make herself available as an ambassador for the cutting edge of Britain's effort against the Soviets – a VIP Sea Day in the Clyde Inners, off the Isle of Arran.

It provided an opportunity for Littlejohns to dazzle some high-powered civilians. He was rather too effective in the case of one top business executive. 'On board was a rather large chairman of a FTSE company – he weighed around 18 to 19 stone. We got under a Royal Feet Auxiliary tanker, which was doing about six knots. We came up from astern and the top of the periscope would have been at 10 feet below the RFA's prop – the standard distance – but we couldn't see very much as the water was quite dirty. I took the boat up four feet and could see much better – just six feet off the RFA's spinning prop. I handed the search periscope over to the guests and while the FTSE chairman was looking through it he asked how far away he was from the prop. When I said six feet he fainted. I can tell you he made quite a crash and was really quite difficult to lift into the wardroom, where he recovered and ate a hearty lunch.'

Sceptre had come a long way, from the half-wrecked 'beached whale' with a rattled crew Littlejohns had found in dock at Devonport.

She could so easily have been a horror story, a career wrecker. After all, he had expected to be given command of the latest S-boat, bringing a brand spanking new HMS *Splendid* out of Barrow. Instead he had received a real hot potato. But rather than plunging Littlejohns into a chasm of despair and failure, commanding *Sceptre* was the pinnacle of his submarine career.

It was, Littlejohns enthused, 'what every baby submarine officer dreams about' and for that reason *Sceptre* holds a special place in his affections.

'I am immensely proud of a number of things. From that wardroom we produced two Vice Admirals, a Rear Admiral, three Commodores and a slew of Captains and Commanders. I worked very hard on one outstanding, but reluctant, Leading Seaman to become an officer – he subsequently passed his Perisher and is now a Commander and a good friend. We won the Submarine Service Periscope Photography competition more than once. We were the first S-boat to win the Sealion Trophy for torpedo-firing proficiency. My relief and good friend, Jonathan Lyall, collected the trophy after I had left but he ensured that I got my tie! That is a partial list of material successes. My overall abiding memory is of a crew that worked hard, played really hard – we won several sporting competitions including a six-a-side cricket cup – but always came up smiling and ready to go. The icing on the cake for them and for me was the award of an OBE for my time in command, which of course stands for Other Buggers' Efforts!'

It was a double-edged sword, for the more of a success Littlejohns made of it, the more likely he was to be selected for another job faster than might otherwise be the case. After the Falklands campaign Sandy Woodward became FOSM. Visiting *Sceptre* for a night at sea with Littlejohns, post-dinner the movie version of the German submarine epic *Das Boot* was shown on a screen in the wardroom. Following the conclusion of the U-boat drama, the admiral asked Littlejohns if he'd like to join him at the Northwood HQ as Operations Officer. This would entail running all non-SSBN operations in CTF 311 – the cell that oversaw Royal Navy attack and patrol submarine operations worldwide. Littlejohns would also perform the same role for Woodward in the admiral's capacity as NATO's Commander Submarines Eastern Atlantic. Littlejohns would soon move on to a job that would see him battling as a Whitehall Warrior to ensure Britain chose Trident for its new nuclear deterrent.

Prior to taking up his CTF 311 job, Littlejohns attended the Joint Services Defence College at Greenwich, for a course that broadened the horizons of naval officers outside their own service for jobs in the MoD. One day the Russian ambassador to the UK came to give a talk on East–West relations.

It was a time of recent high tensions over the Soviets shooting down a Korean airliner, and two years earlier a Russian diesel submarine had been caught in flagrante spying deep inside Swedish territorial waters. Littlejohns was keen to explore the ambassador's views on both incidents.

The airliner had accidentally strayed into Russian airspace but the Soviet boat's intrusion was deliberate.

On 1 September 1983 all 269 aircrew and passengers aboard KAL flight 007 were killed when a Sukhoi fighter of the Soviet air force shot it down over the Sea of Japan. On 27 October 1981 the 24-year-old Whiskey Class *S-363* accidentally ran aground just off Karlskrona Naval Base.

To penetrate deep into the Swedish territorial waters she had to skilfully navigate shallow, hazardous waters but became stuck on a rock.

The crew of a Swedish trawler spotted the skewered submarine as she strained diesel engines to dislodge herself. They could barely believe their eyes. On reporting the discovery to the Navy, they were dismissed as raving alcoholics. Sent to check their claim anyway, the sailors of Swedish naval vessels were similarly incredulous.

When asked what he was up to, the CO of *S-363* said he had experienced malfunctioning navigation and radar equipment. Captain Second Rank Pyotr Gushchin claimed to believe his boat was aground off Poland. After several days of high-level diplomacy the Soviets were allowed to retrieve their submarine – suspected of carrying nuclear-tipped torpedoes – and Capt. Gushchin was sent to Siberia.

At Greenwich after his talk the Russian ambassador took questions but batted away anything too challenging. Littlejohns stood up and asked, with deep irony: 'I fully understand your reasons for shooting down the Korean airliner. Applying the same principles, would you have been upset if the Swedes had blown up the Whiskey submarine that got stranded on the rocks in *their* territorial waters?'

There was a sharp intake of breath and the KGB man with the ambassador flicked through cards to see if there was a stock answer.

With none forthcoming, the ambassador told Littlejohns: 'While the Jumbo was spying, the submarine made a genuine navigational mistake.'

Later, at the ambassador's request Littlejohns sat next to him at lunch in the Painted Hall. They had a lively chat.

The Russian diplomat chided Littlejohns for asking the question. The British submarine captain responded by enquiring why, as someone in his seventies, the ambassador was still working.

The ambassador replied: 'If I retire, I go back to a one-bedroom flat in Moscow, whereas here I have a nice house in London.'

The Soviets did not change their surveillance habits in the Baltic. Safeguarding access to and from Leningrad, and its gateway naval base at Kronstadt, as well as the major facility at Baltiysk in the Kaliningrad enclave, was too important. They still needed to know what was going on, even in the bases and ports of neutral nations. The Russians referred to the Baltic as 'the Sea of Peace', an arrogant assertion of their supposed control of it in the face of militarily weaker and more passive Scandinavians and Germans.

In the summer of 1981 Brezhnev said he would guarantee Baltic nations they would not be attacked with atomic weapons if they declared a so-called 'Nordic Nuclear-Free Zone'. The idea had been under discussion for some years, finding great favour in non-aligned Finland and also support elsewhere. The Soviets were not, though, prepared to consider the Kola Peninsula, which bordered Nordic countries, nuclear-free. While some Scandinavians were enthusiastic about the idea, the Americans and their allies saw it merely as a ploy to destroy NATO. It would inhibit deployment of forces in countries bordering the Baltic (such as Germany, the key battleground). In late July 1981 the state-run Novosti press agency published a statement claiming: 'As far as Soviet territory is concerned, the military potential on the Kola Peninsula is part of the global strategic balance between the United States and the USSR, and is not aimed at the Nordic Countries.' Novosti proposed that if Kola was free then it was only fair that the North Atlantic – prime operating area for submarines of both sides – should be also. That was never going to happen and the Nordic Nuclear-Free Zone idea faded away.

To counter the Soviet naval presence in the Baltic – and find out what was going on in the foe's harbours and bases – the British had for some years deployed diesels. They were smaller and quieter than SSNs and therefore better suited to such shallow waters. Among the Oberon Class boats consequently specialising in Baltic missions was, for example, HMS *Ocelot*, which carried out a deployment there in 1965. Porpoise Class boats also took part. By the late 1970s, the British were sending at least two O-boats a year into the Baltic, a commitment that continued into the early 1990s.

On one deployment *Onslaught* poked around the Baltic for seven weeks, her cramped interior home to 17 intelligence specialists in addition to her 65-strong crew.

The intelligence-gathering O-boats – some of them even carrying Special Forces – dived before making submerged transits of the narrow Belt into the Baltic. NATO allies Germany and Denmark were advised, to avoid accidental attacks by friendly forces.

It was recently claimed that Sweden – despite its neutrality – allowed submerged NATO submarines to transit its territorial waters via cleared lanes. Swedish boats also allegedly carried out covert missions inside Soviet territorial waters. The British O-boats are said to have frequently prowled in the littoral waters of the Soviet Union, using all the old skills of snorting and judicious employment of the periscope. Swedish sources have suggested they even sent ashore SBS teams to conduct close-up surveillance of key installations. HMS *Orpheus* was among vessels fitted with lockout chambers so the commandos could exit while she was submerged.

Unlike Soviet boats based in the Baltic – half a dozen Golf Class diesels, each armed with three short-range ballistic missiles – the British submarines did not carry nuclear weapons.

Britain has always denied they were there.

However, when a sound recording of a suspected underwater intruder in Swedish waters was played back to UK sonar specialists, they agreed it sounded like an Oberon Class boat. In 1996 it was reported some alleged recordings were more likely to have been shoals of flatulent herring. It made a change from claiming Cold War submarines were icebergs.

It was unlikely Dan Conley or any of his crew would ever confuse fart-ing fish with Soviet submarines for, pursuing the cutting edge even further, he had become a fanatical practitioner of towed array sonar.

A sort of electronic sausage, it consisted of a rubberised, flexible sleeve stuffed with sonar sensors towed behind the submarine on a very long cable, hence the name. In the 1970s there had been a high casualty rate, with towed arrays frequently being cut off. It was, though, an idea clearly worth persisting with. The idea of towed array was to put passive sonar at a considerable distance from the self-generated noise of the submar-ine, so it could listen much more effectively than the array in the boat.

It also offered a broader range of additional listening devices.

Towed arrays were able to pick up Soviet submarine reactor machinery noises over vast distances, but there were problems in deploying them.

The towed array had to be attached to one of the after stabilisers of the host submarine, close to the propeller or propulsor. If the connection between the towed array cable and the spigot on the stabiliser was not watertight, data could not be transmitted into the boat's Sound Room.

Also the submarine had to manoeuvre very carefully, not turning too sharply at high speed and running over the towed array. The display screen might go blank for a while until the submarine settled on the new heading. Having it connected throughout a patrol meant the captain had to *always* bear it in mind when manoeuvring. He had to consider his submarine was the length of the boat *plus* the towed array, which itself would be about 3,000 yards long. This, Conley reflected, meant 'care had to be exercised, particularly when on the surface, as the array would only be a few feet under and could be damaged by other ships passing close astern'.

The accursed Soviet spy trawlers might also deliberately try to chop off the towed array if they happened across a British SSN on the surface. Practitioners like Conley had to be aware that, with the tow wire exhib-iting negative buoyancy, the towed array could also sink if the boat was at low speed. It might even hit the seabed.

Conley was well aware of additional challenges.

'A boat fitted with it had to keep moving at all times and was, therefore, not allowed to make port visits unless arrangements were made with a dedicated team aboard a special vessel to remove it prior to entry into harbour.'

Conley had honed his towed array skills on a two-year exchange posting to the US Navy's elite Submarine Development Squadron 12 (SUBDEVRON 12), based at New London, Connecticut. As the Squadron Officer between 1981 and 1983, he had developed tactics for both using towed arrays and close-range submarine versus submarine encounters. Conley went to sea in a number of Sturgeon Class and Los Angeles Class nuclear-powered attack submarines.

He was gifted an ideal opportunity to work in the most demanding hunter-killer environment.

Conley discovered the US Navy's Submarine Force placed 'a high priority on tactical development'. He received whatever resources his team needed to develop Towed Array Target Motion Analysis.

'My ultimate aim was to develop tactics to conduct a successful approach and attack exclusively using towed array data. I had some brilliant Ph.D. mathematicians working for me. We would develop tactics ashore using computer modelling or training simulators and then go to sea in order to try them out for real.'

The American SSNs were fitted with what were called 'noise augmenters', which enabled the boats to mimic the acoustic signatures of Soviet submarines. Going to sea in USN boats for up to three weeks at a time, Conley played a key role in both tactical development exercises and later analysis of results.

'To test new short-range tactics we used 3-D tracking at AUTEC and I embarked with a team in the attack submarine USS *Richard B. Russell*, with the USS *Archerfish* playing the part of a Victor Class SSN. Over 50 runs were carried out to evaluate the best manoeuvres in an underwater dogfight situation. From these were developed rapid-reaction procedures for crews when suddenly confronted with a short-range situation. Obviously when we talk about an underwater dogfight it is in a different order of magnitude to the fighter aircraft scenario. Even so, with two 5,000-ton submarines manoeuvring around each other – with less than 3,000 yards' separation, possibly at over 30 knots closing speed – it can be pretty nerve-racking.'

A fighter pilot fears being 'bounced' by an enemy – suddenly caught unawares by an opponent who comes from nowhere, delivers a killer blow and gets away. It is the same for submarines, and Conley with his COMSUBDEVRON 12 team spent quite some time looking at what he termed 'an unexpected short-range encounter with a Soviet submarine'.

Short range meant detection of the threat at less than 5,000 yards. The ultimate aim was to detect the enemy first, avoid a collision and evade detection while getting into a prime position to shoot and kill.

After careful analysis of exercise results Conley came to recognise that, while there was a good chance a tactical advantage could be achieved, if it appeared the enemy had detected you caution had to be discarded. He summed up the necessity for instant, ruthless aggression: 'If the other guy starts manoeuvring to kill you also, all bets are off. If the opposition gets aggressive, then really close-range passes may happen.'

Conley saw it as high priority to bring home the fruits of his labours to the UK. There was no way in the much smaller and less well-resourced Royal Navy that he would ever have a squadron of attack submarines to play with.

Working and living in American submarines was similar to the British experience, but there were also some notable differences. Conley discovered the 'emphasis upon nuclear reactor operating training for all the officers meant a lot more training and stress upon the junior officer. There tended to be a much more serious atmosphere in the wardroom.'

Even so, he grew accustomed to American ways and made some enduring friendships. 'My last sea-ride was in USS *Atlanta*, where, at a ceremony in the crew's mess, I was made an "honorary US submarine officer". I was presented with the standard set of dark blue coveralls, as worn by American submarine crews at sea, and a submarine brooch.'

On his return to Britain, Conley, who had by now acquired the nickname 'Towed Array Dan', became captain of *Courageous*. He took her down to the Falklands in March 1984, for the boat's fourth three-month deployment to keep an eye on the Argentinians since the Falklands War.

He made it clear to the ship control department that he did not want to lose the towed array under any circumstances. The boat had suffered ill luck with them on several previous occasions.

At least minding out for it would give his men something to keep the inevitable boredom of a South Atlantic patrol firmly at bay. Waters around the Falklands were a long way from premier league action against the Soviets. It was strictly the back end of nowhere in operational terms. To help fight the tedium, *Courageous* also sailed south with 100 movies aboard (Westerns were particularly popular). As an occasional treat, there was Austrian smoked cheese and digestive biscuits.

Conley took with him episodes of the rural radio soap *The Archers*, re-corded onto cassettes by his wife. He religiously listened to one each day as if he was tuning in back home. By late March 1984, *Courageous* was nosing around the Falkland Islands, having taken over patrol duties from *Warspite*. Spending much of her time at periscope depth, her ESM mast picked up whatever intelligence there was to be had. At one stage dolphins and pilot whales surrounded *Courageous*. Conley took the boat down to 8oft, leaving the periscope up, giving sailors a turn studying the creatures gathered around them in their natural environment.

It was an enthralling sight.

The seas were often very rough, with the SSN going deep to get some peace and stability. *Courageous* spent much of her time cruising just out-side the Argentinian 12-mile limit, her sensors monitoring air force and other military activity. The Argentinians only worked during the day, so *Courageous* was able to pull back at night and give her crew a rest. Embarked in the boat, in an echo of the Special Fit missions against the Russians, were two Spanish-speaking intelligence operatives.

They used specialist equipment to tune into Argentinian military frequencies. During her 1984 deployment to the South Atlantic, *Coura-geous* had all six tubes loaded, half with Tigerfish torpedoes and the rest with Sub Harpoon missiles.

Despite the end of hostilities, a 150-mile Tactical Exclusion Zone (TEZ) was still in force around the Falklands. The ROE issued to Conley ad-vised that he was to destroy any Argentinian submarine that transgressed it. Conley thought, with actual hostilities ending two years earlier, that it was unlikely such an action would be welcome either in Argentina or in the UK. Fortunately, the only submarine activity detected was a Type 209 diesel-electric boat alongside in the naval base at Mar del Plata, conducting radar trials. A coast guard vessel was the sole significant military surface contact. Still licking their wounds, the Argentinian forces were staying firmly at home. *Courageous* also staked out waters off the Argentinian air base at Rio Gallegos, and again there was very little, if anything, going on.

Thanks to a mirage effect prevalent off the coast of Argentina, some-times the periscope watch keepers were able to observe what looked like cars and trucks driving along coastal roads. One surface ship sailor embarked in *Courageous* for a short period took a periscope look and claimed to have spotted women in bikinis sunbathing on the beach.

As someone with an interest in maritime history, Conley decided he would take the submarine for a poke around some of the bays that had reputedly been explored by the Elizabethan seadog Sir Francis Drake back in the sixteenth century. One night while doing this he suddenly found *Courageous* surrounded by a fishing fleet heading out to sea. Eyes glued to the periscope, Conley very carefully threaded *Courageous* through the trawlers, taking extra care not to snag their nets.

Aside from movie shows, *Courageous* had quiz nights and reading was a popular off-duty distraction to make up for lacking a decent foe like the Soviets. Conley found he could easily manage around five hours a day reading should he want to, as not all the command decisions needed the captain. He took command of the boat turn about with his XO, as usual also Perisher-qualified, running a shift pattern. Bored with books, Conley tried – and often failed – to beat his Sinclair computer at chess.

Having a shave and keeping hair neat and tidy was neither compulsory nor discouraged. While there was no lack of water to take a shower, there was simply no need for it on a daily basis, except in the case of the back afties in the hot, sweaty machinery spaces. Most of the submarine's men wore whatever elements of uniform they felt comfortable in – for the engineers it was oil-stained overalls unbuttoned to the waist to help with the intolerable heat back aft. The lack of ironing did not help in the smartness stakes. Badges on shirts were frayed, buttons missing, while boots and shoes remained scuffed and dull.

No boot polish was allowed anyway, due to the risk of its carcinogenic fumes being spread throughout the boat by the air conditioning. There was rumoured to be a tin of it somewhere aboard, but it got lost.

The philosophy was that there was no need to look especially smart or adopt regulation dress. There was no likelihood of being needed on parade or inspected by senior officers.

The heavy frequency of deployments to the South Atlantic meant a number of the men aboard had been in the same waters several times since the war. It was all getting a bit too repetitive.

To help relieve the tedium, attempts were made to get some of them ashore on the Falklands, for a spot of sight-seeing and alcohol-infused relaxation. This involved surfacing and lifting people off by helicopter, then returning them via the same method. Stormy weather – including thunder and lightning – sometimes led to a return flight cancellation. This did not disappoint the submariners, as their run ashore was extended by another night consuming more local 'hooch'.

On the business end of life, Conley initiated a series of tactical evaluations, some of which utilised on-station warships that had little else to do. The aim was to see if radar intercept and sonar data could be successfully used to hit targets 60 miles away with Harpoon. Such a long reach brought a whole new dimension to the SSN's utility in war – the maximum range of a torpedo was 15 miles or less. Conley's team detected a software problem in the DCB Action Information and Fire Control System, which might have caused Harpoon to miss. After sending a signal back to the UK a solution was figured out and sent back as a patch for the computer software.

As the deployment came to a close *Courageous* called at San Carlos Water, which two years earlier had been the scene of ferocious combat as Argentinian strike jets bombed British task force ships.

The boat secured to a buoy, there were visits to an army camp ashore and a tanker ship, the MV *Scottish Eagle*, which was at anchor nearby, the latter hosting a hard-drinking party for the *Courageous* lads one evening.

The submarine had a pair of unusual visitors for her two days in San Carlos, with a pair of penguins taking up residence on the casing. They were fattened up by submariners feeding them jam and scones, not to mention quite a few chips.

After a last look at Mar del Plata, *Courageous* headed home in mid-May. The departure was slightly delayed by her replacement on station, *Valiant*, being temporarily sent off in pursuit of a Soviet submarine.

A treat for Conley when the boat came back alongside at Faslane was to see his 18-month-old daughter, Faith. He had to be careful to hold her extra tight when carrying her on board. Unable to get much exercise, his muscles had wasted away during three months on patrol.

In July *Courageous* sailed for Plymouth and a major refit at Devonport, taking a diversion on the way to visit the German port of Bremerhaven.

The submarine made her final approach on the surface in a thick fog, surrounded by a fleet of trawlers. At 4.00, Conley was alerted to a hitch when the speaker in his cabin blared: 'Captain to the bridge!'

Rolling out of his bunk, where he had been reading, he rapidly made his way through the Control Room and climbed up through the fin.

The Officer of the Watch drew his attention to a large merchant ship about 1,200 yards off the boat's starboard beam and bearing down fast.

Conley ordered *Courageous* to speed up, extracting herself from its path. A voice boomed over the VHF radio on the bridge, in English, but with a heavy German accent: 'You – fucking fishing vessel – get clear!'

They had mistaken the SSN's navigation lights for those of a trawler. Taking exception to this description of his SSN, Conley radioed back: 'We are Her Majesty's Nuclear Submarine *Courageous* and we are trying our best to get out of *your* way!' Didn't the cheeky blighter know who he was dealing with?

Dan Conley was eager to tackle the challenge of taking his new command, the veteran SSN *Valiant,* out to meet the Soviets. With both the quality and quantity of Russian Navy submarines improving dramatically, there was increased pressure on the small British nuclear submarine flotilla. Older SSNs, such as *Valiant*, were pushed as hard as ever, despite their advancing years.

Valiant was by now nearly 20 years old and had not received a major refit since 1977. This showed in her mechanical performance. While the Royal Navy would never send a boat to sea if unsafe to sail or fight, successive teams of engineers were challenged on a daily basis to keep her going.

Minor fires in the engineering spaces were not unknown but thankfully all were dealt with swiftly. In the period 1984–86 *Valiant* conducted two patrols in which her main focus was hunting down and closely trailing Soviet submarines.

She fully earned her nickname 'Black Pig', which was bestowed upon her with a mixture of love and loathing – Pig as in a bit of a pig to keep running. *Black Pig* was also the name of the rickety old sailing ship in a popular 1970s cartoon serial. Much beloved by both kids and adults (including real-life sailors), it featured the hapless Captain Pugwash, who led a motley crew of pirates on many ill-fated humourous adventures.

As Conley later reflected, his own 'Black Pig' was the creator of numerous blackly comic moments in which you didn't know whether to laugh or cry. 'There were too many long hours in harbour with the engineers labouring in exceedingly cramped, hot conditions to repair yet another broken bit of machinery; too often there were frustrations experienced from programme change caused by a major defect.'

In short, *Valiant* was a lovable bitch of a boat but Conley and his crew worked extremely hard to make the most of her. In the spring of 1985 she was needed badly for a mission being overseen by Doug Littlejohns.

Nowhere was the essentially close working relationship between the American and British navies more important during the Cold War than in managing the immensely complex business of ensuring friendly sub-marines did not collide with or even attack each other. Water space management was essential to the business of identifying the Soviet foe.

As Submarine Operations Officer (SOO) with CTF 311 co-ordinating missions both for the UK and NATO in the eastern Atlantic, Cdr Littlejohns was deeply involved.

In the 1980s there were lots of submarines in the North Atlantic, not just belonging to fully paid-up NATO nations and Russia but also the contrary French, who had partially withdrawn from the Western Alliance (and liked to do their own thing). French nuclear deterrent submarines, for example, were not committed to anything but control from Paris.

There were five layers to the water space management onion, but the most important one was always British and American SSBNs. Little-johns's first priority, working from the Northwood HQ, was making sure the areas various submarines wanted to enter were free of friendly boats.

Aside from checking with the UK's own SSBN managers Little-johns's team members also visited the senior US Navy officer assigned to NATO's Eastern Atlantic naval command. Based down in 'the hole' – Northwood's nuclear-proof bunker – he wouldn't identify the exact location, but would admit one of two things:

'Yes, you can go in there and beat up some Soviets.'

Or: 'No, you can't.'

The onion layer could run at levels of water, too, depending on what depth an SSBN, for example, might require. Friendly SSNs could in-trude into it but only at certain depths to ensure separation.

In most cases the idea would be to allocate boxes of water for friendly submarines to operate in. Should they trail a Russian, as it moved out of their respective area they would hand over duties to their neighbour.

Once a submarine was on the trail CTF-311 would try its hardest to keep her on it. It would endeavour to somehow predict where the Soviet boat would go next and arrange the cleared water.

Radio silence would only be broken if the Russians all came out on a surge deployment, a situation requiring rapid tasking of available units and swift allocation of water space – coordinating the response like fighter controllers in the Battle of Britain responding to waves of incom-ing Luftwaffe bombers crossing the Channel.

'USN and RN submarine forces worked hand in glove,' observed Littlejohns. There were some areas where attitudes to tactics and other matters diverged. 'American thinking was that if the cat-and-mouse game turned into a shooting war, on a given signal we would sink every Soviet SSBN. The First Sea Lord, Admiral Sir John Fieldhouse, said it was a flawed policy. The British suggested that sort of thing was not part of the West's doctrine of "second strike", but rather a "first strike" idea.'

Fieldhouse asked them: 'What happens if you miss one?'

The Americans saw the sense of this, and their policy was changed to one of *trailing* all SSBNs: trail them, work out their patrol patterns, and then the USN and RN submarines would be in position to pull the trigger if necessary. More importantly, they would *deter the foe*. It was all balanced on a knife-edge but, with careful management, it worked.

In the spring of 1985 Cdr Conley was ordered to take up a patrol position in the Shetland–Faeroes Gap, one of the gateways used by Soviet boats attempting to break out into the Atlantic undetected. *Valiant* was warned by intelligence sources to watch out for a southbound Victor I attack submarine. The target was soon located – using the much-vaunted towed array – and, thanks to close shadowing, good recordings were made of the Russian boat's distinctive signature.

At Northwood, as Staff Operations Officer (SOO) of CTF 311, Little-johns was carefully managing the position of Conley's SSN and others. He could see it was going to be a busy time. 'The Eastern Atlantic was filled with Victors. To begin with there were three other RN boats out there in addition to *Valiant* and one American SSN under our control. It was only the second time the Yanks had given us a boat to control. They sent me a top boat, the Los Angeles attack submarine USS *Minneapolis St Paul*. HMS *Valiant* was tasked against a Victor I and the rest against Victor IIIs. On the British side we ultimately had *Conqueror*, *Churchill*, *Sovereign*, *Valiant* and also finally *Trafalgar* out as well. We also tasked two towed array frigates.'

Throughout the events that unfolded, CTF 311 was sorely stretched to try and stay on top of a rapidly changing situation and the challenges of very complicated water space management. Littlejohns thought that deploying SSNs, surface warships and Maritime Patrol Aircraft against the Soviet surge was like playing three-dimensional chess in slow motion.

The Victor I, apparently heading for the Mediterranean, was said to be fitted with advanced detection capabilities. It was essential to know where she was in order to safeguard NATO's SSBNs against being detected and trailed. The first Soviet attack boat purpose-designed with a true sub-killer mission, the Victor was coated in either rubberised an-echoic tiles or sheets. This reduced the sonar reflection and made the boat harder for surface vessels on active pinging to find. Combined with high underwater speed and agility, the stealth coating also enabled the Victor to stand a better chance of evading a homing torpedo.

Revolutionary though the Victor I had been when the type first entered service in the late 1960s, by the spring of 1985 boats of the early batch were showing wear and tear, much like some British vessels, not least *Valiant*. Other shadowing tasks soon followed on that patrol for Conley's boat, including a more capable (newer) Victor II SSN. *Valiant* also trailed an elderly cruise missile-armed Echo II boat. The latter's deployment was reckoned to be a response to the arrival of American cruise missiles in Europe. *Valiant* also picked up a Victor III – one of the latest batch in that class of attack boat and a formidable vessel – headed back to the Kola.

During a subsequent patrol in the summer of 1985 the 'Black Pig' continued to battle engineering gremlins and keep track of the various Soviet boats. A steady and rising flow of Russian submarines in the north-east Atlantic had been detected. Responding to a CTF-311 tasking the *Valiant*, on sonar trials, was called back to the Clyde for a towed array to be attached.

It was essential the plentiful Russian forces did not find the deployed British SSBN doing her best to continue a deterrent patrol in complete stealth.

Available Fleet submarines were tasked with finding and trailing Russian submarines to keep a handle on them, riding shotgun to see off any Soviets that might stray close to the British SSBN (though nobody knew exactly where the boat they were protecting actually was).

HMS *Churchill* found and hung on to a Soviet SSN, to the west of the British Isles, but was withdrawn. Conley was worried the trail would be cold by the time his boat got there to take over. *Valiant* found a Victor in the area *Churchill* had been withdrawn from. It appeared from the sonar signature this was the specially fitted Victor I that *Valiant* had trailed in the spring, but this time returning home to Russia from the Mediterranean. The Soviet boat withdrew to the north-east, with *Valiant* sticking to her tail for four days. The British submarine's Sound Room picked up another (and even quieter) customer and began a second simultaneous trail.

Just as things were going so well, *Valiant*'s mechanical problems intervened, much to Conley's disgust. 'It was at this moment gremlins struck with a temperature gauge indicating a potentially serious defect in the reactor compartment. It was the sort of problem that on a previous occasion had forced *Valiant* to abandon an exercise and head for home.'

It was unprecedented to lose reactor power while actually trailing a Soviet submarine. There was no choice but to shut down the reactor so the potential problem could be investigated properly.

Conley ordered *Valiant* to switch over to battery drive. Still maintaining a shadowing position, her speed fell to 5 knots. The battery would have limited endurance to both propel the boat and maintain all the life support and weapons systems. An SSN could run for about 40 minutes on the battery before having to run the diesel – and without a fairly well-charged battery it would not be possible to restart the reactor.

This was going to be tricky. Were *Valiant* not trailing Soviet submarines, Conley might well have ordered his boat to surface and cruise on the diesel engines, rather than sap the battery which was meant to be a last resort. It was a risk worth taking for a short while, depending on how serious the reactor problem turned out to be.

Rivalry with other British submarines was always a good driver. *Valiant*'s men were very eager to ensure HMS *Trafalgar*, a comparatively new boat only completed in 1983 – but around 12 hours behind and therefore not in contact with the Soviet submarines – would not be ordered to replace their boat. Conley was confident that, with his towed array, and the excellence of his Sound Room team, he could still stay in the game. To make sure he could remain undetected he manoeuvred the submarine extremely carefully, avoiding a straight course and not keeping to a single heading for too long. Maintaining bearings on the Soviet submarines – using her bow-mounted broadband sonar – *Valiant* stayed just beyond the edge of the Soviet boats' sonar range.

As the captain, Conley was placed at the centre of the Control Room – looking at all the plots, both sonar and navigation, holding the tactical picture in his mind. Keeping a grip on it all the time, he calculated ranges to the target submarines, angles of approach, depth and horizontal separation. He was also trying to figure out what they might do next. 'If counter-detected maybe one of them will come straight towards us at high speed?'

Figures unspooled in his mind, calculations were crunched, as Conley continued to draw all the plots together, thinking in three dimensions and then issuing instructions.

He had to bear in mind the boat was running on battery power. If the reactor problem turned out to be really bad he would have to immediately turn for home. Fortunately only a few minutes passed before there was good news – it was a false alarm. Now came a tricky moment.

While battery drive was silent, the reactor plant would be noisy to re-start. Therefore, Conley let the Russians slip ahead temporarily until *Valiant* was safely back on nuclear power.

Closing down the distance again to maintain the shadowing position, the next day *Valiant* was led into the middle of a Soviet combat exercise. Conley sighted a Udaloy Class anti-submarine vessel on the horizon through his periscope. Shortly afterwards masts of other ships appeared. It looked like they were simulating a NATO convoy.

Conscious the Udaloy was making sonar sweeps and one of the more effective Russian surface combatants, Conley snapped down the periscope and took *Valiant* deep.

The 'Black Pig' continued to shadow the Russians, but in the approaches to the Shetlands–Faroes gap the surface vessels broke up and went their separate ways while the submarine contacts faded. During the same patrol *Valiant* also trailed a pair of Soviet SSBNs heading north as well as a Charlie II Class guided-missile boat. The elderly SSN's expertise with the towed array had been exemplary, again keeping several plates spinning in the air at once. Not bad for an old pig of a boat.

The Americans were very impressed with how the British handled the recent Soviet surge into the North Atlantic. Doug Littlejohns was invited to the USA as a guest of Commander Submarines Atlantic, Vice Admiral Bud Kauderer.

He travelled via Washington DC to the massive fleet base at Norfolk, Virginia. Littlejohns briefed key US Navy players on how Northwood had co-ordinated and controlled the various NATO elements – submarines, surface ships and aircraft – to counter a Russian multi-boat break-out.

While staying at the home of Cdr James Perowne – a former CO of HMS *Superb* and now the assigned submariner with the Commander British Naval Staff (CBNS), Washington – Littlejohns was given a copy of a novel called *The Hunt for Red October*.

Perowne thought it would make ideal bedtime reading for a fellow submariner. Littlejohns started it at 22.30 and finished by breakfast.

He couldn't put it down, realising its author – Tom Clancy – knew as much about submarine operations as he did. 'I have to meet this writer,' he decided, little suspecting it would be within a few days. By coincidence Clancy was in Norfolk for a book signing.

During a subsequent dinner at an American naval officer's home in Virginia, Littlejohns told Clancy he hadn't got everything right, but his book was a pretty good read. With a chuckle, Littlejohns suggested: 'You've put stuff in your book that if I talked about it would see me locked up in the Tower of London.'

It was late in the evening when Clancy decided to take advantage of the amazing array of experience around the dinner table – five British submarine officers and one American – by outlining his ideas for a new book. As Littlejohns relates, some aspects caused horror.

'According to Clancy, chapter one of the new book sees the Soviet cruiser *Kirov* sunk by a French SSN. Six brother submariners are aghast and speak as one against this preposterous idea. They even suggest that if the French boat gets the glory then no Brit will buy the book. In 1986, Clancy's next huge bestseller, *Red Storm Rising*, is published, in which a Norwegian diesel boat sinks the *Kirov*. Join the dots!'

The new novel featured a character named Captain Doug Perrin – captain of an Anti-Submarine Warfare frigate. There was another character named James Little, depicted as CO of the British SSN *Trafalgar*.

It seemed Clancy was having a joke and tipping his hat to two British submariners whom he deeply respected – Doug Littlejohns and James Perowne. 'James Little' was Littlejohns's head on Perowne's body and vice versa for 'Doug Perrin'.

The First Sea Lord, Admiral Sir William Staveley, certainly thought so. One day he appeared by Littlejohns's desk in the Ministry of Defence and thundered: 'I have just read a thinly disguised description of you in Clancy's latest book.' Littlejohns was not entirely sure if the First Sea Lord was impressed or annoyed.

Among those who would also read *Red Storm Rising* was Tim Hale. He was impressed by the realism of episodes in which Swiftsure Class SSNs and American boats ventured into dangerous Arctic waters. One thing that gratified the British SSN captains was to see their tight working relationship with the US Navy reflected. Clancy possessed a genuine and deeply felt respect for the Royal Navy's Silent Service, even placing it above his own nation's. He readily conceded: 'While everyone deeply respects the Americans with their technologically and numerically superior submarine force, they all quietly fear the British. Note that I use the word *fear*. Not just respect. Not just awe. But real fear at what a British submarine, with one of their superbly qualified captains at the helm, might be capable of doing.'

Marine One touched down on the grass at Camp David, its rotors slowly coming to a halt. The front door on the port side of the fuselage of the VH-3D Sea King helicopter was lowered. A young leatherneck in dress blues came down the steps to stand guard at the bottom. Inside the cabin preparing to disembark were the British Prime Minister, Margaret Thatcher, and her party.

A golf buggy came hurtling down the track. At its controls was a former Hollywood actor turned President of the United States, Ronald Reagan. Dressed in a bomber jacket, he was a knight errant coming to calm the Iron Lady's fears of British nuclear emasculation. As he turned in, the President over-steered, the buggy zig-zagging wildly. Reagan straightened it out and pulled in alongside the helicopter.

Mrs Thatcher had flown to the Presidential retreat in mid-November 1986 to ask why the USA felt it could unilaterally offer to disarm the West.

A month earlier, during a summit meeting with the Soviet leader, Mikhail Gorbachev, at Reykjavik in Iceland the President had – without any prior consultation with the British or French – put *everything* on the table.

Watching the evening news on television it dawned on Capt. Doug Littlejohns that something major, and unexpected, was in play. 'Bloody hell,' he thought, 'if that is right Reagan has given away our deterrent.'

Listening to further news broadcasts, Littlejohns became increasingly alarmed. The following morning, instead of arriving at the Ministry of Defence in central London at 08.00 as usual, he was at his desk by 06.30.

The two desk officers who reported to him also came in early, of their own volition. The trio absorbed every MoD signal on Reykjavik, consuming relevant Foreign Office telegrams and scanning newspaper reports.

Before Reykjavik expectations were modest, for it was the first time the two superpower leaders had properly discussed nuclear weapons limitation agreements. It came at a time when the Cold War was heating up again, in a new naval arms race. Reagan's promised '600-ship Navy' was taking shape while the Russians had managed to produce their first truly stealthy submarine, the Akula. They had been behind on the attack boat curve, but now they were on it, or even ahead of it. The advent of the Typhoon SSBN also meant they no longer had to try and even break out into the Atlantic. The Akula and the Bastion concept were not topics that people read about in morning newspapers dominated by other events.

The year 1986 had opened with the space shuttle *Challenger* disaster. In April US Navy strike jets and US Air Force F-111 bombers attacked targets in Libya. It was revenge for terrorist attacks sponsored by the Gaddafi regime against American military personnel. And then there was Chernobyl, a truly terrifying disaster at a Ukrainian nuclear power station not far from Kiev. The Russians meanwhile successfully launched their Mir space station into orbit. Down on planet Earth a grudge match at the World Cup between Argentina and England – the first sporting clash between the two nations since the Falklands War – saw the notorious 'hand of God' victory for the South American football team.

Reagan and Gorbachev had for some time prior to the Iceland meeting been exchanging ideas and views on many things, including getting rid of nuclear weapons.

Negotiations between the two leaders in the Hofdi House near the Icelandic capital entered day two at 10.00 a.m. on Sunday, 11 October. French and British nuclear deterrent forces – both based in submarines – were discussed. Reagan pointed out he considered them independent of any agreement that might be made between the USA and USSR. Gorbachev disagreed, as he suspected the UK integrated its targeting with the USA. Reagan suggested that if the USA and USSR led the way, the British and French would be forced to follow suit. They would also get rid of their strategic nuclear deterrent forces. Reagan envisioned the USA and Soviets 'standing shoulder to shoulder' to tell other nations they must eliminate their nukes. The President recommended practical steps and agreed with Gorbachev 'the heart of the matter was reducing ballistic missile warheads'. Furthermore, Reagan agreed with a suggestion for a 50 per cent reduction on both sides and specifically in sea-based missiles.

The left-leaning British press blamed President Reagan for causing the talks to collapse. They claimed a chance to rid the world of nuclear weapons had faltered because of Reagan's refusal to hobble his proposed 'Star Wars' system. The Strategic Defense Initiative (SDI), as it was more properly described, envisaged Anti-Ballistic Missile missiles working in conjunction with satellites armed with lasers. These would detect launches wherever they occurred and eliminate nuclear-tipped missiles in the early stages of flight. Not only would this nullify the Soviets' nuclear arsenal but also the UK's independent deterrent.

While SDI – if it could be made to work – would enable the USA to destroy most, if not all, incoming Soviet missiles, the President wanted to make its technology available globally. This would level the playing field.

Gorbachev wanted Reagan to keep SDI as a research project and promise not to deploy the system operationally, but the President refused.

In the aftermath of the Icelandic summit, a confidential telegram to Washington DC from the US Embassy said London-based news media were 'painting a far darker picture of gloom than even the Soviets'.

It observed rather despairingly that there was a lot of 'finger-pointing' in the direction of Washington DC – a chance to rid the world of nuclear weapons had been thrown away thanks to Reagan's SDI refusal. Officially the British government was praising Reagan for trying, but privately telling America it was alarmed by 'a lapse in Allied consultation during the summit'.

Just over a month later, Mrs Thatcher came to see Reagan, fully briefed by the MoD on the implications for her country.

As Assistant Director, Naval Warfare (Strategic Systems), Doug Littlejohns was concerned with the nuclear deterrent submarines and matters such as targeting of Polaris missiles. Newly promoted to Captain, he was also involved in getting the Navy and the nation ready for the introduction of Trident missile boats. In the wake of Reykjavik, he had been asked for his input to a briefing for the First Sea Lord about the impact on the UK's independent strategic deterrent.

From what they could glean, via sources in the Foreign Office and back channels to the US Navy, American and Russian leaders at one point did indeed discuss ridding the world of 'strategic offensive arms' by 1996, cutting at least half of them by 1991. Littlejohns took his team's analysis to the Director of Naval Warfare, Capt. Roy Newman, another submariner. It was amended and forwarded to the Assistant Chief of the Naval Staff (ACNS), Rear Admiral Jeremy Black, who with Newman went in to see the First Sea Lord (1SL). Shortly afterwards 1SL took the briefing paper to the Chief of the Defence Staff (CDS), Admiral Sir John Fieldhouse.

Building on this input the Secretary of State for Defence, George Younger, sent an MoD position paper across to 10 Downing Street for Mrs Thatcher to absorb.

She was pretty furious after reading the briefing and receiving analysis from other sources. The Prime Minister had visited Reagan in Washington DC less than a fortnight before he offered to give away the UK's nuclear forces. The President had given no sign of his intentions.

Gorbachev had actually proposed the 'entire triad' of nuclear weapons – sea, land and air – should on both sides be cut completely in half.

The Prime Minister was worried a wily Gorbachev had almost conned Reagan. Mrs Thatcher described her reaction on hearing how far the Americans had been prepared to go as 'an earthquake beneath my feet'. She approved of a 50 per cent cut, but the idea of entirely discarding nuclear weapons within ten years was 'a different matter'.

The British PM feared the system of nuclear deterrence that had kept the peace for four decades 'was close to being abandoned'. Thatcher believed it would be impossible to sell the idea of a cruise missile alternative to the British people. It was more vulnerable to destruction and also more expensive.

When Littlejohns later saw the final MoD briefing document presented to Mrs Thatcher, he was impressed with how she had used a pen to score through the non-essential material, leaving the key points. These included much of his team's analysis of the implications. If the Americans pressed ahead in this vein, it could mean the demise of British nuclear deterrent submarines, both present and future.

Realising that Reykjavik was only the beginning rather than the end of negotiations, the Prime Minister requested an urgent summit with Reagan. While Littlejohns recognises he was but a small cog in the machinery of the UK government's response, his team's analysis played a key part in preventing the Americans from getting carried away with themselves.

They had to pause and think of the impact on their allies. NATO had been set up to defend Europe, not to give the Americans carte blanche over its best defence against Soviet invasion.

Watching the television news and seeing Reagan picking up the Prime Minister in his golf buggy at Camp David, Littlejohns felt confident she would be very persuasive.

'Mrs Thatcher had been armed with expert analysis of the potential consequences, so that she could tell him: "You can't just give away our nuclear deterrent, Mr President." They had to take our deterrent off the table during any future talks.'

Thatcher chided the President that he was selling European security down the river. Mindful of the 'Special Relationship', the President reassured her that was not his intent.

It was a brain-bending Cold War conundrum that the only way to prevent a global war in which millions died ... was to possess the ability to destroy the planet. The idea that getting rid of some nuclear weapons – rather than all of them at once – could make the world a more dangerous one, in which major war and mass slaughter were more likely to happen, was equally difficult to comprehend.

The balance of terror that prevented a Third World War was all about calculation. Should one side think it could get away with a first strike then it might gamble and try. To the Russians SDI provided the Americans with first-strike capability (whereas the USA regarded it as merely defensive).

The Warsaw Pact nations possessed such a massive preponderance in conventional-force numbers that they might think they could overwhelm the West. NATO would be forced to use nuclear weapons to restore the balance in a hot war. By the late 1980s nobody on either side could think of a reason why, in reality, the East would launch a direct attack on the West, or vice versa. But after 40 years of face-off, with two nuclear gunslingers facing each other across the saloon, guns cocked, it wasn't easy to just lay down the weapons.

Margaret Thatcher and Ronald Reagan had built up a truly special rapport, but all that seemed to matter for little during discussions with Gorby at the Hofdi House. Thatcher was concerned the matter of intent – if a foe believes you possess intent to use nukes then he won't gamble on attacking you – was now at stake. A willingness to give up nuclear weapons so easily seemed to signal the USA lacked the intent to use them. The American gunslinger had a chocolate revolver. Still, even Mrs Thatcher thought that if the West could get the Soviets locked into a properly balanced programme of disarmament – with careful verification on both sides – it would be a fantastic achievement. Until that day the doctrine of MAD had to be retained, to safeguard Britain and the rest of Europe.

'It seemed to me that we were poised between a remarkable success and a possible catastrophe,' confessed Mrs Thatcher. She summed up her objective as getting the Americans 'back onto the firm ground of a credible policy of nuclear deterrence'. The result of the November 1986 Camp David meetings between the British and American leaders was a reaffirmation of faith in that policy. They agreed to continue pursuing a carefully calibrated reduction in 'battlefield nuclear weapons' and drawing down conventional forces. This meant keeping the Royal Navy's ballistic missile submarines at sea and proceeding with Trident. Doug Littlejohns would play an important role in steering the SSBN renewal process to success.

While he never commanded an SSBN Littlejohns gained deep insight into the tactical and strategic challenges of deploying such submarines at sea during various appointments in the Northwood HQ.

The dark arts of water space management – hiding a patrolling SSBN like the proverbial needle in the haystack in oceans increasingly crowded with friendly, and unfriendly, submarines – were a rare skill. The longer range of the new Trident missiles provided more hiding room but the challenge of ensuring invulnerability was still considerable.

As a former SSN captain, Littlejohns knew what it took to find, trail and, if necessary, sink an SSBN, so he could feed analysis into how well the new Trident submarines would need to defend themselves tactically.

Littlejohns – who had lived his career in the shadows – was volunteered by the First Sea Lord to be the Navy's official face of Trident. He explained on-camera to an interviewer from *Panorama* (BBC Television's flagship current affairs programme) why it was a good idea. To Littlejohns the fundamental mistake the media always made when looking at Polaris or Trident was to regard them as weapons of war.

In fact, they were weapons for peace.

The whole point of creating a deterrent was 'to make sure you never had a nuclear war by making it unthinkable to ever use them'.

A deterrent, though, had to be real and credible.

Littlejohns at one time supervised the transmitting of test alerts from the Cabinet Office. They were carefully coded to make it clear they were not the real thing. These bolts from the blue prodded the SSBNs to ensure they were ready to respond if and when required.

Even prior to Reykjavik, when it came to the future deterrent, there were all sorts of undercurrents within the Ministry of Defence.

Should a new SSBN not go ahead then the air-launched nuclear-tipped cruise missile option might seem an attractive option.

The RAF wouldn't mind some extra squadrons of strike jets and regaining the deterrent role – great for its prestige and a boost to funding.

The Army could also see something for itself in land-based cruise missile launchers and nuclear artillery.

There were even naval officers who bought into the idea of the entire British attack submarine force being armed with (allegedly cheaper) cruise missiles. They also hoped a good proportion of the billions otherwise spent on Trident could instead be used to build more destroyers and frigates.

Just a few months before the Reykjavik summit Littlejohns and his team had produced a briefing document, which was combined with input from other places, on whether or not the cruise missile option was credible. The Naval Staff concluded that – given the political requirement, reliability and credibility – a ballistic missile submarine was the most suitable platform.

It also offered invulnerability and a guarantee of hitting the right target at the right time.

Littlejohns's assignments on behalf of Trident were sometimes rather convivial. Tasked at one point with meeting a reporter from the Liberal-minded *Guardian* newspaper to discuss various issues, the venue was an expensive Italian restaurant off Leicester Square. Over lunch Littlejohns was able to weigh up the calibre of the journalist. The latter confessed, obviously hoping to establish an air of bonhomie: 'Trust me, I will only let you down occasionally.'

In Littlejohns's world the first time you dropped him in it was the last. When the man joked that he would be able to loosen Littlejohns's tongue on all sorts of things with liberal amounts of alcohol, his fate was sealed.

The *Guardian* reporter failed utterly, finding himself – rather than his naval officer guest – the worse for wear. Somehow, the former submarine captain managed to embed some pro-Trident points in the man's brain, or at least take the edge off the story's likely negative slant.

'Until the submarines were built and in the water, the Trident issue was an open, running sore,' thought Littlejohns, 'so to get the *Guardian* to treat the story even objectively was a result.'

And for former submarine captain Doug Littlejohns the introduction of the new deterrent boats couldn't come soon enough.

'After I had read all the classified reports of the Polaris patrols, I came to the conclusion that we had enjoyed almost 20 years of undetected deterrent missions, but now with new Akula SSNs being fielded by the Soviets, we should think the unthinkable.'

In 18 years of patrolling, British SSBNs had never been detected by the Soviets. Moscow feared retention of the West's SSBNs because they couldn't find them, whereas the British and American hunter-killers regularly found Soviet ballistic missile boats.

Littlejohns asked of his team in the MoD: 'What will happen if Gorby announces: "One of our submarines has counter-detected a Polaris submarine"?'

The Soviets would be unlikely to trail for very long but with their very new and capable Akulas there was a chance they might find one of the Resolution Class SSBNs, which were getting near the end of their careers.

The most likely location for such an interception would be as the Polaris boat either exited on a patrol or returned from one.

Littlejohns believed the Navy should have a PR plan, because the battle for perception was as important in the Cold War as operational reality. Loss of confidence in the so-called invulnerable Continuous At-Sea Deterrent could prove politically disastrous. He broached the topic with ACNS first, during one of their weekly meetings.

'If a Polaris boat is detected it will completely compromise the UK's independent deterrent,' Littlejohns ventured. 'The Yanks will think we are not up to it. It will weaken the Special Relationship.'

The Trident programme might be axed as not worth the time, effort and money. With a gigantic loss of national faith (and nerve) the next time there was a Reykjavik moment Britain might not bother to pull the Americans up on giving away Europe's nuclear protection.

It was a very sensitive issue, so only Littlejohns and his two wingers discussed the contingency plan; the team carefully composed the line that should be taken if a Polaris boat was ever caught.

He took it to ACNS and they presented it to the First Sea Lord. The two of them watched as Admiral Staveley read it, frowning hard and smoking furiously. Not the most relaxed of bosses, but frighteningly efficient and politically savvy, 1SL nodded his agreement. The single page of script was put in the First Sea Lord's personal safe by the man himself.

It was a smart move at a time when submarine operations were a hot topic of debate among the British political classes. There was grave concern about the potential for an incident at sea provoking war. To this day Littlejohns declines to reveal what exactly 'the line' was. It is always wise to have a Plan B. You never know when a totally unforeseen twist will blindside you, as the Royal Navy discovered when a family of American spies gave away secrets that eroded the West's edge in undersea warfare. Littlejohns would play a pivotal role in damage control on a special mission to the Pentagon.

Doug Littlejohns leafed through the latest intelligence report from the Americans about the revolutionary new Soviet submarine and whistled in wonder.

The Victor III is quiet, he thought, *but this Akula is even better.* Studying a grainy photograph apparently taken through a periscope, he mused: *The Russian tractor works is suddenly producing a Maserati.* There had been whispers for years about a radically new kind of boat being laid down at the Leninskiy Komsomol Zavod, a yard on the Amur river in the Soviet Far East.

After launch in the summer of 1984 the beast was moved in a floating transport dock to a yard near Vladivostok and completed.

This first in a class named Akula, or shark, by NATO was commissioned in late December that year. By 1987 she was on sea trials and a prime intelligence objective for American spy submarines. It was said another Akula was now close to completion and construction of a third well under way. The Akula appeared to be very stealthy and fast, approaching Western levels in fact. How had the Russians caught up so quickly?

Admiral Gorshkov's motto – 'Better is the enemy of good enough' – appeared to have been cast aside. After decades of incremental improvements that allowed them to churn out vast numbers of boats, but not of the same quality as the West's, here was this new SSN.

They had to come up with something radical (and reliable) to gain some kind of parity with NATO, for their Golden Fish – the Alfa – had proved a bit of a waste of space. In the end, concluded Littlejohns, what was the *tactical point* of the Alfa?

As he also read reports on its much-vaunted qualities, Littlejohns reflected: 'Nobody can deny that the Alfa was a huge step forward in submarine design – it can go a lot deeper and a lot faster, but it is noisy. But then you have to ask: "What is the point of going down there when there is no one down there? Why spend all that money?" There is concern across NATO that if you fire a torpedo, it won't be able to follow an Alfa down there, due to pressure crushing it. That is a tactical advantage for the Alfa – it can outrun and out-dive a torpedo, but that is about it.'

Littlejohns wondered if the Alfa would be able to hit back from down there. The pressure might be so severe there was a danger that when the bow cap was opened it would blow the rear door off the torpedo tube. 'So, he can go down there,' Littlejohns decided, 'but if the Alfa comes back up then the NATO boat has him cold.'

And the Soviets concluded the same, for after constructing seven of those SSN prima donnas – including the non-operational prototype – the Kremlin ceased production in 1983.

They moved on to a more practical boat, and it seemed something approaching Western standards: the Akula.

In September 1984 the Russians commissioned another new type of titanium SSN, the Sierra, at Severodvinsk. This was also quieter than many previous types of Soviet attack submarine and a second Sierra looked close to completion in 1987. With a similar hull form to the Akula – both were a development of the Victor – the Sierra had a more angular fin, which, so it was speculated, assisted with breaking up through ice.

After the blind alley of the Alfa, this too wasn't just an incremental advance in Soviet submarine technology but an enormous leap. It would turn out the Russians had major assistance from a traitor in American naval ranks.

During his long career Chief Warrant Officer John 'Smilin' Jack' Walker had at one point served in the ballistic missile boats USS *Andrew Jackson* and USS *Simon Bolivar*. In October 1967, while he was serving in the Atlantic Fleet Submarine Force headquarters, Walker climbed in his open-top MG sports car and drove from Norfolk, Virginia, to Washington DC.

Walking into the Russian Embassy he offered photocopied documents as evidence of his willingness to spy for the Soviet Union.

Like Bingham in the UK a few years later, Walker soon settled into a pattern of visiting dead-letter drops to deposit packages of secrets while picking up small parcels containing instructions and cash from KGB handlers. Unlike Bingham, Walker did not suffer any fit of conscience and ultimately hand himself over to a senior officer with a confession of misdeeds.

By 1975, Walker had retired from the Navy but suborned a friend and members of his own family into feeding him secrets for his KGB handlers. Principal among them was Senior Chief Petty Officer Jerry Whitworth, who at one stage was smuggling documents out of an American naval headquarters. Walker – by then a private detective

– photographed them in the back of a van (bought with money from the Soviets).

In 1983 Walker recruited his son Michael, a young seaman serving in the US Navy's nuclear-powered aircraft carriers, and also his older brother Arthur, a retired Lieutenant Commander. An attempt to draw his daughter Laura, serving in the Army, into his espionage ring failed.

Like Bingham it was a woman who figured large in Walker's downfall, in the latter's case his ex-wife, Barbara. Like Maureen Bingham she had accompanied him on a few drop-offs but did not actively participate in the acts of spying. As was the case with Harry Houghton's ex-wife in the Portland Spy Ring case, Barbara did convey her fears about her former husband's pursuits. Visited by an FBI agent in late 1984, Barbara Walker found her claims were treated with suspicion because it was suspected she was acting out of pure animosity towards her former husband.

The FBI agent's file did not lie ignored in a filing cabinet for long, as a supervisor decided it warranted further examination.

Both Barbara and Laura Walker were interviewed again, but it appeared more was needed to build the case. A surveillance operation, including telephone taps, was ordered. Interrogated aboard the USS *Nimitz*, Michael confessed to his crimes and soon not only was John Walker under arrest – with plenty of incriminating documents found at a dead-letter drop and in his home – but so were his brother and also Whitworth.

The arrest of the retired US Navy sailor John A. Walker on 20 May 1985 would ultimately reveal how the Soviet Navy had achieved its sudden leap forward. Walker received two life sentences (running concurrently) in the spring of 1986. Whitworth was sentenced to 365 years in prison and fined US$410,000, while Arthur was fined $250,000 and given a life sentence, eligible for parole the same year as his brother. Michael Walker was sentenced to 25 years in prison. In the aftermath of the sentencing polite enquiries from London asking for a briefing on the implications hit a wall of silence, which ruffled a few feathers in the Royal Navy.

What value the Special Relationship now?

John Fieldhouse had at the time just become CDS and William Staveley, even before he arrived in the MoD to be First Sea Lord (in his previous job as Commander-in-Chief Fleet), had been briefed. Staveley was worried about the impact of the Soviet Union's new SSNs on Polaris operations – more particularly how *exactly* had the West's sea-based nuclear deterrent forces been made vulnerable?

The Americans – still reeling from the shock and shame of the Walker–Whitworth exposure – were not forthcoming. There had to be a way of opening them up, and Littlejohns ended up being the means to that end. 'Within the MoD was a very specialist Int Cell that was cleared to the very highest levels within the Pentagon, but this team was not reviewing the information against the backdrop of deterrent operations. Staveley had been unhappy with this situation as CINC Fleet and now he was unhappy as First Sea Lord – hearing about things via other sources but nothing formal and nothing too detailed.'

As Assistant Director, Naval Warfare (Strategic Systems), Littlejohns was ideally placed to quiz the Americans via joint SSBN talks that happened twice a year. In 1987 he would use them as cover for asking some pertinent questions about the consequences of the Walker–Whitworth case.

'In that job I was in a privileged position because we shared an awful lot of intelligence between the SSBN communities. And, as such, I was the ACNS representative in joint transatlantic SSBN deterrent force talks – held twice a year.'

Captain Littlejohns received a telephone call from the First Sea Lord's office requesting his presence. As he walked up two floors and made his way through the Ministry of Defence rabbit warren, Littlejohns did not immediately connect what he had been reading in the newspapers with the call from on high. Admiral Staveley told him: 'The Yanks have clammed up.'

Staveley had spoken to the US Navy's Chief of Naval Operations – Admiral Carlisle Trost, a submariner. Staveley told him that there had to be a better flow of information, as SSBN targeting was a US–UK endeavour and the Royal Navy needed to know what the state of play was.

In April 1987 Littlejohns flew to the USA at the head of the UK group for the latest joint SSBN force talks, which lasted three days. The team thinned out and he headed for the Pentagon. After he had navigated the security gates, an aide escorted the British submarine captain along some very long corridors to the office of a friendly US Navy officer, Rear Admiral Hank Chiles. The latter had been primed by Trost. Over coffee it was explained the USN had wanted to send Doug's opposite number to the UK to give a briefing but the higher-ups had forbidden the Rear Admiral from doing so. Littlejohns told the Americans that it was all very well reading the Walker–Whitworth trial reports in the press, 'but come on, what about the specifics? What are your SSBNs now doing they didn't do before and how does that translate across the whole trans-atlantic US–UK deterrent partnership?'

Littlejohns discovered the Americans were 'embarrassed, very hesitant to tell me anything. They couldn't believe that one of their own would be a traitor, would betray their country on such a scale. They didn't want to talk about it.' There was still an air of shame in the Pentagon but because Littlejohns had good links with the USN admiral – and the Americans *had* to be part of the nuclear missile targeting arrangement with the UK – they started talking. Nothing was written down during the briefings but, finally, they coughed up the details – 'but don't quote us, buddy'.

On hearing about all this – and more – from his US Navy contacts in Washington DC, Capt. Littlejohns was stunned by the scope of be-trayal that had taken place over the course of 18 years and the impact on deterrent operations.

What the Walker–Whitworth ring had given away enabled the Rus-sians to catch up, making their astonishing technology leap, not only for the Akula and Sierra, but also the earlier Victor III (dubbed unofficially by the US Navy as 'the Walker Class').

From the late 1960s, the former American submariner passed to the Soviets information that also gave them insights into NATO submarine operations, signals codes, SOSUS and US plans in the event of war. When it came to SOSUS, radio reports containing key information on the movements of friendly submarines were thought to have been inter-cepted by the Russians and decoded thanks to Walker.

It has been claimed this enabled the Soviets to send Victor Class SSNs to certain chokepoints, such as the Strait of Gibraltar, in an attempt to detect American SSBNs. Walker's spying let the Russians know how noisy their own submarines were and therefore easy to detect. A Russian admiral would later claim some Victor Class SSNs were able to deploy undetected by SOSUS or NATO submarines and this was also par-tially made possible by the Walker espionage product. Littlejohns flew back to London fully briefed. The message he gave to the First Sea Lord was pretty disconcerting. It was likely the British were exposed to some degree.

'It has given them a leg up onto the leading edge,' was Littlejohns's concise verdict during discussions with Staveley and ACNS.

The information Walker provided enabled the Russians to finally appreciate the worth of quieting measures – and that civilian technol-ogies could be adapted to serve the purpose of submarine stealth. They obtained machinery and computers from Japanese and Norwegian firms to better mill submarine screw edges, so ensuring there was less cavitation (any imperfection would increase it). The KGB worked hard to secure the equipment despite Western export embargos (by pretending it was for civilian use). The Soviets also introduced better shock mountings for submarine machinery rafts to absorb the noise and, again, increase stealth.

In what was dubbed 'The Year of the Spy' the arrest of a National Security Agency communications specialist, Ronald Pelton, on 25 November 1985 had also delivered another body blow on both sides of the Atlantic. It was reckoned he gave away lots of details on what American and British submarines were up to in the Barents, though Operation Ivy Bells – a long-standing US Navy mission to put wiretaps on Soviet communications cables in the Sea of Okhotsk – was the worst exposure. This really knocked the stuffing out of the Americans, who had always regarded treachery as a British disease – and they could point to plenty of examples with a naval connection, from Blake, through Vassall to Bingham.

The array of American traitors uncovered in 'The Year of the Spy' was spectacular and, from a naval point of view, the information given away was far more damaging. Later analysis by some specialists suggested it handed the Russians their best chance of getting on an equal footing with British and American submarines at sea.

The FBI's own verdict was: 'The information passed by Walker and his confederates would have been devastating to the U.S. had the nation gone to war with the Soviets.' The British traitors provided chicken feed in comparison. In his dealings with American colleagues Littlejohns was amazed at the change in their attitude.

'They went from "We're Americans, we love our country" to "Holy shit, we have *our* traitors, too." The entire American people were in disbelief. It was incredible ... suddenly they were finding all these spies in their own ranks.' Littlejohns thought it explained quite a bit: 'In the late 1970s and early 1980s it was a lot easier to gain the advantage over Soviet submarines than it was in the late 1980s, by which time they were harvesting the benefit of the spying. They always had good weapons but their platforms had been basic, agricultural. They were progressing but were battling up a steep curve. Suddenly they made a giant leap forward, gaining about 10 to 15 years.'

The Akula was a stealth submarine on a par with the early Los Angeles Class boats, though not the later ones. It equalled the new Trafalgar

Class SSN the UK was introducing into service in the early 1980s.

It could not rival the stealth of the Ohio Class SSBNs, nor the UK's forthcoming Vanguard Class ballistic missile boats.

There was one area where the British and Americans would retain their edge, of that Littlejohns was sure.

'Our submarine commanders were, on the whole, good. The US Navy guys didn't start thinking about tactics until they were into their 30s, but British submarine officers thought about tactics from day one of their careers. The Americans qualify as nuclear engineers first, but ours are streamed to command straight away. They might have possessed some people who were not top-notch, but they also had people who were absolutely brilliant.'

The Russians must have had some good ones in there, too, among the average and the bad.

'We knew their idiosyncrasies, the reality behind the Soviet façade, but there again we were close to the action. I don't think the surface navy realised entirely, but that is because they didn't get up close like we did. Anyway, part of the game was to play up the power of the opposition – an old gambit to get the Treasury to pay for new kit. British submarine captains were certainly on an individual basis more experienced at operations in the Barents.'

The Americans had many more boats, so their captains would probably only do one patrol round the corner – and this was often the basis on which they were judged for promotion. The Royal Navy, with far fewer submarines, had to send its SSN captains back multiple times. Several British COs did as many as six in some form of command capacity. It gave the Royal Navy a formidable edge in terms of operational experience. In the late 1980s, however, some British politicians were increasingly concerned the cat-and-mouse games at sea could easily lead to a terrible war.

S oviet submarine activity spiked. One Russian officer later explained that while President Reagan might have described the USSR as an 'evil empire', in Soviet eyes it was the USA that menaced the world. The Soviet Navy ran extra indoctrination classes for its submarine crews and doubled deployment of boats to sea. 'We kept a huge number of submarines in the sea all the time as close as possible to the US and British coasts,' confessed Capt. Igor Kurdin. 'And the more submarines we sent out to sea, the more you [the West] sent out. This dangerous concentration and proximity of nuclear submarines could lead to unpredictable consequences.'

Littlejohns had dinner with Kurdin, Capt. Peter Huchthausen USN and Tom Clancy in Baltimore during one post-Cold War visit to the USA. 'Igor could hold his drink and the three of us were reasonably wiped out. Igor is a very nice chap and it would have been sad to have to sink him in war.'

The tipping point nearly came five days before the American and Russian leaders met in Iceland. The elderly Yankee Class nuclear missile submarine K-229 sank off Bermuda while being shadowed by an American attack boat, but the cause of the catastrophe was not a collision.

Structural failure and fire in one of the Soviet SSBN's missile compartments were responsible. Had the Russian submarine not gone down in very deep water then she and her missiles might have exploded. Creating fallout far in excess of the Chernobyl incident, it could have wafted across cities on the eastern seaboard of the USA.

It didn't make any appreciable impact in the Reykjavik summit discussions. A later incident involving the British submarine HMS *Splendid* made a big splash in UK newspapers, provoking heated discussion in Parliament.

On Christmas Eve 1986, the Swiftsure Class boat encountered a Typhoon in the Barents Sea, momentarily making physical contact. *Splendid*'s towed array sonar was ripped away, ending up wrapped around the Russian submarine. A neat little intelligence gift to the Kremlin; the Soviets could now study its secrets to improve their own, less sophisticated, version.

The incident was by no means the most serious but it came at a time of renewed hope and tension in world affairs. There were those who felt nuclear weapons could even now be abolished if only Reagan would give up 'Star Wars' and Thatcher would stop sending submarines into the Barents.

That the British PM was, like her predecessors, authorising such missions was still something nobody in the government or the Navy was prepared to admit.

Some MPs sought to put the issue into the public domain, implying the strain on submariners was increasing and the boats themselves were suffering. Sooner or later, feared the Parliamentarians, there could be an error that led to war. A number of MPs tabled written questions in Parliament and demanded answers in debates about what British submarines had been up to in Arctic seas off Russia.

They wanted a proper inquiry.

In February 1987, during the annual Royal Navy debate, Labour firebrand Tam Dalyell forcefully interrupted a long and detailed boast by the Minister of State for the Armed Forces, John Stanley, about investment in the Navy (including Trident).

'May I suggest that it would be helpful to the House if the Hon. Gentleman's speech could include some reference to what allegedly happened in the Barents Sea with the towed array sonar,' suggested Dalyell, 'so that we can discuss the matter on the basis of information rather than newspaper reports?' Stanley deftly stonewalled Dalyell: 'We follow the practice of all previous Governments and there is no way that we could be drawn into commenting on submarine operations.'

Martin O'Neill, another Scot, and also Opposition spokesman for Defence and Disarmament and Arms Control, disagreed.

'Recent events have highlighted certain questions that require clear answers from the Government,' he said. 'The House is entitled to know what HMS *Splendid* was doing in the Barents Sea.'

There was agreement about 'concern for the services' and everybody desired a proper defence of the nation. O'Neill doggedly persisted: 'I realise that this evening there will be no satisfactory response to the recent reports about lost sonar equipment – it may or may not be significant, and it may or may not be in the Soviet Union's possession – but it is important that we hear today what HMS *Splendid* was doing in the Barents Sea.'

The SDP's defence spokesman and MP for Woolwich, John Cartwright, told his fellow MPs: 'I recognise that submariners are very special people indeed ...' This made him concerned for their lives when carrying out dangerous tasks. 'It is vital to be sure that we are not asking our submariners to undertake unreasonable risks. It has been suggested to me that the HMS *Splendid* incident is not an isolated occurrence and that there have been similar incidents involving HMS *Spartan* and HMS *Sceptre*. If the inquiry shows a need for a review of procedures and methods of operation, the Minister should not hesitate to say so and to carry out the review.'

Returning to the fray, O'Neill criticised what he called the government's 'over-secrecy and paranoia'. He could find out more about what UK naval forces were doing from American sources than he could from anyone in his own country. He worried that too many trespassing NATO submarines might actually provoke the Soviets into firing their ballistic missiles for fear of losing their SSBNs. O'Neill told his fellow MPs: 'If the United Kingdom – and, I presume, the United States – have a presence in the Barents Sea, that will surely threaten the security of the Soviet Union's SSBNs, increase the threat of a Soviet first strike and thus threaten crisis stability. In terms of NATO–Soviet relations at such a sensitive time, when we are supposed to be close to reaching an accommodation with the Soviet Union ... it is foolhardy to be blundering around in the Barents Sea.'

The amazing success of the Royal Navy in covering its tracks for so many decades was reflected in what the Labour Party defence spokesman said next. 'There seems to have been a major change,' said O'Neill. 'Until now we have not been aware of British boats being involved around the Kola Peninsula.' He added: 'The Government's over-secrecy and paranoia on so many issues pollutes and distorts the very basis of discussion on defence matters.' O'Neill overlooked the matter of a Labour government secretly upgrading the Polaris missile system. And was it not Harold Wilson and Jim Callaghan who signed off on SSN missions deep into the Barents? O'Neill came back to the issue of SSNs in the Barents during April and May 1987, with written questions seeking further answers.

The reality was that the Royal Navy's submariners had been there repeatedly since the late 1950s (and before that). There was no official inquiry, open to public scrutiny, on British submarine operations in the Barents. And no government minister confirmed such operations.

There were moves, though, to try and defuse tensions and wind back the arms race. In Washington DC on 8 December 1987, the Americans and Russians signed the Intermediate Forces Treaty. It abolished a whole category of missiles, namely nuclear-tipped land-based cruise missiles and ground-based ballistic missiles with ranges between 300 and 3,400 miles.

The British government had a novel solution to diverting attention away from continuing submarine missions while seeming to offer a gesture towards easing tensions. It would send surface warships specially fitted for spying missions into the Barents and also into the Baltic. In command of one of these daring forays, as Commanding Officer of the brand-new Broadsword Class frigate HMS *London,* would be none other than Doug Littlejohns. Released from driving a desk in the Ministry of Defence he relished the prospect of again causing trouble for the Russians.

Compared with the sleek, black and curvaceous *Sceptre*, this frigate was angular and cluttered. As Capt. Doug Littlejohns drove along the jetty at Devonport in December 1987, the first sight of his new command filling the windscreen achieved a lasting impression. Parking his car in the space allocated to the CO – this time with no challenge from an anxious sailor – Littlejohns climbed out. Running his eyes along the towering slab-sided HMS *London*, he marvelled at her length and height. At 429ft, the boxy frigate was 157ft longer than *Sceptre*. Painted a drab grey, with a gigantic F95 pennant painted on her side, to Littlejohns she was massive, even though at 4,800 tons' displacement she was only 200 tons less than his beloved SSN.

Two thirds of a submarine is below the surface of the water, but with this large, cruiser-sized Broadsword Class warship it was the other way around. Thanks to very thin stressed steel stretched taut over her ribs HMS *London* possessed a starved-dog look. She was festooned with aerials and wires and didn't even have a big gun – her primary self-defence was two six-packs of Sea Wolf medium-range missiles. They were carried in space-age launchers, one on the forecastle and the other aft, on top of her big helicopter hangar. *London* also possessed launchers for the highly effective Stingray lightweight homing torpedo and could carry up to two Lynx helicopters or one Sea King for ASW. The helicopter systems were linked to the ship's when hunting contacts – *London* herself had a powerful bow-mounted sonar system.

The hangar was also designed for the new EH-101 Merlin helicopter. It would be a huge leap forward in submarine-hunting capability, but was late into service and, in the end, would see no Cold War operations.

For attacking surface ships *London* was fitted with four box launchers for Exocet sea-skimming missiles on her forecastle. The only guns on board were two single 40mm anti-aircraft cannons and, when needed, 20mm weapons. To confuse, distract and seduce incoming missiles away from the frigate, there were counter-measures, including chaff rockets and heat-projecting lasers to dazzle (though not burn) the eyes of pilots in attacking aircraft. The laser equipment was always kept carefully shrouded to safeguard against snoopers. HMS *London* had towed array sonar, among the first surface warship types in the Royal Navy to have that capability. In fact, they had been designed from scratch for towed array operations but, as Littlejohns would soon discover, certain flaws somewhat negated that advantage.

The philosophy behind the *London* was pure Cold War. She didn't need a gun because she would be far out in the Atlantic combating Soviet submarines, not engaging other surface ships or bombarding land targets. Most fascinating of all, though, was the sensor fit in *London*, which was big enough to house all the intelligence-gathering systems and people to operate them traditionally shoehorned into submarines.

The American-origin Outboard Electronic Intelligence (ELINT) system was extremely capable. Combined with other sensors and communications equipment, it all fed into a computer in the Operations Room, where it was stitched together to form one combat picture. The Computer Assisted Command System (CACS) could simultaneously track up to 500 contacts, while data from passive sonar and ESM could also be injected.

Just as he had been at the heart of things in *Sceptre*, the *London*'s new Commanding Officer would, when operations required it, sit in a swivel chair at the centre of the frigate's Ops Room (with his own Command CACS Display).

Littlejohns, or the XO if need be, would be the nodal point for all the input from the various officers and senior ratings in charge of the above-water and sub-surface sensors and weapons systems.

As was the case in *Sceptre*, Littlejohns would hold the picture in his head while on the screen also keeping track of what was going on.

As Littlejohns listened in to what was happening on the Ops Room net, if there was ever a situation – a threatening submarine or surface warship – where only the boss could authorise action, then he would decide when (and how) to neutralise it.

It was no accident that SSN captains were being awarded command of the new Type 22 (Batch 2) warships (as *London*'s class was also known). The press regularly referred to them as 'elite fighting ships'.

Due to their size and length they could weather rough seas, with an impressive endurance on patrol of 4,000 miles at 18 knots. *London* was powered by Rolls-Royce Olympus gas turbines for high-speed dashes (up to 30 knots) and RR Tyne engines for normal cruising.

The Olympus was a variant of the jet engine used by the RAF's

Vulcan strategic bomber. The Tyne was a development of a turbo-prop powerplant used in medium-range airliners.

London and her five Batch 2 sister vessels were at the time among the most expensive surface warships ever built for the British fleet. The price tag on Littlejohns's new command, only commissioned in February 1987 but yet to be declared fully operational, was £159m. They were costly because they were tailor-made for ventures into the Russian Bear's backyard at a time when – as we have seen – there was major concern about submarine incidents in political circles.

A number of veteran submarine captains were to demonstrate daring and innovation during encounters with the Soviets as COs of Type 22s, but the poacher-turned-gamekeeper ploy was not restricted to the British.

In both the US Navy and Russian Navy it was also applied. Littlejohns considered it 'a most sensible use' of former submarine captains.

'Most of us, from whichever country, came to similar general tactical conclusions. It was not unusual to find that the "gamekeeper" had an innate feel for where he might find a submarine. And so it proved for me, whether against our own submarines in exercises, or against those of other nationalities.'

Submariners had commanded the British navy's general-purpose surface ships for a number of years. To Littlejohns it 'made complete sense' for them to later command ASW ships. Furthermore, he was proud to observe: 'During the first few years of her life *London*'s captains were either submariners or aviators. I relieved an aviator, was relieved by a submariner who was in turn relieved by another aviator. The last two captains in the first commission were Mark Stanhope and Tim McClement, both submariners, and future admirals.'

Submariners often jokingly referred to their surface brothers as 'targets', or 'skimmers'. Now a band of brothers – former SSN captains – relished the chance to stalk the oceans in surface warships. It was a different means to make life a misery for Soviet submariners.

When he realised that his next sea-going appointment would be to one of the new frigates, Littlejohns began to formulate a cunning plan. He hoped to arrange things so that he was the first former SSN driver who had been North to also command one of the new Type 22s on the same mission.

As he got better acquainted with the personality of his new command, Littlejohns gained an insight into the new wonder warship that was not always reassuring.

'Unfortunately the diesel generators and all auxiliary machinery had been hard-mounted on the hull, which meant they wiped out the low frequencies on our towed array sonar, which wasn't too clever.'

Had rubber spring mountings been used under the machinery, or even shock-mounted rafts, the vibrations (and therefore noise) would have been absorbed. Instead they were transmitted into the hull and then broadcast into the sea. Littlejohns and his team worked out a system that minimised the number of diesels running when trying to use the towed array. News of the necessity to take this measure was not well received by the naval architects in Bath – it showed they had failed to create the perfect towed array frigate.

The noise problem was reduced but would never be entirely overcome. In Littlejohns's view 'the design was flawed from the outset for use of the ship as a towed array platform'. In fact, *London* might have been 'vulnerable in a hot war if she was to meet a surface combatant or a well-handled SSN. She would have done reasonably well against aircraft and missiles of the day.'

A problem with CACS also had to be ironed out before the ship could deploy on front-line missions against the Soviets.

As Littlejohns discovered: 'it had a tendency to crash every forty minutes, or less. Somehow, despite this, we got the ship through sea trials. Later it came to me what the problem was. Every time someone went into the CACS computer room – an equipment compartment not usually manned – and switched the light on, the system crashed. We discovered the ship's builders had used the wrong conduit. It meant the computer busbars were not as protected as they should have been. They were vulnerable to radiation contamination from other electrical cables lying adjacent. This was causing the system to crash. The builders were called in to rectify it by running the cables through the proper conduits. We noticed an immediate and substantial improvement in CACS mean time between failures.'

With *London* declared fully operational in January 1988 she was deployed to the Baltic, which was a backwater in comparison with the North Atlantic and Barents Sea. Even so, for a captain with the aggression and daring of Littlejohns it was a challenge to be embraced. 'The main purpose was to test her against real potential targets. At that time the Russians considered the Baltic to be their own private lake and we set out to prove them wrong.'

Just as he ran submarines on a war footing from the outset of a mission, now Littlejohns instituted a similar regime in his frigate.

He chose darkness to make a passage of the narrow seas between Denmark and Sweden, with all radars off. For further cover, *London*'s lights were arranged to impersonate a merchant vessel and by dawn she was off the coast of the USSR. The Soviets had occupied the Baltic States during the Second World War. Paldiski, on the coast near Tallinn, was a major nuclear submarine training base, with two reactors inside large SSN/SSBN simulators. The major Soviet naval base in the Baltic was at Baltiysk, on territory that prior to Russian occupation in 1945 was East Prussia. The USSR's submarine forces in the region remained second rank, mainly older classes of diesel submarines, but the Baltic Fleet had numerous surface combatants.

The main objective for Littlejohns was 'hanging around sucking in useful intelligence on our sensors, making sure they all operated to specification'.

Once the Soviets realised they had a NATO frigate snooping around – especially of a new sophisticated type – they scrambled aircraft and helicopters to buzz *London*. Not long after a Matka hydrofoil turned up. A small but fast combatant armed with, among other things, a pair of Anti-Shipping Missiles (ASMs) and a 76mm gun, this craft became the British frigate's shadow.

Littlejohns decided to have some 'fun and games' with the Matka.

'He was fitted with high-speed diesel engines so if we went fast then he was OK, but if we went slowly he would coke them up after an hour or so. He would then have to do a high-speed run to burn off the coke.'

A Sunday morning offered a chance to play further tricks on the Soviet shadow. While Littlejohns climbed into a pretty convincing version of a padre's outfit, from the shipwright's workshop was produced a mini-coffin made of plywood. Mock funeral party assembled on the flight-deck, a church service pennant was hoisted. There was a prayer or two, leavened with hymns, before the 'coffin' slid into the sea.

It was deliberately designed to float, *London* moving away to leave it bobbing in her wake. Littlejohns divested himself of his disguise and made his way to the bridge. Grabbing a pair of binoculars, he joined a group of ratings and officers watching gleefully as the Matka moved in to investigate.

Rather than the corpse of some poor oppressed rating flogged to death by his cruel capitalistic officers – as they might fondly imagine – the Soviets were shocked to find a Russian-language copy of *The Hunt for Red October*, courtesy of Littlejohn's good friend Tom Clancy.

For good measure there were also a bottle of whisky and copies of the soft porn mags *Penthouse* and *Playboy*. A note from Littlejohns asked: 'Haven't you got anything better to do?' *London*'s captain was delighted: 'No doubt he had a shock, but I am sure he enjoyed our decadent capitalist gifts. He was certainly less unfriendly thereafter, stopped playing silly rules-of-the-road games and waved cheerily when he made close passes. He even spoke to us a couple of times on the VHF.'

This was all good morale-boosting fun.

Soon far-flung corners of the frigate were alive with feverish activity as various groups of sailors took part in a competition organised by the First Lieutenant. He wanted to see who could design the most realistic fake weapon system. The winners turned out to be a bunch of ratings who used various dustbins and their lids to create a convincing 'monster torpedo'.

It had the biggest fin ever seen on a NATO naval weapon. Mounted amidships, next to the real torpedoes, this striking thing attracted lots of attention from shadowing Soviet vessels. They would swing in past the ship, zoom lenses of their spy cameras zeroing in on the new so-called super-weapon.

Keen to shake down the frigate's sonar, Littlejohns decided to unleash its active mode. Within a short while a clear contact was made, which drew on the frigate captain's 'poacher-turned-gamekeeper' instinct.

'I reckoned if I had been lurking in a submarine that is where I would have gone.'

Capt. Littlejohns thought 'it couldn't have been anything else down there but a Russian boat shadowing us. So, we went back and forth over this poor bugger, getting some very nice traces that revealed it to be a Foxtrot Class diesel-electric submarine. Then we decided to be beastly and sit above him until he ran out of air or needed to come up and recharge his battery.' As a submariner Littlejohns could easily imagine the captain of the Soviet submarine pacing his increasingly fetid Control Room trying to figure out what to do. Littlejohns could second-guess his every move and remained overhead no matter how hard the Foxtrot tried to break away. Come the morning, with batteries running low and air inside the boat almost exhausted, the Russian captain gave the humiliating order to surface.

Opening his hatch and climbing onto the bridge he found HMS *London* circling. Feeling enormous satisfaction, Littlejohns ordered a signal lantern operator to flash a message.

Good morning, hope you are having a good day.

For a former submarine captain command of a frigate requires a real change in mindset not only for himself, but also the sailors he now commands.

The Cold War-era surface navy world was so much larger than the tight-knit community of the Submarine Service. For example, in *Sceptre* the crew was 116, while the *London*'s complement numbered 273.

It was not unusual for a surface warship's crew to know absolutely nothing about their new boss. *They had no idea if he was any good.*

'Submarine crews know their CO has succeeded on the Perisher course,' said Littlejohns, 'so they all realise he has been through the wringer and thoroughly tested. Surface ship COs are a little bit harder for a crew to assess as there is no comparable public test.'

Littlejohns noticed significant differences. 'In surface warships the Commanding Officer is looked upon as the father of the ship and is often the oldest man aboard, whereas in submarines I was never the oldest guy. It seemed to me that surface warship captains were put up on a pedestal. They were distant figures, which was possibly to preserve their air of authority in times of yore. This had worked successfully for centuries and I was not going to rock the boat, so I fell into line with it to an extent. I knew that some surface warship captains stuck to their cabin, the Ops Room, the bridge and sometimes visited the wardroom, if invited. That was about it. This was all a bit strange to a submariner, because on a boat you are always wandering around all over the place.'

The *London*'s men realised Capt. Littlejohns was different when he began to stroll around the ship, visiting almost every part of the vessel to get acquainted with how the frigate ticked and also to meet her people.

'Within a few weeks I think that the crew began to "get it". I was often greeted with a mug of tea and a chocolate biscuit because the word had gone out that I was on the prowl. I did find it strange to have meals on my own in my cabin, which is the custom for surface warships. In submarines, the CO has breakfast on his own and then he eats the rest of the meals with the other officers, in the wardroom. I did see the logic of it in a surface warship. There are many more officers and it is good for them to have somewhere to let off steam without the captain being present. I didn't mind. I was never affected by "the loneliness of command" thing. In fact I quite enjoyed it.'

After so many years in the cramped confines of a submarine, it was a relief to have some privacy, but the responsibilities of command were never more than a few footsteps away. Sometimes, Littlejohns would soon find, split-second decisions would be needed, but to counter the threats of a fanatical foe in the Arabian Gulf rather than the Soviets.

Before leaving for waters East of Suez, the submarine driver turned frigate captain got married for the second time, to Debs, on 4 June 1988. After the honeymoon he was going to knuckle down to what he thought would be a month's worth of settling into a new home on Exmoor.

But then the *London*'s date of deployment to the Gulf was brought forward a month. A Leander Class frigate already out there had suffered fuel contamination. Littlejohns found his ship escorting big fat tankers through the Strait of Hormuz, in one incident facing down menacing Iranian Revolutionary Guard Corps fast-attack craft.

During another tense confrontation he coolly saw off the Iranian Navy frigate *Alborz*. A well-known troublemaker, she approached the starboard beam of *London*, turning to run parallel. The Iranian's 4.5-inch gun turret swung to port, pointing directly at the British warship. Her 30mm and 20mm cannon also swivelled to target the RN frigate. Littlejohns climbed down from his captain's chair, walking out onto the starboard bridge wing. Using binoculars to take a close look at the Iranian, he was not amused.

Stepping back into the bridge, he grabbed the radio's hand mike and hailed *Alborz*: 'I would really prefer you don't do that!'

London kept her course straight ahead, ensuring that the Iranian was 'painted' by the Exocet fire control radar. The British frigate's Lynx helicopter – armed with very effective Sea Skua missiles – was launched to provide added deterrent.

The deployment also saw Littlejohns landing himself in hot water with the Foreign Office by repeating the *Red October* gift set trick with a patrolling Russian frigate. The Soviet defence ministry was enraged and conveyed its displeasure via its own foreign ministry.

'I was already on the dartboard in the Kremlin for my exploits in an SSN,' remarked an older and wiser Littlejohns. 'My sending the package over to their frigate was a step too far for the Russians.'

Not that it bothered Littlejohns in 1988; nor did it affect his career prospects. After bringing *London* back to the UK he took up a new job in the Ministry of Defence as the Principal Staff Officer to the Chief of the Defence Staff. While Littlejohns gained a taste of surface navy command and then returned to the corridors of power in Whitehall, Dan Conley was busy in a frozen clime. He was seeing if the Tigerfish torpedo could run true and destroy Soviet submarines under the ice.

While there had been a number of Royal Navy nuclear-powered and diesel submarines under the ice before, not that many of them had smashed through the roof of the world. HMS *Dreadnought*, commanded by Cdr Alan Kennedy, was the first British SSN to surface at the North Pole, on 3 March 1971. It had been a tricky process. Aside from voyaging 1,500 miles under the ice it took nine hours to find a polynya, requiring the use of periscope looks, sonar pings, an upward-looking echo sounder and even assistance from a searchlight. 'The ice was two feet thick when she emerged through the ice,' one former *Dreadnought* sailor would record. 'Spending seven days under the ice and surfacing six times, she sustained minor damage ... Two small dents noted on her bow and a panel of fibre glass was torn from the fin by the sea when she surfaced outside the Arctic circle. She [had] travelled 5,200 miles in 19 days passing under the ice early on February 28.'

The tall fin of the SSN smashed through the ice, rising like Kubrick's strange black monolith in *2001: A Space Odyssey*, stark and ominous in the primal Arctic wilderness.

Sentries armed with rifles were posted on the ice to protect anyone who ventured out into the hostile environment, where temperatures plunged to –110°F (equivalent to –79°C), in a howling 20 knots of wind chill. Lacerating ice crystals in the air stung any exposed skin. The rifles weren't to deter marauding Soviets, but to see off any polar bears that turned up looking for dinner. None of the creatures appeared that time. Seventeen years later, when Dan Conley ventured onto the Arctic pack ice – to await the arrival of the British submarines *Superb* and *Turbulent* – he was warned to watch out for them, lest he be savaged and devoured. He was on a milestone mission though, to give the Royal Navy a winning edge in the battle against the Soviets.

Having attended the US Naval War College in 1986/87, Conley was now Commander of the Submarine Tactics and Weapons Group, in charge of secret torpedo test firings. His overriding task was to make sure the weapons functioned as expected and perfecting the best tactics for their use in a fight, whether in the open ocean or under ice.

Conley and his team – suitably clad against the severe temperatures – were in March 1988 based on gently shifting pack ice, 120 miles to the north-east of Prudhoe Bay, in the Beaufort Sea, off the northern shores of Alaska. It was a bleak, beautifully clean and pristine white environment. The ice station was a collection of large, heated huts and tents with sturdy frames, established under the auspices of the University of Washington State.

Called the Applied Physics Laboratory Ice Station (APLIS), aside from carrying out ecological research it was a tracking range for test-firing torpedoes, not only the Tigerfish but also the US Navy's Mk48. APLIS had been established on ice flat enough to provide a landing strip for aircraft and helicopters being used to transport people, torpedoes and supplies to and from the site.

'It also offered uniform ice thickness to recover the torpedoes through,' explained Conley. 'Its tracking range, fixed onto the ice, had the complexity of a daily drift of several miles, with a slow anti-clockwise rotation.'

Superb and *Turbulent* made a careful under-ice transit from the north-west Atlantic around the top of the world. More than 1,500 miles from the ice edge, it was further than *Dreadnought*'s. It was a record for the Royal Navy. A US Navy attack boat, USS *Lapon*, was coming north from the Pacific, via the Bering Strait.

Torpedo reliability under the ice was vital to kill the Soviet Navy's ballistic missile boats in their Bastions. Things were dicey enough without the self-inflicted problem of guidance wires breaking and propulsion failures. They had been ironed out in normal, open-ocean conditions, but what about in under-ice extremes? It was a challenge that Conley and his team were eager to tackle during ICEX 88 (as in Ice Exercise 1988). The American submarine was to arrive first and proceed with several test surfacings through the ice monitored by civilian scientists. Conley went with them to watch.

A snowmobile was soon spotted coming at speed from the ice station. On pulling up its driver announced dramatically: 'Two bears are on the way!'

Alarmed looks were cast around, expecting to find hairy beasts lumbering over the horizon, eager to snack on human flesh and bone.

Safety catches were taken off rifles.

People made sure rounds were chambered.

The snowmobile driver shook his head and waved his hands revealing: 'No, not polar bears – Soviet Bears!'

He meant TU-95 Bear turboprop maritime reconnaissance aircraft, coming to snoop on what was going on. The eyes of Conley and others scanned the skies above the pack ice for twinkling silver aircraft. They listened for the distinctive droning roar of the TU-95's four powerful engines and eight contra-rotating propellers – the noisiest military aircraft then in existence.

'Sure enough a few minutes after the USS *Lapon* surfaced the two [Soviet] reconnaissance aircraft flew over at very low altitude pursued by two USAF F-15 fighter jets. With the SSN's sail protruding though the ice and the aircraft framed in a very blue Arctic sky, the scenario was straight out of the Alistair MacLean novel *Ice Station Zebra* – but in this case there were no Russian paratroopers' parachutes blossoming in the sky.'

Now it was down to business and the arrival of the British SSNs was awaited with some anxiety. This was not just the furthest they had ventured under pack ice. They also had to very diligently follow the same track both up to and back from APLIS because of what Conley described as 'limited sonar ice-charting capability'. This, he knew, ruled out them 'having the capability to transit to the closest open water down through the narrow and shallow Bering Straits, especially with the likely presence of ice canyons reaching to the seabed'.

Should there be a serious machinery breakdown or fire under the ice at any stage, things could become very tricky, even for an SSN, which would still have to find a polynya or thin ice to surface through. Conley was sceptical about the alternative. 'In the event of an SSN losing propulsion under the ice, the contingency plan to dig it out presumed that it was able to successfully send a distress signal and that it could be located.'

Conley's heart missed a beat when he heard over the radio from the US base at Point Barrow, Alaska, that *Turbulent*'s electrolysers were defective. They were not producing enough oxygen, so the boat had to burn oxygen-generating candles. These were now running out and must be replenished as a priority. A few days after arrival under the ice at APLIS, the British SSN found a polynya a few miles from the base and surfaced in it. This enabled more candles – including enough for the return voyage home – to be delivered.

During subsequent trials the British submarines fired 16 Tigerfish in carefully coordinated simulations of submarine versus submarine encounters under ice. Conley observed them via real-time displays in a command hut.

Having witnessed how temperamental the Tigerfish could be, he was relieved to see it was now a reliable weapon even in the most demanding of conditions.

'Most of the firings were conducted with each submarine alternating as target, with depth separation to avoid the practice weapons actually hitting the target SSN. Additionally a few weapon runs were against static acoustic targets, which represented a stationary SSBN under the ice. Tigerfish performed extremely well in the quiet Arctic conditions.

'Its passive homing capability came to the fore,' explained Conley. 'Even when used in the active mode the weapon could discern between ice and target returns. American observers were impressed with both their solid performance and precision guidance, which enabled most of them to be parked under suitable flat, thin ice at the end of their run.'

This was all carried out in very deep water where visibility was surprisingly clear. That made it much easier for divers wearing special suits and breathing apparatus to be lowered through the ice to both find and attach a harness to each torpedo. The weapon was than winched up by a hovering helicopter through a specially bored hole. The diver was extracted through another. After recovery the torpedoes were put on board a Casa aircraft, which flew them to the nearby settlement of Prudhoe – described by Conley as 'a frontier town full of oil exploration equipment covered in very solid ice and truck parks full of vehicles with their engines running'.

In residence at a motel was an undercover team from the Royal Naval Armaments Depot at Coulport, near Faslane. They were experts at maintaining and repairing torpedoes. With a workshop at the nearby airfield, they pretended to be researchers from a British university supporting scientists out on the ice.

Conley wondered how many people truly believed that yarn. The 'scientific researchers' wore jungle camouflage uniforms provided by the Royal Marines to make up for their Arctic gear failing to arrive. Most of them also spoke with broad Scottish accents, which surely even some Alaskans would have found strange for an English university.

'I don't think anyone could possibly have been taken in,' Conley observed.

Sometimes to monitor conditions on the ice Conley and his team would venture some distance from APLIS, out to where the wild things roam. It was always best to go armed, especially with recent sightings of bears not far from the ice station.

After listening to one of these warnings Conley made a mental note to be extra wary, but he soon found a serious blunder had been made. 'In the station command hut there was an array of rifles and shotguns. It was normal routine to select a couple of weapons before any foray was made away from the station, in case you had to deal with an aggressive bear. Much to our consternation, having been landed by helicopter at a polynya several miles away from the station – where we were to await the surfacing of a British submarine – we realised that we were without weapons. The next few hours were rather apprehensive, as nobody was keen to be lunch for any stalking polar bear lurking behind the nearest ice ridge.'

If becoming a snack for starving polar bears wasn't risky enough, sometimes Conley found his life could be put in danger by over-enthusiastic snowmobile drivers.

The formation of a polynya at the end of the ice station landing strip provoked much excitement in camp, with several people going out to see it, including Conley.

'On the night it formed I was awakened by an American-Chinese scientist who excitedly told me a large polynya had just appeared. He invited me to take a snowmobile ride to view it. We were soon heading at speed across the runway towards what I could clearly see through the Arctic twilight was open water. I suddenly appreciated that the scientist's goggles and glasses had misted up and his vision was a bit impaired. Self-preservation set in at the prospect of coming to grief in such unusual circumstances. Strong verbal exhortation succeeded in bringing the snowmobile to a halt not far from the edge.'

Other people were not so lucky. The next day, going out with another group of sightseers, Conley was landed with the embarrassing job of making excuses for someone else's mishap.

'On a similar foray to the polynya edge one of the party ended up in the water and a snowmobile was lost to the Arctic depths. Fortunately a helicopter was available, to fly the man who had fallen into the sea back to the camp, where he quickly recovered in a sauna. As senior officer present at the time of the incident, I had to explain to the ice station commander what had happened on my watch, which was a bit embarrassing.'

Beyond snowmobile high jinks on the Arctic ice, the serious objective of ensuring the West could defend itself against the growing menace posed by the Soviet Union's enormous Typhoon and Delta IV SSBNs hiding in ice bastions was achieved.

Conley felt the Tigerfish firings were 'a remarkable achievement, firmly demonstrating the capability of the Royal Navy's SSNs to successfully engage submarines under the Arctic ice pack'. The amazing efforts of *Superb* and *Turbulent* – despite the risks posed by such operations – had, he felt, 'firmly put the Royal Navy on a par with the US Navy in terms of under-ice warfare'. Finally, nearly three decades after Rob Forsyth's nail-biting, extremely hazardous ventures under the ice in the Halifax-based diesel *Auriga*, the British fleet was equal in terms of submarines, weapons and under-ice tactics to the Americans. Conley was disappointed the submariners did not receive more acclaim or recognition, for without their efforts in those frozen waters the West was truly at risk of allowing the Soviets to dominate the Cold War at sea.

As ever, the Submarine Service was the most unheralded part of the traditionally tight-lipped and publicity-averse Silent Service (as the RN is sometimes known). 'As far as I am aware there were no honours awarded,' notes a dismayed Conley, 'and, of course, at the time security precluded any publicity.'

Somehow Conley had for several days survived unscathed in one of the most hostile environments on the planet. The weather was actually rather kind for the time of year, with the temperature never dropping much below 10°F (or –12°C). The downdraft from hovering helicopters could render it a lot colder, though, making it essential to be covered up against frostbite. He had also narrowly avoided taking a dunk in the frozen ocean and hungry polar bears had stayed away. All that remained now was a successful take-off in a twin-prop Casa – provided its skis didn't collapse – and he was headed home.

'I found myself the sole passenger in the back of the aircraft on the way back to Prudhoe, sharing a very noisy hold with two Tigerfish. About half an hour into the flight, I awoke from a doze to a distinct change of pitch on the aircraft's engines. I noted with great alarm that the pilot was wildly gesticulating downwards, pointing to the ice and circling the aircraft to lose altitude. The prospect of a crash landing, seated between two torpedoes, filled me with real foreboding. Then I spotted why the pilot was becoming so excited. There, on an ice floe a few hundred feet below us, were real bears – a magnificent polar bear mother and her two cubs.'

As an idea for a movie, it was kicking around for a few years but a number of Hollywood studios passed on it – even though *The Hunt for Red October* was a massive global bestseller.

They could not see how such an arcane, deeply technical topic could become a mass-market movie. There was also stiff opposition to it in naval circles, for it threatened to give away the secrets of the Cold War under the sea to an even wider audience.

But some far-sighted admirals in the US Navy saw that it could boost the profile of its Submarine Force the way *Top Gun* had for the carrier aviators back in 1986. 'So, let's help them out', they said.

One major element of the book that did not make it to the big screen was the British side of Tom Clancy's original novel. Out went the key role played by the ASW carrier HMS *Invincible*. Also excised was mention of *Sceptre* or any other British ship or submarine. The USN loaned the movie-makers SSNs to take the actors to sea and assist in research to create realistic sets.

It let the actor Scott Glenn – a former US Marine, who would play the captain of the Los Angeles Class attack boat USS *Dallas* – take command of a SSN. This was under strict supervision of her real CO. The USN even allowed some serving sailors to play members of the *Dallas* crew.

In the movie, the hero, naval analyst Jack Ryan, is at least based in England, possibly on loan from the CIA to the Royal Naval College at Greenwich. Sean Connery (a former Royal Navy rating) plays Captain Marko Ramius, the renegade Soviet submarine officer who steals a Typhoon Class boat with revolutionary propulsion and hands it over to the Americans. Ramius reasons that such a powerful stealth boat is a deliberate ploy by the Soviet Union to acquire a first-strike ability and wipe out the USA.

He doesn't think it is fair.

The movie came out just over six months after the Berlin Wall was torn down – heralding the end of the Cold War.

There were fears that it had lost all relevance. It didn't seem to matter, as it harvested a respectable worldwide gross of more than US$300m (a good return on a budget of $30m).

In April 1990, the honour of introducing a private London premiere of *The Hunt for Red October* fell to Tom Clancy's friend Doug Littlejohns.

Standing in front of the massive screen in a private cinema, he neatly managed to simplify aspects of the Cold War that some Hollywood executives found hard to grasp.

'Imagine you are in your submarine here in London,' he told the audience of VIPs. 'You detect an enemy in Birmingham and you intercept him in Bristol.'

And with that thought-provoking indication of the sheer scale across which the undersea contest was waged, the lights dimmed.

The most poignant sequence in the movie – and surely the most insightful to any veterans of the secret war below the waves – is a discussion between Ramius and his XO, Vasily Borodin (played by the Australian actor Sam Neill). As *Red October* clears her baffles – a Crazy Ivan! – unaware the USS *Dallas* is trailing her, Borodin and Ramius are chatting in the captain's cabin. The former is speculating about what his life will be like in the USA once they have successfully defected. Borodin looks forward to journeying from state to state in 'a recreational vehicle' with no need for special permission, also to raising rabbits and 'marrying a round American woman who will cook them for me'. Borodin asks the captain what he will look forward to once *Red October* is safely in America.

Ramius observes, somewhat mournfully: 'I have no such appetites ...'

Borodin suggests: 'There must be something?'

With a sigh Ramius finally concedes: 'I miss the peace of fishing, like when I was a boy.' He pauses, lost in moribund contemplation of his chosen calling: 'Forty years I've been at sea. A war at sea. A war with no battles, no monuments ... only casualties. I widowed her the day I married her ... my wife died while I was at sea ...'

It is a moving moment of reflection amid all the high-tech thrills and surely will always ring true with any real Cold War warriors watching.

What does Littlejohns think?

'Submariners expected a lot of their families and they delivered, but sometimes at a cost.' He also gave his all to that war beneath the waves. *For real.*

It was, though, not quite the end between the Russians and the British. Suddenly it seemed the Cold War might not be over after all. Soviet submarines would stalk Littlejohns's old frigate, including one that decided to fire a torpedo right at her in the old battleground ...

Barents Sea,
August 1991

The Tango Class diesel broke the surface after a few hundred yards or so off HMS *London*'s starboard beam. Water cascading from the casing of the large submarine, a bridge watch team appeared at the top of the broad fin.

A hatch popped open at its base. Two sailors emerged and carefully edged their way around the fin towards the for'ard section of the hull, attaching lifelines to their waists in case they slipped into choppy seas.

This duly happened, one Russian pulling the other back up by his safety line. As officers on the bridge leaned over the side of the fin to shout orders, the conscripts stooped to pull something from the casing. Assembling a saluting cannon, they pointed it in the direction of the British frigate.

They fired off a couple of blank shots – a flash, smoke drifting away, and then the sound of a bang reached the ears of those watching from aboard HMS *London*. Despite one of them again being washed off the casing, and hauled to safety by his comrade, the two Soviet submariners successfully disassembled the saluting gun, and secured it inside the casing. They walked the gauntlet of crashing waves and disappeared back into the fin, the hatch slamming shut behind them. The command team on the bridge made their exit, climbing down into the Tango.

Letting water in her ballast tanks at the bottom and blowing spray through vents, the Soviet boat – large for a diesel, at 302ft long and more than 3,000 tons' displacement – slowly disappeared below the waves, until all that was left was white spume.

In the Operations Room of HMS *London*, sonar operators tracked the Soviet SSK as she moved away, and then turned back towards the frigate. They reported the torpedo tube doors were opening. On the bridge of *London* was Capt. Mark Stanhope. A veteran Cold War warrior, he had allegedly seen these waters from below the surface in command of a nuclear-powered Fleet submarine, seeking to shadow boats like the Tango. Kept apprised of developments, nothing seemed amiss, not yet anyway. Beside him on the bridge was Rear Admiral Bruce Richardson, who retained an abiding affection for Russia despite the Kremlin expelling him from Moscow in December 1982 (as retaliation for Zotov's ejection from the UK).

In the Tango they were about to deliver a shock to the old foe. British submarines and specially equipped Type 22 frigates had been a plague upon Russian waters for years, spying on exercises and hoovering up vast amounts of intelligence. *London* herself was by 1991 an arch miscreant.

Jim Taylor, with Dan Conley as his XO in *Spartan*, had trailed Soviet SSBNs and SSNs in the Arctic during February 1981. Eight years later, as captain of *London*, Taylor intruded right into the middle of a Soviet Navy combat exercise. The frigate's diver even tried to steal a torpedo fired by a Victor Class SSN. The weapon was spent and floating on the surface, so the diver put a wire around it. *London* aimed to haul the heavyweight torpedo on board and make off with it. The arrival of a Soviet warship, signalling the torpedo should be released, frustrated the plan.

Now, in 1991, *London* was about to meet a Soviet tinfish again, only this time under power and aimed straight at her.

The command team of the Tango must have given the instruction 'Fire!' with grim satisfaction. The wire-guided torpedo shot out of the tube and was tweaked onto target by its operator.

Aboard *London* the sonar operators couldn't quite believe their ears or eyes – they had expected the Tango to shadow their warship but not to actually fire a torpedo.

There was a contact on their screens that could only be something deadly heading straight for their warship. It carved a white track across the surface of the sea, passing astern of the Russian hospital ship *Svir*. British war veterans of convoys to the Soviet Union during the Second World War were among those looking on in astonishment. Gathered around the British frigate were a variety of Russian warships and merchant vessels, including the Royal Fleet Auxiliary tanker *Tidespring*. They had assembled to re-enact a convoy run to Murmansk on the fiftieth anniversary of the Second World War-era cruiser *London* escorting the first such shipment to Arctic Russia. Soviet flying boats and Bear and Badger jet bombers had swooped low overhead simulating Luftwaffe attacks. Russian warships unleashed barrages of blank anti-aircraft fire.

British practice torpedoes run like any other, but at the end they surface so they can be seen (thanks to their day-glo orange nose cone) and picked up.

The sonar operators and lookouts aboard *London* realised this thing was very fast and wire-guided. It leapt above the surface, red casing vivid on the grey sea. And it kept on coming. Captain Stanhope judged it would hit his warship if evasive action were not taken. It would be no problem for the welded steel hulls of Soviet Navy warships to shrug such a hit off, but *London*'s stressed steel was mere centimetres thick.

Easily punctured.

She could be seriously damaged or even sunk.

Over the wireless net, *London*'s bridge watch keepers heard a voice aboard *Tidespring* squawk in alarm: 'Someone's trying to torpedo us!'

In the *Gromky* – flagship of Russian vessels taking part in the re-enactment – an admiral was tearing his junior officers off a strip. Furious, from *Gromky*'s bridge he had watched the torpedo skim past the stern of *Svir* and head for *London* and *Tidespring*. It was a career-wrecker and might destroy the notion the Cold War was in any way over.

The hardliners' coup had just been dissolved, with Gorbachev returned to Moscow after being sprung from his imprisonment in a Crimean dacha.

He and the British Prime Minister, John Major, had agreed during a telephone conversation that, as a demonstration that the East–West thaw was for real, *London* and *Tidespring* should still sail for the Barents.

They would voyage down the Murmansk Fjord, past the Polyarny Inlet so recently immortalised in the Hollywood movie *The Hunt for Red October* as the lair of the terrifying Typhoon Class SSBNs.

London and *Tidespring* would be the first Western naval vessels to officially visit Murmansk for five decades – but there remained deep uncertainty. There was still anxiety the Cold War was in place. How far did Gorbachev's influence stretch – would the Russian Navy obey his orders, or would they rebel too?

Setting sail from Rosyth and making passage around the North Norwegian Cape, *London* had penetrated deeper and deeper into the Barents.

Somewhere under the waves she was being shadowed by a Russian Navy attack submarine, which in turn was being trailed by a British SSN.

The old game appeared to be back in play.

On the surface an intelligence-gathering trawler from Murmansk bristling with aerials monitored *London*'s signals traffic (and vice versa).

In the old Cold War days, even a matter of months earlier, *London*'s sonar operators and specially embarked intelligence analysts would have been alert for anything they could record and measure to gain advantage over the Soviets. Could they drop their guard now? It seemed as if their skills were not surplus to requirement after all.

*

The torpedo carved its erratic path through the waves straight at *London*, the noise of its propulsion screaming in the ears of the sonar operators. Lookouts on the bridge wings watched its bobbing red nose getting closer and closer. Were there sympathisers for the hardliners in the Tango? In the old days of the Cold War, such an act would have received a hot reception. A British SSN more than likely would have been right up the Russian submarine's tail, reacting instantly. HMS *London* herself would have launched her own torpedoes.

Instead both *London* and *Tidespring* took evasive action, much as their predecessors had some 50 years earlier during the convoy runs to Murmansk and Archangel under U-boat attack.

The Tango's torpedo passed only 40ft from *London*'s bows.

With destruction avoided the British frigate proceeded down the fjord, past the nuclear submarine base at Polyarny. As the bleak, mostly flat yet rocky, landscape unfolded on each side, mist parted to reveal fabled Severomorsk, the headquarters of the Northern Red Banner Fleet. The carrier *Gorshkov* – named after the remarkable officer who had driven the creation of the massive blue ocean Soviet Navy – received a tribute from *London*'s saluting guns. *Gorshkov* replied – small puffs of smoke spurting from the dark-grey, tiered control tower. On *London*'s upper deck, naval intelligence specialists – quite a number of them ex-submariners – drank in the bleak vista unfolding each side of the frigate. They mentally noted decaying dockyard facilities, the huge number of surface warships tied up alongside. Some of them had seen these shores before, but via a periscope rather than with the naked eye. Most incredible of all was the sight of beached warship hulks, just driven up there and abandoned. This was the reality of the Soviet naval giant – truly a mighty knight who had died inside his armour.

As *London* sailed on, deeper into the lair of the Bear, landscape cameras in the hands of British naval photographers recorded the entire length of the fjord. Overhead a Russian Helix helicopter got closer to *London* than any had previously dared. It was gathering intel data on the frigate's sensors as given away by her aerials. Old habits died hard. Sonar specialists aboard *London* stared at the Soviet submarines whose noise signature they had learned to identify instinctively and felt overcome with awe. Here they were at last, on the surface, exposed and helpless, rather than disappearing into the Atlantic to try and hide.

That *London* and *Tidespring* came close to being torpedoed by a Russian submarine in 1991 is not widely known. I only know about it because I was there, aboard HMS *London* for her entire historic voyage into the Barents. Sometimes during the years since, as the fog of history swallowed up the Cold War, I wondered if I'd imagined it. My fears that the torpedo attack had been a hallucination were eventually dispelled by an acquaintance. A former naval intelligence officer, he enquired after hearing about my trip into the Barents aboard *London*: 'So you were there when a Soviet submarine almost sank one of our warships?'

I had written about it for my newspaper – the evening daily in the naval city of Plymouth, HMS *London*'s home port. My editor was so scared by it that he preferred to consign it to a supporting story with a small headline, rather than the front-page banner treatment it deserved: 'REDS NEARLY SINK ONE OF OUR WARSHIPS!!!!'

It made no impact at a national level perhaps because the Fleet Street papers didn't quite grasp how deadly that 'practice' torpedo was or how remarkable the event. In the middle of a joint naval exercise between the Soviets and the West, a Red Navy submarine aims and fires at British naval vessels. Possibly the powers-that-be – via the intelligence services on each side – asked newspaper editors not to make too much of it, for fear of harming the East–West thaw? Anyway, that was how the Cold War between the Royal Navy and the Soviets ended – with a moment of farce in the Barents.

It is not down in any map; true places never are.

Herman Melville, *Moby-Dick*

S o says Ishmael of the South Seas island the heavily tattooed and en-igmatic Queequeg hails from. Ishmael and Queequeg voyage aboard the whaling ship *Pequod*, under the command of the messianic Captain Ahab. They hunt the great whale that gives his name to the epic novel of nineteenth-century seafaring. Ahab vows at one point to pursue the beast 'round the Norway Maelstrom, and round perdition's flames before I give him up'.

Moby-Dick has already taken his leg during an earlier battle and, so it seems, also robbed him of sanity. Britain's submarine captains did not give up pursuit of their very own Moby-Dick during the Cold War – the Soviet Navy's submarine force. Not even when it dragged them round the corner past Norway and into the potential maelstrom of the Barents.

By the beginning of the second decade of the twenty-first century the Cold War had been over for nearly 20 years and it was some time since the last of the submarine captains had retired from the Naval Service.

Most of the submarines that took the challenge to the Soviets had by the dawn of the new millennium also been pensioned off. Today seven retired nuclear-powered submarines are tied up in a basin at Rosyth and a further ten at Devonport, with reactor fuel still to be removed from some.

All retain radioactive elements that need careful handling; how exactly to carry out that disposal operation remains a thorny problem.

Warspite, in which Tim Hale once stared death in the face, was discarded with unseemly haste. The end came when her innards were open to the skies, halfway through a £100m refit in dry dock at Devonport.

It was cancelled in the autumn of 1990 as part of the defence spending Peace Dividend reaped in the aftermath of the Berlin Wall coming down. There were also claims she had severe propulsion system problems, too expensive to repair. *Valiant*, the notorious 'Black Pig' in which Dan Conley countered the Soviet surge into the Atlantic, sailed on a little longer. In March 1991 she garnered an impressive hole in her casing during a high-speed trench run across the North Norwegian Sea. Though repaired and returned to service, in August 1994 the 'Black Pig' was decommissioned.

Dreadnought – first of the Fleet boats, in which Hale marvelled at the wondrous new world of nuclear-powered submarines – went much earlier, retired in 1980 (worn out before her time). *Swiftsure* was decommissioned in 1992 for similar reasons – she had carried out more deep dives than any of her sister vessels.

The Trafalgar Class was introduced in the 1980s but the Swiftsures continued to shoulder the burden until the end of the face-off with Russia – the *true* seasoned Cold War veterans. In a richly ironic turn of events, it was during the New World Order – as President George H. W. Bush termed the 1990s – that British SSNs finally received their overt baptism of fire. In 1999, an S-boat made history when *Splendid* became the first British submarine to launch Tomahawk Land Attack Missiles (TLAMs) in anger, against Serbian targets during a NATO campaign to halt ethnic cleansing in the Balkans.

Ejected from her torpedo tubes, the rocket motors of the cruise missiles kicked in on reaching the surface. Away they flew, low across the Adriatic and then, using terrain-mapping technology and satellite guidance data, skimming over land.

In 2001, when the UK joined the USA in striking Al-Qaeda terrorist bases in Afghanistan, the T-boats *Triumph* and *Trafalgar* took up position in the Arabian Sea to fire TLAMS. Just under 18 months later *Splendid* fired cruise missiles in the opening moments of the US-led campaign to depose Saddam Hussein from power in Iraq. *Turbulent* later took part in the same bombardment.

The Submarine Service had deviated a long way from Cold War hunter-killers venturing solo into Arctic waters to stalk the Soviet foe.

Now its SSNs were part of a bigger picture, threaded into the strategic tapestry by working to order, receiving up-to-the-minute targeting data for their 1,000-mile-range Tomahawks. They took out enemy command and communications nerve centres deep inland. In spring 2011, *Triumph* played an important part in bringing down that old rogue and friend of the Soviets, Colonel Gaddafi. Lurking off the coast of North Africa she hurled cruise missiles against regime bunkers. *Triumph* fired so many she had to sail back to Devonport and take aboard a fresh load before returning to the Med for another phase of delivering destruction.

*

Most of the Swiftsures were gone not long after *Splendid*'s fire mission against Saddam. Conley's *Spartan* decommissioned in early 2006. *Superb* – commanded by Beastie Biggs when Littlejohns was his XO in the late 1970s – was retired in autumn 2008, slightly earlier than planned. During her final deployment she was in collision with a rock pinnacle in the Red Sea, suffering substantial damage. The *Superb* was brought home but the MoD thought it pointless repairing her – not so near the end of her service life and without an existential threat to the UK on a par with the Soviets.

There was a Cold War warrior S-boat that soldiered on well into the new century, carrying out one more front-line mission to deter a potential foe. More than 30 years after Rob Forsyth brought *Sceptre* into service and pursued *Kiev* across the Med – and just under three decades since Littlejohns brought the boat back to life after her catastrophic collision with *K-211* – the veteran SSN completed an eight-month final deployment.

It stretched from using intelligence-gathering capabilities to hunt pirates and terrorists in the Indian Ocean to operations in the South Atlantic, although you wouldn't get anybody aboard to admit to anything as specific as that. Nevertheless, in March 2010, the highlight of *Sceptre*'s final adventure was splashed all over the front page of one UK national newspaper. 'Navy sends attack sub to Falklands,' screamed the *Sun*. *Sceptre*'s diversion down there was to deter the Argentinian Navy from making any provocative moves against UK companies exploring for oil reserves. There were vociferous objections from Buenos Aires, which also demanded Britain yield sovereignty of the Malvinas (as Argentinians call the Falklands). On *Sceptre*'s return to Devonport, senior officers congratulated the veteran SSN's men on a job well done, even if officially it never happened.

And so, after 32 years at sea, *Sceptre* found herself moored to a buoy close by Plymouth Breakwater. The hunter-killer boat's days were ending in enclosed waters that 236 years earlier saw one of the first, ill-fated, attempts to prove submarining a going concern.

In June 1774 a Norfolk shipwright called John Day managed a well-executed shallow dive in the Sound aboard a submersible based on a converted sloop. He should have stopped there, but foolishly accepted a bet to take his craft down even deeper. Entering the air chamber of the vessel – putting on extra ballast, in the form of stones in special holders bolted to the exterior – Day cheerfully descended again. For light he had a candle and would be sustained by fresh water and biscuits, resting in a hammock if he became fatigued. On reaching a depth of over 100 feet beneath the surface, the fledgling submariner discovered something he had hitherto been ignorant of – the ability of water pressure to crush his submersible. He died as it imploded, the wreckage settling between Drake's Island and Mill Bay.

In May 2010, as she completed her last deployment, *Sceptre*'s somewhat tougher black outer casing was covered in rubberised anechoic tiles meant to make her harder to detect under the water. Some of them had fallen off, dotting rusty squares across the boat's outer skin, giving her a bedraggled look. Yet, even a generation on from the end of the Cold War, the mystique of that time when the great game of submarine versus submarine was played out still exerted its magic. Aboard *Sceptre* the youngsters among her crew talked in reverent tones of the boat's long-ago voyages 'up North' into the Barents Sea. The Cold War hands who served aboard during the SSN's swansong voyage had been youngsters themselves when the East–West face-off ended. They were as reluctant as ever to discuss the fine detail of what they did way back when.

Sceptre slipped the buoy and, escorted by a protective tug, made her way through the deep channel in Plymouth Sound, right over where John Day perished. Heading through the Devil's Narrows, as the SSN carved her way up the Hamoaze, the boat's captain, Cdr Steve Waller, addressed the crew over the speakers.

He quoted Shakespeare's speech by Henry V before Agincourt.

> *'We few, we happy few, we band of brothers;*
> *For he to-day that sheds his blood with me,*
> *Shall be my brother; be he ne'er so vile,*
> *This day shall gentle his condition;*
> *And gentlemen in England now a-bed*
> *Shall think themselves accurs'd they were not here'*

And then *Sceptre* slid gently alongside at Devonport. Sailors in traditional white chunky sweaters – wearing hats displaying 'H.M. SUBMARINES' in gold letters on black ribbon – grabbed thick mooring ropes. The old Cold War warrior was tied up, never again to venture out onto the high seas or plunge into the deep. As the last Commanding Officer of *Sceptre* stepped off the gangway onto the jetty he was greeted by the first. Commander Rob Forsyth had made a pilgrimage from Oxfordshire to Devon in order to see his old boat home.

*

Almost seven months later – on a marrow-chilling December day – it was somehow fitting that the sixteenth (and final) Commanding Officer of *Sceptre* chose the words of a former foe in a speech to formally bring her service life to an end. Commander Waller mounted a podium on the parade ground at Devonport Naval Base and sought to sum up the essence of a submariner's life. Arrayed in ranks before him was *Sceptre's* final Ship's Company – the last of 1,500 sailors to have served in her.

The band of the Scots Guards – the boat's affiliated British Army regiment – provided a soundtrack of seafaring tunes. In the stands were specially invited guests, including veterans of past commissions, not least Forsyth and Littlejohns. Men who had served in other Swiftsure Class SSNs were also there, including Michael Pitkeathly, all paying respects to the last S-boat.

'It's difficult to describe what it is like to be a submariner,' Cdr Waller told his submariners and invited guests, 'but Captain Igor Britanov, a former CO of Russian submarine *K-219*, summed it up perfectly in his memoirs: "Submarine life is not a service it is a Religion."'

Back in October 1986, Britanov – a hero to submariners of all nations – saved the majority of his crew and prevented the nuclear poisoning of the eastern seaboard of the USA. He abandoned *K-219* to a watery grave in very deep water after a severe fire in one of her nuclear missile silos.

Commander Waller touched on the seamless progression of the Submarine Service's human history. 'In many ways today is a sad day, as the old lady is decommissioned – but don't reflect on this, for we should remember the achievements over her long and distinguished history; and the submarine ethos will live on.'

The Royal Navy is notoriously unsentimental when it comes to discarding submarines that have served their purpose and now need to be retired – *Sceptre* was, according to her last captain, 'only steel and pipework'.

Make no mistake, and here Cdr Waller expressed a truth nobody would dispute, 'the heart and soul of *Sceptre* stands before you as her Ship's Company. These men in front of you, and those who went before, have shown undying pride, loyalty and utter professionalism, in their roles and are a credit not only to the service but the country.'

Waller finished by quoting some lines from the legendary 1940s British movie, *In Which We Serve*. They were apt for the final page in *Sceptre's* life, but also for the submariners who held the line at sea during the Cold War. 'Here ends the story of a ship, but there will always be other ships; we are an island race, through all our centuries the sea has ruled our destiny. There will always be other ships and men to sail in them. It is these men, in peace or war, to whom we owe so much.'

Amen to that.

Farewell to *Sceptre*.

Last of the Cold War hunter-killers.

EPILOGUE: 'TREMBLE BOURGEOISIE! YOU'RE SCREWED:)'

The twenty-first century's equivalent of the Barents – the new North – could turn out to be the South China Sea, to which Beijing lays claim in its entirety.

The Chinese are constructing massive bases hidden within coastal cliffs, to hide their boats from snooping satellites. There have been skirmishes between American naval research vessels and Chinese 'trawlers', during attempts by the former to chart potential entry and exit points to the submarine lairs. China's attack submarine force is receiving new hunter-killer boats faster and stealthier than its noisy old SSNs – some have been detected intruding into Japanese waters and off the US Navy base at Guam.

China is engaged in a huge expansion of its entire navy. It is commissioning not only a 'new' carrier (a rebuilt Soviet Navy ship) to counter India's burgeoning maritime power (ditto with regard to a carrier) but also aiming to finally match and supersede the US Navy across the board. To meet the Chinese challenge the Americans are conducting a strategic pivot, committing 60 per cent of their naval forces to Asia-Pacific.

As that rivalry ramps up – with numerous nations competing for oil and gas rights in the South China Sea and also the East China Sea – some well-honed submarine surveillance skills may prove useful again. The Australians – who have grown closer militarily to the Americans in recent years – will bring something to the party. The only non-NATO maritime force to carry out such tasks from the 1970s to 1990s, the Royal Australian Navy has a lot to offer. It emerged recently that the Royal Navy trained the Australian crew of the British-built O-boat HMAS *Orion* in surveillance techniques in the late 1970s. On her delivery voyage to Australia, *Orion* – probably carrying British submarine officers in an advisory capacity – was asked to monitor signals traffic between Soviet Navy ships off the Libyan coast.

It was in the Pacific that the Australians really showed their mettle. *Orion* and her sister vessel *Otama*, also British-built, conducted more than 20 spy missions against both the Soviets and the Chinese, especially in the South China Sea. Australian O-boats carried out underwater looks on Soviet frigates and submarines, including inside Camh Ranh Bay, Vietnam. It was a mission type admitted by one retired admiral who commanded *Oberon* and the SSN *Tireless* in the Royal Navy before transferring to the Australian fleet. He remarked that it was 'a very full-on thing'. A former CO of *Orion* has also confirmed she took on those missions. All the captains of the boats involved were graduates of the UK's Perisher course.

The Australians paused their O-boat patrols when, during a deep penetration of Shanghai harbour in 1992, *Orion* allegedly became entangled in fishing nets. Fortunately, she got away, but with the Cold War over, the Australian government of the day decided it was time to bring such risky endeavours to an end. However, following the election of a new government in 1996, a series of similar missions were run against Indonesia, to seek intelligence on that nation's growing maritime power.

With China once again a target of interest for the USA and her allies, the Australians are operating new-generation Collins Class submarines fitted with Air-Independent Propulsion (AIP). In 2009 a news report claimed that two years earlier HMAS *Farncomb* suffered entanglement with a fishing line when shadowing Chinese submarines off Hainan. She was forced to surface and some of her sailors went out to cut the line away from the screw. The Australian government refused to comment. The Royal Australian Navy continues to recruit British submariners, some of them made redundant under UK defence cuts. Those who have been command-qualified on the Perisher course are particularly sought after to become captains of Australian submarines.

Highly capable diesel-electric boats have since the end of the Cold War proliferated across the globe – many of them of German design and construction – which thanks to AIP systems are more effective than ever.

The Israelis are bringing into service Improved Dolphin Class AIP boats, built in Germany, which they will allegedly use to carry nuclear-tipped cruise missiles. The Improved Dolphins might be deployed on deterrent patrols off Iran (as Tehran moves ever closer to acquiring atomic weapons).

The Dutch fleet's Walrus Class diesel boats have helped track pirates off Somalia. Moving in close to the shore, their officers used periscopes to spot skiffs being launched through the surf to attack merchant vessels. Communications intercepts have also aided the interception and deterrence of so-called Pirate Action Groups.

Britain no longer runs diesels. The last of the Royal Navy's O-boats was retired in 1993, though there was a last chance to show their worth during the 1991 Gulf War. *Opossum* and *Otus* carried out covert operations not dissimilar from their reputed activities in the Baltic against the Soviets.

Their presence has never been officially confirmed by the MoD. The official line in the early 1990s was that submarines never operated in the Arabian Gulf (not the case today when even SSNs are regularly seen). During coalition efforts to evict Iraqi occupiers from Kuwait the O-boats are believed to have landed Special Boat Service reconnaissance teams on the coast to scout out enemy defences. In one incident US Navy strike jets sank an oil tanker, which began to sink on an O-boat hiding underneath while attempting to recover a Special Forces team. She swiftly withdrew.

Opossum, commanded by Lt Cdr Steve Upright, was definitely at Singapore during Christmas 1990, but disappeared until she was recorded passing through the Suez Canal in the spring of 1991. By then *Opossum* sported a new tiger stripe camouflage paint scheme of sandy yellow and black. Returning to Portsmouth, *Otus* both had the tiger stripes and flew a Jolly Roger to signify successful war missions.

The Upholder Class (Type 2400) boats Rob Forsyth helped develop were brought into service to replace the O-boats but in the early 1990s HMS *Dolphin* ceased to be a submarine base. The four Upholders switched to Devonport. For Britain, with its Submarine Service shrinking dramatically in post-Cold War defence spending cuts, a decision was made to go all-nuclear. The Upholders were paid off in the mid-1990s and later sold to Canada, where they continue to serve.

To properly strive for tactical and strategic mastery of inner space, you still need to be in the SSN and SSBN game. And that's why the old Cold War rivals continue to pour billions into nuclear-powered boats.

And the old hunter-killer skills are still as relevant as ever – for the SSN and SSBN club is today growing well beyond the big five of the Cold War years (USA, Britain, USSR, France and China).

India is building her own attack boats and SSBNs, while Brazil (with French assistance) is likely to be the next member of the club, while even Argentina has ambitions to field SSNs (though there is no sign of work starting). In early 2013 President Cristina Fernández de Kirchner of Argentina demanded (not for the first time) that Britain hand over the Falklands. With Britain ready and willing to deploy SSNs to the South

Atlantic (and the Argentinians not yet possessing any) a major deterrent exists against any attempt by Buenos Aires to send its diminished fleet to mount another invasion.

For Britain the future means a new breed of Astute Class SSNs.

At 7,800 tons dived, the A-boats are nearly twice the size of the Swiftsures and six times bigger than Cold War diesels. Serious pieces of machinery, they are costing the British taxpayer more than a billion pounds apiece for the first three (of seven planned). With their long, broad fin and angular casing the Astutes seem more akin to Russian boats than a traditionally sleek British hunter-killer. A very ambitious design, they must handle all the missions demanded of them in the post-Cold War era – from hunting enemy submarines, to land attack, intelligence gathering and Special Forces raids. Their design, construction and introduction into service have been as fraught with difficulty (if not more so) as any previous British SSN.

There is one radical change in *Astute* that seems most strange to the Cold War graduates of Perisher. Two periscopes still cut through the water, but instead of the captain putting his eyes to the cups, cameras transmit an image to a large computer screen. The operator's controls resemble those used by video games consoles. One major advantage is said to be the periscope will break the surface for just a few seconds. Its optronic eye captures an incredible level of detail for analysis, keeping exposure time to an absolute minimum. The image itself can be stabilised using the latest technology, despite conditions prevailing on the surface.

A huge benefit of optronic – or photronic – masts (a type also fitted to the US Navy's latest attack submarines) is that the entire periscope apparatus is within the fin, so does not need to penetrate the pressure hull. The risk from pressure is reduced and the Control Room can be situated wherever best in the boat, rather than always being directly below the fin.

Astute's fighting qualities have already been tested. During late 2011 and early 2012 – in the deep waters of AUTEC off the Bahamas – *Astute* engaged in underwater dogfights with the USS *New Mexico*, one of the American navy's new Virginia Class SSNs. According to the USN the two ran through 'several cat-and-mouse war game scenarios'. *Astute* acquitted herself well as each submarine took it in turns to be the hunter or the hunted.

The USA and UK are also preparing to replace their Trident missile boats in the 2020s (the last operational Polaris submarine was *Repulse*, which was decommissioned by the Royal Navy in 1996).

In London arguments have raged within the government over whether or not current-generation SSBNs should be replaced by air-launched cruise missiles. Another suggestion is that the sea-based deterrent force should be retained, but kept in port largely unarmed. Littlejohns was of course at the heart of a similar debate on the naval side in the MoD three decades ago. It is as true today as it was back then that if the UK wants a truly credible deterrent it has to be provided by ballistic missile submarines.

Both China and Russia are constructing new SSBNs, to keep pace with the West, and while we have looked at the possibility of Cold War-style contests in Asia–Pacific, what of the old rivalry – between the Russians and their Western antagonists?

For a time it receded, but in truth it has never really gone away.

NATO submarines carried on poking around the Barents for some years after the end of the Cold War, continuing to observe and record Russian Navy training and new technology.

It was alleged that British and American attack submarines were trailing the cruise missile-armed Oscar II Class submarine *Kursk* when she was sunk in August 2000. Claims that a NATO submarine was somehow responsible were untrue – the *Kursk* was destroyed by the poor condition of her High Test Peroxide-fuelled torpedoes. One of them is believed to have exploded, setting off a chain reaction in other weapons. Britain and Norway sent teams to try and rescue 24 survivors (from a crew of 118) entombed within the *Kursk*. Russian hesitation to ask the old foe for help in the first place meant by the time they got to work it was too late to save anyone.

When the Russian mini-submarine *AS-28* became trapped on the seabed off Kamchatka in 2005 there was a happier outcome. Rescue teams from Britain, the USA and Japan raced to the scene after a much swifter Russian call for help. It was the Royal Navy that saved the seven crew, using a Remotely Operated Vehicle to cut cables that had snared *AS-28*. This enabled her to surface. It was a rare public demonstration of how men who once trained to kill each other could co-operate to save lives.

For a few years following the break-up of the Soviet Union, the Russian Navy's attack submarines disappeared from the Atlantic. Peace truly had broken out at sea, but in 1996 Akulas were detected prowling off the eastern seaboard of the USA.

Akulas were again to be found off the USA (and also Canada) in August 2009. A year later it was claimed an Akula even attempted to trail a British ballistic missile submarine in the North Atlantic.

Most alarming for the Americans was an alleged foray by an Akula into the Gulf of Mexico in the summer of 2012. Furthermore, it was claimed, the Russian SSN lurked off the American coast for several weeks.

Admiral Jonathan Greenert, Chief of Naval Operations (a submariner by trade), issued a carefully worded rebuttal of the claims. He told a Texan senator who had written to him expressing alarm: 'Based on all of the source information available to us, a Russian submarine did not enter the Gulf of Mexico.' That still fell short of denying a Russian SSN was off the US coast.

In October 2012, the US Navy detected and tracked a Sierra 2 attack submarine less than 300 miles off the eastern seaboard of the USA. She was operating near an American carrier strike group on a pre-deployment exercise. The Sierra 2 was soon heading home to the Kola. Not long after, during Hurricane Sandy, a Russian intelligence-gathering vessel was permitted to seek safe harbour at Jacksonville, Florida, not far from the major American submarine base at Kings Bay, Georgia. Some sources claimed this was conveniently within eavesdropping range of Trident missile boats departing on and returning from deployment.

The Russian foreign minister, Sergei Lavrov, in 2012 said Russia meant to be 'a Pacific power' but nobody could ignore that vast reserves of energy and mineral resources in the Arctic also meant Moscow was interested in dominating that zone.

The Northern Fleet remains the foremost striking force of the Russian Navy and a milestone was reached in January 2013 when its first new ballistic missile submarine for 20 years – named *Yuri Dolgoruky* after the Grand Prince who founded Moscow in 1156 – was officially commissioned into front-line service.

The ceremony took place at a snow-covered Sevmash shipyard, on the shores of the White Sea, where many nuclear submarines were built during the Soviet era. To celebrate the event, the Russian defence industry minister, Dmitry Rogozin – who was once his nation's ambassador to NATO – tweeted: 'Tremble bourgeoisie! You're screwed :)'.

It was meant as a joke, but to some observers – especially Westerners – it was an uncomfortable reminder of the past and possibly a worrying indication of things to come. The former USSR continues to build SSBNs and expand other elements of its armed forces.

Meanwhile, as the SSBN was commissioned President Vladimir Putin was simultaneously aboard the nuclear-powered cruiser *Pyotr*

Veliky (Peter the Great). He used high-tech communications to link in with the *Yuri Dolgoruky* ceremony. *Peter the Great* was moored at the Northern Fleet main base of Severomorsk in the Kola Peninsula and the President told the world: 'We will consistently develop underwater and surface vessels, strengthen conventional forces and naval strategic nuclear forces. In coming years, the fleet will receive over 100 new surface ships and submarines of different classes. We are fully committed to implementing this ambitious programme.'

A videoconference was staged, between Putin in the cruiser and the defence minister Sergei Shoigu and Navy Commander Admiral Viktor Chirkov, aboard *Yuri Dolgoruky*. The minister and naval boss referred to Putin (who was a Cold War KGB officer) as 'Comrade Commander-in-Chief'.

The videoconference concluded with Putin stating: 'This is a great event in the life of the country. This submarine *Yury Dolgoruky* is a serious, powerful weapon that will guarantee the security of our country and enhances our defence capability.' The Russian leader also reaffirmed his determination to see eight new Borey Class SSBNs commissioned by 2020, along with a corresponding number of attack boats. For the Russian counter to the UK's Astute and USA's Virginia is the Yasen (known to NATO as the Severodvinsk Class). A step up from the Akula, the first of these conducted a maiden voyage in the Barents during September 2011. Super-stealthy and fast, capable of firing cruise missiles, the Yasen also costs far more than even the Astutes per boat. The Russians are clearly as keen as ever to gain parity with, if not exceed the capabilities of, NATO submarines.

The possibility remains, though, that Putin's dreams of a powerful, resurgent superpower Russian Navy are destined to fall short. In May 2013, a report from the Federation of American Scientists (using US Naval intelligence data) claimed the Russians – allegedly with nine operationally available SSBNs – could only ever deploy one at a time (if that). They did so only five times in 2012. This compared poorly with the Soviet Navy's 102 nuclear deterrent patrols in 1984. According to the report most Russian SSBN crews never go to sea and deterrent cover may be patchy. By contrast the US Navy operates 14 Ohio Class SSBNs and annually manages up to three deterrent patrols per operational submarine. The British continue to field three Vanguard Class SSBNs (with a fourth in refit) and maintain nuclear deterrent cover all year round, with at least one always at sea. The FAS report suggested the US Navy does not consider hunting Russian SSBNs a primary mission for its 50 attack boats. The Royal Navy, in 2013 possessing ten times fewer SSNs than the USN, sees East of Suez as their primary area of operations.

Nevertheless, if they cannot gain an edge through the toil of their own scientists, engineers and naval architects it appears the Russians still don't mind stealing it from the West. Not only are they willing to turn NATO sailors into traitors, but the would-be turncoats are also keenly aware who is the most likely customer for submarine secrets.

In March 2012, Edward Devenney, a 29-year-old Petty Officer serving in the Trident missile boat *Vigilant* (under refit at Devonport), appeared in a London court charged with breaching the Official Secrets Act.

At his Old Bailey trial it emerged Devenney had one evening repeatedly attempted to telephone the Russian Embassy.

After gaining access to a safe on board the submarine, he used his mobile phone camera to capture encryption codes, which he downloaded to his laptop. This was not for money but due to his disenchantment about being passed over for promotion. He said he wanted to 'hurt the Royal Navy'.

However, the so-called Russian secret service agents 'Dima' and 'Vladimir' whom Devenney met in London were in fact from the British intelligence services. Devenney discussed past and future submarine movements. There were fears that, had he succeeded in making contact with them, the Russians could have waited for submarines to deploy, trailed them and recorded their unique sound signatures.

Pleading guilty to a charge of collecting information for a purpose prejudicial to the safety or interests of the State, Devenney also admitted misconduct in a public office. In December 2012 he was sentenced to eight years in jail. In a statement read out by his solicitor he expressed sorrow at inflicting hurt and shame on his family. Devenney also professed deep regret at the effect of his actions on the Submarine Service and fellow submariners.

An FBI sting operation in December 2012 allegedly prevented a 39-year-old retired US Navy Petty Officer from also passing secrets to the Russians. The indictment said Robert Patrick Hoffman II had served for 20 years in the US Navy, specialising as a Cryptologic Technician, which gave him access to 'classified national defense information'. Furthermore, the indictment claimed, Hoffman was accused of passing on details of 'methods to track U.S. submarines'. An FBI statement on the case pointed out: 'Criminal indictments are only charges and not evidence of guilt. A defendant is presumed to be innocent until and unless proven guilty.' Should Hoffman be convicted he could be sentenced to life in prison. In May 2013, Hoffman pleaded not guilty to a superseding indictment that he also attempted to give away documents revealing how the US Navy tracks ships of foreign navies.

The worst case, though, was in Canada, where secrets were actually successfully conveyed to the Russians over several years. A naval intelligence officer, Sub Lt Jeffery Paul Delisle, potentially revealed how the navies of Canada, the USA, Britain and other allies track Russian submarines. Arrested in January 2012, that October Delisle pleaded guilty to one charge of breach of trust and two charges of 'communicating with a foreign entity'. Four Russian diplomats were expelled from Canada because of the case. The Russian ambassador played it all down, suggesting Canadian secrets were not of that much interest compared with those of other nations, such as Pakistan or even Mali. Delisle allegedly transferred secrets – some downloaded from a shared multinational intelligence system named STONEGHOST – to his Russian handlers via an internet version of the dead-letter drop. A spy for cash, he first offered his services by visiting the Russian Embassy in Ottawa, though he later blamed the mental trauma of his marriage breaking down for his crimes. The 41-year-old officer was said to have passed on a vast amount of material between 2007 and 2011, receiving Can $111,812 in return.

In early February 2013, Sub Lieutenant Delisle was fined Can $111,817 and sentenced to 20 years. He would likely serve 18 years and five months due to time already held on remand in prison.

Delisle made a statement in court apologising to friends, family and colleagues, and in the meantime a NATO nation tried to patch up the damage done to its reputation and build bridges with angry allies. The scenario was familiar to anyone who recalled the spy scandals of the 1960s and 1970s.

But, should there be a new Cold War, it will not be waged between ideological blocs, but rather in the great game of pursuing increasingly scarce natural resources.

In fact, the early rounds have already been played out, with China butting heads at sea with Japan, the Philippines and Vietnam over various islands and resource-rich seas. America has established closer defence ties with these nations, much to Beijing's displeasure. How long before a similar scenario in the northern polar regions? The Russians have planted a metal flag on the seabed of the Lomonosov Ridge in the Arctic, seeking to claim vast oil and gas reserves that have so far remained untapped. Global warming makes them more accessible. To fund its continuing submarine construction programme and fulfil Tsar Putin's dreams of a resurgent superpower Russia, then those resources must be secured and exploited.

America, Canada, Norway and Denmark (the latter via Greenland) are all Arctic powers, too. They are wary of Russian intentions and determined to stake their own interests in the North. Can a North Atlantic power like Britain, reliant on overseas energy sources, keep out of that competition?

Can just seven new Astute Class SSNs cope with commitments both East of Suez and in the Arctic, not forgetting potential trouble in the South Atlantic?

The UK's supply lines these days do not stretch across the Atlantic but rather all the way to the Middle East and Asia–Pacific. More than 90 per cent of Britain's trade still goes by sea, and it remains reliant on energy supplies from Arabia and consumer goods from Asia. Much of its food also comes from abroad. The opening up of the Arctic may or may not create cheaper energy sources closer to home.

In any event, to not possess SSNs with the range and endurance to operate across the seven seas for months at a time would be strategic folly. Therefore, like a snake shedding skin, the Submarine Service has no choice but to bring the Astutes into service come what may.

And, as for the submariners who will take the new-generation boats to sea, in uncertain times, they can reflect with satisfaction on their forebears' victory in the Cold War. But they cannot rest on their laurels.

The new potential battleground for the hunter-killers is global – from the Arctic to the South China Sea – and today there are more players in the top division than just the USA, Britain and Russia.

Surface warships will continue to stake out claims for zones of exploitation, but wherever you find them, somewhere hidden under the sea will be a submarine. And possibly it will be trailed by another submarine ...

GLOSSARY

ABM: Anti-Ballistic Missile.

ACNS: Assistant Chief of the Naval Staff. During the Cold War this was the senior officer who acted as the First Sea Lord's troubleshooter in matters of naval policy.

AGI: Auxiliary Gatherer Intelligence; a Soviet Navy spy vessel.

ASDIC: Anti-Submarine Detection Investigation Committee – an early cover name for sonar.

ASM: Anti-Shipping Missile.

ASW: Anti-Submarine Warfare.

AUTEC: Atlantic Undersea Test and Evaluation Center, a US Navy-run submarine exercise and equipment trials area in the Bahamas.

Baffles: The zone directly behind a submarine in which the noise of screws and turbulent water makes it difficult, if not impossible, to hear whether or not an enemy is following.

Ballast tanks: Tanks external to the pressure hull that are filled with air on the surface to provide positive buoyancy and vented on diving.

Bearing: Direction of a contact measured in degrees of the compass.

Bomber: British naval slang for a ballistic missile submarine.

BRNC: Britannia Royal Naval College. The officer training school of the Royal Navy, located at Dartmouth in Devon.

Bulkhead: A steel 'wall' in a ship, forming a sub-division within the vessel.

CACS: Computer Assisted Command System. As fitted to major surface combatants of the Royal Navy in the latter part of the Cold War, including Broadsword Class (Type 22, Batch 2) frigates.

Casing: Free-flooding superstructure on a submarine, providing a walkway for use when on the surface and a streamlined outer skin around fixtures and fittings.

CDS: Chief of the Defence Staff.

CIA: Central Intelligence Agency.

CO: Commanding Officer, or captain, of a submarine or other naval/military unit.

Control Room: The nerve centre of the submarine, from which the vessel is operated and commanded.

CT: Communications Technician.

DEFCON: American Defense-Readiness Condition. DEFCON 1 was 'at war' (with the possibility of a nuclear exchange) while DEFCON 5 was normal peace conditions ('no threat'). During the Cuban Missile Crisis the USA's armed forces went to DEFCON 2 ('on guard' for war). They were put at DEFCON 3 ('on standby') during the Yom Kippur War. DEFCON 4 was an alert state in which there was intelligence of potential threats (and awareness the status could change at any time).

Diesel: A non-nuclear-powered (also known as 'conventional') submarine, with diesel-electric propulsion. Such a design requires access to air, in order to operate diesel generators and recharge batteries (used for submerged running) and also to ventilate.

***Dolphin*:** Short form for HMS *Dolphin*, the Royal Navy shore base at Gosport, Hampshire, which was the spiritual home of the Submarine Service from 1901 until the early 1990s.

Echo sounder: Downward-pointing sonar used to measure depth beneath the keel. An upward-pointing one is used in under-ice operations.

ESM: Electronic Support Measures. ESM systems detect, locate and identify radiated electromagnetic energy from sources such as radio and radar transmissions, for the purposes of threat recognition. These sources can be countered ('jammed') by the use of Electronic Counter-Measure (ECM) systems.

Fin: The vertical structure on the hull of a submarine enclosing the masts (periscopes, radar, Electronic Counter-Measure, Snort etc.), with a conning (ship control) position (also known as 'the bridge') at the top for navigation on the surface. Connected to the inside of the boat via the conning tower, which is sealed by top and bottom hatches. Known in the US Navy and other navies as the Sail.

First Sea Lord: Uniformed head of the Royal Navy who is responsible for matters of naval policy. Also known as Chief of Naval Staff.

Fleet submarine: Alternate British term for SSN.

FOSM: Flag Officer Submarines, the uniformed head of the Submarine Service.

FOST: Flag Officer Sea Training. Boss of the organisation that to this day prepares all British and some NATO naval units for front-line operations.

FOTI: Fleet Operational and Tactical Instructions.

Galley: A ship's kitchen.

GIUK: Greenland–Iceland–United Kingdom Gap, covering the principal avenues of entry into the North Atlantic used by the Russians – likely to be a NATO-enforced chokepoint in any hot war. *See map.*

Helmsman: Sailor who controls the rudder of the submarine.

HTP: High Test Peroxide. Highly volatile liquid propellant used in some torpedoes and missiles.

Hunter-killer: Nuclear-powered submarine designed to hunt and kill enemy submarines and surface ships using torpedoes. Can launch ASM and also cruise missiles against land targets. *See SSN and Fleet submarine.*

Hydroplanes: Horizontal control surfaces mounted on the bows or fin of a submarine, and also at the stern to control the attitude, and depth, of the vessel under the water.

ICBM: Intercontinental Ballistic Missile.

Kiloton: Expression of explosive yield in a nuclear-tipped weapon. In this case equal to a thousand tons of high explosive. A megaton possesses the same explosive power as 1,000,000 tons of HE.

Knots: Speed of a ship or aircraft expressed at a rate of nautical miles per hour.

MAD: Mutually Assured Destruction. The balance of terror between the two sides in the Cold War, meaning that one could not attack the other with nuclear weapons without guaranteeing its own destruction.

Main Vent: A hydraulically operated valve at the top of a ballast tank that allows air to be vented out, thereby allowing water to free-flood into the tank via holes at the bottom.

MEO: Marine Engineer Officer.

MIRV: Multiple Independently Targetable Re-entry Vehicles, as mounted in nuclear missiles.

Mk8 (or Mk VIII): Unguided diesel-powered British torpedo.

Mk23 and Mk24 ('Tigerfish'): Wire-guided electric (battery-powered) British homing torpedoes.

MoD: Ministry of Defence.

MPA: Maritime Patrol Aircraft.

NATO: North Atlantic Treaty Organisation. A Western defence alliance formed in 1948 composed of European nations, but also including Canada and the USA. Still exists and has since the end of the Cold War expanded to include a number of states previously under the sway of, or occupied by, the Soviet Union.

Nautical mile: Equivalent to 1.15 land miles, 2,000 yards or a minute of latitude.

NIR: Naval Intelligence Reports.

O-boat: Oberon Class diesel submarine operated by the Royal Navy and other friendly navies.

OOW: Officer of the Watch.

P-boat: Porpoise Class diesel submarine operated by the Royal Navy.

Planesman: Sailor who operates the submarine's hydroplanes.

Polynya: Open stretch of water in an ice field.

Pressure hull: Tough inner hull that can withstand pressure at great depth to protect the machinery and equipment of the boat and the lives of the crew.

Rating: Non-commissioned sailor, whether junior or senior, including Petty Officers and Chief Petty Officers.

RCN: Royal Canadian Navy.

Revs: Revolutions per minute on the screw (or screws).

RN: Royal Navy.

RP: Radar Plotter.

SALT: Strategic Arms Limitation Treaty.

S-boat: Swiftsure Class nuclear-powered submarine of the Royal Navy.

SDI: Strategic Defense Initiative.

Sevmash: Russian submarine building yard at Severodvinsk on the White Sea.

Signature: *Noise* (or *Sound*) signature is unique to every vessel and relates to the noise generated underwater by a vessel's propellers, engines and auxiliary machinery. *Electronic* signature relates to the electronic emissions radiated into the atmosphere by a vessel's communications and radar systems. This may be more generic, relating to nationality and/or operational capabilities and missions.

SINS: Ship's Inertial Navigation System.

SLBM: Submarine-Launched Ballistic Missile.

SM: Submarine squadron. For example the Third Submarine Squadron (SM3) was based at Faslane in Scotland, while SM2 was the Devonport squadron and SM6 the Halifax-based unit, and so on.

Snort: The means by which a submerged diesel-engine submarine draws in fresh air for running the engine (to recharge batteries down the induction mast) and exhausts engine fumes (via the exhaust mast).

SOA: Speed of Advance. Average speed maintained as opposed to actual speed at any instant, which may vary from time to time.

Sonar: Sound navigation and ranging. A technology employing underwater sound propagation to detect objects on or under the surface of the water. *Passive* sonar listens for the sound made by vessels. *Active* sonar emits pulses of sound and listens for echoes. The sounds are detected on *hydrophones* and analysed electronically using computers.

SOSUS: Sound Surveillance Underwater System. Passive seabed hydrophones of immense sensitivity linked to land-based listening stations. Used by NATO to detect Soviet submarines and surface warships over vast distances.

SSBN: Nuclear-powered submarine carrying nuclear-tipped ballistic missiles.

SSK: Diesel-electric patrol submarine.

SSN: Nuclear-powered attack submarine.

Super-T: A Second World War-built T-Class submarine converted after the war via insertion of a middle section containing more compartments, including for special intelligence gathering. Super-T modifications also involved installing more-powerful batteries, removal of the 4-inch gun and fitting a new streamlined casing, including fin structure.

T-boat: Trafalgar Class nuclear-powered submarine of the Royal Navy.

Tinfish: Slang for torpedo.

Towed array: Very sensitive hydrophones packed inside a sleeve and towed at some distance behind a submarine to increase their powers of detection.

Trim: Achieving a state of neutral buoyancy whereby the submarine requires mimimal use of hydroplanes to maintain depth.

Type XXI: Advanced Second World War-era German diesel submarine (U-boat). Captured examples proved useful for both sides in the early Cold War as a basis for improving their own submarine flotillas.

USN: United States Navy.

USSR: Union of Soviet Socialist Republics. A highly centralised union of states under the rule of Russia during the Cold War, founded in December 1922 and dissolved in December 1991.

Warsaw Pact: Defence alliance formed by the Soviet Union in 1955 with satellite nations, devised as a counter to NATO. Dissolved in July 1991.

XO: Executive Officer. In a submarine the most senior officer of the Seaman specialisation. He is also variously known as the 'XO', the 'First Lieutenant', the 'Jimmy' and sometimes 'Jimmy the One'. Also second-in-command and in nuclear-powered boats fully qualified for command.

BIBLIOGRAPHY AND SOURCES

Factual

In constructing the narrative of this book, a vast array of relevant literature was consulted, whether to fix the naval waypoints of the era, weave the background tapestry or retrieve relevant technical detail. Not least among them was a surprisingly wide selection of books written by retired British submariners (some rather senior). Published during the Cold War, or shortly thereafter, those books in particular presented a wealth of truly in-depth information on undersea warfare tactics, weapons and strategy.

Admiralty Manual of Seamanship, Volume I, HMSO, 1964

Aldrich, Richard J., *GCHQ*, Harper Press, 2011

Allaway, Jim, *The Navy in the News 1954–1991*, HMSO, 1993

Anderson, Commander William and Chay Blair, *Nautilus 90 North*, Hodder, 1961

Andrew, Christopher and Vasili Mitrokhin, *The Mitrokhin Archive*, Penguin, 2000

Ballantyne, Iain, *Warspite*, Pen & Sword, 2001

—, *HMS London*, Pen & Sword, 2003

—, *Strike from the Sea*, Naval Institute Press, 2004

Barnett, Correlli, *The Lost Victory*, Pan, 1996

Bishop, Chris, ed., *The Encyclopedia of World Sea Power*, Guild, 1988

Blackman, Raymond V. B., *The World's Warships*, Macdonald, 1969

Blake, George, *No Other Choice*, Jonathan Cape, 1990

Bonds, Ray, ed., *The Soviet War Machine*, Salamander, 1977

Brown, Ashley, Sam Elder, Adrian Gilbert and Richard Williams, eds, *War in Peace*, Harmony, 1985

Bulloch, John and Henry Miller, *Spy Ring*, Secker & Warburg, 1961

Chatfield, Admiral of the Fleet, Lord, *The Navy and Defence*, Windmill, 1942

Clancy, Tom, *Submarine,* HarperCollins, 1997

Compton-Hall, Commander Richard, *Sub v Sub*, Crown, 1988

—, *Submarines and the War at Sea, 1914–18*, Macmillan, 1991

—, ed., *The Submariner's World*, Kenneth Mason, 1983

Conway's All the World's Fighting Ships, Conway Maritime Press, 1984

Coote, Commander John, *Submariner,* Leo Cooper, 1991

Courtney, Commander Anthony, *Sailor in a Russian Frame*, Johnson, 1968

Crane, Jonathan, *Submarine*, BBC, 1984

Darman, Peter, ed., *Warfare at Sea*, Blitz Editions, 1997

DeGroot, Gerard, *The Sixties Unplugged*, Pan, 2009

—, *The Seventies Unplugged*, Macmillan, 2010

Edmonds, Martin, *100 Years of the Trade*, CDISS, 2001

Fisher, Admiral, Lord, *Records*, Hodder & Stoughton, 1919

Forsyth, Robert, *A Parish at War,* Oxon Publishing, 2012

Freedman, Sir Lawrence, *The Official History of the Falklands Campaign*, Vol. II, Routledge, 2005

—, *The Cold War*, Cassell, 2001

Friedman, Norman, *The Cold War Experience*, Carlton, 2005

Gaddis, John Lewis, *The Cold War*, Penguin, 2007

Gray, Edwyn, *British Submarines in the Great War*, Pen & Sword, 2001

Ham, Paul, *Hiroshima Nagasaki,* Doubleday, 2012

Hastings, Max, and Simon Jenkins, *The Battle for the Falklands*, Pan, 1983

Hennessey, Thomas and Claire Thomas, *Spooks*, Amberley, 2011

Hennessy, Peter, *The Secret State*, Penguin, 2010

Hervey, Rear Admiral John, *Submarines*, Brassey's, 1994

Hill, Rear Admiral J. R., *Anti-Submarine Warfare*, Ian Allan, 1984

—, ed., *History of the Royal Navy*, Oxford University Press, 1995

Hoffman, David E., *The Dead Hand*, Icon, 2011

Hool, Jack and Keith Nutter, *Damned Un-English Machines*, The History Press, 2003

Hore, Captain Peter, *The Habit of Victory*, Sidgwick & Jackson, 2005

Huchthausen, Peter A., *October Fury*, John Wiley, 2002

—, *K19, The Widowmaker*, National Geographic, 2002

Huchthausen, Peter, Igor Kurdin and R. Alan White, *Hostile Waters*, Arrow, 1998

Hutchinson, Robert, *Weapons of Mass Destruction*, Weidenfeld and Nicolson, 2003

—, *Jane's Warships Recognition Guide*, 2002

Hutchinson, Robert, and Tony Gibbons, *Jane's Submarines: War beneath the Waves*, 2001

Humble, Richard, *The Rise and Fall of the British Navy*, Queen Anne Press, 1986

Hunters of the Deep, Time Life Inc., 1990

International Electronic Countermeasures Handbook 2004, Horizon House/Journal of Electronic Defense Staff

Ireland, Bernard, and Eric Grove, *Jane's War at Sea 1897–1997*, Harper-Collins, 1997

Isaacs, Jeremy, and Taylor Downing, *Cold War*, Abacus, 2008

Jordan, John, *Soviet Submarines*, Arms and Armour, 1989

—, *Soviet Warships 1945 to the Present*, Arms and Armour, 1992

Kemp, Paul, *Submarine Action*, Sutton, 1999

Lee, R. G., *Defence Terminology*, Brassey's, 1991

Lipscomb, Commander F. W., *The British Submarine*, Conway Maritime Press, 1975

Maclean, Malcolm, *Naval Accidents*, Maritime Books, 2008

Marriot, Leo, *Type 22*, Ian Allan, 1986

McGeoch, Ian, *Mountbatten of Burma*, J. J. Haynes and Co. Ltd, 2009

McLaren, Captain Alfred S., USN, *Unknown Waters*, The University of Alabama Press, 2008

Meyer, Christopher, *Getting Our Way*, Weidenfeld and Nicolson, 2009

Miller, David, *U-Boats*, Conway, 2000

Miller, Nathan, *The US Navy*, Naval Institute Press, 1997

Moore, Captain J. E., *The Soviet Navy Today*, PBS, 1975

—, ed., *The Impact of Polaris*, Richard Netherwood, 1999

—, ed., *Jane's 1982–83 Naval Review*, Jane's, 1982

Moore, Captain J. E., and Commander Richard Compton-Hall, *Submarine Warfare*, Michael Joseph, 1986

Moore, Robert, *A Time to Die – The Kursk Disaster*, Doubleday, 2002

Moynahan, Brian, *The Claws of the Bear*, Hutchinson, 1989

Offley, Ed, *Scorpion Down*, Basic, 2007

Parker, John, *The Silent Service*, Headline, 2001

Polmar, Norman, ed., *The Modern Soviet Navy*, Arms and Armour, 1979

Polmar, Norman, and K. J. Moore, *Cold War Submarines*, Potomac, 2003

Polmar, Norman and Michael White, *Project Azorian*, Naval Institute Press, 2010

Pope, Frank, *72 Hours*, Orion, 2012

Prebble, Stuart, *Secrets of the Conqueror*, Faber and Faber, 2012

Preston, Antony, *The Royal Navy Submarine Service*, Conway, 2001

Rankin, Nicholas, *Ian Fleming's Commandos*, Faber and Faber, 2011

Reagan, Ronald, *An American Life*, Threshold, 2011

Ring, Jim, *We Come Unseen*, John Murray, 2001

Roberts, John, *Safeguarding the Nation*, Seaforth, 2009

Rogers, Paul, *Guide to Nuclear Weapons*, Berg, 1988

Rossiter, Mike, *Sink the Belgrano*, Bantam, 2007

Sasgen, Peter, *Stalking the Red Bear*, St. Martin's, 2009

Schofield, Carey, *Inside the Soviet Army*, Headline, 1991

Sontag, Sherry, Christopher Drew and Annette Lawrence Drew, *Blind Man's Bluff*, Arrow, 2000

Southby-Tailyour, Ewen, *HMS Fearless*, Pen & Sword, 2006

Tall, Commander J. J. and Paul Kemp, *HM Submarines in Camera*, Sutton, 1998

Thatcher, Margaret, *The Downing Street Years*, HarperCollins, 1993

Tietjen, Arthur, *Soviet Spy Ring*, Pan, 1961

Tunander, Ola, *The Secret War against Sweden*, Routledge, 2004

Turner, John Frayn, *VCs of the Royal Navy*, Harrap, 1956

Twigge, Stephen, Edward Hampshire and Graham Macklin, *British Intelligence*, The National Archives, 2009

Van der Vat, Dan, *Stealth at Sea*, Weidenfeld & Nicolson, 1994

—, *Standard of Power*, Hutchinson, 2000

Vassall, John, *Vassall – The Autobiography of a Spy*, Sidgwick and Jackson, 1975

Walker, Martin, *The Cold War*, Vintage, 1994

Walmer, Max, *Modern Naval Warfare*, Salamander, 1989

Wapshott, Nicholas, *Ronald Reagan and Margaret Thatcher*, Sentinel, 2008

Weiner, Tim, *Legacy of Ashes*, Penguin, 2008

Weir, Gary E. and Walter J. Boyne, *Rising Tide*, Basic, 2003

Wertheim, Eric, ed., *Combat Fleets of the World*, 15th Edition, Naval Institute Press, 2007

West, Nigel, *A Matter of Trust*, Weidenfeld and Nicolson, 1982

—, *The Illegals*, Hodder & Stoughton, 1994

Wettern, Desmond, *The Decline of British Seapower*, Jane's, 1982

White, Rowland, *Phoenix Squadron*, Bantam, 2009

—, *Vulcan 607*, Corgi, 2007

Whitestone, Cdr Nicholas, *The Submarine: The Ultimate Weapon*, Davis-Poynter, 1973

Winton, John, *The Submariners*, Constable, 2001

Wolfe, Tom, *The Right Stuff*, Bantam, 1980

Woodward, David, *The Russians at Sea*, William Kimber, 1965

Woodward, Admiral Sandy, *One Hundred Days*, HarperCollins, 1992

Ziegler, Philip, *Mountbatten*, HarperCollins, 1985

Fiction

Whether seeking inspiration about the savage sea, insight into the Cold War mentality of suspicion and dread, or the mechanics of submarine life, tactics and technology, these books provided a surprising amount of insight (and, in the case of Tom Clancy's work, some truths cloaked in thrills and spills).

Clancy, Tom, *The Hunt for Red October*, HarperCollins, 1985
—, *Red Storm Rising*, Fontana, 1988
—, *SSN*, HarperCollins, 1997. *SSN* was groundbreaking in being a novel based on a successful computer game devised by Red Storm Entertainment, which was founded by Clancy and Littlejohns in 1996. As such *SSN* includes an interesting Q&A between Clancy, Doug Littlejohns and a journalist, James Adams.
Fleming, Ian, *Moonraker*, Pan, 1963
Hackett, General Sir John, and others, *The Third World War*, Sphere, 1979
le Carré, John, *Tinker Tailor Soldier Spy*, Sceptre, 2009
—, *The Russia House*, Sceptre, 2000
MacLean, Alistair, *Ice Station Zebra*, Fontana, 1963
Melville, Herman, *Moby-Dick*, Wordsworth, 1992
Shute, Nevil, *On the Beach*, Vintage, 2009
Verne, Jules, *20,000 Leagues under the Sea*, Wordsworth, 1992

Privately published memoirs

Jenner, Stephen, with Peter Haydon, *Ambrosia: A Scrapbook of the Sixth Submarine Squadron at Work and Play*, 2004
Middleton, Patrick, *Admiral Clanky Entertains*, 2010
Wixon, David, and Michael Pittkeathley and others, *Submarine Courageous – Cold War Warrior*, HMS *Courageous* Association, 2010

Newspapers, magazines and periodicals

Newspapers (and other news sources)
The Age, 8 September, 2006
    Article on Cold War-era Royal Australian Navy submarine spying missions.
Barents Observer, 6 May 2013
    Report on Russian Navy missile submarines spending most of their time in port. Based on analysis report by the Federation of American Scientists. *See below.*

Belfast Telegraph, 12 November 2012; *Daily Telegraph*, 13 November 2012; *Daily Mail*, 12 December 2012

Court reports on sentencing and the trial of the British submariner Edward Devenney for trying to give secrets to the Russians.

CBC News, 10 October 2012; *Globe and Mail*, 12 October 2012, 22 October 2012, 8 February 2013; *National Post*, 8 February 2013

All the above reports on the Jeffrey Delisle case in Canada.

Daily Telegraph, 24 August 2000

Letter from Ted Johnson (member of HMS *Warspite*'s crew in 1968) referring to the Barents as 'Sea of Collisions' and mentioning his SSN's 'shunt' with a Russian Echo II, and aftermath.

Daily Telegraph, 27 August 2010

According to this news item, 'senior Navy officers' said an Akula Class submarine tried to trail a British SSBN.

Dorset Daily Echo and Weymouth Dispatch, 16 June 1955

HMS *Sidon*'s explosion.

Guardian, 18 September 1962

Anti-nuclear protests in Trafalgar Square and Holy Loch.

Herald, Glasgow, 4 December 1982; *Nashua Telegraph*, 6 December 1982; *The Day*, 6 December 1982

Coverage of Zotov's expulsion from the UK for spying.

Herald, Glasgow, 22 March 2007

Chris Paton on his dad's experiences during HMS *Warspite*'s collision with an Echo II submarine in October 1968.

Independent on Sunday, 1 October 2006

Profile of George Blake.

Japan Times, 17 November 2004

Suspected Chinese submarine tracked off Guam by US Navy.

Miami Herald, 16 July 1998

Feature about the CIA's involvement in the Bay of Pigs invasion.

The News, Portsmouth, 7, 10 and 11 October 1972

Coverage of the Maureen Bingham trial.

The News, Portsmouth, 29 November 1979

Soviet revelations of alleged Bingham secrets.

The News, Portsmouth, 5 April 2002

Maureen Bingham's retrospective account of her husband's espionage exploits and the impact on their family.

The News, Portsmouth, 1 July 2003

Article by Defence Reporter Richard Hargreaves on the exploits of Cold War submarines of the Royal Navy during the 1950s, with a focus on HMS *Turpin*. Includes detailed testimony by Tony Beasley on the perils *Turpin* and her men faced, including attack by Soviet naval forces.

The New York Times, 18 December 1982

News item on the connection between the British naval attaché in Moscow being ordered home and Zotov's earlier exit from UK.

The New York Times, 4 August 2009

Russian submarines detected off the east coast of the USA and Canada.

North West Evening Mail, 5 July 2006

Barrow-in-Furness-based newspaper asks 'Did the Russians Hit Barrow Sub?'

North West Evening Mail, 8 July 2006

Retired submariner Graham Salmon says Echo II doing a 'Crazy Ivan' hit *Warspite*.

Sunday Independent, 14 June 1981

Report on HMS *Sceptre*'s collision with an 'iceberg'.

Sunday Times (Australia), 16 June 2012

Report on the intelligence-gathering exploits against Chinese targets of HMAS *Farncomb* in 2007.

The Times, 14, 15 and 17 March 1972

Reports of David Bingham's trial.

The Times, 22 October 2002

Letter from Vice Admiral Toby Frere, former Flag Officer Submarines, on British submarines in the Cuban Missile Crisis. He also wrote at length on this topic in *Ambrosia*, the privately published account of operations by Sixth Submarine Squadron. *See above.* Frere's contribution to *Ambrosia* was entitled 'Pass the Marmalade – What Missile Crisis?'

Washington Free Beacon, 14 August 2012

Claim of Russian SSN patrolling Gulf of Mexico.

Washington Free Beacon, 5 November 2012

Russian Sierra 2 submarine off US Eastern Seaboard and AGI in Florida port.

Western Evening Herald, 17 and 22 August 1968

Reports on *Warspite*'s first visit to Plymouth and Devonport.

Western Morning News, 25 November 1996

Profile of Lt Cdr Dick Raikes (by the author).

Magazines, periodicals and miscellaneous reports
Australian Financial Review, 28 November 2003
> A very detailed insight – entitled 'The Mystery Boats' – into Australian diesel submarine espionage exploits against the Chinese and Russians during the Cold War, including underwater looks. Written by Geoffrey Barker, who interviewed Rear Admiral Peter Clarke (former RN submarine captain).

Bulletin of the Atomic Scientists, March 1982
> Milton Leitenberg, 'The Case of the Stranded Sub' – a discussion of the issues surrounding the running aground of the Soviet submarine *S-363* in Swedish waters.

Defence Management Journal, July 2009
> Article by Commander Jeff Tall, entitled 'Past and present danger'. It looks at the risks of operating submarines, particularly SSNs. Includes explanation of the 'Operating Envelope'. Also mentions various incidents including HMS *Valiant*'s broaching of the surface in the 1970s due to technical failure.

FAS [Federation of American Scientists] Strategic Security Blog, 3 May 2013.
> Analysis report by Hans M. Kristensen entitled 'Russian SSBN Fleet: Modernizing But Not Sailing Much.' Kristensen used US Naval Intelligence data obtained via the Freedom of Information Act (FOIA).

Global Force 2007
> Official Royal Navy publication, featuring an account of HMS *Conqueror*'s Falklands War deployment by Vice Admiral Tim McClement.

In Depth, October 2010
> Frederick Rodgers' account of HMS *Alcide*'s iceberg peril.

Journal for Maritime Research, September 2001
> Professor Brian Lavery on 'The British government and the American Polaris base in the Clyde [Holy Loch]'.

Metro, April 2000
> US-based magazine, profile of Doug Littlejohns as submarine captain and CEO of Red Storm Entertainment.

Naval History Magazine, June 2010
> Article on the Walker spy case by John Prados in a US-based magazine.

Naval Review, October 1972; October 1973
> Commentaries on the Bingham case and its meaning for the Royal Navy.

Navy News, April 1971

Account of HMS *Dreadnought*'s voyage to North Pole.

Navy News, October 1979

Report on Admiral Lord Mountbatten's visit to HMS *Superb*.

Northern Mariner, April 2007

Peter Haydon on Canada's part in the Cuban Missile Crisis.

Observer magazine, 22 May 1983

Special multi-page article, *The Most Secret Service*, providing a deep look at the Cold War beneath the sea as it unfolded, particularly British aspects.

Proceedings, Naval Review Issue, May 1971

Published by the United States Naval Institute, it includes two relevant items. *The Defense [sic] of Northwest Europe and the North Sea*, by Major General J. L. Moulton RMs, looks at how NATO would respond to Soviet maritime attacks and a land offensive. *Soviet Naval Activities, 1970*, by Robert W. Daly, includes a look at Okean 1970 and other Russian Navy developments. A warts and all chronicle of developments at sea, called *Naval and Maritime Events July 1970 – December 1970*, includes accidents and crashes, the growing Soviet submarine threat, activities of Russian AGIs and HMS *Ark Royal*'s collision with a Soviet warship.

Time, 24 March 1958

Account of Mars Bluff incident.

Time, 5 May 1975

Report on the Soviet Navy's Okean '75 exercise.

Time, 13 December 1982

Zotov's expulsion from the UK mentioned in an item on recent spy cases.

Tribune, 17 February 1967

Article on the visit to the UK of the Soviet Premier, Alexei Kosygin.

WARSHIPS International Fleet Review, September 2009

'Out of the Shadows' – a review of the play *Kursk*, and interview with its creators, revealing the high level of input provided by the Royal Navy on SSN operations. *See below.*

WARSHIPS International Fleet Review, July and August 2012

Two-part profile of the UK's Polaris missile system by Commander John Coker.

World Policy Journal Blog, 26 September 2012

Alleged British submarine operations discussed in an article entitled 'Secrets of the Baltic'.

Obituaries

Vice Admiral Sir Geoffrey Biggs, *Daily Telegraph*, 3 July 2002
Vice Admiral Sir Ian McGeoch, *Daily Telegraph,* 17 August 2007
Captain John Moore, *Scotsman*, 26 August 2010
Lieutenant Commander Dick Raikes, *Daily Telegraph*, 28 June 2005

Museums and others

Royal Navy Submarine Museum
RNSM, A1994/163

Essay on his deployments into the Barents 1959–60 by Lt Cdr Alfie Roake. Detailed first-hand account of early forays into the Barents Sea.

RNSM/A2007/35

Diary kept by Leading Engineer Mechanic M. Hurley during HMS *Taciturn*'s deployments into the Barents 1957–58.

RNSM/A207/302

'Some Light-Heart Memories', unpublished memoir of Lt Cdr Dick Raikes.

RNSM/L/10479

Notes from an interview with Cdr Rob Forsyth for a museum audio-visual project, about his career in the Navy and time as Commanding Officer of HMS *Alliance*.

Canadian Naval Memorial
The Cuban Missile Crisis

Account published 2011.

Hansard

Transcripts of various debates on issues connected with the Cuban Missile Crisis (1962), nuclear submarine construction (especially in the 1960s and 1970s), the state of the Royal Navy (1960s–1980s), and also the potential risk caused by alleged British and NATO submarine missions in the Barents.

House of Commons Debate transcripts: 25 October and 30 October 1962, 15 February and 7 February 1968, 28 January 1970, 16 December 1974, 4 March 1977, 19 June 1978, 21 December 1982, 2 February 1987. Also, House of Lords Debate, 13 June 1961, on issues relating to the Romer Report into the Portland Spy Ring.

Margaret Thatcher Foundation
Cold War: Reykjavik (Reagan–Gorbachev) Summit
Transcripts of meetings between Reagan and Gorbachev in the Hofdi House, Reykjavik, and other relevant documents, including assessment by the American Embassy in London of the UK media's reaction to proposals aired at Iceland.

John F. Kennedy Presidential Library and Museum
A treasure trove of documents relating to the Cuban Missile Crisis and other Cold War issues. *See websites below.*

Central Intelligence Agency
Assessment articles commissioned by the CIA (recently declassified):
Robert Fulton's Skyhook and Operation Coldfeet
Unravelling a Cold War Mystery – The ALFA SSN: Challenging Paradigms, Finding New Truths, 1969–79. Written by Gerhardt Thamm.

The National Archives (UK)
DEFE/69/196–200
David Bingham's testimony to Special Branch and other papers relating to the case, including formerly secret assessments of damage caused by the submariner's espionage on behalf of the Soviets.
PREM 13
Briefing letter on the incident in which the *Dreadnought* and other British units pursued a Russian submarine during a 1967 visit to the UK by the Soviet premier.
PREM/19/416
Papers relating to the defence review carried out by the Secretary of State for Defence, John Nott, in 1981.

Royal Canadian Navy
Profile of Vice Admiral Kenneth Lloyd Dyer
Flag Officer Atlantic Coast at time of Cuban Missile Crisis.

US Navy
Submarine Warfare Division, Chronology
Chief of Naval Operations paper published 1999.
The Third Battle: Innovation in the U.S. Navy's Silent Cold Struggle
Paper by Dr Owen R. Cote, of MIT, available via US Navy and includes a look at the Soviet Navy's bastion concept.

Press releases dated 30 and 31 January 2012, on Exercise Fellowship 2012, during which HMS *Astute* and the USS *New Mexico* engaged in submarine versus submarine combat training.

Richard M. Nixon, Presidential Materials
Declassified US State Department assessment of the nuclear balance of terror, made in 1969.

Federal Bureau of Investigation
Case profiles for John Walker and Ronald William Pelton
Official account of 'The Year of the Spy'
Press release, 6 December 2012, on the indictment of the former US Navy sailor Robert Patrick Hoffman II by a federal grand jury, 'for attempting to provide classified information to individuals who he believed to be representatives of the Russian Federation'. In May 2013 AP reported that Hoffman pleaded not guilty to further espionage charges.

Other
Court document, 5 December 2012
United States District Court, Eastern District of Virginia, Norfolk Division. United States of America v Robert Patrick Hoffman II, federal grand jury indictment.

Personal accounts
In July 1964, when his submarine paused at Gibraltar on her way back to the UK, **Tim Hale** wrote and submitted a piece on *Dreadnought*'s transatlantic voyage (entitled 'The World is Flat') to *Navigation and Direction Bulletin*. In the late 1960s his essay entitled 'The Cruise of the Nuclear Woodpecker', about *Warspite*'s voyage to and from Singapore, was also published in a professional journal. Hale wrote about his time in *Swiftsure* in an article entitled 'Late Runs Ashore', which detailed some of his adventures from the late 1950s to the early 1970s. It was published in *All Round Look*, the journal of the Society of Friends of the Royal Navy Submarine Museum (RNSM).

Dan Conley writes about his time as XO of *Spartan* on a Northern patrol in an essay entitled 'From Barrow to Bear Island', published in the US-based *Submarine Review* (January 2011) and UK-based *The Naval Review* (around the same time). Both are journals for professional naval officers. Dan Conley wrote about his HMS *Valiant* adventures in an article entitled 'The Black Pig and the Red Banner Fleet', first published in *The Naval Review*, February 2009. Dan Conley's article 'Royal Navy Under-Ice Torpedo Firings ICEX 88', published in the *Submarine Review* (January 2010), also details his adventures on the ice. Conley writes about his experiences on assignment with the US Navy's Submarine Development Squadron Twelve in a freely available paper entitled 'A Royal Navy Exchange Perspective 1955 – 2001'. This document also contains detailed insider perspectives on Anglo-American SSN tactics development from other RN submarine captains.

Colin Paton kindly provided a written account of the *Warspite*'s 'iceberg' (Echo II) collision and its aftermath.

At the time of the 10th anniversary of the Falklands War, I was accorded the rare privilege of interviewing **Chris Wreford-Brown** about his time as captain of HMS *Conqueror* during the conflict. A useful secondary source to back-up details during my interview was provided by his own account, entitled *Conqueror's War Patrol*, in John Winston's book, *The Submariners*.

Select websites

For more than just WW2 German submarines:
www.Uboat.net

Various submarines have their own websites, run by former members of their crews. Some that proved useful in fleshing out this book are:
www.hmsresolution.org.uk
www.hmscourageous.co.uk
www.hmsdreadnought.co.uk
www.hms-repulse.co.uk

Barrow Submariners website, which features a profile of SSN *Warspite*'s career including brief details of collision with Echo II and aftermath:
www.rnsubs.co.uk

Account from Soviet Navy perspective of collision between a NATO SSN (HMS *Sceptre*) and the Russian ballistic missile submarine *K-211*:
www.submarine.id.ru
Or
www.shipandship.chat.ru/avar/022.htm

Two accounts of the same collision:
redbannernorthernfleet.blogspot.co.uk/2008/05/soviet-submarine-disaster-of-day_26.html

Submarine and submariner-accented discussion on various topics, including some interesting stuff from retired submariners, not least Ian Wragg on *Warspite*'s collision:

www.subsim.com

Or see:

www.subsim.com/radioroom/showthread.php?t=95492&page=2

For David Krieger's article/Q&A entitled 'Jimmy Carter on Morality and Nuclear Weapons' visit:

www.wagingpeace.org/articles/db_article.php?article_id=47

President Carter's Farewell Address (14 January, 1981):

www.jimmycarterlibrary.gov/documents/speeches/farewell.phtml

President John F. Kennedy papers:

www.jfklibrary.org

Margaret Thatcher Foundation:

www.margaretthatcher.org

For Hansard 1803 – 2005 archive:

www.parliament.uk

Transcript of the video conference [involving President Vladimir Putin] with Defence Minister Sergei Shoigu reporting from the nuclear-powered missile submarine *Yuri Dolgoruky*, 10 January 2013.

www.eng.kremlin.ru/transcripts/4853

Television (documentary) & other visual media

Vice Admiral Tim McClement, video interview with British Forces News, May 2012, about his time as XO of HMS *Conqueror* during the Falklands War. *Viewed via Internet.*

ITN news video. Clip Ref: AS031282009 0/ITN. Trevor McDonald interviews Dr David Owen about the Zotov affair. *Viewed via Internet.*

Cold War, a landmark 24-part series for CNN broadcast in 1998, featuring the inside story from key participants who were on both sides of the East–West confrontation. Includes Captain Igor Kurdin on the dangers at sea in the 1980s. *Viewed on VHS/DD Home Entertainment.*

An officer who had served in HMS *Sceptre*, David Forghan, was interviewed on national television in the UK – *This Week* (aired 19 September 1991) – about the SSN's May 1981 collision with an alleged 'iceberg'. The author has not seen the video – though Forghan is quoted in Prebble's book and elsewhere. *See Bibliography.*

Submarine Patrol (aired September 2011, Channel 5) provided an insight into contemporary British SSN missions. Featuring HMS *Turbulent* and her crew, the operational focus of the series was especially on the boat standing by for cruise missile strikes off Libya and on anti-piracy tasks in the Indian Ocean. *Viewed on DVD/*demand*dvd*

HMS Splendid provided a good insight into life aboard an S-boat, including testing and firing the first-ever submarine-launched cruise missile. The BBC series (aired 1999) also takes viewers aboard HMS *Trafalgar* for a Perisher course. *Viewed on DVD/DD Home Entertainment.*

The US Navy has produced a highly detailed dramatised insight into various intelligence gathering/ASW techniques on a released (declassified) video. Episodes illustrated in detail: the USS *Batfish* trail of a Yankee SSBN in the Norwegian Sea and Atlantic (17 March 1978); a Cold War-era Missile Test Observation mission in 'international waters' by a USN boat (using actual periscope footage of a Soviet Navy surface warship launching a new type of missile and its impact on an aerial target); 'Underhull Survey Training' (including animated graphics and periscope footage of what the RN calls an underwater look on a surface warship). US Navy attack submarines and their crews are used to accurately show how the Control Room would function in such complex missions, from the captain on the scope to the planesmen.

Movies (DVD), TV (drama, DVD) and Theatre (drama)

Of course it is essential to separate fact from fiction, but there is always some interplay between the two. Provided you take a pinch of salt – and know the actual reality – digesting these works can yield a feel for the era and some emotional insight. Some of them are submarine movies, while others are about Cold War espionage or imminent nuclear Armageddon. There has also in recent years been a play that has lifted the veil of secrecy drawn across British submarine operations in the Arctic.

Movies
The Bedford Incident (Sony, 2004)
Crimson Tide (Walt Disney, 2002)
Das Boot – The Director's Cut (Columbia Tristar, 1998)
Dr Strangelove (Sony Pictures, 2002)
Fail-Safe (Sony, 2007)
Farewell (Universal, 2011)
For Your Eyes Only (MGM, 2000)
The Hunt for Red October (Paramount, 2003)
The Ipcress File (Network, 2006)
K-19 – The Widowmaker (Paramount, 2003)

No Way Out (MGM, 2001)
On the Beach (MGM, 2004)
Run Silent Run Deep (MGM, 2004)
The Russia House (MGM, 2004)
The Russians are Coming, the Russians are Coming (MGM, 2005)
The Spy Who Loved Me (MGM, 2006)
Thirteen Days (Walt Disney Studios, 2002)
Tinker Tailor Soldier Spy (Optimum, 2012)

Television
Cambridge Spies (2 Entertain, 2003)
The Company (Universal/Playback, 2007)
Family of Spies (Boulevard, 2006)
A Perfect Spy (2 Entertain, 2005)
Smiley's People (2 Entertain, 2004)
Tinker, Tailor, Soldier, Spy (2 Entertain, 2003)

Theatre
Kursk (a Young Vic and Fuel co-production with Sound and Fury, 2009)
A milestone play, it provided an unprecedented insight into how
British SSNs and their men have operated in Arctic waters. Deeply
immersive technically and tactically, while a work of fiction, it was re-
searched with the full co-operation of the Royal Navy. The Navy gave
the creators unprecedented access to serving and former submariners
(including visits to the Trafalgar Class SSNs *Torbay* and *Trenchant*).
Material recorded aboard those submarines was used in the production. Its storyline includes a tense underwater look operation on a
Russian submarine in the Barents Sea. The target later turns out to
be the ill-fated *Kursk* (sunk in August 2000 when her own weapons
exploded). Critically acclaimed, one of the actors was even a former
Cold War submariner. The use of broad and narrow band sonar
to gather intelligence and under ice operations are also depicted in
Kursk, reproduced step-by-step with complete accuracy. Written by
Bryony Lavery, with technical advice from a veteran Cold War SSN
and SSBN captain, *Kursk* was directed by Mark Espiner and Dan
Jones. It toured the UK in 2010 and gained rave reviews, especially
from old Cold War warriors who felt they were back on patrol.
Website: www.soundandfury.org.uk/kursk/index.php

PHOTO CREDITS

Battle Map © Dennis Andrews
Cutaway of an Improved Valiant Class SSN.
Image courtesy of HMS Courageous *Association*

Section One
The crew of the Royal Navy's first submarine, *Holland 1*, enjoying the
fresh air, circa 1901.
Photo: BAE Systems
The Nazi-origin Type XXI U-boat.
Photo: Dennis Andrews
Tim Hale's first boat, HMS *Subtle*.
Photo: Tim Hale Collection
The young submariner: Sub Lieutenant Tim Hale, 1956.
Photo: Tim Hale Collection
Rob Forsyth as a Midshipman in 1958.
Photo: Rob Forsyth Collection
21 October 1960: Britain's first nuclear-powered submarine, HMS
Dreadnought.
Photo: ©PA Archive/Press Association Images
HMS *Auriga* sails past the towering skyscrapers of New York in 1963.
Photo: US DoD/Navy
A Foxtrot Class diesel submarine of the Soviet Navy.
Photo: Nigel Andrews
The captain of *Auriga* tests the strength of the ice pack.
Photo: Rob Forsyth Collection
Tim Hale's accident-prone submarine, HMS *Tiptoe*, pictured in 1967.
Photo: Jonathan Eastland/AJAXNetPhoto
Midshipman Dan Conley at sea under training.
Photo: Dan Conley Collection
Midshipman Littlejohns in his Whites while serving at sea in tropical
waters.
Photo: Doug Littlejohns's Collection
HMS *Sealion* – which both Rob Forsyth and Dan Conley served in.
Photo: Jonathan Eastland/AJAXNetPhoto

The towering fin of HMS *Warspite*, with officers and ratings on bridge.

Photo: Topfoto

A Polaris missile blasts into the sky after being fired during a test off.

Photo: US DoD/Navy

HMS *Resolution*, the first of Britain's Polaris missile submarines.

Photo: BAE Systems

HMS *Courageous* at speed.

Photo: The Courageous Association

The diesel submarine HMS *Alliance* in dry dock at Devonport in the early 1960s.

Photo: Crown Copyright/Royal Navy

Lt Cdr Forsyth on the bridge of his first submarine command, HMS *Alliance*.

Photo: Rob Forsyth Collection

May 1970: Sub Lieutenant David Bingham with his wife Maureen.

Photo: Keystone/Getty Images

The frigate HMS *Rothesay*, aboard which Sub Lt David Bingham betrayed his country.

Photo: US DoD/Navy

Section Two

A torpedo in one of *Courageous*'s tubes.

Photo: Nigel Andrews Photography

A starboard bow view of a Russian spy vessel observing NATO ships

Photo: US DoD/Navy

HMS *Swiftsure* on sea trials in October 1972.

Photo: BAE Systems

Both Kashin Class and Kanin Class ASW frigates of the Soviet Navy shadowed HMS *Swiftsure* during her sea trials.

Photo: Tim Hale Collection

A torpedo track (right of image).

Photo: Rob Forsyth Collection

After successfully passing the Perisher, Lt Littlejohns at the periscope.

Photo: Doug Littlejohns' Collection

Tim Hale in February 1977

Photo: Tim Hale Collection

Cdr Rob Forsyth at the beginning of his time in command of HMS *Sceptre*.

Photo: Rob Forsyth Collection

HMS *Sceptre* on the surface in 1978.
Photo: Crown Copyright/Royal Navy
A bow view of Soviet Victor II Class nuclear-powered attack submarine under way.
Photo: US DoD/Navy
Dan Conley while XO of HMS *Spartan* in the late 1970s.
Photo: Dan Conley Collection
The British SSN HMS *Conqueror* returns to Faslane from the Falklands War.
Photo: Crown Copyright/Royal Navy
A gigantic Typhoon Class ballistic missile submarine of the Soviet Navy.
Photo: US DoD/Navy
Cdr Littlejohns in his Volvo lorry driver's chair at the heart of the action.
Photo: Doug Littlejohns's Collection
A composite created from an underwater look on a NATO submarine surfaced in a polynya.
Photo: Crown Copyright/Royal Navy
A British sailor from HMS *London* and a Soviet Navy rating at Murmansk.
Photo: Iain Ballantyne
Return of the last of the Cold War warriors.
Photo: Nigel Andrews Photography
The first of a new generation of British hunter killer submarines, *Astute*.
Photo: Nigel Andrews Photography
Built in the Cold War, Sierra Class SSNs of the Russian Navy like this one are today active again off the coast of the USA.
Photo: Royal Norwegian Air Force
The remarkable sight of what appears to be a full-scale submarine on dry land.
Photo: Doug Littlejohns's Collection.

INDEX

ACKNOWLEDGEMENTS

Quite how this book came to be – its genesis – is convoluted, but worth retelling as a means to apportion proper credit where it is due.

Yes, this is my book, but it is the submariners' story and in some ways it began back in the summer of 2000, when I visited Newton Abbot to interview Tim Hale at his law firm's offices.

I was researching another book, whose main focus was the Second World War battleship *Warspite*, with a short epilogue on the submarine of the same name. While he was guarded, Hale provided a few tantalising insights into the Cold War under the sea.

'Wouldn't it be wonderful,' I thought, 'to one day get Britain's Cold War submariners to open up properly and enable me to write a book on their experiences?'

At the time I had no idea Doug Littlejohns and Tim Hale were friends. I had first encountered Littlejohns in 1993 at Plymouth, when I was Defence Reporter of the local evening newspaper. He was in command of the city's Royal Naval Engineering College (RNEC) Manadon. He and I did not meet again until 2002, after his return from working with Tom Clancy in the USA (where they had founded Red Storm Entertainment).

It wasn't until 2008 that I broached the idea of a book that revealed what happened in the Cold War under the sea with Littlejohns. I knew he had been Commanding Officer of the nuclear-powered submarine HMS *Sceptre*.

He agreed it was something that was well worth consideration.

Little did I know, but Littlejohns and Hale were already thinking of telling their stories, though they had yet to decide exactly how to take things forward. As I would eventually learn, it was Tim Hale's son, Robert, who had planted the seed in their minds. On Christmas Eve 2007, father and son Hale had lunch with Littlejohns and his wife, Debs. Tim Hale later recounted: 'Various silly stories were told. On the way home, I apologised to my son, that he had to listen to old men telling stories. "No, Dad," he said, "it was fascinating. You have to get them written down." And that's how it started.'

This notion triggered a round of discussions among a tight-knit group of submarine captains. Books had been published on both the American and Russian sides of the story, but there was hardly anything on British exploits.

It was high time the balance was restored.

Provided it was carefully put together – with an emphasis on the human side of the story – it could work well. There was the question of security, but at 30 years' distance (or more) from many key episodes, certain aspects were emerging into open source areas – and had been there for some time – if you knew where to look for them (or who to talk to).

As a distinguished lawyer Tim Hale was fully capable of putting the Official Secrets Act (OSA) under scrutiny and there were clearly areas where it was possible to tell the story more fully than before without contravening it. Separate to the captains, I had already come into contact with some extraordinary details. With all they had achieved it seemed ridiculous to me that the UK's Cold War warriors risked being airbrushed from history.

Hale and Littlejohns had soon pulled Rob Forsyth into their dialogue.

Coincidentally, Forsyth, in his capacity as a Trustee of the Royal Navy Submarine Museum, was already trying to rouse interest in compiling submariners' Cold War stories with a view to somehow benefiting the museum. It was during a chance conversation with Hale that he heard about this other idea. How it would go from discussion to print remained uncertain, so they all met for lunch at Tim Hale's house in Devon to weigh up the options. Also present as a 'wise head' was distinguished former Flag Officer Submarines, Rear Admiral Frank Grenier. Though he would not feature as a player in the narrative of any resulting book, Rear Admiral Grenier suggested the others found a suitable author – an outsider with some inside knowledge of how submarines, and the Submarine Service, work.*

It was proposed by Littlejohns that Ballantyne might be the chap to knit it together and bring it all to life. He knew I was keenly interested in doing something, and had started hunting for a likely publisher for whatever it was that might emerge.

The submarine captains discussed my qualifications – I had already written some naval history books, my character and track record were known. I had also been to sea in nuclear-powered submarines. My ambition to write a book and their desire to finally tell their stories seemed to be in synchronicity.

I started sketching out what I felt was the means by which their story could be told. The device was simple: Keep the cast of our drama tight and make the story as action-packed as possible, while also providing enough of the broader Cold War context.

In early 2010 the process properly began, with Dan Conley joining the squad of submarine captains, rounding it out to a useful quartet spanning the entire story from the 1940s to the end of the Cold War. Conley had already seen an article or two on his own Cold War adventures published in professional naval journals, though I had not at that time read them.

A few people who had served with the captains in various submarines were also recruited to the cause, broadening the personal element of the story and providing a different perspective.

The redoubtable Michael Pitkeathly (Pitt.k) deserves a special mention for his generous advice on technical matters, Silent Service customs and of course for allowing me to tell the story of his Cold War under the waves.

The following contributed directly or provided general insights over the years and also deserve my gratitude: Alan Cain, J. J. Colling, John Cumberpatch, Alan Jones, Colin Paton (and his son Chris), Keith Sapsed, the late Dick Raikes. There are others who chose not to be named, but who also deserve my gratitude.

Throughout many hours – indeed days – of interviews the submariners were amazingly kind and patient, occasionally exasperated with my non-submariner ways, but always available to advise or otherwise assist (and correct – my technical blunders). Above all it has been a deep honour to be entrusted with telling their stories. I remain in awe that Britain was able to produce such incredible men at the right time and in the right place. Being captain of a nuclear-powered submarine is beyond the ken of us civilians – the responsibilities and stresses are extreme and very few people can handle them. For me, it was daunting enough to be captain of *this* ship, never mind contemplate how to convey what it felt like to be in charge of a nuclear-powered submarine.

I should not forget to make a salute in the direction of both the HMS *Courageous* and HMS *Warspite* veterans associations. Due to my earlier book on the battleship *Warspite* I am even an Associate member of the *Warspite* Association, which is an honour in itself. Both thriving associations are organisations that exert themselves to carry the flame of commemorating Cold War sacrifice.

While so much in this book is fresh, never before told history, archives were drawn on and George Malcolmson at the Royal Navy Submarine

Museum is deserving of my thanks. He kindly hunted down some key papers relevant to the early period of the Cold War.

I have enjoyed the support of some stalwart friends and colleagues, not least Dennis Andrews for his fine work on the illustrative front. Jonathan Eastland, Peter Hore, John Roberts, Martin Robinson and Dave Sloggett chipped in with advice and/or material assistance. The flexibility and understanding of HPC Publishing, for whom I put together *WARSHIPS International Fleet Review* magazine, has been key to meeting the sometimes-tough demands of producing this book.

It has long been my ambition to work with a top team in the upper tier of British publishing and I am happy to report I found it at Orion. Alan Samson provided not only deeply appreciated creative guidance but proved to be fully committed to mastering the challenges of bringing this story out of the shadows. Tasked as editor of this epic, Jillian Young never lost her patience and kept a steady hand on the tiller, while copyeditor Mark Handsley deserves a tip of the hat. I'd also like to thank Rowland White for his early encouragement and seeing the potential for this dramatic true-life tale.

Throughout this whole voyage Tim Bates, my agent at Pollinger, has been a rock, offering wise counsel and enthusiastic support.

Finally, I would like to express my love and admiration for my wife, Lindsey, and our two boys, Robert and James. They have heroically tolerated my total commitment to this project.

* It is worth noting that while Frank Grenier is not a featured player in the expansive narrative of this book, he has applied his talent for glass engraving – for which he has achieved international renown since retiring from the Navy – to creating a remarkable sculpture at the Cold War Submarine Memorial, Patriots Point in the USA. It pays tribute to those who served in British submarines during the Cold War and has a prominent position to reflect the fact that the RN was the USN's primary ally. Frank has also created a similar piece of work for the RN Submarine Museum. Both memorials were funded by donations from British submariners.

EXPERIENCE A SUBMARINE

Two of the submarines that feature in the narrative of this book are still with us and open to visitors. They offer a taste of the unique environment in which Cold War undersea warriors lived and worked.

HMS *Alliance* & the Royal Navy Submarine Museum

While other diesel boats have long disappeared – dismantled and recycled at various breakers' yards – HMS *Alliance* has since the early 1980s been open to the public at Gosport in Hampshire. *Alliance* is also a permanent memorial to the 5,300 British and Commonwealth submariners who have lost their lives. HMS *Alliance* remains the star attraction of the Royal Navy Submarine Museum (RNSM) and was in April 2014 recommissioned following a £7 million 'refit'. The A Class boat now offers a walk-through – and very immersive – sound, vision and even smell experience. Visitors are treated to all the bells and whistles, not least blaring klaxons, vibrating deck plates and even the aroma of 'Pot Mess' in the galley. The recorded voices of her 'crew' are heard throughout, swapping stories, repeating orders and even 'dripping' about the usual things matelots do. To enhance a visit to *Alliance* herself, retired real-life submariners also act as guides to regale tour groups with tales of the unique lives they once led. The museum offers many fascinating exhibits on the Submarine Service, from its establishment in 1901 right up until today. There are also two other submarines on display. *Holland 1* – the first commissioned British submarine – is preserved inside a climate-controlled building. Visitors can even clamber inside *Holland 1* – though they are best advised to mind their heads. *X-24* is the sole surviving preserved Royal Navy mini-submarine that saw active service in the Second World War, operating off the coast of Norway. She has been cut into sections, which enable visitors to view her cramped and technology-packed innards.

- *For more information visit:*
  www.submarine-museum.co.uk
  Tel: 00 44 (0)23 9251 0354

HMS *Courageous*

At Devonport Naval Base in the South West of England, the decommissioned Fleet submarine *Courageous* – retired from service in 1992 – has
also welcomed thousands of visitors. Defuelled and mothballed, *Courageous* was retrieved from a basin at the dockyard, which is in Plymouth,
and first opened to the public in 2002. Like *Alliance* she is a time machine, lovingly restored by a band of dedicated volunteers – including
men who once served in her. She is presented in her 1970s heyday as a
hunter-killer SSN seeking out the Soviets. Due to her position within
a working naval base and dockyard, access to *Courageous* is on a by
appointment basis only. The retired SSN has still attracted more than
100,000 visitors over the past eleven years. A refurbished Control Room
and Sound Room and superbly authentic Wardroom are among high-
lights. It is the attention to period detail throughout three decks that
makes a visit to *Courageous* such an engrossing experience. There are
items of fascinating hardware, uniforms and relevant artefacts throughout. Adding realism in the torpedo room are two neutralised weapons: a
Sub-Harpoon missile and a Tigerfish torpedo. All in all, it's almost as if
the submarine is still in service.

As with *Alliance*, retired submariners act as guides to enliven a tour
and provide essential information. A large memorial board honouring
all Royal Navy submarines (and their men) lost in both war and peace is
displayed on the jetty alongside *Courageous*. It acts as a fitting reminder
of the special dedication required to operate conventional and nuclear
boats since their inception in the British fleet more than a century ago.

• Anyone wishing to visit *Courageous* should telephone:
  00 44 (0)1752 552326.
  Or make contact via e-mail:
  desnbcd-cob-book1@mod.uk
  Further information is also available via:
  www.hmscourageous.co.uk